1993

PRIVACY
and PUBLICITY

Readings from
COMMUNICATIONS AND THE LAW

Edited by
The Honorable Theodore R. Kupferman

1. Defamation: Libel and Slander
ISBN 0-88736-507-8   CIP 1990

2. Privacy and Publicity
ISBN 0-88736-508-6   CIP 1990

3. Censorship, Secrecy, Access and Obscenity
ISBN 0-88736-509-4   CIP 1990

4. Advertising and Commercial Speech
ISBN 0-88736-510-8   CIP 1990

PRIVACY
and PUBLICITY

Readings From *Communications and the Law, 2*

Edited by
The Honorable Theodore R. Kupferman

Meckler
Westport • London

Citations to the original appearance of articles collected in this volume appear at the back of this book.

Library of Congress Cataloging-in-Publication Data

Privacy and publicity / edited by Theodore R. Kupferman.
      p. cm. -- (Readings from Communications and the law ; 2)
    ISBN 0-88736-508-6 (alk. paper) : $
    1. Privacy, Right of-- United States. 2. Publicity (Law)--United States. 3. Freedom of information--United States. I. Kupferman, Theodore R. II. Series.
KF 1262 . A 75P75   1990
342.73 ' 0858 -- dc20
[347.302858]   89-31993
                                      CIP

British Library Cataloguing in Publication Data

Privacy and publicity : readings from Communications
and the law.
1. United States. Right to Privacy. Law
I. Kupferman, Theordore R. II. Communications and the law
347. 302 ' 858

ISBN 0-88736-508-6

Meckler Corporation, 11 Ferry Lane West, Westport, CT 06880.
Meckler Ltd., Grosvenor Gardens House, Grosvenor Gardens,
   London SW1W 0BS, U.K.

Printed on acid free paper.
Printed and bound in the United States of America.

CONTENTS

PREFACE

Of special interest in the area of Privacy and Publicity is the problem of credit reporting, especially in view of the fact that many times people don't even know what is being said about them. Back in 1980, the *Fensterstock* article took on this problem, and the *Moore* article later considered various aspects of financial privacy.

The heart of the problem of privacy is, of course, the desire of people to be let alone. The *Glasser* and the *McLean* articles consider this problem in the light of the public's right to know through an uninhibited press.

The *Foschio* article considers a special aspect of the privacy doctrine in the area of motor vehicle records.

Other special aspects are considered by *Barber* in her discussion of the televising of sensational actual court cases, and by *Maxwell* and *Reinsch* on the Freedom of Information Act and *Donovan* on the difference in the privacy and publicity area between life and death.

Sherer considers the problem with regard to photos and journalism, while *McLean*, a prolific writer, considers the get-a-story-at-any-price problem.

So we have the area covered in depth and yet also parsed. This volume complements those on Defamation and on Advertising and Commercial Speech in this series of readings from *Communications and the Law*.

BLAIR C. FENSTERSTOCK

The Public and the
Fair Credit Reporting Act

Mr. Fensterstock is a litigator with the
New York law firm of Dewey, Ballantine,
Bushby, Palmer & Wood. He graduated
from Columbia Law School as a Harlan
Fiske Stone Scholar and was Associate
Editor of the *Columbia Journal of Law
and Social Problems.* He also graduated
from Bowdoin College with an A.B. in
economics, Summa Cum Laude and Phi
Beta Kappa.

I. INTRODUCTION

The necessity of balancing individual privacy against other legitimate
public and private interests, be they economic, commercial, or social, has
become increasingly important as our society continues to become more
data-generating. This article attempts to discuss the success of the Fair
Credit Reporting Act in accomplishing this goal.

A. The Common Law

Prior to 1971, the common law provided essentially no remedy for
the victims of false consumer reports; most jurisdictions granted consumer reporting agencies a qualified privilege based on the agencies'

function of providing credit information to the commercial sector of the economy.[1] Under the common law, it was necessary to demonstrate actual damages and sufficient abuse of the privilege to warrant a finding of actual malice,[2] the necessary prerequisite for a valid cause of action.

B.   The Fair Credit Reporting Act—Background

The Fair Credit Reporting Act (the Act)[3] was enacted in 1970 and became effective in 1971.[4] It is the first federal statutory attempt to regulate the consumer reporting industry. It is designed to regulate the personal information market—that part of the private sector which includes credit bureaus, investigative reporting companies, and other organizations whose business is the gathering and reporting of reputational information for use by others in making decisions concerning whether to grant credit, underwrite insurance, or grant employment to the individual about whom such report relates information.[5]

The Act established a federal statutory code of conduct for the consumer reporting industry and today is not alone in the regulation of consumer reports. It was followed by a number of state statutory codes, modeled after and authorized by the Act so long as such state laws are not inconsistent with the Act. Thus far, Arizona, California, Connecticut, Florida, Kansas, Kentucky, Maine, Maryland, Massachusetts, Montana, New Hampshire, New Mexico, New York, Oklahoma, Pennsylvania, and Texas have enacted statutes regulating, to some extent, the purposes for which a consumer report may be issued or obtained and the

1. *See, e.g.,* Altoona Clay Products, Inc. v. Dun & Bradstreet, Inc., 367 F.2d 625 (3d Cir. 1966); A.B.C. Needlecraft v. Dun & Bradstreet, Inc., 245 F.2d 775 (2d Cir. 1957).
2. *See, e.g.,* H. E. Crawford Co. v. Dun & Bradstreet, Inc., 241 F.2d 387 (4th Cir. 1957); Hooper-Holmes Bureau, Inc. v. Bunn, 161 F.2d 102 (5th Cir. 1947); Mil-Hall Textile Co. v. Dun & Bradstreet, Inc., 160 F. Supp. 778 (S.D.N.Y. 1958); *see also,* Geltzer, *Current Practice Under The Fair Credit Reporting Act,* 65 ILL B.J. 702 (1977).
3. 15 U.S.C. § 1681 *et seq.* (1970).
4. Section 504(d) of Pub. L. No. 90-321, as amended by Pub. L. No. 91-508, Title VI, § 602, 84 Stat. 1136 (Oct. 26, 1970) provided that: "Title VI [enacting this subchapter] takes effect upon the expiration of one hundred and eighty days following the date of its enactment [Oct. 26, 1970]."
5. Foer, *The Personal Information Market: An Examination of the Scope and Impact of the Fair Credit Reporting Act,* 2 LOY. (L.A.) CONS. L.J. 37, 38 (1974), reproduced, Hearings on S. 2360, p. 695 *et seq.;* R.B. NORRIS, CONSUMER RECORD KEEPING, CONSUMER CREDIT 1975, at 69 (1975) (Com. Law and Prac. Course Handbook No. 123) (Practicing Law Institute).

availability of the report to the consumer to whom it pertains, and providing for civil penalties for violations.[6]

On the federal front, the Act was followed by the Privacy Act,[7] enacted in 1974 for the purpose of expanding the protection of individual privacy and striking a balance in regard to records maintained by federal agencies concerning individuals.[8] The Privacy Act requires federal agencies, except as otherwise required by law, to permit an individual, *inter alia,* to (a) determine what records pertaining to him are collected, maintained, used, or disseminated by such agencies; (b) prevent certain records pertaining to him to be used for purposes other than the purposes for which they were obtained; (c) have access to records relating to him; and (d) have recourse with respect to the accuracy of such records.

The growing material desires of the American consumer compel the necessity of affirming the individual's right to privacy. As he enhances his life style, purchases a larger home, increases the outstanding balance on his credit cards, and expands the various lines of credit available to him, he is without choice more susceptible to the data-gathering and data-disseminating processes than ever before. Records reflecting his life style, preferences, generosity, religious, political, and charitable associations, gathered by consumer agencies, cannot validly be said to be given voluntarily by him to a third party. Rather, it is by economic necessity and adhesion that he must disclose such information, with little pragmatic choice in the matter. The American consumer is living in an "information fishbowl"[9] and is a subject of the ballooning consumer

---

6. For a complete list and analysis of the state statutes, comparing them with the Act, *see* 1 Cons. Cr. Guide (CCH) ¶ 680; *see also* Credit Data of Ariz., Inc., v. Ariz., 602 F.2d 195 (9th Cir. 1979) holding that the Arizona act was not preempted by the Act on the issue of the propriety of a reporting company's charging a fee for disclosures to consumers.
7. Pub. L. No. 93-579, 88 Stat. 1897 (codified in part at 5 U.S.C. § 552a).
8. 33 The Record of the Ass'n of the Bar of the City of New York, *Governmental Access to Privately Maintained Financial, Communications Toll and Credit Records* (Oct. 1978).
9. Statement by Commerce Secretary Juanita M. Kreps, reported in N.Y. Times, Oct. 3, 1979, at A 16, col. 1, referencing legislative proposals by the Carter administration aimed at increasing privacy safeguards for consumers holding insurance policies or using credit cards. Among the new proposals were the following:

(a) Insurance companies would be required to inform consumers what information about them would be collected and to give consumers the right to examine and correct information in their files;

(b) Credit card and check authorization companies would be required to allow individuals the right to challenge a request for disclosure of records when the request is made in the course of a civil lawsuit;

(c) Disclosure of electronic funds transfers could only be made to a government agency after it had obtained a court order.

credit industry, which has increased from under $6 billion at the close of World War II to approximately $184 billion[10] in 1975.

Not ue the developing policy against indiscriminate disclosure of tax records, the underlying policy of the Act is a compelling one which should be supported and emphasized in future legislation and case law developments.

II. GENERAL DESCRIPTION OF THE ACT

A.   Privacy as a Recurrent Theme

The Act balances the commercial need to have easy access to information necessary to make a sound business decision and the consumer's right to know of and correct information being disseminated about him.[11] It stresses the consumer's right to privacy[12] and confidentiality of records[13] while recognizing the need for fair and equitable procedures to meet the needs of consumer credit, insurance, employment, and other legitimate business purposes.[14]

Privacy is a recurrent theme throughout the Act, interwoven in the provisions designed to insure the accuracy of reported information. Its protection is the prime motivation underlying those portions of the Act relating to (a) the distinction between consumer reports (credit reports) and investigative consumer reports,[15] (b) the restriction on access to reports,[16] (c) consumer notification of requests for investigative reports,[17] (d) a consumer's right to access information in his file,[18] (e) prohibition of the reporting of obsolete information,[19] (f) the assurance of maximum possible accuracy,[20] (g) the right to verification and reverification,[21] and

---

10. CONS. CR. GUIDE (CCH), Last Report Letter Nos. 173 at 10 (May 21, 1975), 185 at 3 (Oct. 21, 1975); *see also* Note, *Judicial Construction of the Fair Credit Reporting Act: Scope and Civil Liability,* 76 COLUM. L. REV. 458, 459 (1976). Along with consumer credit reporting agencies has evolved a second type of consumer reporting agency, the investigative reporting agency, which concentrates on gathering information on the consumer's character, reputation, mode of living, and other personal information, through interviews and the like.
11. 5 CONS. CR. GUIDE (CCH) ¶ 11,303 at 59,785 (1977).
12. 15 U.S.C. § 1681a(4) (1970).
13. 15 U.S.C. § 1681(b) (1970).
14. 15 U.S.C. § 1681(a)(1) (1970).
15. Compare 15 U.S.C. §§ 1681a(d) and 1681a(e) (1970).
16. 15 U.S.C. § 1681b(3)(E) (1970).
17. 15 U.S.C. § 1681d(a) (1970).
18. 15 U.S.C. §§ 1681d(b), 1681g (1970).
19. 15 U.S.C. § 1681c (1970).
20. 15 U.S.C. § 1681e(b) (1970); *see* Miller v. Credit Bureau, Inc. of Wash. D.C., [1969-1973 Transfer Binder] CONS. CR. GUIDE (CCH) ¶ 99,173 (D.C. Super. Ct. 1972).
21. 15 U.S.C. § 1681i (1970).

(h) the right to confidentiality.[22] Moreover, each time amendments to the Act have either been proposed or made, privacy is a continuing theme.[23]

The Act limits the reporting of adverse information, the date of which antedates the report by a specific time period depending on the nature of such information. For example, the Act prohibits the reporting of bankruptcies which antedate the report by more than fourteen years; suits and judgments by more than seven years (or until the governing statute of limitations has expired); paid tax liens, accounts placed for collection, records of arrest, indictment or conviction, and any other adverse item of information by more than seven years.[24]

These provisions regulating the reporting of events which antedate the report by a specific time period are constantly being examined. For example, a version of S. 658, a bill to amend the Bankruptcy Reform Act of 1978, has recently been recommended for passage by the Senate Committee on the Judiciary. This measure includes a change in the Fair Credit Reporting Act for the reporting of Chapter 13 cases. By the amendments, credit reports would be permitted to show Chapter 13 filings for a maximum of seven years following the date of the petition, rather than the usual fourteen-year period. The committee's report on the bill states that debtors who attempt to pay their debts under Chapter 13 should be more credit worthy than debtors who have received a straight bankruptcy discharge and it is intended that they should be treated so by the credit community.[25]

With respect to the disclosure of information to a governmental agency, the Act limits such disclosure to a consumer's name, address, former addresses, places of employment, or former places of employment.[26]

Disclosures to consumers are required to be clear and accurate and to be made during normal business hours and on reasonable notice.[27] Consumers are prohibited from bringing defamation, invasion of privacy, or negligence actions regarding information reported about

---

22. 15 U.S.C. § 1681(b) (1970).
23. *See, e.g.,* The Fair Credit Reporting Act Amendments of 1973, S. 2360 (93d Cong., 1st Sess.) proposed amendments before the Senate Subcommittee on Consumer Credit intended in part to enhance the right of privacy and grant consumers control over information about them; § 1681c as amended by Pub. L. No. 95-598, Title III, § 312(a), 92 Stat. 2676 (Nov. 6, 1978); S. 1840 (94th Cong., 1st Sess.), a bill introduced by Senator Proxmire and referred to the Committee on Banking, Housing and Urban Affairs.
24. 15 U.S.C. § 1681c (1970). However, such time limitations do not apply to transactions involving more than $50,000 or to employment whereby an individual is reasonably expected to receive an annual salary equal to or greater than $20,000.
25. CONS. CR. GUIDE (CCH), Last Report Letter No. 288 at 4 (Sept. 18, 1979).
26. 15 U.S.C. § 1681f (1970).
27. 15 U.S.C. §§ 1681g, 1681h (1970).

them "except as to false information furnished with malice or willful intent to injure such consumer."[28]

The Act also provides for civil liability for willful and negligent noncompliance including costs of the action and reasonable attorney's fees,[29] limits the time within which an action may be brought to two years,[30] and provides criminal penalties for obtaining information under false pretenses[31] and for unauthorized disclosures by officers or employees of a consumer reporting agency.[32]

The Federal Trade Commission has general authorization for compliance enforcement, and certain other agencies have been granted limited authorization for compliance in specific areas. Such agencies include the Comptroller of the Currency, Federal Reserve Board, Federal Deposit Insurance Corporation, Federal Home Loan Bank Board, National Credit Union Administration, Interstate Commerce Commission, Civil Aeronautics Board, and the Secretary of Agriculture.[33]

B.   Areas of Noncoverage

The Act, while covering consumer reporting agencies and consumer reports, does not cover commercial credit reports which contain consumer credit information concerning a principal of the business organization about which information is being reported. Thus, a consumer cannot recover under the Act for derogatory information issued about him in connection with a commercial credit report;[34] the reporting of information must be in the context of a business transaction with the consumer *qua* consumer.

28. 15 U.S.C. § 1681h(e) (1970).
29. 15 U.S.C. §§ 1681n, 1681o (1970); *see* text accompanying note 60.
30. 15 U.S.C. § 1681p (1970).
31. 15 U.S.C. § 1681q (1970).
32. 15 U.S.C. § 1681r (1970).
33. 15 U.S.C. § 1681s (1970).
34. Wrigley v. Dun & Bradstreet, Inc., 375 F. Supp. 969 (N.D. Ga.), *aff'd,* 500 F.2d 1183 (5th Cir. 1974) (suit for damages incurred by plaintiff as a result of information on his criminal convictions and the bankruptcy of his old company, Wrigley Sales, Inc., contained in a credit report on his present business, Wrigley Construction Co.); Sizemore v. Bambi Leasing Corp., 360 F. Supp. 252 (N.D. Ga. 1973) (report on key employee of company trying to induce bank to purchase lease); *but see* Anonymous v. Dun & Bradstreet, Inc., 40 U.S.L.W. 2162 (N.Y. Sup. Ct., Sp. Term 1971), where the Court enjoined the dissemination of twenty-year-old criminal information concerning a corporate official in a report issued for business and commercial purposes; Ley v. Boron Oil Co., 419 F. Supp. 1240 (W.D. Pa. 1976) (report on attorney representing buyer of land from user of a consumer report); *see also* § 1681a(c) of the Act defining "consumer" in "consumer report" as "an individual," thus emphasizing the fact that the Act is not intended to cover commercial reports.

The Act does not prohibit a bank from responding to a subpoena issued by the Internal Revenue Service to produce certain records of named depositors since it was not designed to apply to tax investigations.[35] Nor does the Act cover adoption agencies which gather information on prospective adoptive parents.[36]

The key to the strengths and weaknesses of the Act lies in the interpretation of what is or is not a consumer report or a consumer reporting agency. The answer to this question should be gleaned from the purpose for which a reporting agency originally filed the information.[37] The importance of the purpose for which information was filed in interpreting the Act was emphasized in an opinion letter of the Federal Trade Commission,[38] but has been ignored in the cases concerning reports on businesses.[39] By utilizing this method of determining whether or not information is in a consumer report, the pendulum-like inconsistency, at least on this subject, could be laid to rest.

III. ADMINISTRATIVE PROPOSALS TO STRENGTHEN THE RIGHT TO PRIVACY

A. Interpretations by the Federal Trade Commission

In accordance with its administrative duties under the Act, the Federal Trade Commission, in 1973, issued six interpretations, five of which had a bearing on the right to privacy:[40]

(1) One interpretation prohibits publication and distribution by credit bureaus of "credit guides" containing consumer credit ratings unless encoded to ensure anonymity.

(2) Another interpretation allows publication and distribution of certain kinds of "protective bulletins" which identify check-forgers and others, provided that no information in them is used in establishing the subject's eligibility for credit, insurance, or employment.

(3) A third interpretation requires that when insurance companies

---

35. United States v. Bremicker, 365 F. Supp. 701 (D. Minn. 1973).
36. Porter v. Talbot Perkins Children's Service, 355 F. Supp. 174 (S.D.N.Y. 1973); see also Compliance with the Fair Credit Reporting Act, 4 Cons. Cr. Guide (CCH) ¶11,302 et seq. at 59,781-818.
37. Note, Judicial Construction of the Fair Credit Reporting Act: Scope and Civil Liability, 76 Colum. L. Rev. 458, 475 (1976); see text accompanying note 52 et seq.
38. FTC Informal Staff Opinion Letter of May 19, 1971, [1968-1972 Transfer Binder] Cons. Cr. Guide (CCH) ¶ 99,424.
39. See Leo Foundation v. Dun & Bradstreet, Inc., 5 Cons. Cr. Guide (CCH) ¶ 98,798 (D. Conn. 1974); Wrigley v. Dun & Bradstreet, Inc., 375 F. Supp. 969 (N.D. Ga. 1974); Sizemore v. Bambi Leasing Corp., 360 F. Supp. 252 (N.D. Ga. 1973).
40. 38 Fed. Reg. 4945-47 (Feb. 23, 1973), 5 Cons.Cr.Guide (CCH) ¶ 11,351-56.

use a state motor vehicle report to alter a consumer's insurance cost, such companies inform the consumer of that fact and of the state agency's identity.

(4) A fourth interpretation permits consumer reporting agencies to prescreen prospects' names for credit worthiness for direct-mail solicitations so long as the user of the report certifies that every person on the list furnished will receive the solicitation.

(5) A fifth interpretation concludes that reporting activities of federal agencies are not within the scope of the Act.

With respect to the prohibition of credit guides, the Federal Trade Commission ruled that a corporation distributing weekly "Alert Lists" to merchants of consumers who allegedly passed bad checks, violated the Act because subscribers to the list service did not have a legitimate business need for the information regarding all the individuals on the list. The lists contained more information than was permissible under the Act and were disseminated to law enforcement agencies. Certification from subscribers and law enforcement agencies that the lists would be used only for permissible purposes was not obtained. Nor was there verification that the lists were only being used for such purposes.[41]

B. Relationship of the Act with the Equal Credit Opportunity Act

On 8 March 1978, the Federal Trade Commission issued a statement interpreting the requirements under the Act which deal with the utilization of reasonable procedures to assure maximum possible accuracy of information concerning individuals.[42]

Section 202.10 of Regulation B, implementing the Equal Credit Opportunity Act,[43] requires creditors, on or after 1 June 1977, to report account information to credit bureaus in such a way as to reflect the participation of both spouses in joint accounts or user accounts and in such a way as to provide access to information in the name of each spouse.[44] This is intended to stop the practice of having credit history reported only in the name of the husband, with the wife's name as a mere identifier, like a social security number. In addition, Regulation B requires creditors to ascertain whether accounts established prior to and in existence on 1 June 1977 are joint or separate, and to adjust their reporting of these accounts accordingly.[45] For accounts opened after 1 June 1977, creditors

41. In the Matter of Howard Enterprises, Inc., 5 CONS. CR. GUIDE (CCH) ¶ 97,717 (FTC, June 12, 1979).
42. 43 Fed. Reg. 9471 (March 8, 1978).
43. 15 U.S.C. § 1691 (1977).
44. 12 C.F.R. 202.10(a) (1977).
45. 12 C.F.R. 202.10(b) (1977).

are required to determine, when the accounts are opened,[46] how the credit history is to be reported. Further, the regulation requires creditors, to the extent to which they consider credit history, to consider the credit history, when available, of any account reported in the name of the applicant's spouse or former spouse which the applicant can demonstrate accurately reflects the applicant's ability or willingness to repay.[47]

Under the Act, a consumer reporting agency may report information contained in the file of spouse A when spouse B applies for a separate extension of credit, if such information relates to accounts on which spouse B is either a joint user or contractually liable. Conversely, a consumer reporting agency may not report information from spouse A's file which relates only to his or her individual credit history when spouse B applies for credit, unless the creditor has a permissible purpose for the report under the Act.[48]

Other Federal Trade Commission interpretations permit a creditor to access a consumer report of an applicant's spouse in the following cases:[49]

(a) if the spouse is permitted to use the account;

(b) if the spouse is contractually liable on the account; or

(c) if the applicant resides in a community-property state or property upon which the applicant is relying as a basis for repayment of the credit requested is located in such a state.

IV. THE GROWTH OF THE FAIR CREDIT REPORTING ACT

The Act, in its brief eight years of existence, has been no exception to the normal American routine; it has experienced a pendulum-like interpretation of legislative intent. For the most part, case law has focused on the definitional parameters of consumer reporting agencies and consumer reports — the core of the Act.[50] For example, a state motor vehicle agency disseminating accident reports has been found to be a consumer reporting agency,[51] while a police department collecting records used in employment has been found not to be a consumer reporting agency.[52] In

46. 12 C.F.R. 202.10(a) (1977).
47. 12 C.F.R. 202.6(b)(6)(iii) (1977).
48. 15 U.S.C. § 1681b(3)(A) (1970).
49. 12 C.F.R. 202.5(c)(2)(i), (ii), (iv) (1977).
50. It is interesting to note that during the House discussion of the conference report, Representative Brown asserted that "[T]he definitions are so vague that no one is certain what is included as a "consumer credit report" or who or what is to be construed as a "consumer reporting agency," 116 Cong. Rec. 36,576 (1970).
51. Op. Atty. Gen. Pa., August 7, 1975, Cons. Cr. Guide (CCH) ¶ 98,549 (1975).
52. Mattingly v. D.C. (D.D.C. No. 74-1296, April 23, 1975) Cons. Cr. Guide (CCH) ¶ 98,604.

the latter situation, an individual claimed he was denied several jobs because of his record being distributed, upon request, by a local police department. The court noted that the information was being disseminated for employment purposes, not for credit purposes, and was therefore without the purview of the Act.

Reports from federal agencies, including the Federal Bureau of Investigation, were found not to be within the scope of the Act on the rationale that only those reporting agencies that garnered material for the purpose of furnishing consumer reports to third parties were governed by the Act.[53] The court concluded that agencies such as the F.B.I. do not compile information on persons particularly for the purpose of furnishing consumer reports to third parties.

Nevertheless, a Florida court has found that a report prepared for use in connection with a state court civil action involving an increase in child support and medical expense payments was not a consumer report under the Act since it was not used for any of the purposes expressly set out in the Act.[54]

One of the more interesting cases to come out of the courts regarding the definition of a consumer reporting agency involved Gulf Oil Company's directions to the Holiday Inn to repossess an individual's credit card.[55] In *Wood* v. *Holiday Inns, Inc.,* the plaintiff, an executive vice president of a manufacturing company, attempted to use his credit card issued by Gulf to pay his hotel bill at a Holiday Inn. When the Holiday Inn telephoned to confirm the propriety of the plaintiff's charge, it was directed to repossess the card and thereby to receive a reward. The Holiday Inn seized the card pursuant to Gulf's directions. Wood paid his bill in cash and checked out of the Holiday Inn. Upon returning home, Wood telephoned Gulf, explained that he used the credit card for business purposes and that his account was current. Three days later, with his frustration building, Wood suffered a heart attack while relating the incident to a friend. Thereafter, Wood sued Gulf. The court noted that the Holiday Inn would have, had it completely ignored Gulf's directions, extended Gulf's credit, not its own. As such, the revocation by the Holiday Inn did not involve a communication "for the purpose of furnishing consumer reports to third parties." The communication was merely reasoned to be directed from Gulf to its local representative, made for the purpose of protecting Gulf rather than influencing the Holiday Inn's own credit

53. Ollestad v. Kelley, 573 F.2d 1109 (9th Cir. 1978), citing the interpretation of the Federal Trade Commission, concluding that federal agencies are not consumer reporting agencies within the meaning of the Act, 16 C.F.R. § 600.6 (1977).
54. Gardner v. Investigators, Inc., 413 F. Supp. 780 (M.D. Fla. 1976).
55. Wood v. Holiday Inns, Inc., 508 F.2d 167 (5th Cir. 1975).

decision. Under these circumstances, Holiday Inn was not considered a credit reporting agency. Furthermore, Gulf did not violate the Act in not notifying the consumer of a credit report "unfavorable" to him. Gulf's credit report on the plaintiff was entirely favorable. Rather, revocation was based on Gulf's decision that too much was being charged.[56]

Like the cases involving the definitional parameters of consumer reporting agencies, cases involving consumer reports have also suffered inconsistent interpretations. On one hand, internal bank records have been held not to be covered by the Act,[57] whereas bank records received from third parties have been held to be covered by the Act.[58]

Strict adherence has been paid to the liability sections providing for penalties for violations of the Act. For example, in one case, a newspaperman was denied automobile insurance because of a credit report that he was a worthless hippie. His demands to see his file resulted only in the oral reading of a disclosure sheet. The court held the information-gathering methods of the agency deficient in that only one person was the source of the adverse information despite statements in the report that three persons provided the information. This failure to assure reasonable accuracy together with the failure to give the consumer access to the report, the court found, entitled the plaintiff to an award of $40,000 including punitive damages of $25,000.[59]

Consistent with the growing trend to find civil liability based on criminal provisions of federal statutes, the Ninth Circuit, in *Hansen* v. *Morgan*,[60] held that the obtaining of a consumer report in violation of the Act, without disclosing the impermissible purpose for which the report was desired, constituted obtaining consumer information under false pretenses. In that case, third parties obtained a credit report on a political candidate, allegedly not for the purpose of extending credit but rather for the political purpose of assisting the House Administrative Committee in its investigation of alleged improper campaign financing procedures. The court reasoned that the Act explicitly provided for civil

---

56. *See, cf.* Bain v. May Dept. Stores Co. 421 U.S. 947 (1975) where a retail store reported an out-of-court settlement for less than the amount owed to a credit bureau. This information was subsequently reported to another creditor who refused to grant credit. The court found that there was no cause of action against the retailer.
57. United States v. Lake County, N.B. (N.D. Ohio No. C75-55, March 18, 1975), Cons. Cr. Guide (CCH) ¶ 98,621.
58. United States v. Puntorieri & First Nat'l City Bank, 379 F. Supp. 332 (E.D.N.Y. 1974).
59. Carroll v. Exxon Co., U.S.A., 434 F. Supp. 557 (E.D. La. 1977); Millstone v. O'Hanlon Reports, Inc., 383 F. Supp. 269 (E.D. Mo. 1974), *aff'd,* 528 F.2d 829 (8th Cir. 1976).
60. Hansen v. Morgan, 582 F.2d 1214 (9th Cir. 1978).

liability for willful[61] or negligent[62] noncompliance by a consumer reporting agency or user of information who fails to comply with "any requirement imposed under this subchapter with respect to any consumer." The criminal provision of the Act,[63] the court reasoned, stated a "requirement imposed under this subchapter." Therefore, its violation formed a basis for a finding of civil liability. Civil liability was imposed since the obtaining of the consumer report under false pretenses was found to be violative of the defined permissible purposes of consumer reports.

Although the Act, then, provides for civil liability under certain circumstances, it clearly does not cover others. Although it mandates "maximum possible accuracy"[64] and allows for reinvestigation,[65] nowhere does the Act provide for civil penalties for furnishing an inaccurate report. It is clear that if a reporting agency had no procedures at all to verify the accuracy of its reports, it would be in violation of the Act.[66] But it is not clear whether an agency which had procedures, but didn't follow them, would be in violation of the Act.

In two cases where this latter question arose, the courts used the prescribed procedures of the respective agencies as a benchmark against which to establish a standard of reasonableness.[67] In both cases, the agencies were found liable for violations of the Act.

61. 15 U.S.C. § 1681n (1970) provides:
"Any consumer reporting agency or user of information which willfully fails to comply with any requirement imposed under this subchapter with respect to any consumer is liable to that consumer in an amount equal to the sum of:
(1) any actual damages sustained by the consumer as a result of the failure;
(2) such amount of punitive damages as the court may allow; and
(3) in the case of any successful action to enforce any liability under this section, the costs of the action together with reasonable attorney's fees as determined by the court."
62. 15 U.S.C. § 1681o (1970) provides:
"Any consumer reporting agency or user of information which is negligent in failing to comply with any requirement imposed under this subchapter with respect to any consumer is liable to that consumer in an amount equal to the sum of:
(1) any actual damages sustained by the consumer as a result of the failure;
(2) in the case of any successful action to enforce any liability under this section, the costs of the action together with reasonable attorney's fees as determined by the court."
63. 15 U.S.C. § 1681q (1970) provides:
"Any person who knowingly and willfully obtains information on a consumer from a consumer reporting agency under false pretenses shall be fined not more than $5,000 or imprisoned not more than one year, or both."
64. 15 U.S.C. § 1681e(b) (1970).
65. 15 U.S.C. § 1681i(a) (1970).
66. See generally W.F. WILLIER, THE FAIR CREDIT REPORTING ACT: WHAT IS AN ATTORNEY TO DO? (1971).
67. King v. The Credit Bureau, Inc. of Ga. (D.D.C. 1975) 2 POVERTY L. REP. (CCH) ¶ 20,619; Millstone v. O'Hanlon Reports, Inc., 383 F. Supp. 269 (E.D. Mo. 1974), aff'd, 528 F.2d 829 (8th Cir. 1976).

Another problem with the Act arises when reporting agencies issue reports which contain factually-accurate information but which are also misleading. In two cases,[68] courts held that consumer reporting agencies are under an obligation to follow reasonable procedures to discover mitigating circumstances regarding adverse data. Yet, in another case, a court held that civil liability under the Act will not be found unless the report sought to be attacked is inaccurate.[69]

V. CONCLUSION

The Act, the first federal step in the regulation of the consumer reporting industry, is awkward, vague, ambiguous, subject to varied interpretations, and less inclusive than necessary to protect individual consumers from invasion of their privacy. Central to its weaknesses are its basic definitions of "consumer reports" and "consumer reporting agencies." Until these rudimentary concepts are narrowed, interpretation will continue to be inconsistent. Future amendments to the Act should focus on definitions, with an increased emphasis on the purposes of the Act.

Nevertheless, as a first step in regulating the consumer reporting agency, the Act is worthy of applause. Like other statutory schemes intended to protect our inalienable civil rights, the strength of the Act lies in its interpretation. Privacy is a right which has come of age. Courts should accept that right, acknowledge its importance, and construe ambiguity in its favor.

68. Green v. Stores Mut. Protective Ass'n., 74 Civ. 4607 (S.D.N.Y., Oct. 7, 1975); Miller v. Credit Bureau, Inc. of Wash., D.C. (D.C. Super. Ct. 1972) [1969-1973 Transfer Binder] Cons. Cr. Guide (CCH) ¶ 99,173.
69. Peller v. Retail Credit Co., Civ. A. No. 17900 (N.D. Ga., Dec. 6, 1973). A summary of the opinion can be found at 5 Cons. Cr. Guide (CCH) ¶ 98,648.

THEODORE L. GLASSER

Resolving the Press-Privacy Conflict: Approaches to the Newsworthiness Defense

Theodore L. Glasser (Ph.D., University of Iowa, 1979) is a visiting assistant professor at the University of Minnesota School of Journalism and Mass Communication, on leave from the University of Hartford Department of Communication. An earlier version of this paper was presented to the Mass Communication Interest Group of the Eastern Communication Association, Pittsburgh, April 1981. Research for this paper was completed while the author was a Visiting Faculty Fellow at Yale University; the author extends his appreciation to Yale's Thomas I. Emerson, Lines Professor of Law Emeritus, for many stimulating discussions on the conflict between privacy rights and a free press.

The right of privacy and freedom of the press may come in conflict in a variety of ways, but the oldest controversy — and the most serious from a journalistic perspective — arises from the unauthorized publication of true but embarrassing facts. To be sure, when private facts are both offensive to a reasonable person and of no legitimate public concern, their publication constitutes a civil tort, a wrongful act for which the press is fully accountable under the common law of privacy.[1] While the First Amendment protects a robust and uninhibited press,[2] there

---

1. See *Restatement (Second) of Torts* § 652D (1977). In the United States, recognition of the right of privacy is virtually universal; see Peter L. Felcher and Edward L. Rubin, "Privacy, Publicity, and the Portrayal of Real People by the Media," *Yale Law Journal*, 88 (July 1979): 1581-1583.
2. *New York Times v. Sullivan*, 376 U.S. 254, 270 (1964).

may be only a limited Constitutional privilege to pander to vulgar curiosity by publishing lurid gossip.

Unwanted and unnecessary publicity lies at the core of the common law of privacy. Its history begins in 1890 with the publication of Samuel Warren's and Louis Brandeis' *Harvard Law Review* article on "The Right to Privacy," a scathing attack on journalism's invasion of "the precincts of private and domestic life."[3] When in 1960 William Prosser reformulated privacy into four distinct torts,[4] public disclosure of embarrassing facts — what Kalven calls the "mass communication tort of privacy"[5] — retained its status as the "true" or "pure" invasion of privacy; the other torts, one commentator suggests, "are offspring from the wrong side of the blanket, scions of meretricious liasions between privacy and the torts of trespass, defamation, and . . . trademark infringement."[6] In short, embarrassing facts *as news* remain the principal privacy controversy, an issue of Constitutional proportion insofar as "news" falls within the purview of the First Amendment.

Although the Supreme Court let pass a recent opportunity to examine the Constitutionality of the public disclosure tort,[7] the courts ordinarily protect any press report "of public or general interest," including stories "concerning interesting phases of human activity."[8] Under the common law privilege of "newsworthiness," embarrassing facts as news do not, in principle, qualify as an invasion of privacy. In practice, however, the newsworthiness defense offers a confused and problematic answer to the question of what constitutes a tortious public disclosure. Understandably, the courts are reluctant even to define

3. Samuel D. Warren and Louis D. Brandeis, "The Right to Privacy," *Harvard Law Review*, 4 (December 1890): 195. For a review of the early development of privacy law, including excerpts from "illustrative cases," see William G. Hale, *Law of the Press*, 3rd ed., St. Paul, Minn.: West Publishing Co., 1948, pp. 298-323.
4. In addition to public disclosure of private facts, privacy could be invaded through (i) intrusion upon an individual's seclusion or solitude, (ii) publicity which places an individual in a "false light," and (iii) appropriation of an individual's name or likeness. See William Prosser, "Privacy," *California Law Review*, 48 (1960); 389.
5. Harry Kalven, Jr., "Privacy in Tort Law — Were Warren and Brandeis Wrong?" *Law and Contemporary Problems*, 31 (Spring 1966): 326-341.
6. Dorsey D. Ellis, Jr., "Damages and the Privacy Tort: Sketching a 'Legal Profile'," *Iowa Law Review*, 64 (July 1979): 1111.
7. In *Cox Broadcasting Corp. v. Cohn*, 420 U.S. 469 (1975), the Supreme Court evaded the broader issue of the Constitutionality of publishing true but embarrassing facts and focused instead on the Constitutionality of publishing embarrassing facts obtained from public records.
8. See for example *Ann-Margret v. High Society*, 6 Med. L. Rptr. 1774, 1776 (S.D.N.Y. 1980).

news or newsworthy, especially since the Supreme Court expressly advised against "committing this task to the conscience of judges."[9] But with the press as the sole arbiter of its own defense, newsworthiness is defined descriptively, not normatively, and the judiciary is left with a strictly empirical and hopelessly tautological view of the newsmaking process: news is whatever journalists say it is.[10] As attractive as this view may be to the press, it presents an almost insurrmountable barrier for the plaintiff. Realistically, how can an individual demonstrate invasion of privacy by the press when virtually everything published by the press qualifies as news and is therefore privileged as "newsworthy"? As Kalven observes, the defense of newsworthiness may be "so overpowering as virtually to swallow the tort."[11]

Since the courts have neither advanced nor adopted a unified theory of news, the concept of newsworthiness "has no generally accepted meaning, nor one that can be poured into it."[12] And yet, without a workable and defensible definition of newsworthy, judges and juries are afforded no realistic guidance and plaintiffs are extended no effective protection.

While much has been said about privacy and the defense of newsworthiness,[13] there appear to be only three broadly distinguishable — and largely disparate — theories, none of them in circulation long enough to have influenced the courts. In an effort to assess these theories, this paper begins with a brief overview of the conflict between privacy and a free press, with an emphasis on the legal and moral tension created by an individual's desire to conceal embarrassing facts and the journalist's proclivity to disclose them. Preceded by a description of

---

9. *Gertz v. Robert Welch, Inc.,* 418 U.S. 323, 346 (1974).
10. See generally Comment, "The Right of Privacy: Normative-Descriptive Confusion in the Defense of Newsworthiness," *University of Chicago Law Review,* 30 (Summer 1963): 722-734. Curiously, even journalism educators often prefer the descriptive definition of news: "There is no need to belabor the point that news is what journalists say it is," advised one recent textbook. In the "final analysis," the authors propose, "any definition of news is going to be a tautology." See David J. LeRoy and Christopher H. Sterling, *Mass News,* Englewood Cliffs, N.J.: Prentice-Hall, 1973, p. 123.
11. Harry Kalven, Jr., "Privacy in Tort Law — Were Warren and Brandeis Wrong?" *Law and Contemporary Problems,* 31 (Spring 1966): 336.
12. Thomas I. Emerson, *The System of Freedom of Expression.* New York: Random House, 1970, p. 533.
13. See for example Don R. Pember, "Privacy and the Press: The Defense of Newsworthiness," *Journalism Quarterly,* 45 (Spring 1968); 14-24. Also, Linda N. Woito and Patrick McNulty, "The Privacy Disclosure Tort and the First Amendment: Should the Community Decide Newsworthiness?" *Iowa Law Review,* 64 (July 1979): 185-199.

the three theories of newsworthiness, the concluding section offers an appraisal of each theory in terms of its contribution to legal theory and, more pragmatically, as a contribution to a workable compromise between newsworthiness and invasiveness.

PRIVACY RIGHTS AND A FREE PRESS

Privacy has been defined in a variety of ways, from a broad right "to be let alone"[14] to what Westin believes is an essential aspect of self-determination.[15] It has been said that privacy insures "autonomy, identity, and intimacy";[16] it preserves human dignity and fosters individuality;[17] it is "the right not to participate in the collective life — the right to shut out the community."[18] At the very least, privacy is concerned with an individual's accessibility to others: "the extent to which we are known to others, the extent to which others have physical access to us, and the extent to which we are the subject of others' attention."[19] Broadly and ultimately, privacy has been described as a *natural* right, what Marnell calls the "inalienable right of the individual to hold inviolate the fortress of self."[20]

Natural right or not, the Supreme Court did not recognize privacy as a *Constitutional* right until 1965.[21] Like many other Constitutional protections, however, the privacy right created by the Court in *Griswold v. Connecticut* serves only to protect individuals from an overbearing and too powerful government. Just as the First Amendment does not ordinarily function as a safeguard against private abridgement of expression, the *Griswold* Court's construction of a privacy right offers no protection against private — as opposed to governmental — intrusion. As the New York Supreme Court recently held, "There is no legal extension of the Constitution so as to afford protection to one private party

---

14. The "right to be let alone" was introduced by Judge T. Cooley in 1888 but was popularized by Warren and Brandeis in their 1890 *Harvard Law Review* article.
15. Alan Westin, *Privacy and Freedom.* New York: Atheneum, 1967.
16. Tom Gerety, "Redefining Privacy," *Harvard Civil Rights — Civil Liberties Law Review,* 12 (1977): 236.
17. Edward J. Bloustein, "Privacy as an Aspect of Human Dignity: An Answer to Dean Prosser," *New York University Law Review,* 39 (December 1964): 962-1007.
18. Emerson, p. 549.
19. Ruth Gavison, "Privacy and the Limits of Law," *Yale Law Journal,* 89 (January 1980): 423.
20. William H. Marnell, *The Right to Know.* New York: Seabury Press, 1973, p. 145.
21. *Griswold v. Connecticut,* 381 U.S. 479 (1965).

from acts of another private person or corporate entity."[22]

Whatever protection might exist from invasion of privacy by the press is, therefore, a matter of common law or statutory law, not Constitutional law. But since any law that restricts or inhibits free expression is likely to come in conflict with the Constitution, particularly the First Amendment, the conflict between privacy and freedom of the press is typically a lopsided conflict between common law and Constitutional law. Almost inevitably, a free press prevails because the Constitution and its amendments necessarily take "precedence over any competing, nonconstitutional policy."[23] Consequently, the common law of privacy — especially the public disclosure tort, which often runs counter to the demands of the First Amendment — appears to be Constitutionally infirm. To protect effectively an individual from publication of embarrassing facts would require the courts to limit the scope of the First Amendment, a Constitutional controversy in which few judges are anxious to become involved.

Under the guise of "newsworthiness," the courts have thus extended exceptionally broad protection to the press, even under those circumstances when the press simply caters to the public's insatiable appetite for the trivial and sensational. The foremost public disclosure case, *Sidis v. F-R Publishing Corp.,*[24] serves well to illustrate the tension between privacy claims and a free press, and underscores as well the judiciary's resolve to define newsworthiness so broadly that, as Kalven feared, not much remains of the privacy tort. *Sidis* involves a one-time child prodigy, William James Sidis, who sued for invasion of privacy when the *New Yorker* magazine published an article that not only "dredged up the public past of a person who wanted the world to forget his past" but exposed the more recent past of a person who "gave up all professional ambitions for a life as a semi-recluse employed in relatively mindless jobs."[25] One of a series of articles on formerly prominent individuals, "Where Are They Now? April Fool,"[26] recounted Sidis' early days as an eleven year-old Harvard mathematics lecturer, his gradua-

22. *Kahn v. News Group Publications,* 6 Med. L. Rptr. 1429, 1430 (N.Y.S.Ctr., 1980).
23. Felcher and Rubin, p. 1588.
24. 113 F.2d 806 (2d Cir. 1940). For a worthwhile review of the *Sidis* case, see Emile Karafiol, "The Right to Privacy and the *Sidis* Case," *Georgia Law Review,* 12 (Spring 1978): 513-534.
25. Karafiol, p. 519.
26. Sidis' birthday was April 1. *See New Yorker,* August 14, 1937, p. 22.

tion from Harvard College at sixteen, his three years at Harvard Law School, and his faculty position at a university in Texas. But the truly intrusive aspects of the article focused on Sidis' physical characteristics, his mannerisms, his living conditions, and, ironically, the fact that Sidis scorned publicity. Accordingly, the thirty-nine year-old eccentric — who had lived in relative obscurity for nearly eleven years — charged that the *New Yorker* article exposed him to "unwanted and undesired publicity" and subjected him to "public scorn, ridicule, and contempt."[27]

Finding no relevant case "which held the 'right of privacy' to be violated by a newspaper or magazine publishing a correct account of one's life or doings," the District Court of Southern New York dismissed Sidis' privacy claims.[28] The Second Circuit Court of Appeals dismissed the dismissal; so long as the press confines itself to the "unembroidered dissemination of facts," the Court held, "prying of the press" deserves protection.[29] Only when the public relevations are "so intimate and so unwarranted in the view of the victim's position as to outrage the community's notion of decency" would privacy claims outweight the public's interest in information.[30]

The "community's notion of decency" standard was clarified somewhat by the Ninth Circuit Court of Appeals in *Virgil v. Time Inc.,*[31] a case involving a *Sports Illustrated* account of the strange behavior[32] of a body surfer named Mike Virgil. The *Virgil* Court flatly rejected the proposition that the newsworthiness privilege extends to all true statements:

> To hold that privilege extends to all true statements would seem to deny the existence of "private" facts, for if facts be facts — that is, if they be true — they would not (at least to the press) be private, and the press would be free to publicize them to the extent it sees fit. The extent to which areas of privacy continue

27. *Sidis v. F-R Publishing Corp.,* 34 F. Supp. 19, 20 (S.D.N.Y. 1938).
28. *Ibid.* at 21.
29. 113 F.2d at 808.
30. *Ibid.*
31. 527 F.2d 1122 (9th Cir. 1975).
32. Virgil's strange behavior included reports about him eating spiders and insects, biting off the cheek of a man in a "six-against-30" gang fight, extinguishing a lighted cigarette in his mouth, and burning a hole in a dollar bill while the bill rested on the back of his hand.

to exist, then, would appear to be based not on rights bestowed by law but on the taste and discretion of the press. We cannot accept the result.[33]

Instead, the Court of Appeals in *Virgil* proposed that a line be drawn between information to which the public is entitled and publicity which becomes nothing more than "a morbid and sensational prying into private lives for its own sake, with which a reasonable member of the public, with decent standards, would say that he had no concern."[34] Nonetheless, a district court in California, to which *Virgil* was remanded, found the *Sports Illustrated* article "simply not offensive to the degree of morbidity or sensationalism" necessary for an actionable privacy claim.[35] "Any reasonable person reading the *Sports Illustrated* article," the lower court concluded, "would have to conclude that the personal facts concerning Mike Virgil were included as a legitimate journalistic attempt to explain Virgil's extremely daring and dangerous style of bodysurfing."[36]

Thus if the Court of Appeals in *Sidis* and *Virgil* recognize the importance of — and perhaps even promote — a sense of decency on the part of the press, it is not clear that the courts have come to grips with the morality of unauthorized and unwanted publicity. Does the press lose its "sense of decency" because it deprives someone of privacy or because it defies community standards? More to the point, can privacy be defined in terms of community standards? From this judiciary's perspective, what are the questions and issues relevant to a *prima facie* case? Indeed, it is not always clear that the courts — especially the *Sidis* and *Virgil* courts — fully appreciate that the right of privacy "refers to the right of the individual to exclude society from his private life, not the right of the community to be spared unpleasant and seamy stories."[37]

When are Embarrassing Facts "News"?
  While the Supreme Court recognizes a "zone of privacy surrounding

33. 113 F.2d at 809.
34. *Ibid.* at 808.
35. *Ibid.*
36. *Ibid.*
37. Karafiol, p. 525. The distinction between a privacy right intended to protect an individual's private life and a privacy right intended to protect an individual from unwanted communication blurs to the extent that the courts confuse the right of privacy with the right not to know. The former — the right of privacy — is intended to guard against the unwanted disclosure of private facts, whereas the latter — the right not to know — is rooted in the proposition that the First Amendment ought to protect individuals from being part of a captive audience.

every individual," and while the Court further recognizes the state's legitimate interest in protecting an individual from "intrusion by the press,"[38] little has been done to define the contours of such a "zone" or to retard the journalist's ability to penetrate it. There are, of course, those few instances when the courts have upheld the plaintiff's privacy claims. In *Barber v. Time, Inc.,*[39] for example, the press enjoyed no privilege to publish intimate details — along with a photograph — of a hospitalized woman's exotic disease. Similarly, in *Daily Times Democrat v. Graham,*[40] publication of a photograph of a woman whose dress had been blown above her waist by a jet of air at a fun house proved to be an invasion of her privacy. In *Melvin v. Reid,*[41] a court found in favor of a reformed prostitute whose privacy had been violated by a movie depicting her as a prostitute and dramatizing her real-life role in a murder trial; despite the essential accuracy of the movie portrayal, the successful rehabilitation of the plaintiff proved to be more important than the public's interest in her former activities. Finally, in *Briscoe v. Reader's Digest,* the California Supreme Court upheld recovery for the truthful disclosure of a man's conviction for a hijacking 11 years previous to publication.[42] But for the most part these are the exceptions,[43] not the rule; even judicial tolerance has its limits.

Significantly, since *Time, Inc. v. Hill* in 1967,[44] when the Supreme Court applied to privacy the Constitutional fault standard used to protect the press in libel litigation, there has been no reported case "in which a plaintiff has succeeded in finally recovering damages for truthful disclosure by the press."[45] Although *Hill* involves the "false light" tort, it is significant that the Court cites with approval a number of non-actionable cases brought to court under the public disclosure tort.[46] As in libel, truth may soon emerge as an unqualified defense

38. *Cox,* 420 U.S. at 487.
39. 348 Mo. 1199, 159 S.W.2d 291 (1942).
40. 276 Ala. 380, 162 So.2d 474 (1964).
41. 112 Cal. App. 285, 297 P. 91 (1931).
42. 4 Cal.3d 529, 483 P.2d 34 (1971).
43. See also *Feeney v. Young,* 191 N.Y.S. 481 (1920); *Banks v. King Featᵤ ₃s Syndicate,* 30 F. Supp. 352 (S.D.N.Y. 1930); and *Johnson v. Evening Star Newspaper Co.,* 344 F.2d 507 (D.C. Cir. 1965).
44. 385 U.S. 374 (1967).
45. *Briscoe* would appear to be an exception. But this 1971 case was subsequently removed to a federal court and dismissed because the publication was newsworthy. See Ellis, p. 1133, n. 163.
46. 385 U.S. at 383, n. 7 (1967). Some of the more recent "representative cases" cited by the Court include *Afro-American Pub. Co. v. Jaffee,* 366 F.2d 646 (D.C. Cir. 1966); *Wagner v. Fawcett Pubs.,* 307 F.2d 409 (7th Cir. 1962); *Jenkins v. Dell Pub. Co.,* 251 F.2d 447 (3d Cir. 1958); *Miller v. N.B.C.,* 157

against an individual's privacy claims. Both the press and the courts seem to agree that the First Amendment stands out as "the predominant factor in determining the scope of an individual's right to sue the media for portrayals that impinge upon his privacy."[47] Ellis' observation offers a succinct summary of the present state of the public disclosure tort: "An attorney who accepts a disclosure case on a contingency fee basis is either desperate or extremely dedicated."[48]

If the newsworthiness privilege appears to be overwhelming in *Sidis,* its scope is virtually boundless today. Not only must the plaintiff prove the lack of newsworthiness of the disclosure but must demonstrate its invasiveness as well. Apparently, newsworthiness is not "an issue or privilege which must be urged defensively but an element which must be negated by the plaintiff when meeting her burden of proof."[49]

The vague and ambiguous defense of newsworthiness typically fails to protect an individual's interest in privacy not only because the plaintiff — as opposed to the press — must identify the limits to the newsworthiness privilege but because the terms used to define "newsworthiness" are themselves vague and ambiguous. While it is clear that "the dissemination of news does not constitute an actionable invasion of privacy,"[50] it is uncertain whether "news" is limited to — or extends far beyond — "issues about which information is needed or appropriate to enable the members of society to cope with the exigencies of their period."[51] When, for example, the courts use a "public interest" standard to distinguish between news and other kinds of freshly ac-

F.Supp. 240 (D.C. Del. 1957); *Buzinski v. Do-All Co.,* 175 N.E.2d 577 (1961); and *Hubbard v. Journal Pub. Co.,* 368 P.2d 147 (1962). Since *Time v. Hill,* relevant cases include *Pearsen v. Dodd,* 410 F.2d 701 (D.C. Cir.), cert. denied, 395 U.S. 947 (1969); *Rawlins v. Hutchinson Pub. Co.,* 281 Kan. 295 (Kan. 1975); *Howard v. Des Moines Register and Tribune Co.,* 283 N.W.2d 289 (Iowa 1979).

47. Flecher and Rubin, p. 1585.
48. Ellis, pp. 1134-1135.
49. *Howard v. Des Moines Register and Tribune Co.,* 283 N.W. 2d 289, 300 (Iowa 1979).
50. *Id.* at 300. See also *Bremmer v. Journal-Tribune Pub. Co.,* 76 N.W.2d 769 (Iowa 1956).
51. *Thornhill v. Alabama,* 210 U.S. 88, 102 (1940). Perhaps the broadest interpretation was put forth in *Campbell v. Seabury Press,* 614 F.2d 395, 397 (1980), where the Fifth Circuit identified a broad constitutional privilege "not merely limited to the dissemination of news either in the sense of current events or commentary upon public affairs. Rather, the privilege extends to information concerning interesting phases of human activity and embraces all issues about which information is needed or appropriate so that individuals may cope with the exigencies of their period."

quired information, do they mean "*of* public interest" or "*in* the public interest"?[52] Since information "of public interest" is a simple empirical question to which the press is more than willing to provide its ready answer,[53] the courts ordinarily reject the "in the public interest" interpretation or, on occasion, accept it without elaboration.

Thus the *Virgil* Court, with its emphasis on information "of legitimate *concern* to the public,"[54] fails to explicate a workable doctrine that might reasonably define such terms as "concern" and "public". Does "concern" denote a *need* to know or merely a keen interest? And does "public" refer to a publication's general audience or, as political scientists and sociologists use the term, a collectivity of individuals "who regard themselves as likely to become involved in the consequences of an event and are sufficiently concerned to interest themselves in the possibility of control"?[55]

Should the courts opt for protecting only information "in the public interest" are they prepared to distinguish between publications which entertain or amuse and publications which inform and educate? And would such a distinction be of any Constitutional consequence? In other words, does the First Amendment apply with less force to a "frivolous" press as opposed to a "serious" press?

These are only a few of the questions to which a coherent theory of newsworthiness might address itself. If nothing else, such a theory must identify — conceptually and operationally — the limits to the newsworthiness defense. Moreover, a theory of newsworthiness would need to reconcile society's interest in protecting an individual's privacy with society's interest in free expression.

THEORIES OF NEWSWORTHINESS

In light of the concern over the conflict between privacy and freedom of the press, the courts may soon be ready to adopt — if not formulate on their own — a theory of newsworthiness. To this end, three existing theories may prove instructive: (i) the Black-Douglas doctrine, which gives almost exclusive weight to First Amendment concerns; (ii) Emerson's definitional approach, which calls for full protection of privacy,

---

52. For an insightful examination of the ambiguities of the public interest concept, see Everette E. Dennis, "The Press and the Public Interest: A Definitional Dilemma," *De Paul Law Review,* 23 (Spring 1974): 937-960.
53. See Pember, pp. 16-20.
54. 527 F.2d at 1129 (emphasis added).
55. Tamotsu Shibutani, *Improvised News.* New York: Bobbs-Merrill, 1966, p. 38.

even when privacy runs counter to a free press; and (iii) a Meiklejohnian standard — refined by Bloustein and operationalized by Bezanson
— which defines newsworthiness in terms of the purpose of self-
government.

The Black-Douglas Doctrine

As absolutists, Justices Black and Douglas preferred a strict and
literal interpretation of the First Amendment. There is, Douglas said in
his concurring opinion in *Cox Broadcasting Corp. v. Cohn,* "no power
on the part of government to suppress or penalize the publication of
'news of the day.' "[56] The First Amendment, from the perspective of
Black and Douglas, means *no* laws abridging freedom of the press, and
that would include the common law of privacy as well as efforts by state
legislatures to protect their citizens from an intrusive press. When
Douglas expressed his support for privacy in *Griswold,* it was state intrusion, not private intrusion, he sought to eliminate. Decidedly, the
privacy right articulated by Douglas in *Griswold* serves to enhance
freedom of expression by protecting freedom of choice; within the narrow context of *Griswold,* privacy appears to be fully consistent with an
absolutist's reading of the First Amendment.

When freedom of the press is at stake, it is, for Douglas, "irrelevant
to talk of any right of privacy."[57] Both Douglas and Black reject the
"weighing process" whereby a compromise might be reached between
privacy rights and a free press. In his concurring opinion in *Time, Inc.
v. Hill,* in which Douglas joined, Black wrote:

> If the judicial balancing choice of constitutional
> changes is to be adopted by this Court, I could wish it
> had not started on the First Amendment. The
> freedoms guaranteed by that Amendment are essential
> freedoms in a government like ours. That Amendment
> was deliberately written in language designed to put its
> freedoms beyond the reach of government to change
> while it remained unrepealed. If judges have, however,
> by their own fiat today created a right of privacy equal
> to or superior to the right of a free press that the Con-
> stitution created, then tomorrow and the next day and
> the next, judges can create more rights that balance
> away other cherished Bill of Rights freedoms. If there
> is any one thing that could strongly indicate that the

56. 420 U.S. 469, 501 (1975) (Douglas, J., concurring).
57. *Time v. Hill,* 385 U.S. 374, 401 (1967) (Douglas, J., concurring).

146, 55-1

> founders were wrong in reposing so much trust in a
> free press, I would suggest that it would be for the
> press itself not to wake up to the grave danger to its
> freedom, inherent and certain in this "weighing pro-
> cess."[58]

Both justices even reject the "actual malice" standards as essentially unconstitutional since it expressly narrows the ambit of the First Amendment. As a standard of liability, "knowing or reckless falsity" is, in
Douglas' words, an "elusive exception" to the First Amendment, an
abridgement of speech which gives the jury "broad scope and almost
unfettered discretion."[59] Thus, while many commentators see *Hill* as an
important step toward protecting the press, Black and Douglas view it
as one more attempt to constrain what would otherwise be a free press.

Given their views on the viability of Prosser's "false light" tort and
the standard of liability used by the Court in *Hill,* there is little doubt
that Black and Douglas would not support in any way press liability for
publishing true but embarrassing facts. To be sure, Black and Douglas
stand firm in their conviction that a free press cannot withstand the
kind of balancing approach the courts must use if the common law of
privacy is to survive. That the newsworthiness defense seems to be
decimating the public disclosure tort would be of little concern to Black
and Douglas. "The press will be 'free' in the First Amendment sense,"
Douglas once said, "when the judge-made qualifications of that
freedom are withdrawn."[60] Under the Black-Douglas doctrine, in short,
the press would have an unqualified privilege to report the day's news,
even if such reportage invaded the privacy of those individuals on
whom the press reports. Black and Douglas thus offer a simple but effective resolution of the conflict between privacy and publicity: no
liability for the press.

---

58. *Ibid.* at 400 (Black, J., concurring). Black seemed to have developed what
    one commentator describes as a "crabbed view of privacy," a somewhat
    confusing and inconsistent effort to "exclude privacy from the Constitu-
    tion by a strict construction or narrow interpretation of that document's
    language." See Donald M. Gillmor, "Black and the Problem of Privacy," pp.
    81-93 in E.E. Dennis, *et al., Justice Hugo Black and the First Amendment.*
    Ames, Iowa: Iowa State University Press, 1978, p. 82.
59. *Ibid.* at 402 (Douglas, J., concurring).
60. *Cantrell v. Forest City Pub. Co.,* 419 U.S. 245, 255 (1974) Douglas, J., dissen-
    ting).

Emerson's Definitional Approach

Like Black and Douglas, Emerson rejects a balancing or weighing approach. Unlike Black and Douglas, however, Emerson confronts the conflict between privacy and freedom of the press by delineating the privacy right and by reserving full protection for it; that is, he uses a definitional approach, an effort to define the right of privacy and then "accord that right full protection against claims based on freedom of the press."[61] For Emerson, the right to privacy calls for "protection for the individual against all forms of collective pressure."[62] Not limited to state or governmental intrusion, Emerson's theory would support press liability — albeit strictly limited liability — for invading an individual's zone of privacy.

In Emerson's view, freedom of the press serves social interests, whereas privacy serves the individual; and "the individual right of privacy would plainly take precedence over the collective interest."[63] Indeed, Emerson would go so far as to protect the individual "against intrusion by any rule, regulation, or practice of the society in its collective capacity"; thus the First Amendment "would be subordinate to the requirements of the privacy right."[64] Interestingly, Emerson's concern for privacy is rooted in his desire to maintain an effective system of freedom of expression. More often than not, freedom of expression and privacy are mutually supportive, especially when they combine to enhance individual self-fulfillment. When the two are in conflict, however, Emerson uses as his guiding principle the need to protect only that right which does not injure another person. For this reason, when privacy and freedom of the press come in conflict with each other, Emerson believes the right of privacy should prevail.

The privacy Emerson wants to protect extends only to "matters related to the intimate details of a person's life: those activities, ideas or emotions which one does not share with others or shares only with those who are closest."[65] Although Emerson does not offer an exhaustive list of protected "activities, ideas or emotions," he cites, for example, family relations, bodily functions, and sexual relations. He would unequivocally exclude from protection any violation of privacy

---

61. Thomas I. Emerson, "The Right of Privacy and Freedom of the Press," *Harvard Civil Rights-Civil Liberties Law Review,* 14 (Summer 1979): 342.
62. *Ibid.*
63. *Ibid.,* p. 341.
64. Thomas I. Emerson, "Legal Foundations of the Right to Know," *Washington University Law Quarterly,* 1976 (Number 1): 22.
65. Emerson, "The Right of Privacy and Freedom of the Press," p. 343.

resulting from publication of any officially public document or proceeding. Moreover, Emerson would afford the press some "breathing space" when discussing the public conduct of public figures or public officials; individuals "who operate in the limelight," Emerson reasons, "cannot expect the same degree of privacy about their personal lives."[66] Finally, Emerson would guard against self-censorship by "imposing strict limitations upon the liability of the press"; to avoid uncertainty and to encourage legitimate expression, Emerson believes the "basis for recovery against the press can and should be held to narrow grounds."[67]

In sum, the protection Emerson would extend to the press is broad and encompassing; the press would be held liable for disclosing embarrassing facts only when those facts "touched the inner core of intimacy."[68] Privacy would indeed prevail over the First Amendment, but privacy, for Emerson, is narrowly defined and, in theory, defined precisely enough for the courts to be able to decide when and where the newsworthiness defense applies.

A Meiklejohnian Standard

Bloustein and Bezanson, in separate but related articles, put forth a theory of newsworthiness rooted in the First Amendment theory of Alexander Meiklejohn. In brief, Meiklejohn's interpretation of the First Amendment rests on the fundamental importance of the right to know, not the right to speak. For Meiklejohn, the right to speak is essentially a private right, whereas the right to know is a public right; and it is only the public's right to know, in Meiklejohn's view, which deserves full First Amendment protection. "What is essential," he argues, is "not that everyone shall speak" but that "everything worth saying shall be said."[69] The goal of the First Amendment, Meiklejohn is convinced, is not to sustain "unregulated talkativeness"[70]. From Meiklejohn's perspective, First Amendment protection for the right to know is justified as a necessity of self-government; it is essential that citizens be exposed to expressions which bear upon "issues with which voters have to deal."[71] As Bloustein understands it, Meiklejohn's contention is this:

---

66. *Ibid.*, p. 347.
67. *Ibid.* pp. 344, 360.
68. Emerson, *The System of Freedom of Expression*, p. 557.
69. Alexander Meiklejohn, *Political Freedom: The Constitutional Power of the People.* N.Y.: Oxford University Press, 1965, p. 26.
70. *Ibid.*
71. *Ibid.*, p. 79.

> The test for freedom of speech under the first amendment is whether discussion of the given subject matter contributes to the public understanding essential to self-government. If the communication fulfills this purpose, it should not be restricted. If it does not fulfill this purpose, the communication may be subject to reasonable limitation in the public interest just like the exercise of any other private right.[72]

Accordingly, Bloustein proposes a "test of relevance" which, if not met, would justify reasonable restrictions on the public disclosure of embarrassing facts. Bloustein's relevance test is, simply, "whether what is published concerning a private life is relevant to the public understanding necessary to the purposes of self-government."[73] Thus while Bloustein would support an "unqualified first amendment right of the public to learn about those aspects of private lives which are relevant to the necessities of self-government," he would support only a qualified First Amendment right of a publisher to "satisfy public curiosity and publish lurid gossip about private lives."[74]

Bloustein's test of relevance is greatly enhanced by Bezanson's efforts to demonstrate that not all public disclosures are "equally entitled to constitutional privilege."[75] Although, curiously, Bezanson makes no explicit reference to Meiklejohn, his distinction between the *communicative* value of a disclosure and its *impact* value closely parallels Meiklejohn's distinction between the public and private uses of speech. In Bezanson's attempt to balance privacy claims and freedom of the press, the role of the disclosure — its communicative value versus its impact value — will decide its constitutional value.[76] He would accept at face value the "newsworthiness" of whatever appeared in the press. "But to conclude that every article and every invasive public disclosure published by the press is newsworthy," Bezanson cautions, "is not to conclude that every newsworthy disclosure should be constitutionally privileged."[77]

---

72. Edward J. Bloustein, *Individual and Group Privacy*. New Brunswick, NJ.: Transaction Books, 1978, p. 61.
73. *Ibid.,* p. 62.
74. *Ibid.,* p. 64.
75. Randall P. Bezanson, "Public Disclosure as News: Injunctive Relief and Newsworthiness in Privacy Actions Involving the Press," *Iowa Law Review,* 64 (July 1979): 1073.
76. *Ibid.,* p. 1069.
77. *Ibid.,* p. 1099.

Specifically, Bezanson distinguishes between the First Amendment protection of the news story and First Amendment protection of the tortious dislosure — a distinction between the *substance* and *means* of expression.[78] Bezanson would want the courts to examine the nexus between the disclosed facts and the substance of the article.[79] Does the disclosure narrow the reader's perspective or foreclose reader understanding?[80] Is the disclosure used to enhance the subject matter of the article or is it used to attract reader interest?[81] In other words, if the disclosure is reasonably communicative, it deserves First Amendment protection; if, however, its principal value is impact, privacy rights would prevail.

Both Bloustein and Bezanson are concerned with the *need* to know; they differ, however, on their level of analysis. While Bloustein talks about the public's need to know, Bezanson refers to the reader's need to know. The difference between "public" and "reader" is, perhaps, more apparent than real: whether the analysis focuses on the value of the disclosure to society in general or the reader in particular, its value — what Bezanson calls its communicative dimension — will determine its First Amendment protection and, in the end, impose limits on the defense of newsworthiness.

NEWSWORTHINESS RECONSIDERED

The Black-Douglas doctrine is an appealing solution to the press-privacy controversy only to the extent that society has no interest in freedom *from* the press. Given the pervasive presence of modern media of communication, public disclosure of private facts is today far more damaging than it was nearly a century ago when Warren and Brandeis introduced the "right to privacy." For Black and Douglas to argue against any liability for the press — even when the press aimlessly turns private life into a public spectacle — is to deny the need to hold the press accountable for its actions. If the press remains responsive only to marketplace forces, as Black and Douglas would prefer, what incentive is there for journalists to protect what Warren and Brandeis call the "inviolate personality" of the individual?[82]

78. *Ibid.,* p. 1091
79. *Ibid.,* p. 1074.
80. *Ibid.,* p. 1070.
81. *Ibid.,* p. 1074.
82. Warren and Brandeis, p. 205.

More importantly, the Black-Douglas doctrine of "no liability for the press" indiscriminately protects all journalistic expression, regardless of quality or value. As attractive as this approach may be to the press, the unfortunate implication is that anything the press may publish is, *ipso facto,* of value to society. While there is good reason not to provide government, including the judiciary, an opportunity to decide *at whim* what constitutes quality journalism, there is a pressing need to adopt an objective standard to which the courts might turn when faced with a press more damaging to individuals than valuable to society. Without such a standard — without a theory of newsworthiness — there can be no protection against invasion of privacy by the press. The Black-Douglas doctrine, therefore, does not offer a solution to the problem of an intrusive press; instead, Black and Douglas contend that the problem is not of sufficient consequence to justify any liability for the press. Black and Douglas thus offer a theory of the First Amendment wholly at odds with a society struggling to define "vital information,"[83] a view of the Constitution in which the public is unable to direct or channel, let alone constrain, the awesome power of the press.

In contrast to Black and Douglas, Emerson recognizes the need for the individual to know "to what extent privacy will be protected," the need for the press to be able "to assess its potential liability for infringement," and the need for the courts to have "appropriate guidelines for accommodating these often conflicting areas."[84] Emerson is concerned with protecting "certain areas of individual autonomy, identity, and intimacy";[85] his approach to the problem of an intrusive press focuses on the individual, not society, and the success of his theory rests on an operationally clear definition of "matters related to the intimate details of a person's life."[86]

As conceptually compelling as Emerson's definitional approach may be, it is not quite what Emerson hopes will someday be a workable theory of privacy. For Emerson, privacy is a "developing right," and one "cannot expect it to take final, concrete shape at this point in our history."[87] Although Emerson prefers a legal doctrine that expresses itself in definitional terms, he is unable to articulate with sufficient

---

83. For a worthwhile discussion of this issue, see Clifford G. Christians, "Jacques Ellul and Democracy's 'Vital Information' Premise," *Journalism Monographs,* No. 45 (August 1976).
84. Emerson, "The Right of Privacy and Freedom of the Press," p. 341.
85. *Ibid.*
86. *Ibid.,* p. 343.
87. *Ibid.,* p. 340.

precision the limits to the privacy right he wants to protect. In his most recent effort to reconcile the right of privacy with freedom of the press, Emerson concludes:

> in strict theory the reconciliation should be accomplished through development of a careful definition of privacy, and material falling within that carefully defined sphere would then be afforded full protection. This approach would seem to follow from the very nature of the right to privacy — protection for the individual against all forms of collective pressure. Unfortunately there has been no agreement on such a definition. Hence no unified theory of the right of privacy, which would serve as the foundation for constitutional protection of the various kinds of interests, which we intuitively group under the notion of privacy, has been forthcoming. This Article has not solved that problem.[88]

Consequently, Emerson is willing to settle for the very approach he initially rejects. "Accepting a balancing theory," Emerson writes, "the effort should be directed toward developing, refining, and giving specific weight to the various considerations which go into the balancing process."[89] The further development of the privacy tort will not, Emerson believes, "pose a serious threat to freedom of the press."[90] A "fair accommodation" between privacy claims a free press and a little more concentration on the "privacy side of the equation" would, in Emerson's view, yield a satisfactory standard of liability for the press.[91]

Whether balancing is used or not, however, Emerson offers some insightful clues as to where privacy begins and ends; and conceptually, he offers an important rationale for giving serious consideration to the individual first and then to the collective interests of society. Clearly, Emerson would not extend the newsworthiness privilege to any expression "of public interest." Unlike Black and Douglas, Emerson advocates a basis for recovery against the press, although, regrettably, a full understanding of what constitutes an invasive public disclosure

88. *Ibid.*, p. 359.
89. *Ibid.*, p. 360.
90. *Ibid.*
91. *Ibid.*

must await a more careful delineation of privacy in general, intimacy in particular.

If Emerson gives considerable weight to individual interests, Bloustein and Bezanson focus on the other side of the continuum; their approach calls for an emphasis on the social or public value of private facts. Bloustein, following Meiklejohn, successfully unravels the "confusion between the public's constitutional right to be informed . . . , the publisher's constitutional right to publish private gossip, and the public's thirst for lurid details of any private life";[92] and Bezanson identifies with great clarity the precise role of the disclosure, its value to the reader, and thus "the extent of constitutional protection to which it is entitled."[93] Together, they offer an impressive outline of a theory of newsworthiness based on a "right to know" interpretation of the First Amendment.

Bloustein's understanding of the First Amendment involves both an appreciation for the privacy of the individual and respect for society's need for an informed electorate. He appreciates the "anguish and mortification," the "blow to human dignity" that may result from an "unwanted witness" to private life.[94] At the same time, he recognizes the importance of a press free to inform and enlighten its readers. To establish an effective compromise between freedom of the press and the often countervailing interest in privacy, Bloustein identifies and resolves the ambiguities of "newsworthiness." He thus calls for a distinction between "public interest," meaning curiosity, and "public interest," meaning the "value to the public of receiving information of governing importance."[95] Only the latter, in Bloustein's view, deserves full First Amendment protection; the former — the public's curioisity — may be restricted when privacy is threatened. "The privacy of an individual may only be invaded by mass publication when that publication is relevant to the purposes of self-government," Bloustein argues. "In all other cases the right of the publisher should be subject to reasonable restriction in order to protect the public interest in privacy."[96]

92. Bloustein, p. 83.
93. Bezanson, p. 1075. See pp. 1093-1108 for Bezanson's application of his analysis to a recent public disclosure case in Iowa, see *Howard v. Des Moines Register and Tribune Co.*, 3 Med. L. Rptr. 2304 (Iowa Dist. Ct. 1978). Using, in part, Bezanson's analysis, the Iowa Supreme Court affirmed the lower court's dismissal. See *Howard v. Des Moines Register and Tribune Co.*, 283 N.W. 289, 303 (1979).
94. Bloustein, p. 55.
95. *Ibid.*, pp. 82-83.
96. *Ibid.*, p. 65.

For both Bloustein and Bezanson, newsworthiness is defined in terms of the quality and relevance of the public disclosure. As Bezanson puts it, "a public disclosure that narrows the reader's perspective or forecloses reader understanding ought to be entitled to less constitutional protection than one that deepens and enhances understanding and perspective."[97] Thus the Meiklejohnian standard advanced by Bloustein and Bezanson's useful distinction between the communicative and impact values of the disclosure combine to protect not only the vital information the public needs to know but an individual's solitude as well.

Until and unless Emerson's theory is developed to the point where privacy is fully and clearly defined, the works of Bloustein and Bezanson — or a creative synthesis of the two — would appear to be the most attractive solution to the conflict between privacy and freedom of the press. It would appear to be the most attractive solution in part because it recognizes that freedom of choice requires a satisfactory blend of privacy and free expression; and, in part, because it offers judges and juries a workable plan for accommodating both.

97. Bezanson, p. 1070.

LESLIE G. FOSCHIO

Motor Vehicle Records: Balancing Individual Privacy and the Public's Legitimate Need to Know*

Leslie G. Foschio, General Counsel and
Secretary, Barrister Information Systems
Corporation, is a former Commissioner of
Motor Vehicles of the State of New York
and a former Corporation Counsel of the
City of Buffalo. He was at one time Assistant
Dean and Associate Professor of Law at
the Notre Dame Law School, and prior to
that was an Assistant District Attorney of
Erie County, New York. He is a graduate
of the State University of New York at
Buffalo Law School and was an editor of
its *Law Review*. Mr. Foschio is President
of the Theodore Roosevelt Inaugural Site
Foundation in Buffalo and is a member of
the American, New York State, and Erie
County Bar Associations.

The purpose of this presentation is to supply a factual frame of reference within which to consider the possible need for broader regulation of access to state-compiled data, particularly as regards the New York Department of Motor Vehicles records, which is the most frequently accessed databank in state government. In addition, I will seek to illustrate the tensions created between existing statutes touching upon Department of Motor Vehicles records and principles of the State Freedom of Information Law and the recommendations of the Federal Privacy Commission. Finally, I will outline some suggested ways to reconcile the apparent conflicts in the public interest.

*Based on remarks given at a program sponsored by The Association of the Bar of the City of New York on Thursday, November 18, 1982, on the subject "My Right to Know Versus Your Right to Privacy—Government Release of Information." The author gratefully acknowledges the able assistance of his former special counsel and executive assistant, Edward A. Sheridan, in the preparation of the original remarks.

LESLIE G. FOSCHIO

I. INTRODUCTION: THE DATA COLLECTORS AND USERS

New York State government maintains literally tens of millions of records on individuals within its various record-keeping departments, including the Division of Criminal Justice Services and Departments of Taxation, Labor, Social Services, Education, and State.[1]

The Department of Motor Vehicles alone has more than 10 million vehicle, boat, and snowmobile registrations and 10.8 million driver's license records. In a single month, the Department computer processes more than 7 million inquiries—over 1 million from the state police; 300,000 from other law enforcement agencies; 175,000 (2 million annually) from service companies providing information primarily to insurance carriers on driving records; and over 150,000 to other state and local government agencies. The balance of the inquiries are departmental internal, data processing, and enforcement.

II. MOTOR VEHICLES: TYPES AND CONTENT OF THE MAJOR RECORDS

The major types of records maintained by the Department of Motor Vehicles include the license file, which contains personal identification information, but not the individual's social security account number. The license file incorporates such information as military service, the status of the license (whether it is a conditional or a restricted-use license, for example), accidents involving the licensee during the past three years, convictions and reversals for the past three years (ten years for offenses of driving under the influence of alcohol or drugs), and any suspensions or revocations against the license during the past three years. In another major type of record, the vehicle registration file, the Department maintains personal identification information concerning the registrant, vehicle and boat identification information, suspensions and revocations against the registration, scofflaw data, the ownership record, lienholders, if any, and stolen vehicle status, if applicable, under the vehicle identification number.

Pursuant to Vehicle and Traffic Law, section 202(3)(b), the Department's registrations list compiled from all registrations is sold to the highest responsible bidder. This provision of law was added by the legislature in 1940 by chapter law 691. The present contract for such registrations information is held by the R. L. Polk Company of Detroit. This information is used for

---

1.   *E.g.*, the New York Department of State maintains licensee disciplinary files, but retains only final agency decisions; the Department of Education maintains files on professional misconduct warnings and investigations, which are not subject to disclosure (Education Law § 6510(2)(b))—other final determinations of misconduct and penalties are disclosable.

government-related activities, highway safety and consumerism statistics, and commercial mail solicitation. For example, in the past the United States Department of Transportation has received monthly statistical reports from the Polk Company based on the registration list, as has the United States Department of Commerce, which has received truck data by weight group for its census of transportation. Also, the United States Department of Treasury has, on occasion, sought selected registration data on trucks subject to the federal highway use tax. An important use of this information furnished by R. L. Polk and Company is the mailing of manufacturers' warranty and emission recall notices.

R. L. Polk Company uses the list itself for commercial mail solicitation, serving approximately 1100 users for this purpose. The list is rented, not sold, so that Polk maintains control. Nine hundred fifty New York State automobile dealers use such information for sales solicitation, as do one hundred fifty other commercial users, including automobile and insurance companies, oil companies, stock brokerages, marketing research firms, mail order and catalog sales businesses, and travel and vacation users.

It has been estimated that approximately seven pieces of commercial mail per year, per registrant, are attributable to the Department's sale of this list to the Polk Company. The annual revenue to the state general fund from the sale of the departmental registrations list is approximately $290,000.

Interestingly, we find that other state departments do not provide such commercial lists, and this is one main issue for continued consideration of the justification for generating such lists. The New York State Department of State does not provide any list for commercial or fund-raising purposes, relying on the provision of the State Freedom of Information Law in that regard. Lists of professional licensees are furnished to nonprofit groups for appropriate purposes, however.[2] The State Education Department provides no list for commercial purposes.[3] Furthermore, although both agencies are major state licensing agencies like the Department of Motor Vehicles, none of the information they compile is available in terms of enforcement unless there has been a final agency determination and adjudication.

III. BALANCING FREEDOM OF INFORMATION AND PRIVACY IN MOTOR VEHICLE RECORDS

The Department, in attempting to balance the freedom of information and privacy concerns in motor vehicle records, deals with a number of statutory provisions that are in conflict.

2. N. Y. Public Officer's Law § 389.
3. *Id.*

LESLIE G. FOSCHIO

The Vehicle and Traffic Law in section 354 specifically mandates for driver and registration records that the Commissioner of Motor Vehicles furnish any insurance carrier or any person the abstract of operating record of any person. Simply put, this means that anyone can have access to anyone else's operating record upon payment of the two-dollar — or, if the request is submitted in machine readable form, one-dollar — fee. The state general fund grosses approximately $3.5 million annually from the sale of such information.

Juxtaposed against this disclosure provision in the Vehicle and Traffic Law is the State Freedom of Information Law, which in Public Officer's Law, section 87, broadly defines "record" and mandates disclosure except where disclosure would constitute "an unwarranted invasion of personal privacy."

As I have noted with respect to registration lists, the Vehicle and Traffic Law in section 202(3)(b) authorizes the Commissioner to sell the list to the highest responsible bidder. Both statute and contract prohibit resale or use contrary to "public policy, morals or welfare." The Commissioner may require a report on the use made of such list. In this latter respect, the Vehicle and Traffic Law is inconsistent with the State Freedom of Information Law, which in Public Officer's Law section 89(2)(b)(iii) defines "unwarranted invasion of personal privacy" to include the sale or release of names and addresses for commercial or fund-raising purposes, one of the known uses of the list by the R. L. Polk Company.

Balanced against the individual's interest in privacy and protection of the information contained in the motor vehicle license and registration record is government's legitimate need to know. Law enforcement officials, for example, must have access to vehicle license and registration records to perform stolen car checks and for safety enforcement. Similarly, parking violations bureaus must have access to registrations and license files for scofflaw enforcement. Prosecutors and courts must be able to verify driving records and convictions to lay the proper charge or impose the appropriate sentence. And the Department of Motor Vehicles requires such information for highway safety research and program administration.

Other governmental and public uses must also be accounted under the government's legitimate need to know. Welfare fraud enforcement, for example, sometimes requires access to identification information in the motor vehicle record. And, in the past, the Department of Motor Vehicles has cooperated with the Selective Service System in identifying draft-eligible persons based upon the driver's license record and date of birth.

There is, as well, a private need to know. Highway safety interest groups, for example, may have legitimate reason for access and disclosure of motor vehicle license and registration records. Automobile insurance carriers, under provisions of Insurance Law sections 167(a) and 176, are empowered to make coverage and premium decisions based upon the three-year driving record for which they should have—and indeed do have by express provision of law—access to the driving record. Under the First Amendment, the press also may have a legitimate right and need for access to certain motor vehicle records—for example, accident information.

But a balance must be drawn at some point to protect the individual's privacy. After all, the Department of Motor Vehicles collects information to accomplish its highway safety mission. Should unrelated information requests from government and private sectors be allowed? That is to say, should the driving record affect credit or employment decisions, or should there be any obligation on the Department to furnish such information to service bureaus and others to facilitate such uses? Also, should your neighbor—out of curiosity, whim, or caprice—be entitled to a copy of your driving record merely upon payment of the two-dollar fee?

The Federal Privacy Commission addressed some of these concerns and made specific recommendations. First, it recommended that government agencies restrict access to records on individuals. In this regard, the Privacy Act of 1974[4] provides a federal model for possible state application. It sets forth a "routine use" requirement, the essence of which is that no disclosure should be allowed unless for a use compatible with the purpose for which the record was collected, or for agency use, or for criminal or civil law enforcement.

The New York State Department of Motor Vehicles is now reviewing its information disclosure policy within these guidelines and recommendations for possible incorporation into the Vehicle and Traffic Law and for restriction of access to records on individuals in accordance with the principles stated by the Privacy Commission.

In balancing the individual's interest in privacy and legitimate State Freedom of Information Law concerns, the accuracy of the record must be addressed. Any person may obtain a copy of his or her license or registration record and, upon verification, the Department will correct errors therein.

In the delicate balancing of contending interests, registration lists and their sale present a special problem. In *Lamont v. Commissioner*,[5] the court rejected a constitutional challenge to the authority of the Commissioner under Vehicle and Traffic Law, section 202, to sell registrations information, stating that the information was in the category of public records, that the state had tapped a small source of needed revenue, and that it reflected a rational and allowable balancing of values by the legislature.

Thirty-six states presently sell registrations information. In New York State, the sale of registrations information annually yields $290,000 for the general

4.   5 U.S.C., § 552(a).
5.   269 F. Supp. 880 (S.D.N.Y. 1967).

fund. Some have justified such sales on the basis of governmental uses, safety, warranty recalls, and even commercial value to the mail order industry, which exceeds $60 billion annually in the United States. And although we attribute approximately seven pieces of unsolicited commercial mail per year per registrant to the sale of the registrations file to the Polk Company and the uses made by that company of it, no abuses of this list have come to the Department's attention.

Nevertheless, appropriate recognition of the privacy interest and the "right to be left alone" requires, at a minimum, that the registrant have the right to opt out by (1) the negative check-off on a registration document or (2) notification of the uses of registration and instruction on how to remove his or her name from a list by writing to the contractor. The negative check, recommended by the Privacy Commission, permits the motorist to indicate on the annual renewal document that he or she does not wish his or her name used for commercial solicitation purposes. As the Privacy Commission recommended, by so informing or indexing the registrations list it would then be incumbent upon the mail order house—which relies upon that industry's expressed policy and interest not to mail to someone who is not going to be responsive—to in fact not mail to that individual.

IV. CONCLUSION

Some have said that we as a nation are approaching an unsought but inescapable "dossiered society" and that it is the rare American who does not dwell in the shadow of his or her dossier. If privacy, as the cradle of the active soul, of vital personality and the social distance necessary to maintain effective citizenship, is to thrive, government as the trustee of vast individual information systems has the high responsibility to take steps to ensure they are administered in the public interest and that privacy continues to nurture the common foundation of individual dignity and public freedom.[6]

---

6.   On July 25, 1983, chapter 652 of the Laws of 1983 (S. 6936/A. 8176), a new Article 6-A of the Public Officer's Law, the New York Personal Privacy Law, was approved. It establishes guidelines for the acquisition and disclosure of information about individuals by state and municipal agencies generally consistent with the Federal Privacy Commission's recommendation regarding routine use. Under § 96(1)(e) and (f) of the statute, however, the unfettered access to motor vehicle records allowed under Vehicle and Traffic Law § 354 still appears to be available, as does access to accommodate the needs of federal agencies which are enabled to grant themselves access to state records by authority of their own regulations. The new law also appears to continue implied authorization for the compilation of vehicle registration data for commercial lists.

DEBORAH MANSON

The Television Docudrama and the Right of Publicity

Deborah Manson received her B.A. in
Political Science from New College of the
University of South Florida in 1980 and
her J.D. from The University of Santa
Clara in 1984. She was an editor on the
Santa Clara Law Review.

> No matter who portrays me, she will not be me, I will not
> be she. I am my own commodity. I am my own industry. The
> way I look, the way I sound, that is my industry, and if
> someone else portrays me and fictionalizes my life, it is taking
> away from me.[1]

The docudrama, a recent television phenomenon, is a blend of truth and fiction[2] that portrays the lives of public figures.[3] Do living public figures have the right to prevent this portrayal?[4] Elizabeth Taylor used the right of publicity[5] to sue American Broadcasting Companies (ABC) and David Paradine

1. Elizabeth Taylor *quoted in* Lewin, *Whose Life Is It?,* N. Y. Times, Nov. 21, 1982, § 2, at 1, col. 2, *reprinted in* L. A. Daily J., Nov. 25, 1982, at 1, col. 6.
2. "Neither fiction nor straight documentary, the 'docudrama' liberally tailors real people and events to fit the TV entertainment format." *Elizabeth Taylor vs. Tailored Truth,* TIME, Nov. 8, 1982, at 71.
3. In recent years, Jacqueline Kennedy Onassis, Gloria Vanderbilt, Prince Charles and Princess Diana, and Grace Kelly have been portrayed in docudramas. *See id.* at 71. The story of Grace Kelly's life began filming before her death and was aired in February 1983.
4. The public figure can try to collect damages under the right of publicity, once the docudrama has been televised. Damages, however, will not erase the confusion in the minds of viewers nor will damages remove the injury to the image and reputation of the public figure. Therefore, an injunction is a more satisfactory remedy. *See supra* text accompanying notes 36–45.
5. The right of publicity is the right of a person to "own, protect, and commercially exploit his own name, likeness, and persona." Lerman v. Chuckleberry, 521 F.

Productions because of their plans to televise a docudrama based on her life.[6] She sought declaratory relief and preliminary[7] and permanent injunctive relief. Taylor wanted to prevent the docudrama from airing because she contended that, "her life story is a commercial property which she alone has the right to exploit . . . ."[8] Thus, she alleged that the film would cause "irreparable injury" to her since the defendants would be misappropriating her life story for their own commerical use thereby damaging her "valuable interests in her name, likeness, and public and professional image and reputation."[9] She contended that these interests are part of the "goodwill" associated with a successful business enterprise.[10] In addition, Taylor wanted to "maintain and

---

Supp. 228, 232 (S.D.N.Y. 1981). For a public figure suing under the right of publicity, New York provides the best chance of recovery. To begin with, New York is an accessible forum to cases that are national in scope, as in the Taylor case, because defendants, such as production companies and national television networks, are generally located there. In addition, a plaintiff may sue under the New York right of privacy statute, New York Civil Rights Law, §§ 50, 51 (McKinney, 1976). The privacy statute allows recovery where a living person's name, portrait, or picture is used for advertising purposes or for the purposes of trade, without written consent. *Id. But cf.* CAL. CIV. CODE § 3344 (West, 1981) (allows recovery only where a person's name, photograph or likeness is used for advertising purposes, without consent). Many New York cases have used the statute since its enactment in 1903. Finally, the court may look at right of privacy cases to help them resolve cases brought under the right of publicity because the two rights are interrelated. *See infra* text accompanying note 74. Taylor's complaint also alleged violation of her right of privacy under New York law, New York Civil Rights Law §§ 50, 51 (McKinney, 1976): "false representations . . . of origin in connection with goods and services used in commerce which raise a significant likelihood of public confusion . . . ." § 43(a) of the Lanham Act, 15 U.S.C. § 1125(a), damage to her professional and business reputation under New York law, New York General Business Law § 368(d) (McKinney, 1976), and unfair competition under the common·law of New York. Complaint at 7–10.

6. Taylor sued the defendants because of their "planned exhibition and broadcast of a fictional, made for television movie exploiting the name, likeness, and public and professional reputation and image of plaintiff, Elizabeth Taylor, without her approval or consent." Complaint at 1. Taylor notified the defendants of her "objections to their unauthorized use of her name [and] likeness . . . ." The defendants, however, decided "to proceed with the production, exhibition and broadcast of the film without her consent." Complaint at 6–7.
   The suit was dismissed on April 29, 1983, because ABC decided not to pursue the project.

7. "Each case must stand on its own facts. An injunction will not issue when it is not in the public interest." Mazzacone v. Willing, 246 Pa. Super. 98, 369 A.2d 829 (1976). Thus, newsworthy presentations, since they are in the public interest, *see infra* text accompanying notes 78, 79, and 81, will always prevail over prior restraint. But how important is it that the public know about the life of a public figure when the account of this life is a clever blend of truth and fiction as in the docudrama? *See supra,* note 2.

8. Lewin, *supra*, note 1, at 26, *reprinted in* L. A. DAILY JOURNAL at 18.

9. Complaint at 1.

10. Complaint at 3.

enhance her distinctive public and professional reputation and image, which constitute the source of her livelihood and are of great personal value to her."[11]

Motion pictures (for example, docudramas), however, are a form of speech.[12] The first amendment strongly protects freedom of speech,[13] a fact to be carefully considered when examining the docudrama under the right of publicity. The courts presently follow two tests, with regard to books and movies, to determine if the right of publicity[14] will overcome the first amendment-protected freedom of speech. In order to prevail over the first amendment and therefore obtain an injunction or damages or both, the substantially false presentation is subject to the following test: The plaintiff must prove that the presentation contains "material and substantial falsification and that the work was published with knowledge of such falsification or with a reckless disregard for the truth."[15] However, for the first amendment right usually *granted* novels and movies to outweigh the plaintiff's publicity rights, a fictionalized account of events in the life of a public figure must adhere to this test: The court must find that "it is evident to the public that the events so depicted [in the novel or movie] are fictitious."[16]

This article explores the unresolved question of whether or not a public figure can use the right of publicity to successfully enjoin the showing of

11. Complaint at 3. Taylor contended that she

> carefully controls the use of her name and likeness in connection with commercial and entertainment ventures in order to preserve her professional reputation and the economic value attached to her name and likeness. She also carefully selects the activities in which she herself participates. Over the course of her career she has received and rejected numerous offers to endorse products, appear in movies and plays, and cooperate in writing, publishing or producing books, articles, and films concerning her life and career.

Complaint at 3–4.
12. *See* University of Notre Dame v. Twentieth Century Fox, 22 A.D.2d 452, 457, 256 N.Y.S.2d 301, 306 (1965). The court in this case stated that "[m]otion pictures . . . are 'a significant medium for the communication of ideas;' their importance 'as an organ of public opinion is not lessened by the fact that they are designed to entertain as well as to inform . . . .'" *Id.* at 457, 256 N.Y.S.2d at 306 (quoting Joseph Burstyn v. Wilson, 343 U.S. 495, 501 (1952); Jocobellis v. Ohio, 378 U.S. 184 (1964)).
13. U.S. Const., amend. I. *See generally* NAACP v. Button, 371 U.S. 415 (1963).
14. *See supra,* note 5.
15. Spahn v. Julian Messner, 21 N.Y.2d 124, 127, 233 N.E.2d 840, 842, 286 N.Y.S.2d 832, 834 (1968), *appeal dismissed,* 393 U.S 1046 (1969).
16. Hicks v. Casablanca, 464 F. Supp. 426, 433 (S.D.N.Y. 1978); *see* 22 A.D.2d at 455, 256 N.Y.S.2d at 304–5. Thus, the "absence or presence of deliberate falsifications or an attempt by a defendant to present the disputed facts as true determines whether the balancing process shall tip in favor or against protection of the speech at issue." 446 F. Supp. at 433.

a docudrama based on his or her life. The article examines the right of publicity and the right of privacy because the two are interrelated; the interests protected by the right of publicity are similar to those protected by the right of privacy.[17] In addition, this article looks at the relationship of the first amendment to the right of publicity. After considering the tests stated above, the article concludes that neither test is applicable to the docudrama.

A living public figure who has an interest in maintaining a professional and public image and reputation is his or her own commodity. Taylor or any other living public figure should have the right to decide when and how others may portray his or her life. The docudrama poses a unique problem since it is "neither fiction nor straight documentary."[18] It is a clever blend of truth and fiction, thus creating an ambiguous distinction in the viewer's mind between reality and fabrication as depicted in the docudrama. Viewer confusion diminishes and thereby damages the value of the public figure's name, likeness, and personality.[19] This article proposes that the figure should have recourse to the right of publicity and its privilege of enjoining the exhibition of a docudrama based on his or her life, unless the public figure provides express permission for this docudrama to be presented.

I. THE RIGHT OF PUBLICITY

A. Evolution and Definition

The right of publicity is the right of a person to "own, protect, and commercially exploit his own name, likeness, and persona."[20] *Haelen Laboratories v. Topps Chewing Gum*[21] was the first case to expressly recognize and apply the right of publicity. The appellate court reversed the trial

17. *See infra* text accompanying note 74.
18. *See supra,* note 2.
19. *See* Complaint at 6.
20. Lerman v. Chuckleberry, 521 F. Supp. at 232. *See also* Felcher and Rubin, *Privacy, Publicity, and the Portrayal of Real People by the Media,* 88 YALE L. J. 1577, 1589 (1979) (a person's right in the use of his name, likeness, activities, or personal characteristics).
21. 202 F.2d 866 (2nd Cir. 1953). The facts of *Haelen Laboratories* are as follows:

> The plaintiff and defendant were rival chewing gum manufacturers. Plaintiff Haelen Laboratories made an agreement with a baseball player granting the plaintiff the sole right to use the player's photograph in connection with the sale of the plaintiff's gum. The ballplayer agreed not to give any other gum manufacturers a similar right as long as he was under contract with Haelen Laboratories. The defendant then persuaded the ballplayer to allow the defendant to use the player's photo in connection with the sales of defendant's gum during the term of the plaintiff's contract with Haelen Laboratories. The plaintiff

court's decision for the defendant[22] and held that the right of a man in the publicity value of his photograph, that is, the privilege to authorize the sole right of publishing his picture, might be called a right of publicity.[23] The court stated that this right of publicity was "in addition to and independent of [the] right of privacy."[24] The defendants had claimed that

> none of plaintiff's contracts created more than a release of lia-
> bility because a man has no legal interest in the publications
> of his picture other than his right of privacy, [that is], a
> personal and non-assignable right not to have his feelings hurt
> by such a publication.[25]

The court said, however, that a public figure is not very likely to have his personal feelings hurt from public exposure. Rather, he is more likely to be injured from not receiving compensation for granting the right for his likeness to be used in advertisements.[26]

In a right of publicity cause of action, a plaintiff must demonstrate:

(1) "that his name or likeness has publicity value;"[27]

---

claimed that the defendant had infringed upon the plaintiff's exclusive right to use the photos of prominent baseball players. The defendant countered that the plaintiff's contract did not give the plaintiff a property right or any other legal interest which the defendant's contract had invaded.

22. The appellate court remanded the case to the trial court for further determinations regarding the contracts that the baseball player made with the plaintiff and defendant. The appellate court said that the defendant was not liable for a breach of the plaintiff's contract and therefore was not liable for an induced breach. However, the court decided that the plaintiff "in its capacity as exclusive grantee of a player's right of publicity ha[d] a valid claim against the defendant if defendant used that player's photograph during the term of grant and with knowledge of it." *Id.* at 869.
23. *Id.* at 868.
24. *Id.*
25. *Id.* The right of privacy "belongs to the broad field of injury to feelings." S. HOFSTADER AND G. HOROWITZ, THE RIGHT OF PRIVACY 2 (1964). This right was first formulated in 1890 in an article by Samuel Warren and Louis Brandeis. *The Right of Privacy,* 4 HARVARD L. REV. 196 (1890) They stated:

> The design of the law must be to protect those persons with
> whose affairs the community has no legitimate concern, from
> being dragged into an undesirable and undesired publicity and
> to protect all persons, whatsoever; their position or station, from
> having matters which they may properly prefer to keep private,
> made public against their will. *Id.* at 214–15.

26. 202 F.2d at 868.
27. 521 F. Supp. at 232.

(2) that he has "exploited" this name or likeness;[28] and

(3) that the defendant has used this right of publicity without the plaintiff's consent for advertising or trade purposes.[29]

In order for a celebrity to have a marketable public personality, he must dedicate years of "practice and competition" to developing his personality.[30] "That identity, embodied in his name, likeness...and other personal characteristics, is the fruit of his labors and is a type of property."[31] The interest in this property is unique.[32]

The right of publicity encompasses the marketability of the picture or representation of a public figure and protects his right to the financial profits in his public image and reputation.[33] His name is commercially profitable because the public is aware of the person's name and associates goodwill and certain accomplishments to that individual.[34] Furthermore, the right of publicity can be compared to a commercial enterprise's right to benefit from the "goodwill" it has created in its name.[35] Therefore, the interest in protecting the right of publicity is "the straightforward one of preventing unjust enrichment by the theft of goodwill."[36]

B. Remedies

Under the right of publicity, a public figure may obtain injunctive relief, damages, or both.[37] While a public figure may collect monetary damages

28. 464 F. Supp. at 429; see Factors, Etc. v. Pro Arts, 444 F. Supp. 279, 283 (S.D.N.Y. 1977); Factors, Etc. v. Pro Arts, 444 F. Supp. 288 (S.D.N.Y. 1977), aff'd, 579 F.2d 215 (2d Cir. 1978), cert. denied, 440 U.S. 908 (1979). In order to show exploitation, the person claiming the right of publicity must demonstrate that he acts in such a way as to openly recognize the "extrinsic commercial value of his or her name or likeness." 464 F. Supp. at 429.
29. 521 F. Supp. at 232; Ann-Margret v. High Society Magazine, 498 F. Supp. 401, 406 (S.D.N.Y. 1980).
30. Uhlaender v. Henrickson, 316 F. Supp. 1277, 1282 (D. Minn. 1970).
31. Id.
32. Id. at 1283.
33. See Zacchini v. Scripps-Howard Broadcasting Co., 433 U.S. 562, 573 (1977); Ali v. Playgirl, 447 F. Supp. 723, 728 (S.D.N.Y. 1978).
34. 316 F. Supp. at 1283.
35. Grant v. Esquire, 367 F. Supp. 876, 879 (S.D.N.Y. 1973).
36. 447 F. Supp. at 728–29 (quoting Kalven, Privacy in Tort Law — Were Warren and Brandeis Wrong? 31 LAW & CONTEMP. PROBS. 326, 331 (1966) quoted in 433 U.S. at 576.
37. See, e.g., Cher v. Forum Int'l, 692 F.2d 634, 640 (9th Cir. 1982) (damages); Ali v. Playgirl, 447 F. Supp. 723, 729 (S.D.N.Y. 1978) (injunctive relief); Grant v. Esquire, 367 F. Supp. 876, 881 (S.D.N.Y. 1973) (damages); Uhlaender v. Henrickson, 316 F. Supp. 1277, 1283 (D. Minn. 1970) (injunctive relief); see also Spahn v. Julian Messner, 21 N.Y.2d at 129, 233 N.E.2d at 844, 286 N.Y.S.2d at 836 (right of privacy case; damages and injunctive relief).

The Television Docudrama and the Right of Publicity

(that is, the fair market value)[38] for the use of his or her photograph by the defendant,[39] it is difficult to attach a monetary amount to the value of the dilution of the public figure's name, likeness, and personality.[40] Injunctive relief, therefore, may be a more satisfactory remedy. For example, in *Uhlaender v. Henrickson*[41] the court said:

> It seems clear to the court that a celebrity's property interest in his name and likeness is unique, and therefore there is no serious question as to the propriety of injunctive relief.
>
> Defendants have violated plaintiffs' rights by the unauthorized appropriation of their names and statistics for commercial use. The remedy at law, considering particularly the difficulty in determining and measuring damages, past or future, is inadequate.[42]

In *Ali v. Playgirl,*[43] the court stated "To the extent that defendants are unlawfully appropriating this valuable commodity [that is, Ali's "commercially valuable proprietary interest in his likeness and reputation"][44] for themselves, proof of damages or unjust enrichment may be extremely difficult."[45] The court stated that in addition,

> defendants appear not only to be usurping plaintiff's valuable right of publicity for themselves but may well be inflicting damage upon this marketable reputation...Damages from [the] evident abuse of plaintiff's property right in his public reputation are plainly difficult to measure by monetary damages.[46]

38. 367 F. Supp. at 881.
39. *See* 202 F.2d 866; 367 F. Supp. 876.
40. *See* 447 F. Supp. at 729; 316 F. Supp. at 1283.
41. 316 F. Supp. 1277.
42. *Id.* at 1283.
43. 447 F. Supp. 723. In *Ali,* former heavyweight boxing champion Muhammad Ali sued the defendants for injunctive relief and damages after *Playgirl Magazine* published and distributed an objectionable portrait of Ali in one of its issues. The portrait showed "a nude black man seated in the corner of a boxing ring." *Id.* at 725. "Although the picture is captioned 'Mystery Man' the identification of the individual as Ali is further implied by an accompanying verse which refers to the figure as 'the Greatest.'" *Id.* at 726–27. The court noted that "the Greatest" is a name that "Ali has regularly claimed for himself and that his efforts to identify himself in the public mind as [such] have been so successful that he is regularly identified as 'the greatest' in news media." *Id.* at 727.
44. *Id.* at 729.
45. *Id.*
46. *Id.* Furthermore, the court found that "in the preliminary injunction context 'difficulty [in computing damages] is especially common when damage to reputation, credibility or good will is present.'" *Id.* (quoting Dino DeLaurentis Cinematografica v. D–150, 366 F.2d 373, 376 (2d Cir. 1966) (citing cases)).

DEBORAH MANSON

C. Interrelationship of Right of Publicity and Right of Privacy

The New York Right of Privacy Act[47] was enacted in 1903 as a result of *Roberson v. Rochester Folding Box Company.*[48] In *Roberson,* the court denied recovery to a woman whose photo was used by the defendant, without her consent, to advertise its brand of flour. The court stated that the so-called right of an individual to "pass through this world" without having his picture published (the right of privacy), whether favorable or not, does not exist at law.[49]

The first case to apply the new statute to motion pictures was *Binns v. Vitagraph,*[50] where the defendant produced a series of short movies portraying

---

Because it is difficult to resolve monetary damages, the plaintiff is left without an "adequate remedy at law." 447 F. Supp. at 729. In addition, this difficulty in determining damages "satisfactorily establishes irreparable injury for purposes [of] preliminary equitable relief." *Id.* The following test is used to decide whether a preliminary injunction should issue:

> [A] preliminary injunction should issue only upon a clear showing of either (1) probable success on the merits *and* possible irreparable injury, *or* (2) sufficiently serious questions going to the merits to make them a fair ground for litigation *and* a balance of hardships tipping decidedly toward the party requesting the preliminary relief. *Id.* at 726 (quoting Sonesta Int'l Hotels v. Wellington Associates, 438 F.2d 247 (2d Cir. 1973)).

47. N.Y. Civil Rights Law §§ 50, 51 (McKinney, 1976), Section 50, states:

> A person, firm or corporation that uses for advertising purposes, or for the purposes of trade, the name, portrait or picture of any living person without having first obtained the written consent of such person . . . is guilty of a misdemeanor.

Section 51 states:

> Any person whose name, portrait or picture is used within this state for advertising purposes or for the purposes of trade without the written consent first obtained as above provided may maintain an equitable action in the supreme court of this state against the person, firm, or corporation using his name, portrait or picture, to prevent and restrain the use thereof and may also sue and recover damages for any injuries sustained by reason of such use. . . .

48. 171 N.Y. 538, 63 N.E. 442 (1902) The decision in *Roberson* led to a "storm of professional and popular disapproval." S. HOFSTADER AND C. HOROWITZ, THE RIGHT OF PRIVACY 27–28. A *New York Times* editorial was so vehement that a member of the court wrote an article justifying the *Roberson* decision. Therefore, in order to remedy what was perceived as an erroneous decision, the Right of Privacy statute was enacted by the legislature at its next session. *Id.* at 28.
49. 171 N.Y. at 544, 63 N.E. at 443.
50. 210 N.Y. 51, 103 N.E. 1108 (1913).

the plaintiff, a wireless operator who became a hero during a rescue at sea.[51] Most of the movies were taken in the defendant's studios, and an actor portrayed the plaintiff. Pictures of Binns appeared in the series five times and his name was used in the subtitles six or more times. The court held the following:

> A moving picture company, which uses the name and pictures of a person as a feature and not as incidental to the film, and are not designed to instruct or educate those who see it, but only to amuse them and to make money for the company, is using the portrait and name of the person for the "purposes of trade" within Civil Rights Law § 50, 51.[52]

In reaching their decision, the court found that the movies were not "true pictures of a current event, but mainly a product of the imagination...."[53] Futhermore, the court said that the picture did not necessarily have to be a photograph of a living person in order to meet the requirements of the statute, but could be any representation of that person.[54]

However, in another New York case, *Humiston v. Universal*,[55] the court decided that using the plaintiff's name and picture in a motion picture of current events did not violate the statute, since the right of privacy did not prevent the use of one's name and picture in accurate news presentations. The plaintiff, an attorney, sued to enjoin exhibition of newsreel. She also sued for damages because of the suffering incurred as a result of the film's presentation. The plaintiff had been filmed as she went about her task of investigating and solving the mysterious disappearance and subsequent discovery of the body of a woman named Ruth Cruger.[56] The court found that the picture was a true account of a current event filmed at the time it occurred.[57] The court stated

51. The facts of the rescue are as follows:

> On January 23, 1909, the steamships Republic and Florida collided at sea. The plaintiff was a telegraph operator on the Republic. Immediately after the collision, he sent a signal which was received by telegraph operators on the steamship Baltic and on Nantucket Island. Because of the messages sent from the plaintiff to the Baltic, the Baltic rescued the passengers and crew on the Republic and Florida. According to the court, "The plaintiff was the first man to use wireless telegraphy at a time when its use resulted in saving hundreds of lives." *Id.* at 52, 103 N.E. at 1109.

52. *Id.* at 51, 103 N.E. at 1108.
53. Id. at 56, 103 N.E. at 1110.
54. *Id.,* 103 N.E. at 1110.
55. 189 A.D. 467, 178 N.Y.S. 752 (1919).
56. *Id.* at 470, 178 N.Y.S. at 755.
57. *Id.* at 470–71, 178 N.Y.S. at 755.

that there was a definite difference between a newsreel (as in this case), which shows only actual photos of current events of public interest, and a motion picture, which is "inherently a work of fiction."[58]

In *Blumenthal v. Picture Classics,*[59] a film depicted various scenes of New York City inlcuding one showing the plaintiff engaged in selling bread on the street. The only professional people used in the film were four actors who portrayed two guides and two teachers on a tour of the city. Yet, the court held that, since the defendants had used the film for purposes of trade and profit, the plaintiff had the right to enjoin the scene in which she had appeared.[60]

In applying the New York statute to the above cases, the courts found that films used for purposes of trade[61] fell within the statute. The plaintiff could enjoin a series of motion pictures in which he was portrayed by an actor and where his name and picture were used several times in the films.[62] If a film showed actual life scenes but also employed professional actors, the plaintiff could enjoin the scene in which she appeared.[63] But, the court found that the use of the plaintiff's name and likeness in a newsreel did not violate the statute since the statute does not prevent the use of one's name and likeness in an accurate presentation of current events.[64]

Cases brought under the New York privacy statute[65] must be examined if dealing with the right of publicity with regard to motion pictures and books. Although the privacy statute deals with injury to personal feelings[66] and

58. *Id.* at 470, 178 N.Y.S. at 755. The distinction between a newsreel and a feature picture was also stressed in Redmond v. California Pictures, 23 A.D. 708, 1 N.Y.S.2d 64 (1937), *aff'd,* 277 N.Y. 707, 14 N.E.2d 636 (1938). In *Redmond,* a golfer presented a trick shot display that was filmed, with his consent, as a newsreel. The defendant bought the film and used it (without Redmond's consent) in a short feature. Since the plaintiff had originally given permission, the trial court awarded him six cents. The appellate court increased this to $1,500; *see also,* Sharkey v. National Broadcasting Co., 93 F. Supp. 986 (D.C.N.Y. 1950), where a former heavyweight boxing champion sued the defendant under the New York Right of Privacy statute for showing the plaintiff without his consent in a program called "Greatest Fights of the Century." The court held that the plaintiff's complaint was sufficient to state a claim on which relief could be granted since "[n]othing in the complaint support[ed] defendants' argument that the challenged program was merely dissemination of news." *Id.* at 987.
59. 235 A.D. 570, 257 N.Y.S. 800 (1932).
60. *Id.* at 571, 257 N.Y.S. at 801. According to the dissent, the film was not "inherently a work of fiction" since the dialogue of the four actors was incidental to the film. Rather, it was an "actual photograph of current events of public interest." *Id.* at 574, 257 N.Y.S. at 804 (O'Malley, J., dissenting).
61. *See supra* note 47.
62. 210 N.Y. 51, 103 N.E. 1108.
63. 235 A.D. 570, 257 N.Y.S. 800.
64. 189 A.D. 467, 178 N.Y.S. 752.
65. New York Civil Rights Law §§ 50, 51 (McKinney, 1976).
66. *See supra* note 25 and accompanying text.

publicity applies to the right of the public figure to commercially exploit himself or herself,[67] both are concerned with the use of the name and likeness of a living person for commercial purposes.[68]

In *Hicks v. Casablanca,*[69] the court explained why it is helpful to look at right of privacy cases, under the New York statute, when resolving the issue of "whether the right of publicity attaches where the name or likeness [of a public figure] is used in connection with a book or movie."[70] The court stated that it did not know of any other cases having a similar fact pattern or posing a similar constitutional question[71] regarding the right of publicity. Therefore it would look to cases involving the right of privacy under section 51 of the New York Civil Rights Act[72] to help resolve the issue of whether the right of publicity applies where a name or likeness is used in a book or movie.[73] According to the court, even though the right of publicity is not statutory, both the rights of privacy and publicity are "intertwined" because of the "similarity between the nature of the interests protected by each."[74] The court found that earlier decisions regarding the limits on the right of privacy would help it decide what restrictions, if any, should be placed on the right of publicity.[75] The court found that the same "privileges and exemptions" that are part of the privacy statute are part of the right of publicity.[76]

II. THE FIRST AMENDMENT AND PORTRAYALS

"The primary social policy that determines the legal protection afforded to media portrayals is based on the first amendment guarantee of free speech

67. *See supra* text accompanying note 20.
68. *Id. See supra* note 47.
69. 464 F. Supp. 426. *Hicks* involved a suit by the heirs and assignees of the mystery writer, Agatha Christie, to enjoin movie producers and a publisher from distributing a movie and a book dealing with an incident in Christie's life. *See infra* note 138.
70. 464 F. Supp. at 430.
71. The constitutional question was "whether movie or novel fictionalizing events in lives of public is entitled to First Amendment protections of speech . . . ." *Id.* at 427.
72. New York Civil Rights Law § 51 (Mckinney, 1976).
73. 464 F. Supp. at 430.
74. *Id.*
75. *Id.*
76. *Id.* In interpreting the New York statute, the New York Supreme Court, Appellate Division, in Spahn v. Messner, 23 A.D.2d 216, 260 N.Y.S.2d 451 (1965), stated that:

> Although the statute makes no express provision therefor, the courts have engrafted upon it certain privileged uses and exemptions. Generally, the privileged uses are concerned with leaving untrammeled matters of news, history, biography, and other factual subjects of public interest despite the necessary

and press."[77] Implicit in freedom of speech is the "prevailing view" that free speech offers certain advantages to society.[78] For example, without free speech we could not preserve our "system of self government" based on a free "political process" and an open political dialogue.[79] Another advantage inherent in free speech is the contribution toward cultural enrichment.[80]

In examining how the first amendment relates to media portrayals, it is necessary to look at two types of portrayals: those that inform and those that entertain.

Informative portrayals are considered news. Since news encourages public debate, it enjoys the highest degree of first amendment protection.[81] Informative portrayals are found in newspaper, magazine, and radio or television reporting.[82] Such portrayals also are encountered in books (for example, biographies), scholarly articles, and television or motion picture documentaries.[83] These portrayals "attempt to describe, interpret or assess the real world."[84]

Biographies are considered informative and therefore enjoy first amendment protection. In *Rosemont Enterprises v. Random House*,[85] the defendants, publisher and author of a biography on Howard Hughes, sought summary judgment dismissing Rosemont Enterprises'[86] complaint. The complaint had alleged that the defendants were planning "to exploit commercially the name, likeness, and personality of Hughes without the

---

references to the names, portraits, identities, or histories of living persons.

      Id. at 219, 260 N.Y.S.2d at 453.

77. Felcher and Rubin, *Privacy, Publicity, and the Portrayal of Real People by the Media*, 88 YALE L. J. 1577, 1598 (1979).
78. *Id.* at 1596–97.
79. *See id.* at 1597.
80. *Id.*
81. *Id.*
82. *Id.*
83. *Id.* A documentary is defined as "having or claiming the objective, quality, authority, or force of documentation in the representation of a scene, place, or condition of life." WEBSTER'S THIRD NEW INTERNATIONAL DICTIONARY 666 (15th ed. 1966).
84. Felcher, *supra* note 77, at 1597.
85. 58 Misc.2d 1, 294 N.Y.S.2d 122 (1968).
86. Rosemont Enterprises was described in the complaint as "engaged 'in the business of developing and acquiring literary and dramatic properties and rights, biographical material and the right to use such material . . .'" *Id.* at 2, 294 N.Y.S.2d at 124. Hughes learned in 1965 that Random House was planning a biography of his life. He warned Random House that he was opposed to the biography. Subsequently, Rosemont Enterprises was formed by associates of Hughes in order to prepare an authorized biography. However, the real purpose of Rosemont Enterprises was to prevent unauthorized biographies of Hughes, especially the Random House biography.

consent of either Hughes or plaintiff and to capitalize upon the achievements of Hughes and upon his life story or incidents therein. . . ."[87] In addition, the plaintiffs contended that the "book. . .would not be written or published in order to disseminate newsworthy information."[88] Rather it would be written and published in order to "exploit commercially the name, likeness, and personality of Hughes."[89] The court held that when the right of publicity conflicted with the "free dissemination of thoughts, ideas, newsworthy events and matters of public interest," it must give way to public interest.[90] The court found that the biography of Hughes came within "those 'reports of newsworthy people or events' which are constitutionally protected. . . ."[91] Thus, a public figure has no exclusive rights to his life story. In addition, consent from the public figure is not required before a biography on his or her life is written.[92]

In *Koussevitsky v. Allen, Towne and Heath*,[93] a world-famous symphony conductor[94] sought to enjoin the publication of an unauthorized biography. The book contained very little about his private life but dealt mainly with his musical career. The plaintiff claimed that the book "falsely and wrongfully portrayed his life and musical career."[95] The court stated that there was "nothing repugnant to one's sense of decency or that takes the book out of realm of the legitimate dissemination of information on a subject of general interest."[96] The court, in holding that the plaintiff was not entitled to an injunction, said that the right of privacy statute did not pertain to a biography of a public figure, written without his permission, unless the biography was a fictional or novelized version.[97] "That it may contain untrue statements does not transform it into the class of fiction."[98]

The second category of portrayals refers to works with artistic and entertainment value. This category includes "fictionalized history, stage, motion picture or television simulations of real events, mimicry, parody, and purely fictional works set against an historical background."[99] Since these

87. *Id.* at 3, 294 N.Y.S.2d at 125.
88. *Id.* at 4, 294 N.Y.S.2d at 126.
89. *Id.,* 294 N.Y.S.2d at 126.
90. *Id.* at 7, 294 N.Y.S.2d at 129.
91. *Id.,* 294 N.Y.S.2d at 129.
92. *Id.,* 294 N.Y.S.2d at 129.
93. 188 Mis. 479, 68 N.Y.S.2d 779 (1947).
94. Serge Keussevitzsky was conductor of the Boston Symphony from 1924 to 1949.
95. 188 Misc. at 481, 68 N.Y.S.2d at 780.
96. *Id.* at 485, 68 N.Y.S.2d at 784.
97. *Id.* at 484, 68 N.Y.S.2d at 783.
98. *Id.* 68 N.Y.S.2d at 783.
99. Felcher, *supra* note 77, at 1598. Drama is defined as "a composition in verse or prose arranged for enactment and intended to portray life or character or to tell a story through the actions and usually dialogue of the enactors." WEBSTER'S THIRD NEW INTERNATIONAL DICTIONARY 685 (15th ed. 1966).

portrayals involve actual persons, the content will often be informative.[100] The distinction between informative portrayals and entertaining portrayals is that while the former is informative in a newsworthy sense, the latter consciously departs from accurate reporting.[101] The first amendment protects entertainment that is both informative and culturally rewarding.[102]

Courts are hesitant to make "fine distinctions" between speech that is for entertainment purposes and speech that is strictly informative.[103] "The line between the informing and the entertaining is too elusive for the protection of [the First Amendment]."[104] "Consequently, any difference in the protection afforded news and entertainment portrayals is likely to be a question of subtle shadings rather than explicity different standards."[105]

In resolving the question of whether or not speech contained in movies and books is deserving of first amendment protection, courts must weigh and balance "society's interest in the speech for which protection is sought [against]...the...commercial interests seeking to restrain such speech"[106] (for example, the public figure who is asserting the right of publicity). "And unless there appears to be some countervailing legal or policy reason, courts have found the exercise of the right of speech to be protected."[107]

A. Tests Applied to Portrayals of Public Figures

The courts follow two tests, *Spahn* and *Notre Dame-Hicks,* to determine whether the right of publicity will overcome the first amendment-protected freedom of speech. These tests will be examined in order to evaluate whether or not they are applicable to the docudrama.

1. Spahn

The test in *Spahn v. Julian Messner*[108] is as follows: Before a public figure may recover for an unauthorized presentation of his or her life, he or she must show (1) that "the presentation is infected with material and substantial falsification" and (2) that "the work was published with knowledge of such falsification or with a reckless disregard for the truth."[109]

---

100. Felcher, *supra* note 77, at 1598.
101. *Id.*
102. *See id.*
103. *Id.*
104. *Id.* (quoting Winters v. New York, 333 U.S. 507, 510 (1948)).
105. Felcher, *supra* note 77, at 1598.
106. 464 F. Supp. at 431.
107. *Id.*
108. 21 N.Y.2d 124, 233 N.E.2d 840, 286 N.Y.S.2d 832, *appeal dismissed,* 393 U.S. 1046.
109. *Id.* at 834, 233 N.E.2d at 842, 286 N.Y.S.2d at 834. The court said that these requirements must be proven in addition to the requirements of New York Civil Rights Law §§ 50 and 51. *Id.,* 233 N.E.2d at 842, 286 N.Y.S.2d at 834.

Spahn involved a fictionalized biography of the well-known baseball player, Warren Spahn. The plaintiff, Spahn, sued for injunctive relief and damages because he claimed that the book was a violation of sections 50 and 51 of the New York City Civil Rights Law. The trial judge found for the plaintiff and stated that the portrayal of Spahn contained "all pervasive distortions, inaccuracies, invented dialogue, and the narration of happenings out of context."[110] The appellate court affirmed the findings of the trial court in favor of the plaintiff and stated that, "it is conceded that use was made of imaginary incidents, manufactured dialogue, and a manipulated chronology."[111] Upon appeal to the United States Supreme Court,[112] the Court remanded *Spahn* to the appellate court so that it could be resolved according to the standards decided on in *Time v. Hill.*[113]

On remand, the court of appeals, in *Spahn,* found that the book had used fabricated dialogue, made up incidents and "attributed thoughts and feelings,"[114] and was therefore not protected by the first amendment.[115]

The court's reasoning for their holding was based on the defendants' failure to make clear how an all-pervasive use of incidents which had never taken place, dialogue which was purely fabrication, and made up thoughts and feelings could not be considered knowing falsity.[116]

The defendants had also argued that their literary techniques were often used in children's literature. In their brief,[117] the defendants had stated that

110. *Id.*, 233 N.E.2d at 842, 286 N.Y.S.2d at 834 (quoting Spahn v. Julian Messner, 43 Misc.2d 219, 230, 250 N.Y.S.2d 529, 541 (1964)).
111. Spahn v. Julian Messner, 23 A.D.2d 216, 219, 260 N.Y.S.2d 451, 454 (1965). The court stated that "[t]his liberty . . . was exercised with respect to plaintiff's childhood, his relationship with his father, the courtship of his wife, important events during their marriage, and his military experience." *Id.* at 219, 260 N.Y.S.2d at 454.
112. Julian Messner v. Spahn, 387 U.S. 239 (1967).
113. 385 U.S. 375 (1967). In *Time v. Hill,* the plaintiff sued under the New York privacy statute for damages. He alleged that *Life* magazine had published an article that falsely reported that a new play portrayed an experience suffered by the plaintiff and his family when they had been held hostage in their home by escaped convicts. The Court held that the "constitutional protections for speech and press preclude the application of the New York statute to redress false reports of matters of public interest in the absence of proof that the defendant published the report with knowledge of its falsity or in reckless disregard of the truth." *Id.* at 388.
114. 21 N.Y.2d at 127, 233 N.E.2d at 841, 286 N.Y.S.2d at 833.
115. *See id.* at 129, 233 N.E.2d at 843, 286 N.Y.S.2d at 835. (The court stated that to allow publication of the "knowing fictionalization presented here would amount to granting a literary license which is not only unnecessary to the protection of free speech but destructive of an individual's right . . . to be free of the commercial exploitation of his name and personality.")
116. *Id.* at 127–28, 233 N.E.2d at 842, 286 N.Y.S.2d at 834. "Indeed, the arguments made here are, in essence, not a denial of knowing falsity but a justification for it." *Id.* at 128, 233 N.E.2d at 842, 286 N.Y.S.2d at 835.
117. The defendant's brief was discussed by the court. *Id.* at 128, 233 N.E.2d at 842–43, 286 N.Y.S.2d at 835.

invented dialogue was considered mandatory for a respected critic, teacher, and author of children's books.[118] The court did not accept this explanation as a defense, but they said that even if they could accept the explanation, the defendants' argument could not succeed because the author had never interviewed Spahn, his family, or any baseball players who knew him. The only research the author had done was to read newspaper and magazine articles.[119]

True accounts of the lives of public figures are protected by the first amendment, since the public is entitled to hear more than the public figures' description of the events of their lives.[120] In addition, holding authors or publishers responsible for inaccuracies that are a consequence of "mere negligence" would severely inhibit the exercise of free speech and press.[121] However, when a so-called biography is substantially and materially false and is "published with knowledge of such falsification or with a reckless disregard for the truth,"[122] then the biography is no longer a dissemination of news or a matter of public interest, "for there is no legitimate public interest in false statements concerning public figures."[123] The fictionalized biography is a commercial product and therefore "contains no matter sought to be protected by the first amendment."[124]

2. Notre Dame *and* Hicks

In order for the first amendment right usually granted novels and movies to outweigh the plaintiff's publicity rights, a fictionalized account of events in the life of a public figure must adhere to the test applied in *Notre Dame v. Twentieth Century Fox*[125] and *Hicks v. Casablanca:*[126] The court must find

118. *Id.* 233 N.E.2d at 842–43, 286 N.Y.S.2d at 835 (quoting defendant's brief). Furthermore, he claimed that biographies for children cannot be "straight narrative" since they have to be stories that will take children away from "television and all other distractions.'" *Id.* at 128, 233 N.E.2d at 843, 286 N.Y.S.2d at 835 (quoting defendant's brief).

119. *Id.,* 233 N.E.2d at 843, 286 N.Y.S.2d at 836. The court stated that the author had made little effort to check the authenticity of these articles. Even when he did check out a source, he ignored it. For example, he was told by the Army that Spahn was not awarded a Bronze Star during World War II but that the records were not completely accurate and "that if Mr. Spahn said he won the Bronze Star, it was likely that he did." The author, however, described Spahn as a recipient of the award. He did concede that Spahn had never said that he had won the Bronze Star. *Id.* 233 N.E.2d at 843, 286 N.Y.S.2d at 836.

120. Berkman, *Right of Publicity,* 42 BROOKLYN L. REV. 527, 553–4.

121. *Id.* at 554.

122. 21 N.Y.2d at 127, 233 N.E.2d at 842, 286 N.Y.S.2d at 834.

123. Berkman, *supra* note 120, at 554.

124. *Id.* The biography that is published with knowing falsity or a reckless disregard for the truth is therefore just a commercial product that is using the public figure's name in order to benefit financially. *Id.*

125. 22 A.D.2d, 452, 256 N.Y.S.2d 301.

126. 464 F. Supp. 426.

that "it is evident to the public that the events so depicted [in the novel or movie] are fictitious."[127]

a. *Notre Dame.*

In *Notre Dame,* the plaintiffs—the university and its president—sued the defendants to enjoin the release and distribution of a movie called *John Goldfarb, Please Come Home* on the basis that the defendants had illegally appropriated the names and reputations of Notre Dame and its president. The plaintiffs also requested that further distribution of the novel be prevented. Neither the president's name nor his picture were used in the movie. In addition, the use of his name in two places in the book was incidental in nature.[128] Thus, the court found that the defendants had not violated sections 50 and 51 of the New York Civil Rights Law,[129] and as a result held that an injunction should not be granted.[130]

The court stated that viewers and readers are aware that they are not seeing or reading about real Notre Dame happenings or about actual characters.[131] The court based this on the fact that the "novel and photoplay both fall in the category of broad farce in which, among other blunderbuss travesty, collegiate football is depicted as having attained such magnified importance today that it may affect religious barriers and influence international relations."[132]

In applying the test[133] to decide whether the plaintiffs should prevail over

127. *Id.* at 433; *see* 22 A.D.2d at 455, 256 N.Y.S.2d at 304–5.
128. 22 A.D.2d at 454, 256 N.Y.S.2d at 304.
129. *Id.* at 455.
130. *Id.,* at 457, 256 N.Y.S. 2d at 307.
131. *Id.* at 455, 256 N.Y.S.2d at 305.
132. *Id.* at 453, 256 N.Y.S.2d at 303. The plot is as follows:

> The son of the King of the Arab country Fawzia is a student at Notre Dame. When the King finds out his son has been denied a spot on the football team, he organizes a team of his own subjects at Fawz University. The King hires a former football star ("Wrong-Way Goldfarb") to train the King's team so that they can beat Notre Dame. Goldfarb is an American pilot who works for the Central Intelligence Agency and who landed by mistake in Fawzia. The King exerts pressure by saying that if the U.S. wants to lease an oil base in his country, it must arrange a game between Fawz U. and Notre Dame. Notre Dame finally consents and its team travels to Fawzia. Notre Dame loses because the night before the game they indulge in spice mongoose at a dinner given by the King and also because the chief of the Central Intelligence Agency acts as referee. The winning touchdown is scored by an American woman reporter who joins the game last minute on the side of Fawzia U. She is carried over the goal line by an oil gusher which erupts on the football field.

Id. at 454, 256 N.Y.S.2d at 303–4.
133. *See supra* text accompanying note 127.

the first amendment, the court asked the following: "Is there any basis for any inference on the part of rational readers or viewers that the antics engaging their attention are anything more than fiction or that the real Notre Dame is in some way associated with its fabrication or presentation?"[134] The court stated that there was "none whatsoever." The viewers and the readers "know they are not seeing or reading about real Notre Dame happenings or actual Notre Dame characters and there is nothing in text or film from which they could reasonably infer 'connection or benefit to the institution.'"[135] Therefore the court found that nobody is "deceived" or "confused."[136]

b. *Hicks.*

Hicks v. Casablanca[137] involved a suit by the heir and assignees of the mystery writer Agatha Christie to enjoin movie producers and a publisher from distributing a movie and book dealing with an incident[138] in Christie's life. The court found that Christie had exploited[139] the right of publicity during her life and, therefore, that right survived her death.[140]

The court held for the defendant and stated that the right of publicity does not apply where "a fictionalized account of an event in the life of a public figure is depicted in a novel or a movie, and in such novel or movie, it is evident to the public that the events so depicted are fictitious."[141]

The court stated that the book and movie presented a fictionalized account of a true incident in Christie's life.[142] The defendants had claimed that *Agatha* was a biography and thus protected under *Spahn.*[143] The court disagreed with this contention and said that the only accurate facts in the book were the following: the names of Mrs. Christie, her husband, her daughter, and Ms. Neeley, and the fact that Christie disappeared for eleven days.[144] "The remainder is mainly conjecture, surmise, and fiction."[145] Furthermore, the court stated that since the word "novel" was used on the cover of the book

134. 22 A.D.2d at 455, 256 N.Y.S.2d at 304.
135. *Id.,* 256 N.Y.S.2d at 305 (quoting Cornell Univ. v. Messing Bakeries, 286 A.D.490, 492, 138 N.Y.S.2d 280, 282, *aff'd* 309 N.Y. 722, 128 N.E. 421 (1955)).
136. 22 A.D.2d at 455, 256 N.Y.S.2d at 305.
137. 464 F. Supp. 426.
138. After Christie married her first husband, she disappeared from her home in England. Her disappearance received wide publicity. After eleven days she was reported missing, but she then reappeared. She never explained the reason for her leaving or her whereabouts during the disappearance. *Id.* at 429.
139. *Id.* at 429. *See supra* text accompanying note 28.
140. 464 F. Supp. 430.
141. *Id.* at 433.
142. *See* 464 F. Supp. at 430–31.
143. It would be more difficult for the plaintiffs to overcome the first amendment if they had to prove knowing falsity or a reckless disregard for the truth. *See supra* text accompanying note 109.
144. 464 F. Supp. at 431.
145. *Id.*

and no mention was made of sources or references, the defendants could not claim that the book was a biography.[146]

After comparing the facts of *Spahn* with those of *Notre Dame,* the court decided that *Notre Dame* should dictate the result in the present case.[147] The court stated that *Spahn* involved the distribution of a book that was held out, by the defendant, as a biography. Therefore, *Spahn* appeared to be similar to *Hicks.* The court went on to say, however, that the Spahn biography contained "deliberate falsifications of events represented to be true, manufactured dialogue, and erroneous statistical data."[148] *Notre Dame,* on the other hand, involved a movie that "satirized modern-day events, people, and institutions, including a football team, identified as that of Notre Dame."[149] The court decided that the *Spahn* holding "should be and was intended to be limited to its facts."[150] Thus, *Hicks* should follow the test set out in *Notre Dame.*[151] The court stated:

> It is clear from the review of these two cases that the absence or presence of deliberate falsifications or an attempt by a defendant to present the disputed events as true, determines whether the scales in this balancing process shall tip in favor of or against protection of the speech at issue.[152]

III. PROPOSAL

This article proposes that the public figure should have the privilege to invoke the right of publicity to enjoin the presentation of a docudrama based on his or her life unless he or she grants written consent for the televising of this docudrama. In determining whether or not the first amendment protects the docudrama, a balancing test must be used. "[I]n addressing the scope of first amendment protections of speech, [courts] have engaged in a balancing test between society's interest in the speech for which protection is sought and the . . . commercial . . . interests seeking to restrain such speech."[153]

Thus, in *Spahn,* the court balanced the plaintiff's privacy rights against the public's interest in the first amendment protection of fictionalization (in

146. *Id.*
147. *See id.* at 432.
148. *Id.*
149. *Id.* at 432.
150. *Id.*
151. *See id.* at 432. The court reached this conclusion based on the fact that *Hicks* was similar to *Notre Dame* since there were no deliberate falsifications, and the reader of the novel *Agatha* would know that the book was fictitious. *Id.* at 433.
152. *Id.*
153. *Id.* at 431.

this instance, falsification).[154] The court found no such protection and as a result granted the plaintiff relief.[155] The court stated that in order for the plaintiff to overcome the first amendment-protected freedom of speech and therefore recover for an unauthorized portrayal of his life, he must prove that the "presentation is infected with material and substantial falsification and that the work was published with knowledge of such falsification or with a reckless disregard for the truth."[156] The *Spahn* test would not be helpful in the docudrama situation for the following reason: The public figure seeking to enjoin the docudrama under the right of publicity usually has no way of knowing what will be in the docudrama, thus making it extremely difficult to prove "material and substantial falsification" or knowing falsity.

In *Hicks*, the court weighed the public figure's publicity rights against the public's right to benefit from the first amendment protection of fictionalization (that is, a fictionalized account of events in the life of the public figure).[157] The court found that the first amendment outweighed the right of publicity because it was apparent to viewers that the events shown in the movie were fictitious.[158] The *Hicks* test is not applicable to the docudrama because it is extremely difficult for the viewer to differentiate between what it true and what is false in the docudrama.[159] Therefore, it will not be evident to the public that the events shown in the portrayal are fictitious.

To determine whether or not the first amendment protects the docudrama, the following balancing test is imposed: Society's interest in the docudrama must be weighed against the public figure's interests in restraining this type of portrayal. Society greatly benefits from the informative nature of the first amendment-protected freedom of speech. The public has an interest in portrayals that inform (e.g., biographies and documentaries); since biographies and documentaries disseminate information, they are accorded the highest degree of first amendment protection.

Society also has an interest in portrayals that entertain (e.g., drama) because of their cultural value. Drama, however, is protected only where the viewer realizes that the events portrayed are fictitious.[160]

The docudrama, because it is "neither fiction nor straight documentary,"[161] does not fall within the first amendment protection of biographies and documentaries; it does not provide a dissemination of information. Furthermore, the docudrama does not come under the first amendment protection of drama;

154. *Id.* at 432.
155. *Id.*
156. 21 N.Y.2d at 127, 233 N.E.2d at 842, 286 N.Y.S.2d at 834. *See supra* text accompanying note 109.
157. *See* 426 F. Supp. at 433.
158. *Id. See supra* text accompanying note 127.
159. *See supra* note 2 and accompanying text.
160. *See* 426 F. Supp. at 433; 22 A.D.2d at 455, 256 N.Y.S.2d at 304–5.
161. *See supra* note 2.

it is not evident to the public that the events depicted in the docudrama are fictitious.

The viewer cannot clearly distinguish between truth and fiction in the docudrama because of its very nature. Viewer confusion is not in the public interest. Because the court in *Hicks* found that it was evident to the public that events presented in the movie were fictitious,[162] the public figure's value in her name, likeness, and personality was not damaged. The viewer confusion created by the docudrama, however, damages and dilutes the value of the public figure's interests in his or her name, likeness, and personality.[163] For these reasons, the public figure has the right to prevent the docudrama from being televised without his or her consent.

IV. CONCLUSION

Society benefits from the first amendment-protected freedom of speech and therefore has an interest in portrayals that may inform or entertain. To determine whether or not the docudrama should be accorded first amendment protection, society's interest in the docudrama is balanced against the public figure's interest in enjoining the exhibition of the docudrama under the right of publicity.

The docudrama does not profit from the first amendment protection of biographies and documentaries or dramas. Neither pure fiction nor documentary news reporting, the docudrama is a cleverly contrived merging of truth and fiction. By its very nature, the docudrama tends to confuse the viewer, making it difficult to discern when true events in the life of the public figure portrayed merge and blend with purely fanciful fabrications. To confuse the viewer is a disservice to the public—to society. Further, confusion also diminishes and thereby damages the value of the public figure's "name, likeness, and persona."

Thus, after weighing the interests of society against those of the public figure, this article finds that unless the public figure expressly permits the presentation of his or her life in a docudrama, he or she can use the right of publicity to enjoin this type of presentation.

162. 426 F. Supp. at 433.
163. *See* Complaint at 6.

SUSANNA R. BARBER

The Big Dan's Rape Trial: An Embarrassment for First Amendment Advocates and the Courts

Susanna R. Barber is an assistant professor of mass communication at Emerson College in Boston. She received her Ph.D. from Bowling Green State University in Ohio, and has been awarded grants from the Kaltenborn Foundation for her research on cameras in the courtroom. She is the author of a book, *News Cameras in the Courtroom,* which will be published by Ablex later this year.

When Judge Paul Baker helped to open Florida courts to cameras in the late 1970s, he noted optimistically that there should be a dialogue of give-and-take, a relationship based on "mutual understanding," between the needs of the courts and the goals of the media.[1] Occasionally, however, media indifference to the courts (as well as to trial participants) has sharply juxtaposed the interests of these two institutions. The hoped-for dialogue sometimes turns to feelings of resentment, if not open confrontation.

One recent, highly publicized case, the Big Dan's barroom rape trial in Fall River, Massachusetts, has triggered heated debate over whether cameras should be allowed to remain in the nation's courtrooms. During the past four

---

1. *See* Judge Paul Baker's views expressed in *Cameras in Courtroom Two-Way Street*, 33, no. 9 NEWS PHOTOGRAPHER 11 (September 1978); his *Report to the Florida Supreme Court re: Conduct of Audio-Visual Trial Coverage*, (State v. Zamora), 1977; and in *Photojournalism Stands Trial With Ronny Zamora in Florida*, 32, no. 11 NEWS PHOTOGRAPHER 11 (November 1977).

SUSANNA R. BARBER

years since the U.S. Supreme Court decided *Chandler v. Florida*,[2] this and other sensational trials, such as the Wayne Williams case in Georgia, the Claus von Bulow case in Rhode Island, and the McMartin child molestation case in California, have fueled and refueled discussion of this free press/fair trial issue.

Today's debate, however, presents a new set of arguments from those heard in either *Chandler* or its predecessor, *Estes v. Texas*.[3] *The issue of televised trials has moved beyond the courtroom and into the audience.*

What concerns the latest anti-cameras lobbyists are not the potentially prejudicial impacts of camera coverage *inside* the courtroom *during* the trial, but possible adverse effects on the viewing public and viewer perceptions of trial participants. Arguments that cameras are physically disruptive, distracting, and detrimental to the dignity and decorum of the courtroom have been laid to rest, as have the equally tenuous arguments that cameras turn witnesses into hysterics, lawyers into flamboyant actors, judges into political sycophants, and jurors into puppets of local public opinion. In their place has arisen a series of concerns that have less to do with trial prejudice, and much more to do with audience reactions to the participants and cases that are televised.

These new concerns can generally be defined as follows: (1) privacy rights of witnesses, particularly victims of physical and sexual abuse; (2) the extent to which televised trials damage the reputations of defendants, and (3) the impact of broadcast trial coverage on the viewing public, particularly children in the audience.

This article will look at each of these issues in turn and examine them in the broader context of the "courtroom cameras" debate as a whole and in the narrower context of the Big Dan's trial. Since hundreds, if not thousands,[4] of cases have been televised in the past decade without causing much anxiety, it might be interesting to see why this particular case appears to present problems that many others do not.

PRIVACY

The question of a right to privacy in the context of judicial proceedings has prompted mixed decisions from the courts and strongly polarized arguments from interested parties. Those who support camera access to courtrooms claim that defendants and witnesses take on "public figure" and "public

2. Chandler v. Florida, 449 U.S. 560 (January 26, 1981).
3. Estes v. Texas, 381 U.S. 532 (1965).
4. Davis, *Courtroom Television: It's Here, It Works*, 18, no. 3 TELEVISION QUARTERLY 7 (Fall 1981); and Davis, *Television in Our Courts: The Proven Advantages, the Unproven Dangers*, 64, no. 2 Judicature 85 (August 1980).

interest" status, and thereby surrender a right to privacy.[5] They also argue that since the public's interests are involved in every criminal trial, the public should have access to those trials, whether in person or through a surrogate in the form of a camera.[6]

Those opposed to camera access contend that the public's right to attend trials is being met, not only because people can visit courtrooms, but also because the press can send reporters to cover trials. *Cameras*, they emphasize, are not covered under the first amendment. They also argue that privacy rights of defendants and witnesses are violated when cameras enter courtrooms: these participants are subjected to humiliation in an atmosphere resembling a public pillory rather than a dignified judicial arena.

THE SIXTH AND FIRST AMENDMENT CHALLENGE TO PRIVACY

Ironically, the privacy issue, one of the most widely promoted "emotional" arguments for keeping cameras out of courtrooms, is also one of the weakest arguments from a purely constitutional point of view.[7] The Florida Supreme Court discussed the privacy issue with specific regard to camera access in *Petition of Post-Newsweek Stations, Florida, Inc.*, the case which first opened Florida courts to cameras on an experimental basis without the need for

5. *See* Gertz v. Robert Welch, Inc., 481 U.S. 323 (1974), and New York Times v. Sullivan, 376 U.S. 254 (1964).
6. *See* Red Lion Broadcasting Co. v. FCC, 395 U.S. 367 (1969), where Justice White, writing for a unanimous Court, emphasized the licensees' responsibility is to serve listeners and viewers for whom they act in proxy; and CBS v. Democratic National Committee, 412 U.S. 94 (1973), where Chief Justice Warren Burger described the licensee as a "public trustee" whose duty is to fairly and impartially inform the listening and viewing public.
7. For a discussion of privacy, among other issues, in the context of televised trials *see*: Lindsey, *Cameras in Court: An Assessment of the Use in State and Federal Courts*, 18 GEORGIA LAW REVIEW 393–97 (Winter 1984); Kuriyama, *The 'Right of Information Triangle': A First Amendment Basis for Televising Judicial Proceedings*, 4 UNIVERSITY OF HAWAII LAW REVIEW 116–30 (1982); *Television in the Courtroom — Limited Benefits, Vital Risks*? 3, no. 1 COMMUNICATIONS AND THE LAW 35–50 (Winter 1981); Kulwin, *Televised Trials: Constitutional Constraints, Practical Implications, and State Experimentation*, 9 LOYOLA UNIVERSITY LAW JOURNAL 913–19 (1978); Roberts and Goodman, *The Televised Trial: A Perspective*, 7 CUMBERLAND LAW REVIEW 331–32 (1976). Although a right to privacy is not a constitutional right, *per se*, it has been acknowledged and protected under common law for about a hundred years. In his 1888 *Treatise on the Law of Torts*, Thomas Cooley defined privacy as the "right to be let alone" [cited in DON R. PEMBER, MASS MEDIA LAW (3d ed. 1984)]. Two years later, Samuel Warren and Louis Brandeis published their seminal article, *The Right to Privacy*, 4 HARVARD LAW REVIEW (1890), in which they argued that an individual's right to privacy is the right to preserve "one's inviolate personality," [at 205] and that an individual should not be subjected to "mental pain and distress" [at 196] as a result of press disclosure of information that is of no concern to the public at large.

defendant consent. In his opinion, Justice Alan Sundberg noted: "First, a judicial proceeding... is a public event which by its very nature denies certain aspects of privacy. Second,...there is no constitutionally recognized right to privacy in the context of judicial proceedings."[8]

Since the privacy argument when applied to the courts is generally regarded as weak, it has not yet been used by the judiciary as the *single* criterion for excluding the press (or television cameras) from criminal courtrooms. If applied at all, it has been done so only when coupled with arguments focusing on the dangers of pretrial publicity and juror prejudice. In an attempt to protect due process, the courts have held that the right to choose a public trial rests with the accused, not the public or the press.[9]

However, while the Supreme Court has noted an *implicit* constitutional guarantee to privacy,[10] and has at times limited public and press access to courtrooms, it has more often upheld public and press access to trials, emphasizing that "[w]hat transpires in the courtroom is public property;"[11]

8. *Petition of Post-Newsweek Stations, Florida, Inc.*, 370 So.2d 764, 799 (1979). *See also* Cox Broadcasting Corp. v. Cohn, 420 U. S. 469 (1975), involving a suit filed against an Atlanta, Georgia, television station for broadcasting the name of a young woman who was raped and murdered. The Court held that the press is not liable for invasion of privacy for reporting information that is already part of the public record, *i.e.*, part of a criminal prosecution. *Cox* was later implicitly affirmed in Paul v. Davis, 424 U.S. 693 (1976), where the Court held that publication and circulation of flyers containing the photograph of a shoplifter did not violate privacy concerns, and in: Landmark Communications, Inc. v. Virginia, 435 U.S. 829 (1978); Smith v. Daily Mail Publishing Co., 443 U.S. 97 (1979), and Globe Newspaper v. Superior Court, 457 U.S. 596 (1982). Another interesting case is Doe v. Sarasota-Bradenton Television, 436 So.2d 328 (Fla. App., 1983) where the Florida Supreme Court held that a rape victim who is identified, and whose testimony is videotaped in open court and then broadcast, cannot sue the television station for invasion of privacy. However, the Court severely criticized the prosecution for making no effort to keep the victim's name out of the records, and for not recommending that the judge bar cameras while the victim was on the witness stand, although it had promised anonymity. The Court also criticized the television station for being insensitive to the distress it caused the woman, saying that broadcasting her name and footage of her testimony added little to the story about the trial.
9. Early clarification of this point appeared in re Oliver, 333 U.S. 257 (1948); United Press v. Valente, 308 N.Y. 71, 123 N.E.2d 777 (1954), and was implied in Estes v. Texas, 381 U.S. 532 (1965). More recently, a stronger declaration of this argument arrived in Gannett Co. v. DePasquale, 443 U.S. 368 (1979) upholding the right of a state court to close a pretrial hearing. In its holding the Court emphasized that the press has no affirmative right of access to pretrial proceedings, and that the sixth amendment guarantee of a public trial is for the benefit of the defendant alone, not the public or the press.
10. *See* Eisenstadt v. Baird, 405 U.S. 438 (1972), and Griswold v. Connecticut, 381 U.S. 479 (1965) where, in his separate concurring opinion, Justice Goldberg said that privacy had a place in the ninth amendment; *cf.* Whalen v. Roe, 429 U.S. 589 (1977).
11. Craig v. Harney, 331 U.S. 367, 347 (1947).

that a public trial is a "safeguard against any attempt to employ the courts as instruments of persecution,"[12] and that public scrutiny helps to ensure trial fairness.[13]

The prevailing stance of the Supreme Court appears to rest on the side of first amendment freedoms and the view that a public trial means both spectators and the press must be allowed to attend.[14] Only very carefully tailored restraints or specific time, place, and manner restrictions can be applied, and then only in the event that the information disclosed would have harmful or dangerous results on government interests.[15]

---

12. *In re* Oliver, 333 U.S. 257, 270 (1948).
13. *See* Waller v. Georgia, 10 MEDIA L. REP. 1714 (1984), a case involving racketeering charges, where the Court held that a defendant's sixth amendment right to a public trial must extend to pretrial suppression hearings. Writing for a unanimous Court, Justice Powell dismissed prosecution claims that privacy interests of not yet indicted persons might be infringed if such a hearing were open to the public (at 1715). *See also* People v. Jelke, 123 N.E.2d 769 (1954), where the New York Court of Appeals held that exclusion of press and spectators from a trial for compulsory prostitution violated the defendant's sixth amendment rights. The case is particularly interesting in view of the trial judge's reasons for closure, which included safeguarding public morals against disclosure of "obscene and sordid details" (at 770). The Appeals Court noted: (1) though the statute in question authorized closure in cases of divorce, seduction, abortion, rape, sexual assault, sodomy, bastardy, or filiation, it did not apply to a case involving charges of compulsory prostitution; (2) anticipation of evidence "of an indecent or filthy nature" (describing a sodomous act) was not sufficient to trigger imposition of the statute; (3) "demands of public morality do not . . . justify judicial nullification of the right of public trial, even in cases of an obscene or indecent nature, . . ." (at 771–73).
14. *See, e.g.,* Press Enterprise Co. v. Superior Court, 52 U.S.L.W. 4113 (1984) supporting qualified access to *voir dire* jury selection proceedings; Globe Newspaper Co. v. Superior Court, 457 U.S. 596 (1982); Richmond Newspapers, Inc. v. Virginia, 448 U.S. 555 (1980) announcing a qualified right to attend criminal proceedings; and Landmark Communications v. Virginia, 435 U.S. 829 (1978) confirming a right to report about judicial conduct. *Globe Newspaper* is particularly relevant to the present discussion. It involved a first amendment challenge to a Massachusetts statute requiring closure of rape and sexual assault trials during the testimony of victims who are minors. The Court held that even though the statute was applied with the good intentions of protecting the well-being of such victims, *mandatory* closure was unjustified. Justice Brennan, writing for the majority, explained that: (1) minors who are victims of sex crimes could be protected from "further trauma and embarrassment" by allowing judges to close trials on a case-by-case basis (at 597); (2) it is both speculative and illogical to close a trial in the interests of protecting a victim's identity, and thereby "encouraging [other] such victims to come forward and testify," (at 597) since (a) the press could obtain an account of a victim's testimony from the trial transcript, court personnel, or other sources, and (b) the statute did not prevent publication of a victim's identity or the testimony's substance.
15. Nebraska Press Association v. Stuart, 427 U.S. 539 (1976); Clark v. Community For Creative Non-Violence et al., 104 S. Ct. 3065 (1984); and Regan v. Time, Inc., 104 S. Ct. 3262 (1984).

SUSANNA R. BARBER

COVERAGE OF SENSITIVE CASES

Although in the context of judicial proceedings privacy is considered only an interest and not an absolute right, there are those who stress that in certain sensitive cases, judges should close their courtrooms to all media, or certainly to cameras if not to newspapers, in the interests of the participants concerned.

The circumstances under which this philosophy becomes compelling, they emphasize, are in cases involving testimony from victims of physical or sexual abuse. In such cases, witness privacy (or at least anonymity) is crucial, not only to protect the victim from further trauma and embarrassment, but also to reduce the possibility that other victims of such crimes would be deterred from coming forward due to fear of public humiliation.[16]

They further argue that the particular threats to privacy that surface in sensitive cases warrant narrow views of the public's right to know and the media's right to televise trials:

> Traditional methods of trial coverage secure both the media's First Amendment interests and the defendant's constitutional right to a fair and public trial. *The guarantee of freedom of the press should not be confused with freedom to use every available communications technology in every setting.*[17]

At times, then, the issue becomes one of "qualitative difference" between

16. *See* discussion of Massachusetts General Laws, chapter 278, section 16A in *Globe Newspaper v. Superior Court*, majority opinion. *But see also* Chief Justice Warren Burger's dissenting opinion in *Globe Newspaper* in which he was joined by Justice Rehnquist. It appears that Chief Justice Burger and Justice Brennan had very different views about the issues involved in this case. The Chief Justice understood the purpose of the closure statute as follows: "[It] is intended not to preserve confidentiality, but to prevent the risk of severe psychological damage caused by having to relate the details of the crime in front of a crowd which inevitably will include voyeuristic strangers. In most states, that crowd may be expanded to include a wide television audience, with reruns on the evening news" (at 618). However, in a footnote to his opinion, Chief Justice Burger included a portion of the prosecutor's report about interviews she conducted with the three victims regarding their privacy concerns. From a reading of this note, it is clear that the victims were not so much afraid to testify in front of members of the press as they were extremely worried about any resultant publicity, i.e., they would agree to press attendance only if the press would guarantee "not to print their names or where they go to school or any personal data or take pictures of them or attempt to interview them . . . ." (footnote 1 at 612).
17. Boone, *TV in the Courtroom: Is Something Being Stolen From Us?* 9 HUMAN RIGHTS 26 (Summer 1981), emphasis added; *see also* Ares, *Chandler v. Florida: Television, Criminal Trials, and Due Process*, 6 SUPREME COURT REVIEW 182 (1981), citing Alfred Hill, who suggests that a right to privacy should be recognized when the trial record would include "revelations so intimate and unwarranted as to outrage the community's notions of decency."

the potentially adverse results of electronic versus traditional news coverage. Specifically, two important questions are raised: (1) Are there cases in which privacy interests should override first amendment freedoms? (2) Should certain witnesses be protected from all forms of media coverage or from broadcast though not newspaper reporting?

WITNESS PROTECTION

Big Dan's is an example of a case where the presiding judge allowed broadcast and newspaper reporters a free rein in covering the trial, but the shocking aftermath of the coverage has led to some strong self-examination by the courts and the media.

Controversy arising from the "on air" naming of the alleged rape victim in the Big Dan's case prompted Senate Judiciary Committee hearings about the privacy rights of certain sensitive witnesses, such as victims of sexual and physical abuse.

At the hearings, rape victims described their traumatic ordeals of not only testifying in front of courtroom crowds but also of knowing that their testimonies, and perhaps even their faces, would be broadcast locally and maybe nationally. The newspaper as well as broadcast publication of such personal details as their names and places of work resulted in an assortment of crank phone calls, poison pen letters, and even personal insults directed at the victims and their families and relatives. So horrific were the hostilities and humiliations resulting from media coverage that, for many victims, they constituted a "second rape."

Without going into excessive detail about the events of the Big Dan's trial, a discussion of certain elements of the media coverage is in order. The case was covered by several newspapers and broadcast media organizations, including Ted Turner's Cable News Network and three other television news enterprises, which were hooked up to the courtroom's "pooling" camera for live coverage of the trial. As soon as the rape victim's name was mentioned by the judge and the prosecutors, it was heard throughout America.[18]

Using the argument that any ethical considerations about naming the witness were now moot, three local newspapers and a television station started to include the name in their daily reports of the trial. Gavel-to-gavel coverage by the Providence, Rhode Island Colony Communications cable system reached 44,000 households in the New Bedford area—home of the victim

18. De Silva, *The Gang-Rape Story*, COLUMBIA JOURNALISM REVIEW 42 (May/June 1984). For similar details *see When News Becomes Voyeurism*, TIME, March 26, 1984, at 64; *New Bedford Rape: Rejecting 'the Myth'*, NEWSWEEK, March 26, 1984, at 39; and *Rape Trial: 'Justice Crucified'?* NEWSWEEK, April 2, 1984, at 39.

and several defendants. Within forty-eight hours, the Providence *Evening Bulletin, The Providence Journal*, the Fall River *Herald News*, the Portuguese-language paper, *O Journal*, and WLNE-TV, the CBS affiliate in Providence, began using the name in reports. Within four days, United Press International (UPI) distributed wire copy containing the name to its 1,000 subscribers. [19]

The result was a barrage of complaints from the public, the legal profession, and even the media. Representatives of media organizations that maintained the policy of withholding the victim's name argued that its publication "adds nothing to the reader's understanding of the story. Furthermore, . . . public identification can needlessly add to the pain of the victim and is likely to deter other victims from reporting the crime." [20]

Call-in comments to radio stations and casual comments to the press that the victim "asked for it" and that she "led the men on" prompted Scott Charnos, the victim's lawyer, to point out that public incriminations indicate "it is more odious to be the rape victim than the rapist." [21]

At the close of the trial, Judge William C. Young had some strong words of reprimand for both the broadcast and print media. He told them: it was "an abysmal error of judgment" to publish the victim's name; it was a decision for which there was "utterly no reason," and it was a step taken "only for the poorest motives," [22] — prurient commercial ones. Perhaps adding insult to injury, the offending media responded nonchalantly: that they were simply broadcasting what the microphone picked up; that they did not realize the name would be mentioned, and that they "could not justify" spending money for a tape delay system to bleep out the name. [23]

Although in this particular instance the primary offenders were broadcasters (i.e., live television coverage was the first to disclose the victim's name), newspapers followed suit very soon afterwards. In other cases the situation might well be reversed, with broadcasters following the example of newspapers.

In the aftermath of this disturbing media event, it does little good to try to lay the blame on individual parties that contributed to the problem, but it does serve a purpose to try to analyze how the situation could be prevented in the future. One way to avoid the problem is through the adoption and enforcement of guidelines for media trial coverage. Better still would be a commitment on the part of newspapers, television and radio organizations to withhold the names of rape victims. If the media will not refrain from this of their own volition, the restraints may be applied by the courts. It is

---

19. De Silva, *supra* note 12 at 42.
20. *Id.* at 43.
21. *Id.*
22. *Id.* at 44.
23. *Id.* at 42.

surely better to permit electronic coverage of trials within the framework of protective guidelines than to ban such coverage entirely because of potential abuses by the media.

COURTROOM CAMERA GUIDELINES

The issue of protecting sensitive witnesses existed before *Chandler* was handed down and provision was made for these participants in state canons, as well as being mentioned explicitly in the *Chandler* majority opinion. Most of the forty-one[24] states that now allow some form of audio-visual coverage of trial and/or appellate courts have strict guidelines about the types of proceedings and participants that can be recorded, televised or photographed. These guidelines are sometimes incorporated in a state's Canons of Judicial Ethics, and at other times are simply written as a separate set of rules.

In almost every state, ultimate discretion regarding camera coverage rests in the hands of individual judges and is dealt with on a case-by-case basis. Many states also require formal written notice to be submitted to a lower court and/or the state Supreme Court for approval: twenty-six states have made prior consent of the court/judge an absolute precondition to coverage, and five states require that the court receive notice of intent to cover a proceeding *prior* to its commencement. In thirteen states, official written consent is not required, although informal notice is *pro forma* when broadcast media expect to cover trials.[25]

The rules of several states emphasize that broadcast coverage will not be permitted when media access is otherwise restricted by law, and a number of states have rules which explicitly prohibit or limit coverage of particular types of cases or specific participants. Of particular interest to the present discussion are guidelines pertaining to witnesses. In Massachusetts, for example, "[a] judge may limit or temporarily suspend such news media coverage, if it appears that such coverage will create a substantial likelihood of harm to any person or other serious harmful consequences."[26]

Other guidelines are more explicit: in Alabama, Iowa, Maryland, Minnesota, New Mexico, Ohio, Oklahoma, Pennsylvania, Rhode Island,

24. There is a slight discrepancy between available figures on the number of states that allow some form of electronic media coverage of courtrooms. A Radio-Television News Directors Association (RTNDA) report, "News Media Coverage of Judicial Proceedings With Cameras and Microphones: A Survey of the States," July 1, 1984, indicates forty-three states; information compiled by the National Center for State Courts, (summary of cameras in state courts), July 1, 1984, indicates forty-one.

25. *See* RTNDA report, "News Media Coverage of Judicial Proceedings..." July 4, 1984, at A1–A62.

26. THE MASSACHUSETTS CODE OF JUDICIAL CONDUCT (3:09), Canon 3A(7), revised January 1, 1983.

SUSANNA R. BARBER

Tennessee, Utah and Washington, the presiding judge can exclude electronic media coverage during any part of a proceeding at the request of a witness. In Alaska, it is forbidden to broadcast any portion of a trial to which a victim or witness of sexual abuse objects. Even in states where witness consent is not specifically required, judges are advised to prohibit, or at least restrict, camera coverage of police informants, undercover agents, children, certain juveniles, the family of a victim or the accused, custody suits, and victims of sexual crimes.[27]

The majority of states, then, have managed to deal successfully with the witness protection issue and are adamant that certain witnesses should not be exposed to unnecessary dangers or pressures. In fact, it is generally regarded to be the trial judge's responsibility to inform *all* witnesses that they have the option to request not to be photographed or televised if they can show cause, and some states "permit the court to order that a witness not be filmed *even absent a request.*"[28]

In his *Post-Newsweek* opinion, Justice Sundberg made clear and careful reference to the duties of trial judges when considering whether certain categories of witnesses may be adversely affected by electronic coverage. His ultimate point was that the potential for adverse impacts on some witnesses does not constitute sufficient grounds for an absolute ban on camera access to all courtrooms. As he explained, problems that may arise with regard to sensitive witnesses are not insurmountable: "What is called for is an articulated standard for the exercise of the presiding judge's discretion in determining whether it is appropriate to prohibit electronic media coverage of a particular participant."[29]

Furthermore, Justice Sundberg stressed that it is the duty of the judge to weigh the possible dangers against the principle of open justice. If necessary, the judge should use discretionary authority to bar electronic media coverage of certain participants, *but only if it can be shown that broadcast coverage would have substantially different or more deleterious effects upon that person than traditional newspaper reporting.* This standard, known as the "qualitative difference" test,[30] is an important recognition by the courts

27. See RTNDA report, supra note 25 at B1–B17.
28. Brief of the Attorneys General of Alabama et al. as Amici Curiae, submitted to the U.S. Supreme Court in Chandler v. Florida, October Term 1979, at 27 (emphasis added).
29. See Petition of Post-Newsweek Stations, Florida, Inc., 370 So.2d 764, at 778 (Fla. 1979).
30. The "qualitative difference" test as outlined by Justice Alan Sundberg in Post-Newsweek at 779, states that cameras may be excluded only "upon a finding that such coverage will have a substantial effect upon the particular individual which would be qualitatively different from the effect on members of the public in general and such an effect will be qualitatively different from coverage by other types of media."

that newspapers can just as easily be responsible for disclosing harmful trial-related details as broadcast media.

SOME CONCLUSIONS ABOUT WITNESS PROTECTION

Given the recent heated debate over television coverage of the Big Dan's case, it might appear that cameras have been permitted in courtrooms without careful consideration by individual judges or collaborative decisions by judicial committees. This is an entirely unrealistic picture. A more appropriate assessment could be reached by asking: (1) whether or not judges use their discretionary powers frequently or strongly enough, and (2) whether or not the media are willing to do a little self-policing "in matters of taste and decency."[31] The consequences could make headstrong commercial exploitation of trials a dangerous path for broadcasters to follow. Ultimately, a little self-restraint could protect the first amendment freedoms of the press as well as the privacy interests of sensitive witnesses.

Few would deny that testifying at a trial, even without media coverage, is a highly emotional and perhaps frightening experience for victims as well as their families. There are fears of embarrassment, humiliation, or even retribution from parties involved in the case, or from those who may learn about the case. But while privacy *interests* of witnesses (particularly victims of sexual crimes such as rape or child molestation) must be protected, the renewed cry for a ban on all broadcast coverage dismisses the issue with an all too simplistic response. There are rational remedies to situations such as the one caused by media insensitivity in the Big Dan's case and these remedies protect both witnesses and the first amendment rights of broadcasters.

1. While allowing broadcast coverage of inherently sensational cases, courts must continue to make provisions for restricting coverage of sensitive witnesses.
2. Newspapers as well as broadcast media must be encouraged to police themselves on questions relating to the publication of information

---

31. *See* Benson, *Do Cameras in the Courtroom Hurt the Cause of Justice?* UPDATE 54, published by the ABA Special Committee on Youth Education for Citizenship (Spring 1984). *See also Report of the Chief Court Administrator on the "Cameras-in-the-Court" Experiment of the State of Connecticut*, May 1, 1983, at 8: "We would hope the media would police themselves . . . so that it will be unnecessary for the judges to consider more restrictive regulations to remedy such problems." *And see* Judge Paul Baker, *Report to the Florida Supreme Court . . .* (1977) at 9, referring to the relationship between the press and the courts in cases involving children, or rape or sexual assault victims: "Rather than face these issues in a confrontation . . . , the better practice would appear the media itself establish an enforceable code of ethical conduct to be adhered to by all members of their profession. . . ."

which may identify victims or witnesses of sexual crimes.
3. The installation of tape delay systems should be mandatory for media organizations wishing to broadcast "live" coverage of a case.
4. Courts should require prior written notice describing the specifics of intended media coverage so that participants may be given time to apply for exemptions.
5. The activities of the print as well as broadcast media should be carefully and equally scrutinized by trial judges.

As the Big Dan's case so well shows, the trial judge plays a crucial role in monitoring who is televised and what kinds of testimony may be broadcast, and while broadcasters may resent the power judges hold to limit or refuse camera access, it may be wiser to have restricted coverage than no coverage rights at all.

PREJUDICIAL PUBLICITY

The Big Dan's case has also triggered renewed debate about the effects of pretrial and trial publicity on defendants. Those opposed to camera coverage have charged that mere knowledge of the Big Dan's trial being televised only served to make the case highly notorious, incite local community feelings against the defendants, and prejudice potential jurors. They also claimed that media coverage, particularly live television broadcasts, would so sensationalize the case that community presumptions against defendants, even if they were later acquitted or granted a retrial, would be irreversible.

The first of these two claims is clearly exaggerated. The televising of the Big Dan's case cannot be blamed for making the trial any more notorious than it already was prior to coverage. The case was inherently sensational: it involved a gang rape, and it also questioned the culpability of witnesses who watched the crime and not only failed to prevent it, but actually "cheered on" the rapists. These facts alone are surely sufficient to attract public attention if not incense a nation.

Furthermore, the case drew heated public interest long before cameras entered the courtroom. Only a week after news of the alleged gang rape was first reported in March 1983, some 2,500 people marched through New Bedford protesting violence against women, and similar gatherings took place around the country. Once the defendants were indicted, the press picked up coverage again, and for several weeks before the trial began the *print* as well as broadcast media carried stories about (though not the name of) the victim, the defendants, the police investigation, and the bar's patrons.[32]

32. *See* the Boston Globe, March 4–8 and 13–19, 1984, and the New York Times, March 15–17, 1984.

No doubt this kind of pretrial coverage added to an already inflammatory jury selection process, but the case presented some inherent administrative problems in any event. For example, jury sequestration was compounded by the fact that there were multiple defendants, necessitating two separate trials—one in the morning and one in the afternoon—because the testimony of some defendants implicated others.

DEFENDANT REPUTATION

While the argument about pretrial and trial notoriety is a fairly easy one to refute, challenges to camera coverage based on concerns about defendant reputation are more difficult to parry. In any trial, but particularly in highly publicized cases, personal reputations are at stake.[33] What happens to a defendant who has been tried and found "not guilty" and who must then return to the community? Are feelings of animosity extended toward this person and, if so, are they exacerbated by television coverage of the case? Would attitudes be the same if the case were only reported in newspapers?

Answers to these questions are hard to find, since few "courtroom cameras" studies have made any meaningful reference to the impacts of camera coverage on defendants, either during the trial or after the event. A survey by Kermit Netteburg (1980) found that even after extensive television coverage of a highly sensational murder trial, only sixteen percent of respondents could recall the name of the defendant unaided, only five percent could recall the trial outcome, and only seven to fifteen percent could recall the names of the judge and attorneys involved in the case. It seems—from this study, at least—that broadcast trial coverage does not necessarily make participants well known in the local community or have potentially serious prejudicial effects on defendants or future trials.[34]

Only one piece of research, a case study, has actually sought direct, open-ended responses from a defendant. In this instance, the defendant said he

33. Several arguments surround the defendant reputation issue. One contends that since defendants are considered innocent until proven guilty, they must be accorded the same privacy considerations as witnesses or victims, i.e., if a trial is closed during a rape victim's testimony, it must also be closed during the defendant's; likewise, if a victim is granted anonymity, the accused should enjoy the same privilege. It should be noted, however, that some defendants have claimed that their right to a public trial means that public and press (including television) access *must* be allowed, either because they want pressure placed on witnesses, or because they want vindication among a wide public audience. *See* Cody v. Oklahoma, 361 P.2d 307 (Okla. Crim. App. 1961); U.S. *ex rel.* Latimore v. Sielaff, 561 F.2d 691 (7th Cir. 1977), *cert. denied* 434 U.S. 1076 (1978); and United States v. Hastings, 695 F.2d 1278 (11th. Cir. 1983), *cert. denied*, 103 S. Ct. 1188 (1983).
34. Netteburg, *Does Research Support the Estes Ban on Cameras in the Courtroom*, 63, no. 10 JUDICATURE 472 (May 1980).

was not intimidated by the cameras while testifying, but he thought television and radio coverage would result in his receiving more letters and phone calls than if the trial had been covered only by newspaper reporters.[35] In a more recent California survey, twenty-nine percent of defendants surveyed said they feared physical, psychological, financial, or reputational harm as a consequence of electronic media coverage of proceedings, but no follow-up was conducted to see if such fears were warranted.[36]

While these studies throw a little light on the defendant reputation issue, they can hardly be regarded as sufficient documentation of the problem. The lack of convincing empirical research on the psychological effects of televising trials did not go unnoticed by the court in *Chandler*. Worried about possible mental harassment of defendants, the Court emphasized that "[p]articular attention should be paid to this area of concern as the study of televised trials continues."[37]

IMPACTS ON VIEWERS

Closely related to questions about viewer reactions to trial participants are those concerning potential adverse impacts of televised trials on the public – particularly children in the audience. The argument against permitting a case to be broadcast because of possible adverse effects on viewers is not a new one. It was first used in 1982 as a reason for banning cameras from the Wayne Williams trial in Atlanta, Georgia. (Williams was accused of murdering two of Atlanta's missing children.)

Judge Clarence Cooper, of the Fulton County Superior Court, reached his decision to block cameras after holding a hearing to which he called "expert" witnesses in the fields of sociology, psychology, psychiatry, and mental health. In general, these witnesses testified that televising Williams's trial might adversely affect children and adolescents in the viewing audience, reminding them of the disturbing ordeal that had enveloped Atlanta during the preceding two years.

The judge's report of the hearing included the following comments from the expert witnesses. A psychiatrist noted that live coverage "would tend to aggravate, reopen and reawaken those fears, concerns, and cause more emotional difficulties at a time when we're expending funds and resources

35. *See Report of the Supreme Court Committee to Monitor and Evaluate the Use of Audio and Visual Equipment in the Courtroom,* Wisconsin, April 1, 1979.
36. *See Evaluation of California's Experiment With Extended Media Coverage of Courts,* submitted to the Administrative Office for the Courts, the Chief Justice's Special Committee on the Courts and the Media, and the California Judicial Council, by Ernest H. Short and Associates, Inc., September 1981.
37. Brief of the Attorneys General of Alabama *et al.* as *Amici Curiae* at 40; cited in Chandler v. Florida, 449 U.S. 560 at 578.

to cope with the trauma that has already occurred." A developmental and clinical social psychologist said that the court should "think more about not only the children here who are in Atlanta, but also children across the nation." A sociologist argued that "social costs" would outweigh the public's right to know. The social costs were defined as "the cost to the families of the murdered and missing children, the cost to the family of the accused, the cost of [sic.] the children emotionally. . . ." Finally, a mental health official expressed concern about "what certain segments of the public would do with the information they received from televising the trial." He noted that "in the past some children experienced fears and nightmares after seeing reports of related events."[38]

Judge Cooper's decision to block cameras was prompted by these expert testimonies as well as by conclusions of law. Regarding the audience impact issue, he concluded ". . . we must weigh and balance the desire for a televised trial against the potential harm or danger that might be done to those children and families who were adversely affected by the ordeal."[39] The legal conclusions stemmed from his reading of *Chandler* which, he emphasized, "does not state that a trial may *always* be broadcast over the objections of the defendant," nor does it "expressly limit the inquiries which a trial court may make in reaching a decision on whether it will permit broadcast coverage of a trial."[40]

Cameras, of course, were not barred from the Big Dan's case for reasons of audience impact or for any traditional reasons. A subsequent event, however, involving a child's imitation of facts mentioned during broadcasts of the trial prompted a rally of anti-camera sentiments based on arguments similar to those brought forward by Judge Cooper in Atlanta. On April 17, 1984, a twelve-year-old boy from Pawtucket, Rhode Island, was arraigned on charges that he sexually assaulted a ten-year-old girl on a pool table while other children watched. The boy had apparently picked up the idea from watching the Big Dan's rape trial on television.[41]

Controversy stemming from this incident could have new, negative implications for future televised trials. Some might suggest that broadcast trial coverage be regulated along the lines of "indecent" programming, especially when children may be in the audience. The general argument of the Court in *FCC v. Pacifica Foundation*,[42] better known as the "seven dirty words"

38. Report of Judge Clarence Cooper re: *Petition for Extended News Coverage,* August 25, 1981, at 6.
39. *Id.* at 4.
40. *Id.* at 4, 6.
41. *See* New York Times, April 18, 1984, at A14, and NEWSWEEK, April 30, 1984, at 25.
42. FCC v. Pacifica Foundation, 438 U.S. 726 (1978). *But see also* League of Women Voters v. FCC, 8 MEDIA L. REP. 2081 (1982) in which Pacifica Foundation challenged a Public Broadcasting Act prohibition on editorializing by public

case, was that radio and television are "pervasive" media that should be regulated because they are easily accessible to children. Newspapers and magazines, on the other hand, need less restriction and are not regarded as pervasive because the reader must make a conscious decision to purchase printed materials and read them. Fewer children, it is thought, are interested in reading than in watching television.

Could *Pacifica's* rationale be applied to televised trials if explicitly sexual details or offensive language are broadcast as witness testimony? Though the question is purely conjectural, it invites some interesting speculation, particularly since the issue might become more complicated when a cable system rather than a broadcast station carries a trial.

However, a more fundamental assessment of the Big Dan's incident is that an isolated example of media imitation should neither be regarded as the norm nor elevated to a precedent-setting agenda. Even the most sophisticated experimental research has not proven conclusively that television viewing, *per se*, is to blame for children's delinquent behavior. While under certain circumstances children may imitate televised behavior, research focusing on a cause and effect relationship between a television set and a child can rarely be generalized to everyday settings, like children's home viewing environments. There is usually a concession that other factors, such as socio-economics and family communication patterns, have substantial bearing on how children interpret and relate to what they watch.[43]

The incident in Rhode Island is not the first time a child has imitated acts learned from television, and it will probably not be the last. Ironically, the first trial to be televised in Florida in 1977 involved fifteen-year-old Ronny Zamora who pleaded that television "intoxication" led him to rob and shoot his eighty-five-year-old neighbor. Zamora was found guilty, despite expert testimony that watching excessive amounts of "Kojak" (and other cops and robbers shows) may lead to maladjusted perceptions of violent behavior.[44]

---

television and radio stations that receive federal funds through the Corporation for Public Broadcasting. The California District Court held that funded noncommercial broadcasters have a right to editorialize under full first amendment protections.

43. *See, e.g.*, Report of the Surgeon General's Scientific Advisory Committee on Television and Social Behavior, "Television and Growing Up: The Impact of Televised Violence," 1972; J. R. MILAVSKY, R. C. KESSLER, H. H. STIPP, AND W. S. RUBENS, TELEVISION AND AGGRESSION (1982); CHILDREN'S UNDERSTANDING OF TELEVISION (J. BRYANT AND D. R. ANDERSON eds. 1983).

44. *See Did TV Make Him Do It?* TIME, October 10, 1977, at 27, and *TV On Trial*, a transcript of the program "TV On Trial," aired by the Public Broadcasting Service, May 23, 1978. *See also* Niemi v. NBC, 74 Cal. App.3d 383 (1977), *cert. denied*, 46 U.S.L.W. 3659 (1978), No. 681-035 (Cal. Super. Ct. Aug. 9, 1978, dimissed), involving an eleven million dollar suit filed against NBC and its local affiliate KRON-TV, San Francisco. The suit resulted from the broadcast of "Born Innocent," which depicted a scene of a girl being raped by other girls using a "plumber's

Ultimately, we may need to ask where the responsibility of parents begins and that of broadcasters ends. Perhaps parents have a duty to supervise their children's viewing habits in the same way that judges have a responsibility to monitor the types of cases and trial participants to be televised. Or perhaps parents should consider whether they would take a child to watch a particular trial inside the courtroom. If the answer is "no," then why allow that child to watch it on television?

NEED FOR MORE RESEARCH

As this debate continues, there is a pressing need for more comprehensive critical and social scientific analysis of audience reaction to televised trials. Research needs to address the broader issue of educational versus entertainment qualities of broadcast trial coverage, as well as the narrower perspective of viewer attitudes toward trial participants. Questions that could be applied to this area of concern include the following:

- Is the public better informed or even adequately informed by electronic versus conventional media coverage of a case?
- Can gavel-to-gavel broadcasts serve to educate the public about the administration of justice in general?
- Do time constraints imposed on many broadcast news stories mean that a case is treated either unfairly or inadequately?
- Does the public get a distorted picture of the judicial system, or a biased view of a particular trial, if news stories are edited to highlight sensational testimony, cross-examination, or simply the closing arguments of attorneys?
- How does the public's understanding of the courts and specific cases differ when broadcast versus printed news is the medium of communication?
- Which type of news coverage has consistently provided the most balanced coverage of legal issues, trial participants, and court administration?
- What kinds of legal news coverage are "educationally" valuable to the public at large?
- Do viewers primarily perceive televised trials as a form of entertainment programming?

helper." Shortly after the program was aired, nine-year-old Olivia Niemi was raped with a bottle by a gang of three young girls and a boy on a San Francisco beach. The lawsuit alleged that NBC was negligent in showing a program that might stimulate viewers to imitate its content. The case was finally dismissed because Niemi's lawyer could not show that NBC *intended* to incite the rape.

SUSANNA R. BARBER

CONCLUSIONS

The courtroom cameras controversy is a complex issue with important legal, sociological and psychological implications. Those who would dismiss it with a simplistic rally to "ban all broadcast coverage" forget that broadcasters are entitled to the same first amendment rights to cover trials as their newspaper counterparts (though they also have the same responsibilities to report cases fairly and without harming those involved).

In the heated debate over televised trials, emotional arguments have often superceded reasonable discussion. Arguments, for example, which attempt to claim that because broadcasters prefer to cover more sensational types of cases they should be excluded from courtrooms, miss the point that traditional newspaper coverage has similar biases, with a similar aim of selling more newsprint. Few would suggest, however, that *responsible* reporting of trials by both the broadcast and print media is not in the public interest and is not a fundamental freedom of the press.

Equally tenuous arguments focus on the negative feelings trial participants have about being photographed or televised. It should be noted, however, that trial participants have anxieties about appearing in court regardless of media coverage. Witnesses, for example, are often more nervous about the process of giving testimony in general, especially the cross-examination of attorneys, than about being covered by television or still cameras.[45] No doubt defendants and witnesses (especially victims) would feel *more* comfortable if they could be assured complete protection from *all* forms of news coverage — newspaper as well as broadcast. But since a courtroom is a place of public business, and since the privacy argument does not generally apply to trials, it is hard to argue that there should be no news coverage at all. Certainly jurors must remain anonymous if they are to be shielded from community pressures, and the same applies to certain witnesses who may be exposed to vengeful attacks. But state guidelines governing camera use can provide protection to these parties, as can carefully imposed judicial authority.

As for defendants, while sympathy for their emotional and potentially embarrassing plight is obvious, cameras are not necessarily responsible for causing uneasiness; traditional newspaper coverage would mean that the defendant's reason for being in court would be widely known in the local community. Hopefully, it is not the intention of broadcast coverage to humiliate any trial participant, but simply to cover the proceedings in as impartial and informative a manner as possible.

45. *See, e.g., Report and Recommendations of the Ad Hoc Committee of the Greater Cleveland Bar Association on the Effects of Cameras in the Courtroom on Participants in Such a Trial,* 1980; and Brief of the Attorneys General of Alabama *et al.* at 28.

The picture of courtroom cameras, though, should not be painted in one direction only. Problems arise when media representatives circumvent the camera coverage guidelines established by courts. In ignoring the rules, whether by failing to follow procedures, or by "hounding" sensitive trial participants, a few broadcast organizations jeopardize the rights and reputations of all media representatives. The struggle to obtain camera access to courtrooms has been a long one, and it seems a pity that the selfish interests of a small minority might tarnish the reputation of the majority. As a safeguard, it might be appropriate to restrict *all* forms of media coverage of witnesses and victims of sex crimes, such as rape or child molestation. Television, however, should not be singled out as the "offending" medium when newspapers are often responsible for publicizing details such as victims' names, areas of residence or places of work.

In *Chandler*, the Court was quick to point out that "[f]urther research may change the picture"[46] and that broadcasters should therefore proceed cautiously in covering trials. As one commentator has perceptively hinted: "Just how the news media *use* the material they gather in courts with cameras and recorders will be a weighty factor in deciding whether to allow broadcast coverage to continue."[47]

Perhaps the last word belongs to Judge Baker whose affirmative first amendment stance has often been wisely tempered with some down-to-earth advice for the media. Referring to the question of whether "unfettered access to news becomes synonymous with unfettered dissemination," he noted that the answer "lies equally between the inherent powers of the Court and the *conscience of the media*."[48] Broadcasters should take heed!

46. *Chandler, supra* note 2 at 576, footnote 11.
47. Hughes, *Chandler v. Florida: Cameras Get Probation in Courtrooms*, 26, no. 1 JOURNAL OF BROADCASTING 443 (Winter 1982).
48. Judge Paul Baker, *Report to the Florida Supreme Court . . . , supra* note 1 at 8, emphasis added.

KIMERA MAXWELL
ROGER REINSCH

The Freedom Of Information Act Privacy Exemption: Who Does It Really Protect?

Kimera Maxwell is the Assistant Director of Information Services and Roger Reinsch an assistant professor of business at Emporia State University.

The right of the individual to privacy generally has been accepted as an implied Constitutional right since the earliest days of the Constitution. That right was best stated by the U.S. Supreme Court in 1968 in *Griswold v. Connecticut*. This implied right recognizes the personal privacy of the individual, not the privacy of government agencies.

This article reaffirms that implied right of privacy, examines the Freedom of Information Act (5 U.S.C. § 552) ("the Act"), and by using the history of the Act, shows that its main purpose was to provide access to the workings of government. However, government agencies using this act have hidden behind Exemption (b)(6) in order to protect their own privacy. A variety of federal and Supreme Court cases show that, instead of protecting only the privacy of individuals, this exemption has been used by custodians in government agencies to protect the privacy of the agencies. These agencies also abuse the rights of the individuals they profess to protect by citing this exemption, even though the individuals may have no objections to the release of the information.

A solution to some of the abuses of the exemption is offered here. It is suggested that individuals be contacted to ask their permission to release information that may be protected by this exemption. Not only does this solution maintain the integrity and intent of Exemption (b)(6), but it gives individuals the freedom to have some control over the dissemination of records maintained by government agencies. This solution also would remove from the courts some of the burden of determining if records fall under Exemption (b)(6). In many instances, this solution would expedite the requests for information under the act and avoid the inevitable court cases that result from the abuse of Exemption (b)(6) of the Freedom of Information Act.

INDIVIDUAL RIGHT TO PRIVACY

The individual right to privacy, although not specifically guaranteed in the Bill of Rights, has long been upheld as a fundamental right implied in the first and fourth amendments. *Griswold v. Connecticut*[1] establishes grounds for the protection of the individual's right to privacy. *Griswold* involved a Connecticut law forbidding the use of contraceptives. The Supreme Court held that the law, as it applied to married persons, was unconstitutional. Writing for the court, Justice Douglas said, "We deal with a right of privacy older than the Bill of Rights—older than our political practices, older than our school system. Marriage is a coming together for better or for worse, hopefully enduring and intimate to the degree of being sacred."[2]

More important in the Court's decision was Justice Douglas's definition of the many rights that, although not implicitly stated in the Bill of Rights, are protected fundamental rights. He said:

> The association of people is not mentioned in the Constitution nor in the Bill of Rights. The right to educate a child in a school of the parents' choice—whether public or private or parochial—is also not mentioned. Nor is the right to study any particular subject or any foreign language. Yet, the First Amendment has been construed to include certain of those rights.[3]

Douglas strengthened the concept of the protection of the right to personal privacy when he stated, "[t]he First Amendment has a penumbra where privacy is protected from governmental intrusion."[4]

In *Roe v. Wade*,[5] the Supreme Court further supported a constitutionally

---

1. 381 U.S. 479, 85 S. Ct. 1678 (1965). *See generally* Eisenstadt v. Baird, 92 S. Ct. 1029 (1972); Terry v. Ohio, 392 U.S. 1, 8–9 (1968); Doe v. Bolton, 410 U.S. 179 (1973); Palko v. Connecticut, 302 U.S. 319, 325 (1937).
2. Griswold v. Connecticut, 381 U.S. 479 at 486.
3. *Id*. at 482.
4. *Id*. at 483.
5. 410 U.S. 113, 35 L.Ed.2d 147 (1972).

guaranteed right of individual privacy. In *Roe*, a pregnant, single woman challenged the constitutionality of the Texas criminal abortion laws, arguing that they abridged her right of personal privacy as protected by the first, fourth, fifth, ninth and fourteenth amendments.

The Court's opinion addressed the privacy question when it said: "The Constitution does not explicitly mention any right of privacy. In a line of decisions, however, going back as far as *Union Pacific R. Co. v. Botsford*,[6] the Court has recognized that a right of personal privacy, or a guarantee of certain areas or zones of privacy, does exist under the Constitution."[7]

And, although he did not specifically mention the right of privacy, Justice Douglas, in a concurring opinion in *Roe*, talked about the broader concept of various sacred rights that come under the protection of the Constitution. He wrote:

> The Ninth Amendment obviously does not create federally enforceable rights. It merely says, "The enumeration in the Constitution of certain rights, shall not be construed to deny or disparage others retained by the people." But, a catalogue of these rights includes customary, traditional, and time-honored rights, amenities, privileges, and immunities that come within the sweep of "the Blessings of Liberty" mentioned in the preamble to the Constitution. Many of them, in my view, come within the meaning of "liberty" as used in the Fourteenth Amendment. . . . These are rights protected by the First Amendment and, in my view, they are absolute, permitting of no exceptions.[8]

A final case that reaffirms the constitutional protection of individual privacy is *Stanley v. Georgia*,[9] in which a private citizen was convicted for possession of obscene matter. Stanley appealed, claiming that the Georgia law was unconstitutional because it punished private possession of obscene matter. The Supreme Court strengthened the privacy concept when it said: "[F]or also fundamental is the right to be free, except in very limited circumstances, from unwanted governmental intrusions into one's privacy."[10]

---

6. 141 U.S. 250 (1891): "No right is held more sacred, or is more carefully guarded, by the common law, than the right of every individual to the possession and control of his own person, free from all restraint or interference of others, unless by clear and unquestionable authority of law."
7. Roe v. Wade, 410 U.S. at 152.
8. 93 S. Ct. 756 at 757.
9. 394 U.S. 557 (1968).
10. *Id.* at 564.

KIMERA MAXWELL and ROGER REINSCH

FREEDOM OF INFORMATION ACT

The Freedom of Information Act, passed in 1966, established by statute the public's right to know. The Supreme Court upheld the constitutionality of the Act, saying, "Disclosure, not secrecy, is the dominant objective of the Act."[11] The main purpose of the Freedom of Information Act, which amended Section 3 of the Administrative Procedure Act (APA), was to guarantee the right of persons to know about the business of their government. The House of Representatives addressed this purpose when it said: "The right of the individual to be able to find out how his Government is operating can be just as important to him as his right to privacy and his right to confide in his government. This bill strikes a balance considering all these interests."[12]

Before passage of the Freedom of Information Act, agency and department heads enjoyed broad discretion in suppressing information. Under Section 3 of the APA, agencies were able to hide behind the APA to protect their own privacy.[13] In many instances they were able to withhold information for "good cause,"[14] thereby abusing Section 3 to conceal agency error or impropriety. By focusing on officials' efforts to prevent release of information in order to hide mistakes or irregularities committed by the agency,[15] the Freedom of Information Act established the policy of full agency disclosure and closed loopholes that had long allowed agencies to avoid disclosing information about their dealings.

When the Freedom of Information Act went into effect in 1967, it established the statutory right of access for the first time by transferring from the agencies to Congress and the courts the responsibility for determining whether information could be withheld. Agencies were ordered to disclose all their records unless specifically exempt.[16] Under the Act, special provisions for the release of information included: (1) agencies were required to disclose all records that did not come within one of nine specific exemptions in the act; (2) courts had the authority to review *de novo* any denial of access to decide the propriety of the agency's action and prevent review from becoming meaningless judicial sanctioning of agency discretion; and (3) agencies were

---

11. Dept. of Air Force v. Rose, 425 U.S. 352 (1976).
12. Subcommittee on Administrative Practice and Procedures, Freedom of Information Source Book, S. Doc. (No. 98–82), 93rd. Cong., 2nd. Sess. (1974) [hereinafter cited as Source Book].
13. S. REP. NO. 813, 89th Cong., 1st Sess. (1965) at 9. Also H. R. REP. NO. 1497, 89th Cong. 2d Sess. (1966) at 11.
14. Ch. 324, § 3, 60 Stat. 238 (1946).
15. H. R. REP. NO. 1497 at 6; Source Book 69.
16. 1982 EDITION OF LITIGATION UNDER THE FEDERAL FREEDOM OF INFORMATION ACT AND PRIVACY ACT 1 (M. Halperin and A. Adler ed. 7th ed. 1981), [hereinafter cited as LITIGATION UNDER THE FEDERAL FOIA].

required to prove their actions were proper.[17]

The Act sought to control executive secrecy by establishing three categories for disclosure: (1) publication; (2) making available for inspection; and (3) release pursuant to a request for access from "any person."[18] While the act required disclosure, the nine exemptions still allowed agencies to withhold information required under the Act.[19] But these exemptions, which were to be "specifically made exclusive. . .and must be narrowly construed,"[20] were discretionary, not mandatory.[21]

Following passage of the Act, agencies avoided opening their records by creating broad definitions of the exemptions, claiming they could not find the material, charging very high fees, and instituting long delays to discourage use.[22] In 1974, Congress addressed these problems through a series of amendments that required agencies to index documents not in the Federal Register, identify records for purposes of Freedom of Information Act requests, charge fees only for actual costs for the search and copy, expedite requests, and release segregable portions of exempt material.[23] The 1974 amendments also made more explicit the *in camera* and *de novo* reviews by the courts.[24]

While the 1974 amendments further denied and strengthened the Freedom of Information Act, Exemption (b)(6) remained unchanged. This exemption upheld the constitutionally guaranteed right of personal privacy by prohibiting the disclosure of records that constitute a "clearly unwarranted invasion of personal privacy."[25] In the legislative history of the Act, both the U.S. Senate

---

17. 5 U.S.C. § 552 (c)(a)(3), (a)(3).
18. LITIGATION UNDER THE FEDERAL FOIA, *supra* note 16, at 1.
19. 5 U.S.C § 552 (b)(1)–(b)(9).
20. Air Force v. Rose, 425 U.S. 352, 361 (1976); *see also* Post Company v. New York State Insurance Department, 580 F. Supp. 808 (1984).
21. Chrysler Corp. v. Brown, 441 U.S. 281, 293 (1979).
22. LITIGATION UNDER THE FEDERAL FOIA, *supra* note 16, at 4.
23. *Id.* at 5.
24. 5 U.S.C. § 552 (a)(4)(B):

> On complaint, the district court of the United States in the district in which the complainant resides, or has his principal place of business, or in which the agency records are situated, or in the District of Columbia, has jurisdiction to enjoin the agency from withholding agency records and to order the production of any agency records improperly withheld from the complainant. In such a case, the court shall determine the matter *de novo*, and may examine the contents of such agency records *in camera* to determine whether such records or any part thereof shall be withheld under any of the exemptions set forth in subsection (b) of this section, and the burden is on the agency to sustain its actions.

25. 5 U.S.C. § 552 (b)(6): "[p]ersonnel and medical files and similar files the disclosure of which would constitute a clearly unwarranted invasion of personal privacy."

and the House Committee Reports said the purpose of the exemption was to balance interests between the individual's privacy and the public's right to information.[26] Nowhere in the reports on the discussion of the exemption is there a concern about the balance of individual privacy and the privacy of government agencies.

In discussing Exemption (b)(6), the House Committee report on the Act said, "The limitation of a '**clearly** unwarranted invasion of personal privacy' provides a proper balance between the protection of an individual's right to privacy and the preservation of the public's right to government information by excluding those kinds of files the disclosure of which might harm the individual."[27] The Senate Committee report echoed this sentiment: "The phrase '**clearly** unwarranted invasion of personal privacy' enunciates a policy that will involve a balancing of interests between the protection of an individual's private affairs from unnecessary public scrutiny and the preservation of the public's right to government information."[28]

Although Exemption (b)(6) seems to provide for a simple task of withholding records to protect individual privacy, agencies frequently have attempted to broaden it to insure their own protection. Since the passage of the Act, government agencies have time and again attempted to use Exemption (b)(6), claiming protection of the individual's right to privacy. In reality, the agencies were attempting to protect their own privacy. The following cases illustrate this.

One of the reasons government agencies have tried to hide behind Exemption (b)(6) has been the difficulty in defining the term, "clearly unwarranted invasion of personal privacy." In her article on "Privacy and the Freedom of Information Act,"[29] Mary Hulett wrote:

> The (b)(6) exemption has been criticized for requiring disclosure under circumstances that would be an "unwarranted invasion of personal privacy," but not "clearly" so. For others, there seemed to be an inconsistency between the notion of a "right of privacy" and the notion of a "warranted" invasion of that privacy . . . . The courts have had difficulty with "clearly unwarranted invasion of privacy."[30]

Although the term "clearly unwarranted" seems unclear, the courts have

---

26. S. REP., *supra* note 13. Also H.R. REP. No. 1497, 89th Cong. 2d Sess. (1966) at 11.
27. Subcommittee on Admin. Practice, *supra* note 12.
28. S. REP., *supra* note 13.
29. Hulett, *Privacy and the Freedom of Information Act*, 27 ADMINISTRATIVE LAW REVIEW 275–94 (Summer 1975).
30. *Id.* at 279–80.

attempted to define its meaning. In *Sims v. CIA*,[31] the federal court said, "Exemption (b)(6) was developed to protect intimate details of personal and family life, not business judgments." In *Getman v. NLRB*,[32] the federal court said:

> The use of the term "clearly," . . . which was not inadvertent, but purposeful on the part of Congress, was itself, a "clear" instruction to the Courts that, in determining that whether a disclosure would constitute a "clearly unwarranted invasion of personal privacy," they should tilt the balance in favor of disclosure.[33]

The landmark case about a government agency attempting to hide behind the privacy exemption is *Department of Air Force v. Rose*.[34] Here, law review editors sued to compel disclosure of ethics code violation hearings conducted by the Air Force. Student editors of the *New York University Law Review*, researching disciplinary systems and procedures at the military service academies, were denied access to case summaries of honor and ethics code hearings. The Air Force denied access even though personal references and other identifying information were deleted. The editors were denied access on the grounds that, even with the names deleted, "[s]ome cases may be recognized by the reader by the circumstances alone without the identity of the cadet given," and "[t]here was no way of determining just how the facts will or could be used."[35]

The Supreme Court held that:

> Congressional concern for the protection of the kind of confidential personnel data usually included in a personnel file is abundantly clear. But Congress also made clear that nonconfidential matter was not to be insulated from disclosure merely because it was stored by an agency in its "personnel" files. Rather, Congress sought to construct an exemption that would require a balancing of the individual's right of privacy against the preservation of the basic purpose of the Freedom of Information Act "to open agency action to the light of public scrutiny." The device adopted to achieve that balance was the

31.   642 F.2d 569 (1980).
32.   450 F.2d 670 (1971).
33.   *Id.* at 674.
34.   425 U.S. 352 (1976).
35.   *Id.* at 355.

limited exemption, where privacy was threatened, for "clearly unwarranted" invasions of personal privacy.[36]

Because the Supreme Court found that the files did not contain the "vast amounts of personal data" that constitute a personnel file, nor was access to these files drastically limited, the Supreme Court held the Exemption (b)(6) claim was not relevant.[37]

In addition to addressing the problem of government agencies hiding behind the privacy exemption for their own protection, *Rose* discussed the procedure for an *in camera* inspection of records denied under the exemption. The Supreme Court agreed with the appeals court that the agency would have to provide the records for an *in camera* inspection: "[W]e think it highly likely that the combined skills of court and agency, applied to the summaries, will yield edited documents sufficient for the purpose sought and sufficient as well to safeguard affected persons in their legitimate claims of privacy."[38]

Writing for the court, Justice Brennan also strengthened the wording of "**clearly** unwarranted invasion of **personal** privacy" in Exemption (b)(6). He wrote, "[J]udicial interpretation has uniformly reflected the view that no reason would exist for nondisclosure in the absence of a showing of a clearly unwarranted invasion of privacy, whether the documents are filed in "personnel" or "similar" files."[39]

In *Getman v. National Labor Relations Board*,[40] another case where a government agency attempted to hide behind the privacy exemption, the federal court ordered a balancing of interests of the requestor with the interest in protecting privacy by holding that even if the information fell within Exemption (b)(6), the invasion of privacy would be minimal, and it still would be in the agency's best interest to disclose the information.[41]

In this case, law professors studying National Labor Relations Board (NLRB) voting patterns requested names and addresses of employees eligible to vote in elections. The NLRB denied the request, citing Exemptions (b)(4), (6), and (7) of the Freedom of Information Act. In its decision, the federal court traced the history of the Act, defining the real thrust of Exemption (b)(6) as a "[g]uard against unnecessary disclosure of the files of such agencies . . . which would contain 'intimate details' of a 'highly personal' nature."[42] The federal court never mentioned the need to protect the agency's privacy. Instead, it specifically pointed to the NLRB's attempt to hide behind Exemption (b)(6):

36. *Id*. at 372.
37. *Id*. at 377.
38. *Id*. at 358.
39. *Id*. at 371.
40. *Supra* note 32.
41. *Id*. at 670.
42. *Id*. at 675.

We agree with appellees that it is ironic that the Board should attempt to use speculation about added delays in the prompt resolution of questions of representation as a basis for preventing this study....Thus the Board is taking a too shortsided view in its own self-interest.[43]

In *Arieff v. U.S. Dept. of Navy*,[44] the federal court made its strongest statement about the real purpose of the privacy exemption. Here Arieff, a journalist, requested all records on releases of any prescription drugs to the Office of Attending Physicians to the U.S. Congress (OAP) from the National Naval Medical Center (NNMC, a division of the Navy). Although Arieff was willing to accept the material with all information deleted that could identify the recipients of the drugs, the Navy still denied the request, citing Exemption (b)(6). The federal court disputed this claim:

The text of the exemption [(b)(6)] does not apply to an invasion of privacy produced **as a secondary effect** of the release. It may be predictable that the release of certain agency information will cause the agency head to be bothered at home with irate phone calls, but that, like consequent public speculation, is not the sort of invasion of privacy that can support an Exemption 6 claim. According to the statute, it is the very "production" of documents which must "constitute" a "clearly unwarranted invasion of personal privacy." Obviously that can only occur when the documents disclose information attributed to the **individual**.[45]

Probably the most blatant attempt of a government agency to hide behind Exemption (b)(6) and also the federal court's strongest statement on agency abuse of the exemption occurred in *Vaughn v. Rosen*.[46] Here a law professor, doing research on the Civil Service Commission, requested reports of the Bureau of Personnel Management. The Commission refused access, claiming that the documents fell within Exemptions (b)(1), (2), (5), and (6) of the Freedom of Information Act's general requirements of disclosure.

The federal court supported previous judicial interpretations of the importance of disclosure as a main purpose of the Act.[47] A more important outcome of *Vaughn* was the court's statement on burden of proof and *in camera*

43. *Id.* at 676.
44. 712 F.2d 1462 (1983).
45. *Id.* at 1468.
46. 484 F.2d 820 (1973), *cert. denied*, 415 U.S. 977, 94 S. Ct. 1564, 39 L.Ed.2d 873 (1974).
47. *Id.* at 823.

inspections. In previous cases, it was the court's burden of determining the validity of an agency's claim for exemptions through the *in camera* inspection. The court had to make its own investigations.[48] In *Vaughn*, the federal court disputed this method, saying the *in camera* inspection encouraged the government agency to claim large masses of information as exempt when that information should be disclosed:

> There are no inherent incentives that would affirmatively spur government agencies to disclose information. Under current procedures, government agencies lose very little by refusing to disclose documents. . . . [T]here is little to be gained by making the disclosure. Indeed from a bureaucratic standpoint, a general policy of revelation could cause positive harm, since it could bring to light information detrimental to the agency and set a precedent for future demands for disclosure. . . .
>
> [S]ince the burden of determining the justifiability of a government claim of exemption currently falls on the court system, there is an innate impetus that encourages agencies automatically to claim the broadest possible grounds for exemption for the greatest amount of information. Let the courts decide![49]

So far, the court's *in camera* obligation to determine if records actually fall within Exemption (b) (6) tilts the scales in favor of the government agency, since the requestor of the information has no way of ever finding out what information remains exempt. The federal court recognized this problem in *Arieff v. Navy*:

> FOIA cases as a class present an unusual problem that demands an unusual solution: One party knows the contents of the withheld records while the other does not; and the courts have been charged with the responsibility of deciding the dispute without altering that unequal condition, since that would involve disclosing the very material sought to be kept secret.[50]

The *in camera* inspection places a major burden on the court to determine

48. *Id.* at 825.
49. *Id.* at 825; *see also* Stein v. Department of Justice and FBI, 662 F.2d 1245 (7th Cir. 1981); Gerash v. Smith, 580 F. Supp. 808 (1984).
50. 712 F.2d 1462 (1983) at 1471.

what records fall under Exemption (b)(6). In fact, immediately after the passage of the Freedom of Information Act, many courts declined to conduct the *in camera* review because of its "nonadversarial nature, its burdensomeness to the court, and the danger that it will permit the agency to shift its burden of proving exemption claims to the courts."[51]

The *in camera* approach, although intended to protect the rights of an individual, severely limits his or her control over the disclosure of records. In the cases filed under Exemption (b)(6), the main concern has been for maintaining the balance between the protection of the individual's right to privacy and the public's right to know.

What has never been covered is the issue of the right of the individual to have input in releasing information about himself or herself. Under the Freedom of Information Act, individuals do not get a chance to waive their rights under Exemption (b)(6). The exemption was created to strike a balance between the individual's right to privacy and the public's right to know, but it never took into consideration the possibility that individuals would not object to the government's releasing records about them.

Usually in a routine request for personnel, medical or similar records under the Freedom of Information Act, no attempt is made to contact the individual identified in the record in question for his or her permission to release the information. Agency personnel, as custodians of the records, assume the responsibility for those decisions. They can and do deny access on behalf of the individual, citing Exemption (b)(6), providing simultaneously an avenue for the agency to protect its own privacy.

And, if the requestor objects to that denial, the records custodian has another option before a trip to district court. 5 U.S.C. § 552 permits government agencies to delete identifying details and present segregated files.[52] Again, agencies have the opportunity to protect their privacy.

The main problem with agencies using Exemption (b)(6) to protect their privacy is that the exemption calls for a "**clearly** unwarranted invasion of privacy." Unless the records custodian contacts the individual in question, there is no real way of determining how **clearly** unwarranted that invasion of privacy is. At the very least the individual whose privacy is in danger of being invaded should have some input in deciding whether there is an invasion and if it is **clearly** unwarranted.

Granted, the Act does place the burden of proof on the agency to disclose

---

51. LITIGATION UNDER THE FEDERAL FOIA, *supra* note 16 at 152.
52. 5 U.S.C. § 552 (a)(2): "[T]o the extent required to prevent a clearly unwarranted invasion of personal privacy, an agency may delete identifying details when it makes available or publishes an opinion, statement of policy, interpretation, or staff manual or instruction."

the information,[53] but the agency can still rely on the court's *in camera* inspection to uphold its determination of exempt status. In many instances, this *in camera* inspection would not be necessary if the individual named in the record were contacted for his or her permission, thereby expediting the general public's requests for information.

At first glance, the idea of requiring agency custodians to contact individuals for their permission to release information seems simplistic and burdensome. The two immediate objections are: (1) it is time consuming, costly and would create an extra bureaucratic layer; and (2) there is no guarantee individuals will waive the right to protection under the exemption. A further examination indicates that this solution would be relevant in many situations where standard information is requested. And, it also gives individuals an element of control over the information maintained on them.

Even the federal court recommended this as a possible path of action, in *Sims v. CIA*.[54] In *Sims*, an attorney and doctor from the Nader Group requested a list of names of institutions and researchers who had conducted research under a special Central Intelligence Agency (CIA) project.[55] The list contained 265 names—eighty institutions and one hundred eighty-five individuals. When the CIA received the request, it contacted the eighty institutions to ask if they would consent to disclosure of their identities. The Agency made no effort to communicate with the individuals. Of the eighty institutions contacted, fifty-nine agreed to disclosure. The agency released those names, but continued to refuse to release the other names.[56]

The attorney and the doctor filed suit in district court, where the court said it could not accept the position of the Agency without additional information as to whether "any researcher had any reasonable expectation that his or her participation would be anonymous, as to whether any researcher had any other privacy interest which might be compromised by disclosure...or whether any researcher had any other objection or reason for objection to disclosure of his or her name."[57]

Even though the district court suggested that the CIA contact the researchers, the CIA refused, maintaining that its Exemption (b)(6) claim required no communication with individual researchers.[58] The attorney and doctor appealed, and the federal court responded:

53.   5 U.S.C. § 552 (a)(4)(B), *supra* note 24.
54.   642 F.2d 562 (1982).
55.   "Research concerning chemical, biological and radiological materials capable of employment in clandestine operations to control human behavior." S. REP. No. 755, 94th Cong., 2d Sess., Book I at 389 (1976).
56.   *Supra* note 54, at 565.
57.   *Id*. at 566.
58.   *Id*. at 566.

Eschewing suggestions by the District Court that it communicate with individual researchers, the agency has failed to particularize their objections to disclosure or to establish the likely consequences of disclosure in individual cases. In the absence of a more detailed and conclusive factual showing, we could hardly find that the agency had shown an invasion of personal privacy so deep and severe as to count as "clearly unwarranted" when measured against the countervailing public interest in full disclosure.[59]

Exemption (b)(6) was developed to protect intimate details of personal and family life, not business judgments and relationships. Surely, it was not intended to shield matters of such clear public concern as the names of those entering into contracts with the federal government.[60]

That right of privacy, in substance, is the same as the right of privileged communication. In everyday situations, individuals exist in a variety of client-professional relationships (i.e., the attorney-client, doctor-patient and accountant-client relationships) that respect the right of privileged communication. The federal court has upheld this right between accountant and client in the landmark case, *United States v. Arthur Young and Company*.[61] In this case, the Internal Revenue Service requested a series of papers from Arthur Young, accountant for the Amerada Company.   Even though the company agreed to release certain papers, the accounting firm attempted to claim that they could prevent the release based on the right of privileged communication. To that claim, the court responded:

Moreover, we do not understand whose interests AY [Arthur Young] seeks to protect by this claim of an enhanced burden. Amerada does not need this protection: it can intervene in its own behalf under §7609. And, in fact, it has done so. Since Amerada does not object to production of the audit workpapers, it would be anomalous to deny enforcement on the strength of its accountant's objection. Nor can AY assert any particular burden on it.[62]

59. *Id*. at 573.
60. *Id*. at 575.
61. 677 F.2d 211 (1982).
62. § 7609, *see generally*, Kenderine, *The Internal Revenue Service Summons to Produce Documents: Powers, Procedures, and Taxpayer Defenses*, 64 MINN. L. REV. 73 (1979) (as quoted from 677 F.2d 211 (1982) at 216).

Just as privileged communication belongs to the individual, not the accounting firm, the right to privacy belongs to the individual, not a government agency. Granted, contacting individuals might create a burden, especially in situations where the requested records concern many individuals, but it is not impossible; the CIA did not seem to find it burdensome to contact eighty institutions. It might cost the agency additional money in employee time, paper work, and other expenses, but the cost to the agency and the public would be far less than taking the case to court and wasting the court's time and the public's money in a conflict that easily could have been resolved in a short period of time.

Although the Freedom of Information Act does provide for expedited treatment of challenges to FOIA denials,[63] it is a reasonable assumption that contacting an individual for permission to release a record would be easier, take less time, and be less expensive than a court case before the district court or an *in camera* inspection.

Contacting individuals for their permission to release information would not create an extra layer of bureaucracy in an already overburdened system. Agencies themselves have seen this as a possible course of action. In a handbook for local governments on the 1983 Kansas Open Public Records Act, the League of Municipalities recommended that government officials contact, in writing, the individuals listed in the records, notifying them of the intent to release their records.[64]

This suggestion even follows the lead of the 1974 Privacy Act,[65] which requires an agency to: "[m]ake reasonable efforts to serve notice on an individual when any record on such individual is made available to any person under compulsory legal process when such process becomes a matter of public record."[66] Obviously Congress did not see it as an unneeded layer of bureaucracy when it created this section.

In some instances, contacting individuals for their permission to release records may even cause problems for the individual and the requestor of the information. It could place the individual in a difficult position if he or she were employed by the agency denying access to the records. The individual may not object to releasing the information but may feel compelled to deny

63. 5 U.S.C. § 552 (a)(4)(D): "Except as to cases the court considers of greater importance, proceedings before the district court, as authorized by this subsection, and appeals therefrom, take precedence on the docket over all cases and shall be assigned for hearing and trial or for argument at the earliest practicable date and expedited in every way."
64. League of Kansas Municipalities, Open Public Records—A Manual for Local Governments on the 1983 Kansas Open Public Records Act 33 (September 30, 1983) (preliminary draft).
65. 5 U.S.C. § 552 (a).
66. *Id.* at (e)(8).

the access in order to protect his or her job.

In addition, it is possible that the individual might object to releasing information, forcing the request to the courts. This objection gives agencies added leverage in their claim that it is a "clearly unwarranted invasion of privacy," when they can say the individual objected to the release. However, the Supreme Court, in *Getman v. NLRB* did instruct the courts that, "in determining that whether a disclosure would constitute a 'clearly unwarranted invasion of personal privacy,' they should tilt the balance in favor of disclosure."[67]

The suggestion of contacting the individuals to ask their permission to release records is so basic it seems simple. But, it is not a new or unworkable idea. Mary Hulett wrote: "It would be appropriate for agencies and courts to . . . require advance notice in some instances under the FOIA even though the [Privacy] Act excludes the FOIA from such a requirement."[68]

Contacting individuals for their permission to release records under the Freedom of Information Act is the most logical and the easiest way to avoid prolonged delays and lengthy and expensive court cases. Not only does it give individuals some control over the release of information on them, but it takes away the temptation for government agencies to hide behind Exemption (b)(6). The remedy of the court case and the *in camera* inspection exists in those instances where it is impossible to contact the individual, or where the individual denies access, but the public's right to know clearly outweighs the individual right to privacy. Although agency personnel may see this as an extra burden on them, contacting the individual, in the long run, will save time and government funds. It also is more in keeping with the fundamental rights implied and guaranteed in the Constitution's Bill of Rights. It comes closer to the true spirit of the Freedom of Information Act.

67.   *Supra* note 32 at 674.
68.   Hulett, *supra* note 29 at 290.

DECKLE MCLEAN

Privacy Invasion Tort: Straddling the Fence

Deckle McLean is a member of the
journalism faculty at Western Illinois
University. He has also been a writer for
the *Providence Journal-Bulletin* and the
Boston Globe.

American legal jurisdictions should abolish the privacy invasion tort lawsuit
if Americans are serious about protecting privacy, or as an alternative,
strengthen the lawsuit. Both courses of action would have the same effect:
they would enhance the respect given privacy in public discourse.

Currently, the effectiveness of the lawsuit is questionable. While it discourages the media from taking responsibility for privacy, it fails to provide
invaded persons a solid opportunity to vindicate their claims.

EXAMPLES OF PRIVACY INVASION

Prior to the beginnings of the American privacy tort lawsuit, American
newspapers had begun what could be called "invasive reporting." It was this
kind of reporting on wealthy social figures that provoked Louis D. Brandeis
and Samuel D. Warren to write a crucial 1890 *Harvard Law Review* article,
"The Right To Privacy."[1] In this article Brandeis and Warren argued that
the press' obsession with the marital and sexual activities of the Boston aris-
tocracy and others called for legal restraints.

Warren and Brandeis were not specific about the press activities that
provoked them to write their article. They cited the facts of a then current
New York case in which an actress appearing in tights was photographed

1   4 HARVARD LAW REVIEW 193 (1890).

from a theatre box. She sought an injunction to prevent use of the picture. Warren and Brandeis also complained about press gossip, saying it appealed to what is lowest in everyone, tended to crowd out robust or delicate thought, and created a climate in which strong mental effort cannot flourish. They criticized the press for having a prurient taste for sexual details.

Recent examples of media privacy invasions include the facts of a 1982 case brought by a Cleveland woman against ABC News.[2] ABC had recorded with a concealed camera and microphone her statement that she had traded sex for lenient treatment from a judge. The recorded statement was broadcast. A jury found for ABC after well-known investigative reporter Robert Greene of *Newsday* testified that, under certain circumstances, hidden equipment is a valid reporting device. But was it necessary to name or picture her in the story?

In 1984, *U.S. News and World Report* settled out of court a privacy suit brought by four men pictured in a photograph used to illustrate a story about unemployment among black teenagers.[3] The photo had been taken by a free lancer and forwarded to the magazine by a photo agency. The men in the picture were employed and the picture had been taken at a Washington, D.C. street festival. The magazine's caption to the picture read: "For unemployed young blacks, many empty hours are spent hanging out on city streets."

In a similar case, which reached the New York Court of Appeals in 1981, a black man sued for privacy damages after his photograph was used to illustrate a *New York Times Magazine* article about middle-class Blacks. The plaintiff was not interviewed for the article, which made a point that middle-class Blacks had turned their backs on other Blacks. Instead, his picture was taken at random on the street without his consent by a photographer working for an independent photo agency, which sold the photo to the *Times*. The plaintiff claimed he had been falsely portrayed as having turned his back on other Blacks.

The court ruled the publishing of the photo did not violate the state's privacy statute, which provides a cause of action for privacy invasions made for "purposes of trade," that is, commercial purposes. The picture had been published for editorial, not commercial, purposes, the court said. The court also noted that such an interpretation of the statute served free speech and press objectives. It said the plaintiff might have a privacy invasion action available against the photo agency or photographer on grounds their sale of the picture amounted to a use for a commercial purpose.[4] With the suggestion

2. Boddie v. ABC, No. C80-675A (N.D. Ohio, E.D., May 10, 1982).
3. Reid v. U.S. News and World Report, No. 6828-82 (D.C. Sup. Ct., 1983).
4. Arrington v. New York Times, 55 N.Y.2d 433, 449 N.Y.S.2d 941 (1982), *rearg. denied*, 57 N.Y.2d 669, 454 N.Y.S.2d 75 (1982), *cert. denied*, 459 U.S. 1146,

that a suit against the agency might succeed, the court at least recognized that the plaintiff may have been hurt.

A federal court jury awarded damages to a New Mexico prison guard who had been tortured during a riot at New Mexico State Penitentiary in 1980.[5] A story identifying him by name reported that he had been sodomized with an axe handle. The award was being appealed in 1984.

In 1983, higher appeals courts refused to review a Florida appeals court decision vacating an award to a woman hostage victim who was pictured semi-nude in a published photograph. The woman had been held hostage by her former husband, who had made her undress so that she would not try to escape. After the man shot himself, police escorted the woman to a squad car; she was photographed as she struggled to conceal herself behind a dish-towel. The appeals court said the picture was newsworthy.[6]

Other evidence that some of the media are unwilling to control themselves might be found in the reporting of the British press. England allows no privacy invasion lawsuits. But the British press is little better, if at all, than the American press in avoiding invasions of privacy.

For example, the *London Times*, in March 1982, carried a story about a physician censured for having an affair with a patient. The story reported on the action of the General Medical Council of London; it also carried names of the woman patient and of her husband, who had bugged his own phone to intercept his wife's conversations with the doctor. The story also reported that the wife had refused sex with her husband because he was revolted by a sexual act she wanted him to perform, and that she and the doctor had built their affair around sodomy.

The story also reported that the doctor had derived pleasure from listening over the phone as the woman described her masturbation. All parties were in their fifties. The story was accompanied by head photos of the husband and of the doctor.

In February 1982, two London papers, the *Sun* and the *Daily Star*, pub-

74 L.Ed 2d 994 (1983). The New York Legislature amended its Right of Privacy Statute, Civil Rights Law Section 51, to protect the photo agency and photographer:

> But nothing contained in this article shall be so construed as to prevent any person, firm or corporation from selling or otherwise transferring any material containing such name, portrait or picture in whatever medium to any user of such name, portrait or picture, or to any third party for sale or transfer directly or indirectly to such a user, for use in a manner lawful under this article. . . .

5. Schmitt v. Times-Herald, No. 82-2275 (D. N.M., 1980).
6. Cape Publications v. Bridges, 423 So. 2d 426 (1982), petition for review denied by Florida Supreme Court without opinion, 431 So. 2d 988 (1983), *cert. denied*, 104 S. Ct. 239, 78 L. Ed 2d 229 (1983).

lished pictures of Princess Diana of Wales in a bikini, five months pregnant, on a beach in the Bahamas. The picture had been taken surreptitiously with a long lens.

The Press Council, a news industry organism whose function is to maintain professional standards and freedom, condemned the pictures as a privacy invasion. Fifty percent of the Council's membership is press affiliated; fifty percent is non-press. Its declaration on privacy states, "Publication of information about people's private lives or concerns without their consent is only permissible if a legitimate public interest overrides their right to privacy. The public interest is not synonymous with 'of interest to the public'."

When newspaper editors were invited to Buckingham Palace, not long before the picture's publication, to be asked not to intrude on the princess' privacy, the *Sun* did not attend. However, it headlined its report on the meeting, "Leave our Princess Di alone says the Palace." After the Press Council's protest on the bikini picture, the *Sun* published a front page apology, along with a republication of the photograph.

MEDIA'S NEW MATURITY

Clearly, an effort to enhance privacy respect by freeing the media from legal restraints would be a gamble. Perhaps, like a child not yet grown, the media simply would not be able to handle it. Or perhaps self-control in the private field is too much to ask of an industry that is often desperately competitive. If the media could single-handedly carry the responsibility of protecting privacy, it would be something new—a new expectation of the media by the public and the media themselves.

But mass media have recently and rapidly been reaching a new maturity. One clear signal of this came in a speech by Michael J. O'Neill, then *New York Daily News* editor, to the American Society of Newspaper Editors at the group's 1982 annual meeting. O'Neill, the outgoing president, said that the media's power had increased substantially over the previous decade, but that media had a tendency "to revel in the power and wield it freely, rather than to accept any corresponding increase in responsibility." Muckraking had been "overemphasized," he said. Investigative reporting had sometimes "run off the ethical tracks."

"Individuals and institutions have been needlessly hurt when the lure of sensational headlines has prevailed over fairness, balance and a valid public purpose," O'Neill told his colleagues. "We should begin with an editorial philosophy that is more positive, more tolerant of the frailties of human institutions and their leaders, more sensitive to the rights and feelings of individuals—public officials as well as private citizens," he said.[7]

7. EDITOR & PUBLISHER 52, May 15, 1982.

A year later, *Editor & Publisher*, the leading newspaper industry journal, published an editorial quoting O'Neill's speech and adding comments from more recent speeches by David Shaw, the *Los Angeles Times* media critic, and Donald D. Jones, the *Kansas City Star*'s ombudsman. Said Shaw,

> [O]ne of the gravest ethical problems confronting the press today is our own arrogance—our hypocritical resentment of questions and criticism, our insularity, our solipsism, [our] almost giddy rush to envelope ourselves in the sacred mantle of the First Amendment, our refusal to be held accountable for our shortcomings, large or small.

Jones told an audience that readers "see reporters and editors trying to set themselves up as a privileged class." *Editor & Publisher* concluded that O'Neill had struck a theme which would occupy editors for years to come.[8]

American media have acted with some restraint over the years. For example, in the forties, fifties and sixties, the media ignored provocative personal habits of some leading figures. Franklin Delano Roosevelt's interest in his wife's former assistant was known to some members of the press but was not published. John F. Kennedy's assignations were known among the press in New England as well as in Washington, but these remained outside public discussion. J. Edgar Hoover's excessive fastidiousness—he often used a hankerchief to wipe his hands after shaking hands—did not appear in print.

Similar forebearance continued into the seventies and eighties. The palimony or galimony support suit against tennis figure Billy Jean King by a former lesbian lover received only routine media coverage, except for reporting and commentary on King's press conference to acknowledge that a lesbian affair had occurred. When Juanita Kreps resigned for personal reasons as Jimmy Carter's commerce secretary, the media merely noted that her husband had recently made a suicide attempt. Generally, the media declined to discuss Nelson Rockefeller's relationship to the woman in whose apartment he died. Similarly, the media declined to discuss former Urban League Director Vernon Jordan's relationship to his woman companion at the time an assassination attempt was made on him. As a few congressional pages testified to investigators that some congressmen had sought and received sexual contacts with them, the media refused to release the identities of the legislators named.

Another sign of media restraint in the past decade has been the policy followed by most publications and broadcasters of not using the names of rape victims. Legally, the press is entitled to use rape victims' names when

8.   *A challenge for editors*, EDITOR & PUBLISHER 4, May 7, 1983.

obtained from public records.[9]

There has been a striking change in American media over the past thirty years. In 1950, most American media were low-class businesses. Reporters and editors were working-class people with lower middle-class attitudes. In general, they were not college graduates, and their pay was poor. Most news sources and educated readers did not expect reliable reporting from publications or broadcasters because they knew the news personnel did not have the necessary training to understand complex issues. Journalism was a seedy occupation in most cases.

As Gay Talese pointed out in his *The Kingdom and The Power*, a study of the *New York Times*, most journalists exploited the hunger of their lower middle-class backgrounds and rose on their craving to rub shoulders with the famous, the connected and the powerful.

During the next thirty years, media became a middle- and upper middle-class field. A recent study indicates that editors and reporters on major eastern papers are of higher class status—measured by their own educations and the number of relatives in the professions—than high corporate managers.[10] Journalists now choose their field as an alternative to law, medicine or academia. In 1980, media work was no longer a trade; it was a profession. To get a job, you needed at least a college degree. When hiring was tight, a graduate degree was essential. News organizations had begun to send staff members to graduate schools if they had not been already. Journalism schools had proliferated. They had not reached the stature in the profession that law schools had reached in the legal profession, but hiring editors often wanted to see journalism degrees, professional degrees, master's degrees or at least undergraduate degrees from rigorous colleges. Journalism schools require law courses, and ethical discussions occur throughout journalism programs.

The parents and siblings of these journalists are members of the older professions. So are their friends, spouses and children. The journalism schools are bulging, not only in news areas, but in all parts of the mass media, including broadcast production and film. It is wealthy, swank or highly intelligent students who are entering these fields. Newspaper unions have contributed to the change by raising salaries to the point where a privileged kid willing to trade-off against high income can make ends meet. Media work is no longer a seedy field.

The changeover has not been entirely positive. It has not improved the quality of writing. It has brought into the media moralistic crusaders who sometimes do more harm than good. And it has reduced the occasions of literary excellence, because the demand for credentials has closed the doors to brilliant individuals without credentials.

9.   *See* Cox v. Cohn, 420 U.S. 469 (1975).
10.   18, no. 4 PSYCHOLOGY TODAY 73 (April 1984).

But American media are soon to be dominated by highly educated, high-minded persons, uniquely committed to their business, due to their willingness to sacrifice some of the income that is at their fingertips in other lines of work. Such people should be able to conduct themselves ethically. They are the maturity of American journalism. But they are pressured out of exercising this maturity in privacy matters by legal threats that do not give them room to carry responsibility. Unfortunately, they may never get that room because the media world also includes Rupert Murdoch's newspapers, the *National Enquirer*, and TV docudramas, none of which clearly appear to be a part of the upward trend in privacy ethics.

STRENGTHENING THE PRIVACY INVASION SUIT

The previously mentioned signs indicate the mass media might now adequately protect privacy, even without the spur of legal sanctions. However, a strong privacy invasion tort lawsuit is the surest way to protect individuals from media privacy invasions. Creation of a strong lawsuit is the course of action that has been followed in continental European civil law countries. Brandeis and Warren, in their 1890 *Harvard Law Review* article, cited French law, which even then considered privacy—including that of celebrities—to be protection-worthy.

The U.S. should also adopt a strong privacy invasion lawsuit if American courts cannot go back to the policy of rejecting all claims for privacy invasion damages. American judicial authorities seem to be committed to legally protecting privacy from media invasion—committed to such a degree that retreat may be impossible. For example, consider the following quotation from 62 *American Jurisprudence* 2d, Privacy, sec. 4, p. 683:

> One of the principle arguments advanced in support of the doctrine of privacy by its original exponents is that the increased complexity and intensity of modern civilization and the development of man's spiritual sensibilities have rendered man more sensitive to publicity and have increased his need for privacy, while the great technological improvements in the means of communications have more and more subjected the intimacies of his private life to exploitations by those who pander to commercialism and to prurient and idle curiosity. A legally enforceable right of privacy is deemed to be a proper protection against this type of encroachment upon the personality of the individual.

Strengthening the American privacy invasion lawsuit would require weakening the newsworthiness defense, the traditional media defense to privacy invasion claims. It has embodied and protected first amendment interests although it has not been considered a constitutional defense. The defense can be traced to the 1890 Warren and Brandeis article, in which the authors, relying on the French model, asserted that the privacy right should be limited so that it does not prohibit publication of matter in the public or general interest.

As American courts recognized the privacy right, they also recognized this "public interest" limitation on it. In addition, newsworthiness was a question judges usually retained for themselves to decide as a matter of law. They did not pass the question on for jury decision. As a result, potential privacy invasion plaintiffs could expect that in most cases, judges would find a published remark newsworthy and dismiss the action for failure to state an adequate claim or grant summary judgment to the defendant media prior to trial.

For example, in the *Sidis v. F-R Publishing Company* case of 1940,[11] a trial judge dismissed the complaint of a former child prodigy described in a *New Yorker* profile as then living in shabby isolation. The judge found the article was in the public interest. A federal appeals court agreed and affirmed the dismissal of the suit.

In *Virgil v. Time, Inc.* in federal courts in California in 1975,[12] a trial judge granted summary judgment to Time after Virgil claimed that *Sports Illustrated* had invaded his privacy by revealing his peculiar personal habits in an article on surfing. Virgil was known on his beach for eating spiders, snuffing out cigarettes in his mouth and other unusual acts. The judge found as a matter of law that the article was newsworthy. The appeals court reversed this decision after finding that the judgment of newsworthiness should have been sent to jurors as a fact question to be answered through a community standards test.

This *Virgil* decision was an atypical ruling; it has not been widely imitated. Advocates of a stronger privacy invasion lawsuit (such as Linda N. Woito and Patrick McNulty, writing in 64 *Iowa Law Review* 185 in 1979) argue that this type of ruling be broadly adopted. But in the *Virgil* case, the trial judge found a way to skirt the appeals court's decision. After the case was sent back to him, the trial judge ruled that reasonable jurors would answer such a fact question of newsworthiness negatively. As a result, he again granted summary judgment to Time, and the litigation ended.

In privacy lawsuits, such as the *Sidis* and *Virgil* cases, in which the truth of the published remarks is acknowledged by plaintiffs, the newsworthiness defense can be overcome, courts have said, only where the revelations have

11. Sidis v. F-R Publishing Co., 113 F.2d 806 (2nd Cir. 1940).
12. Virgil v. Time, Inc., 527 F.2d 1122 (9th Cir. 1975), *cert. denied*, 425 U.S. 998 (1976).

been unconscionable in that they have shocked community sensibilities. Some examples of unconscionability have been: disclosing a wife's former and repudiated career as a prostitute;[13] revealing a rehabilitated man's former career as a bank robber;[14] and describing a woman hospitalized for a blood sugar problem as a "starving glutton."[15]

In false light privacy suits, where the revelation has been inaccurate as well as invasive, the newsworthiness defense has been given constitutional stature. If the subject matter of a false light invasive statement is in the public interest, the newsworthiness defense can be overcome only with a showing that the media defendant was actually malicious, which means reckless disregard for the truth in making the false disclosure. This is the actual malice test created in libel cases, fused with the newsworthiness defense and employed since 1967 in privacy cases, even when the plaintiff is clearly a private person.[16]

These kinds of privacy cases—false light and public-disclosure-of-true-facts—are the crucial privacy invasion cases. They result from media invasions that do not appear to have commercial motivations; in short, they result from the most common privacy invasion grievances.

The other types of privacy invasion suits—misappropriation and physical intrusion—are less troublesome for courts. A misappropriation case is one in which a plaintiff claims his privacy has been invaded, for example, by the unauthorized use of his picture in an ad.[17] Misappropriation cases have received clear statutory endorsement in some jurisdictions, and, according to the U.S. Supreme Court in *Zacchini v. Scripps-Howard* in 1977,[18] are essentially unjust enrichment cases. Unjust enrichment has stronger legal roots than the purer privacy right seen in false light and public disclosure cases. The interest at stake in unjust enrichment situations is a property interest, and being so, is the type of interest common law has long been comfortable in addressing.

A privacy invasion by physical intrusion occurs when, for example, a reporter bugs an office to gather news. Common law provides a model for physical privacy invasion lawsuits; eavesdropping was a common law offense for centuries. Some physical intrusion privacy cases—such as those in which journalists cross thresholds with concealed electronic devices or through bribes or lies—can be handled as trespass cases or on a trespass model.[19]

13. Melvin v. Reid, 112 Cal. App. 285 (1931).
14. Briscoe v. Readers Digest, 4 Cal. 3d 529 (1971).
15. Barber v. Time, 348 Mo. 1199 (1942).
16. *See* Time v. Hill, 385 U.S. 374 (1967).
17. *See* Roberson v. Rochester Folding Box, 171 N.Y. 538 (1902).
18. Zacchini v. Scripps-Howard, 433 U.S. 562 (1977).
19. *See* Dietemann v. Time, 449 F.2d 245 (9th Cir. 1971); Galella v. Onassis, 533 F. Supp. 1076 (1982).

It is the false light and public disclosure lawsuits that would demand attention if the right to privacy were enhanced for potential damage suit plaintiffs. The public disclosure lawsuit would be strengthened if the approach to newsworthiness used by the Ninth Circuit Court of Appeals in the *Virgil* case were widely adopted. In fact, after the *Virgil* decision, some media lawyers expressed fear that the *Virgil* ruling would be used widely to increase the media's courtroom losses.

The community standards test advocated in the *Virgil* opinion requires that a juror base his decision on what he knows the view of the average person in his community to be, but not on his own personal view. The test is used as the basis of jury instructions in obscenity cases.[20]

The pure privacy public disclosure lawsuit also might be enhanced by bringing to it something like the *Gertz v. Welch*[21] approach used in libel cases. The *Gertz* rules require a distinction be made between public figure and private person plaintiffs. Public figure plaintiffs are prohibited from winning any libel damages unless they can show that the media defendant had exhibited actual malice in publishing or broadcasting the offending statement. Actual malice is defined as reckless disregard for the truth. Private person plaintiffs, on the other hand, are allowed to win limited damages if they can merely show that the media defendant had been negligent.

The *Gertz* rules do not directly apply to public disclosure suits because these rules are geared to false publications, whereas in public disclosure suits true publications are involved. But the *Gertz* rules could be used as a model. The unconscionability test could be reserved for public figure plaintiffs just as the actual malice test is reserved for public figure plaintiffs in libel cases. Private person plaintiffs in public disclosure lawsuits might then be awarded compensatory, but not presumed or punitive damages, upon satisfying a jury that published statements offended community sensibilities, though to a degree less than shock or unconscionability. Such a private person privacy plaintiff, in line with the *Gertz* model, might also be required to show he had actually been injured by the revelation.

False light lawsuits could be enhanced by applying to them directly the rules used in libel suits as of 1984. False light privacy invasion is akin to libel in that it arises from false statements, but in most states, it is easier for a private person plaintiff to win a libel suit than a false light privacy suit. This situation can perhaps be traced back to the common law deception that a libelous remark damaged a property right while privacy invasion claims touched only personal rights.

Fusing false light and libel rules would enable the privacy suit plaintiff without celebrity status to succeed on a showing that the media was negligent

20. Hamling v. U.S., 418 U.S. 87 (1974); Jenkins v. Georgia, 418 U.S. 153 (1974).
21. Gertz v. Welch, 418 U.S. 323 (1974).

and that he had been injured. Presently, such a privacy plaintiff in a false light suit must show that the media recklessly disregarded the truth of the disclosure. This is a substantially more difficult standard to meet. Examples of reckless disregard drawn from famous privacy and libel cases are: quoting and paraphrasing a story source without actually talking with the source;[22] and basing a published assertion on unchecked information given by a person of doubtful reputation, under circumstances providing adequate time to check.[23]

From 1971 to 1974, the U.S. Supreme Court applied the same constitutional standards of proof to false light and libel cases. But the objective in fusing the rules in 1971 – in *Rosenbloom v. Metromedia*[24] – was to weaken the libel lawsuit in order to better protect media. In 1974, the Supreme Court decided in *Gertz v. Welch* that it had gone too far in weakening the libel lawsuit. It then bolstered libel, divorcing it from false light.

It would be useful now to once again fuse the libel and false light rules, but for the purpose of strengthening the privacy invasion lawsuit. An example for doing so has already been provided by a Kansas federal district judge in *Rinsley v. Brandt* in 1977,[25] in which the judge applied the *Gertz* rules to a false light claim. A federal district judge in Washington, D.C. ruled the same way in 1981 in *Dresbach v. Doubleday.*[26]

One persistent obstacle to bolstering the privacy lawsuit has been the traditional common law reluctance to award damages for violation of a personal right. For example, in the old Rhode Island case of *Henry v. Cherry & Webb* in 1909,[27] the state supreme court took pains to stress that the privacy right was not a property right because a property right passes to heirs while a privacy right does not. The court was answering the argument of a dissenting New York judge in the *Roberson v. Rochester Folding Box* case of 1902.[28] This dissenting judge had said that privacy should be handled as a property right because law should recognize that people have a property-like interest in their personalities. The Rhode Island Supreme Court rejected the privacy claim in the Henry case.

The Rhode Island judge did note, however, that libel had long been anomalous in tort law in that, unlike other mental anguish torts, it was actionable without a showing of special damages. In other words, in libel cases, the law would assume there had been pecuniary loss but it would not make the same assumption in other mental anguish areas. In these other mental

22. *See* Cantrell v. Forest City, 419 U.S. 245 (1974).
23. *See* Curtis v. Butts, 388 U.S. 130 (1967).
24. Rosenbloom v. Metromedia, 403 U.S. 29 (1971).
25. Rinsley v. Brandt, 446 F. Supp. 850 (D. Kan. 1977).
26. Dresbach v. Doubleday, 518 F. Supp. 1285 (D. D.C. 1981).
27. Henry v. Cherry & Webb, 30 R.I. 13 (1909).
28. Roberson v. Rochester Folding Box, 171 N.Y. 538 (1902).

anguish areas, the showing of pecuniary loss where violation of a mere personal right was claimed gave the case the desired property loss element. In libel, however — that is, in libel per se or direct libel — the property loss was assumed. A libel per se is a statement that is libelous on its face, as in saying, "Smith is a gambler," but unlike saying, "Smith visits 25 Vegas Avenue," where some readers know or believe that 25 Vegas Avenue is a bookie headquarters.

The Supreme Court's constitutional libel rules now require that private figure plaintiffs show special injury. But the Supreme Court in its *Gertz* opinion defined this "actual injury" in a way that alters the required proof from the common law property standard of pecuniary loss to an enlightened twentieth century standard of personality damages not necessarily measured by dollar value.

"We need not define 'actual injury' as trial courts have wide experience in framing appropriate jury instruction in tort actions," the Supreme Court said in its *Gertz* opinion.

> Suffice it to say that actual injury is not limited to out-of-pocket loss. Indeed, the more customary types of actual harm inflicted by defamatory falsehood include impairment of reputation and standing in the community, personal humiliation, and mental anguish and suffering. Of course, juries must be limited by appropriate instructions, and all awards must be supported by competent evidence concerning the injury, although there need be no evidence which assigns an actual dollar value to the injury.[29]

Such modification of the special damage requirement indicates American law has reached a degree of maturity in which an injury to personality rights is legally recognizable. Moreover, requiring private libel plaintiffs to offer proof of actual injury as well as proof that the media defendant was negligent not only meets first amendment press protection interests, but also makes libel more consistent with mental anguish torts as cautiously recognized under common law. Add to this the current constitutional rules forbidding presumed or punitive damages except on showings of actual malice, and you have a nicely balanced arrangement. Why it has not been eagerly endorsed for the false light privacy suit strains the understanding.

PROTECTION FOR CELEBRITIES

But the balance struck in the *Gertz* ruling has a flaw. It does not attribute

29.   Gertz v. Welch, 418 U.S. 323 at 349–50 (1974).

validity to the private lives of celebrities and public figures. A change in American privacy law to protect the private lives of public figures would break an established pattern. American personality law has assumed that when a person accepts celebrity status, he/she relinquishes most claims to privacy. The rationale has been that the media have a first amendment mandate to report thoroughly on the private lives of celebrities because these are in the public sphere.

This rationale has probably had an unhappy consequence by discouraging talented persons who value their privacy from entering public life. This represents a loss of talent and also a loss of diversity. As a loss from the field of entertainment, this does not have far-reaching consequences. But in the field of politics and diplomacy, the loss is frightening.

In addition, the level of political campaigning is lowered. In 1982, a candidate for governor of Ohio was attacked by an opponent for having gone to a prostitute ten years before. However, there are so many things worse, legal and illegal, that the candidate could have done, and might in fact have done. It is not saints or inflexible moralists that are needed in public office, but good managers and people with understanding.

How many persons who might enter public life would risk such exposure? A fling with a married woman at twenty-five. A fight in a bar at age twenty-four. A wife or brother who drinks too much. A visit to a psychiatrist during college. Under normal circumstances, revelations of any of these are privacy invasions.

American libel law, like American privacy law, is not designed to protect the private lives of public figures. But the Supreme Court has indicated its willingness to decide   cases with an eye toward protecting celebrities' privacy.

In the 1976 case of *Time v. Firestone*,[30] the Supreme Court was presented with a gray area case involving press comment on the divorce of a socialite couple. The Court defined the divorcing wife as a private person plaintiff, not as a public figure. The decision, taken as a whole, seemed to embody the fact that the claimed defamation involved divorce, a private-like matter. The plaintiff did appear to be a public figure in that she was covered on society pages and had given several press conferences during the divorce proceedings. One justice argued in a dissenting opinion that these press conferences made her a public figure plaintiff. The majority seemed to be signaling that the *Gertz* rules left them little room to base a libel decision on a published comment's being private while the plaintiff was public. But the Court seemed to take the private nature of the comment into consideration in defining the plaintiff as private.

In this libel decision, the Supreme Court has indicated sensitivity to the private zones of public persons' lives. To give effect to this sensibility, it

30.   Time v. Firestone, 424 U.S. 448 (1976).

needs to add a new rule to its *Gertz* rules. The new rule would require that, where a libel plaintiff is a public figure, a check must be made to determine if the published remark touched a private zone of his/her life. If the remark did touch a private zone rather than a public one, then the plaintiff should be handled as a private plaintiff rather than as a public figure. He/she should be permitted to recover limited damages on a showing that the defendant media was faulty in publishing the statement and that the plaintiff was actually injured.

Determining whether statements touch private zones could be done under some of the same tests now used to decide whether a plaintiff is public or private. Did the plaintiff voluntarily thrust himself into the limelight on the subject touched in the statement? Did the plaintiff already have fame or notoriety in his community on the subject touched?

Some court decisions using the *Gertz* rules must inevitably, though not avowedly, include consideration of whether statements about an apparently public plaintiff are private or public. According to the *Gertz* opinion, a person can become a public figure for a limited issue. This rule implies that, for other issues, the person may remain a private person. As a result, courts have room to conclude that a plaintiff may not be a public figure regarding the subject matter broached in any particular irritating publication. Some observers might argue, in fact, that these *Gertz* rules allow courts to make the recovery of damages easier for public figures whose private lives have been touched, simply by calling them private persons for the purposes of the suits. This seems to be what happened in the *Firestone* case.

But nowhere in the *Gertz* opinion does the Supreme Court straightforwardly say a public figure may become a private one for a limited issue, or that a public figure should be handled as a private one for certain kinds of defamatory remarks. This is the kind of new rule courts should make if celebrities' private lives are to be protected.

The addition of such a rule to the *Gertz* defamation rules would enhance libel protection in a modest way. Transferring such a new rule to false light privacy invasion suits would be a bigger step. It would be a striking modification of the newsworthiness defense. It would, however, be an important step in rounding out legal protection of privacy in manner consistent with the European model, which American courts have been very cautiously approaching since 1890.

A CHANGE IS NEEDED

One might ask why it is necessary to tamper with the existing privacy tort lawsuit, either to destroy or enhance it. Doesn't it work well enough? The truth is, it doesn't work well enough. When the law provides a cause of action—a lawsuit—it encourages a fight. There is a wise and ancient purpose to encouraging fights in this way: if people will come to court and fight over damages, they are less likely to resort to barbarian resolutions for their grievances. In a 1916 slander case, a South Carolina judge explained to his jury,

> Now, it is true that we don't have many of this kind of cases in South Carolina because, unfortunately for us and our State, when men use words which are insulting and opprobrious and defamatory against each other, the prevalent idea is that such should be remedied by a blow or with a bullet, and that is one of the reasons why it has been said so frequently that human life in South Carolina is cheaper than five-cent cotton.[31]

When law encourages bringing disputes to court, it does itself a disservice if it arranges the rules so that the odds of success run heavily against one side. Such an arrangement discourages bringing grievances to court and encourages barbarian solutions. Law is very simple at root. It exists only to keep the peace and vindicate principles. In those instances where, in trying to anticipate a dispute or to effectuate a principle, law creates fights where no true disputes exist, it again does itself a disservice if it balances the rules toward one party. In this case, it turns non-combatants pugnacious, then gives one side cause for arrogance.

The false light and public disclosure lawsuits turn the press combative by permitting privacy invasion suits against them and then encourage media arrogance by rigging the rules in the media's favor. The tendency among many editors and reporters is to regard privacy as a club with which the courts and crabby members of the public beat them. The media then take an us–them attitude, overlooking their own responsibilities. In fact, many media practitioners may conclude it is their duty to oppose privacy rights in order to preserve a balance of power. But there is no balance of power in this matter of privacy; media have most of the power—the financial power to absorb the burden of adjusting the grievances and court rules favorable to them.

The puny privacy lawsuit is not a counterweight; it is like a fly irritating a bear. When the bear lashes out at the fly—in defiant neglect of privacy interests—it gets away with it and privacy is damaged as a value. Better to keep the fly away from the bear, or, as an option, turn the fly into another bear.

If privacy invasion is an area of true grievances, the law is discouraging civilized resolution of them by overly handicapping plaintiffs. If it is an area

31.   Lewis v. Williams, 89 S.E. 647 at 649, 105 S.C. 165 at 167 (1916).

of artificial grievances, the law is creating a fight and producing a bully where none previously existed.

There are only two possible solutions here: make the legal forum a fair one, or convert the media from being the favored combatant into being the forum itself. If the law withdraws, the fight may disappear. But if law must provide a forum to honor a principle, the forum must be fair.

VALERIE B. DONOVAN

Unauthorized Use of Deceased's Persona: Current Theories and the Need for Uniform Legislative Treatment

Valerie B. Donovan is an associate editor
for the American University Law Review
and has worked as program manager
and communications liaison for the
U.S. Department of Energy.

A play opened on Broadway in 1980 in which actors clearly imitated the style and appearance of Groucho, Chico, and Harpo Marx.[1] The star of a live, musical stage production imitated the delivery, appearance and distinctive stance of the late Elvis Presley.[2] A company sold plastic busts of the deceased Dr. Martin Luther King, Jr.[3] A Coors beer advertisement featured the likeness of deceased country-western musician, Lester Flatt.[4] In each of these scenarios, taken from actual cases, a commercial enterprise used a deceased celebrity's popular name, likeness, or image to promote the sale of a product. These enterprises had not obtained authorization from the celebrities' estates or representatives to appropriate the distinctive attributes, or personae, of the celebrities.

These situations illustrate a problem intrinsic to a growing and substantive area of tort and property law. The problem concerns the amount of control

1. Groucho Marx Prods. v. Day & Night Co., 523 F. Supp. 485 (S.D.N.Y. 1981), *rev'd on other grounds*, 689 F.2d 317 (2d Cir. 1982).
2. Estate of Presley v. Russen, 513 F. Supp. 1339 (D.N.J. 1981).
3. Martin Luther King Jr., Center for Social Change, Inc. v. American Heritage Prods., Inc., 694 F.2d 674 (11th Cir. 1983).
4. Commerce Union Bank v. Coors, 7 Media L. Rep. (BNA) 2204 (Tenn. Ch. Ct. 1981).

a person's estate has to prevent the unauthorized commercial use of the deceased individual's persona.[5] Courts have been inconsistent in defining the rights of the estate in such situations. The great variety in state law regarding protection of the right of publicity has resulted in suits determined merely by choice-of-law decisions.[6] For example, under New York common law, if the deceased was domiciled in New York at the time of death, the estate or representative of the celebrity would be able to bring a suit and possibly enjoin publication of the advertisement.[7] New York common law recognizes a descendible right of publicity.[8] If the celebrity was domiciled in California, however, his/her estate would have no cause of action, as California does not recognize a descendible right of publicity, unless that right has been

5. The use of public figures in advertisements to stimulate sales has become a large industry. It has been estimated that annual royalties from licensing agreements are over thirty-five million dollars. See Brenner, What's in a Name and Who Owns It? 6 BARRISTER 42, 42–43 (1979).
6. See Haelan Laboratories, Inc. v. Topps Chewing Gum, Inc., 202 F.2d 866 (2d Cir.) (This was the first case to establish a right in the publicity value of a photograph which could be transferred for commercial purposes, and the first case to coin the term, "right of publicity."), cert. denied, 346 U.S. 816 (1953). The right of publicity provides celebrities with an exclusive right to the pecuniary value of their names and likenesses. See also Rosemont Enters., Inc. v. Random House, Inc., 58 Misc. 2d 1, 6, 294 N.Y.S.2d 122, 129 (Sup. Ct. 1968) (defining the right of publicity as a pecuniary right), aff'd mem, 32 App. Div. 2d 892, 301 N.Y.S.2d 948 (App. Div. 1969); infra notes 18–34 and accompanying text (discussing the right of publicity).
7. See Price v. Hal Roach Studios, Inc., 400 F. Supp. 836 (S.D.N.Y. 1975) (Actors had publicity rights in their names and likenesses that descended to their heirs.); Southeast Bank. N.A. v. Lawrence, 104 A.D.2d 213, 483 N.Y.S.2d 218 (N.Y. App. Div., First Dept. 1984) (holding that "Tennessee Williams'" right of publicity survived his death).
8. See Groucho Marx Prods. v. Day & Night Co., 523 F. Supp. 485 (S.D.N.Y. 1981), rev'd on other grounds, 689 F.2d 317 (2d Cir. 1982) (Right of publicity is a property right and as such is both assignable and descendible.); Factors Etc., Inc. v. Pro Arts, Inc., 444 F. Supp. 288 (S.D.N.Y. 1977), aff'd, 579 F.2d 215, 221 (2d Cir. 1978), cert. denied, 440 U.S. 908 (1979) (Factors I). The court held in Factors I that, according to New York law, the Elvis Presley estate's licensee had the right to use Presley's name and likeness in connection with the manufacture and marketing of consumer products. Pro Arts was enjoined from marketing Presley memorabilia. This decision was reversed on appeal by the circuit court in Factors Etc., Inc. v. Pro Arts, Inc., 496 F. Supp. 1090 (S.D.N.Y. 1980) (Factors II). The circuit court in Factors II applied Tennessee law, rather than New York law, reasoning that Tennessee was where Presley had been domiciled. See Memphis Dev. Found. v. Factors Etc., Inc., 616 F.2d 956 (6th Cir. 1980), cert. denied, 449 U.S. 953 (1980) (holding that the right of publicity was not descendible in Tennessee). But see Commerce Union Bank v. Coors, 7 Media L. Rep. (BNA) 2204 (Tenn. Ch. Ct. 1981) (trial court holding that the right of publicity was descendible in Tennessee). See also Price v. Worldvision Enters., 455 F. Supp. 252 (S.D.N.Y. 1978), aff'd, 603 F.2d 214 (2d Cir. 1979) (enjoining impersonation of physical likenesses, voices, and mannerisms of Stan Laurel and Oliver Hardy in television series).

assigned, transferred or otherwise exploited prior to the celebrity's death.[9] In Tennessee, the celebrity's name and likeness would be considered part of the public domain, thereby barring any one person's exclusive right to its exploitation.[10] If the celebrity had a long period of retirement and had been domiciled in Florida, his/her estate could sue under the Florida publicity statute. That statute provides a specific cause of action and damages to the celebrity's estate for unauthorized publication of his/her name or likeness for any commercial or advertising purpose.[11]

The implication of this wide range of judicial response is that, although commercial exploitation may be controlled in one state, such exploitation may simultaneously proliferate in other states.[12] As a result, there are many unanswered questions regarding the right of a person to control the use by others of his/her name, likeness, or image, the duration of the right, and the descendibility of the right.[13]

Currently, no uniform federal law governs this area. The Copyright Act of 1976 protects literary and artistic work from appropriation by anyone other than the copyright holder or his/her assignee.[14] Trademark law, specifically

---

9. *See* Lugosi v. Universal Pictures, 25 Cal. 3d 813, 603 P.2d 425, 160 Cal. Rptr. 323 (1979).

10. *See* Memphis Dev. Found. v. Factors Etc., Inc., 616 F.2d 956 (6th Cir.), *cert. denied*, 449 U.S. 953 (1980).

11. FLA. STAT. ANN. § 540.08 (West 1979).

12. *Compare* Memphis Dev. Found. v. Factors Etc., Inc., 616 F.2d 956 (6th Cir.) (Under Tennessee law, right of publicity does not survive death.), *cert. denied*, 449 U.S. 953 (1980), *and* Lugosi v. Universal Pictures, 25 Cal. 3d 813, 603 P.2d 425, 160 Cal. Rptr. 323 (1979) (Right to exploit name and likeness is personal to an artist and must be exercised during his/her lifetime.), *with* Factors Etc., Inc. v. Pro Arts, Inc., 579 F.2d 215, 220–22 (2d Cir. 1978) (Under New York law, right of publicity survives death.), *cert. denied*, 440 U.S. 908 (1979), *rev'd on other grounds*, 652 F.2d 278 (2d Cir. 1981), *and* Price v. Hal Roach Studios, 400 F. Supp. 836, 844–47 (S.D.N.Y. 1975) (Actor's death did not extinguish right of publicity held by plaintiff.). *See generally* Felcher and Rubin, *The Descendibility of the Right of Publicity: Is There Commercial Life After Death?* 98 YALE L. J. 1125, 1130 (1980) (Publicity rights should be limited to fulfilling the social policy of promoting creative effort.); Sims, *Right of Publicity: Survivability Reconsidered*, 49 FORDHAM L. REV. 453 (1981) (favoring descendible right of publicity); Note, *Lugosi v. Universal Pictures: Descent of the Right of Publicity*, 29 HASTINGS L. J., 751, 767–68 (1978) (recommending that California should recognize right of publicity as descendible); Note, *Inheritability of the Right of Publicity Upon the Death of the Famous*, 33 VAND. L. REV. 1,291 (1980) (Courts should consider advocating the right of publicity as a property right that should survive death.).

13. One court referred to the state of the law as "that of a haystack in a hurricane . . . ." Ettore v. Philco Television Broadcasting Corp., 229 F.2d 481, 485 (3d Cir.), *cert. denied*, 351 U.S. 926 (1956).

14. 17 U.S.C. §§ 101–810 (1982). The underlying policy behind federal copyright law is to provide an incentive for enterprise and creativity by allowing individuals to benefit from their efforts; *see infra* notes 68–70 and accompanying text (discussing federal copyright law).

VALERIE B. DONOVAN

section 43(a) of the Lanham Act (the federal trademark statute), protects trademark interests as well as interests functioning like trademarks.[15] Neither copyright law nor trademark law is consistently applicable to the issue of descendibility of commercial use of a celebrity's persona.[16] This article proposes a federal statute to prohibit the unauthorized use of deceased individuals' personae by others. A uniform law would preempt conflicting state law, ending the confusion that now exists, and would alleviate the confusion over which state law should apply in a particular case.[17]

Section I of this article provides an overview of the various remedies that courts have applied to define the limits of control an estate has over a deceased person's name, likeness, or image. These remedies include the right of publicity, the right of privacy, trademark violation and copyright infringement. Section II presents an analysis of remedies and affirmative defenses. Section III suggests elements to incorporate into federal legislation to create a descendible right of publicity.

I. REMEDIES FOR UNAUTHORIZED USE OF PERSONA

A. Right of Publicity

The familiar names and faces of celebrities have strong commercial value, as demonstrated by their use in national, multi-media advertising campaigns for consumer products. Legal remedies invoked by celebrities to protect their interest in the use of their unique personae include the right of privacy, unfair competition (trademark law), copyright infringement, and, most recently, the right of publicity. It is this last right that has afforded the celebrity the most effective protection.

The right of publicity emerged thirty years ago as a means to protect the value of a celebrity's name, likeness, or image from unauthorized use.[18] Courts continue to grapple with the parameters of this right, focusing in

15. 15 U.S.C. §§ 1051–1127 (1982).
16. See infra notes 47–82 and accompanying text (discussing copyright and trademark law).
17. See Groucho Marx Prods. v. Day & Night Co., 523 F. Supp. 485 (S.D.N.Y. 1981), rev'd on other grounds, 689 F.2d 317 (2d Cir. 1982) (The Second Circuit Court of Appeals found that the district court erred by relying on New York law. The court determined that California law was controlling.); see infra notes 84–115 and accompanying text (discussing choice-of-law issues).
18. The right of publicity was first promulgated in Haelan Laboratories v. Topps Chewing Gum, 202 F.2d 866 (2d Cir.), cert. denied, 346 U.S. 816 (1953). The court recognized a personal, non-assignable, and non-exploitable right of privacy. In addition, the court determined that the plaintiff had a distinct right of publicity. This right included the exclusive right to control the publishing of a person's photograph. This right could be assigned to others; whether it was a property right was not considered to be relevant. Id. at 868.

particular on whether the right survives the death of the celebrity.[19] The U.S. Supreme Court and many state jurisdictions have recognized the right of publicity.[20] Plaintiffs have used it to secure legal[21] and equitable[22] relief in claims ranging from commercial endorsements[23] to imitations of a celebrity in a performance.[24]

19. *See* ACME Circus Operating Co. v. Kuperstock, 711 F.2d 1538 (11th Cir. 1983); Martin Luther King Jr., Center for Social Change, Inc. v. American Heritage Prods., 694 F.2d 674 (11th Cir. 1983); Memphis Dev. Found. v. Factors Etc., Inc., 616 F.2d 956 (6th Cir.), *cert. denied*, 449 U.S. 953 (1980); Groucho Marx Prods. v. Day & Night Co., 523 F. Supp. 485 (S.D.N.Y. 1981), *rev'd on other grounds*, 689 F.2d 317 (2d Cir. 1982); Price v. Worldvision Enters., 455 F. Supp. 252 (S.D.N.Y. 1978), *aff'd*, 603 F.2d 214 (2d Cir. 1979); Factors Etc., Inc. v. Pro Arts, Inc., 444 F. Supp. 288 (S.D.N.Y. 1977), *aff'd*, 579 F.2d 215 (2d Cir. 1978), *cert. denied*, 440 U.S. 908 (1979); Estate of Presley v. Russen, 513 F. Supp. 1339 (D.N.J. 1981); Lugosi v. Universal Pictures, 25 Cal. 3d 813, 603 P.2d 425, 160 Cal. Rptr. 323 (1979); Guiglielmi v. Spelling-Goldberg Prods., 25 Cal. 3d 860, 603 P.2d 454, 160 Cal. Rptr. 352 (1979); Commerce Union Bank v. Coors, 7 Media L. Rep. (BNA) 2204 (Tenn. Ch. Ct. 1981).
20. *See, e.g.*, Zacchini v. Scripps-Howard Broadcasting Co., 433 U.S. 562, 569 (1977) (A celebrity has control over commercial exploitation of his/her personality and talents); Martin Luther King Jr., Center for Social Change, Inc. v. American Heritage Prods., Inc., 694 F.2d 674 (11th Cir. 1983); Winterland Concessions Co. v. Silieo, 528 F. Supp. 1201 (N.D. Ill. 1981); Groucho Marx Prods. v. Day & Night Co., 523 F. Supp. 485 (S.D.N.Y. 1981), *rev'd on other grounds*, 689 F.2d 317 (2d Cir. 1982); Estate of Presley v. Russen, 513 F. Supp. 1330 (D.N.J. 1981); Uhlaender v. Henricksen, 316 F. Supp. 1277 (D. Minn. 1970); Cepeda v. Swift & Co., 291 F. Supp. 242 (E.D. Mo. 1968), *aff'd*, 415 F.2d 1205, 1206 (8th Cir. 1969); Sharmon v. Schmidt & Sons, 216 F. Supp. 401 (E.D. Pa. 1963); Cher v. Forum Int'l., 213 U.S.P.Q. 96 (C.D. Cal.), *rev'd in part*, 692 F.2d 634 (9th Cir. 1982); Delan v. CBS, Inc., 91 A.D.2d 255, 445 N.Y.S.2d 898 (1981); Brinkley v. Casablancas, 80 A.D.2d 428, 438 N.Y.S.2d 1004 (1981); Madison Square Garden Corp. v. Universal Pictures Co., 255 App. Div. 459, 7 N.Y.S.2d 845 (1938).
21. *See, e.g.*, Grant v. Esquire, Inc., 367 F. Supp. 876 (S.D.N.Y. 1973) (Cary Grant sued to recover full market value of unauthorized use of his identity by *Esquire* magazine.).
22. *See, e.g.*, Ali v. Playgirl, Inc., 447 F. Supp. 723 (S.D.N.Y. 1978) (A preliminary injunction issued to restrain publication of a magazine containing a photograph of a nude male recognizable as Muhammad Ali.).
23. *See, e.g.*, Commerce Union Bank v. Coors, 7 Media L. Rep. (BNA) 2204 (Tenn. Ch. Ct. 1981) (violation of celebrity's right of publicity by putting his picture on calendar advertising defendant's beer).
24. *See, e.g.*, Price v. Worldvision Enters., 455 F. Supp. 252 (S.D.N.Y. 1978), *aff'd*, 603 F.2d 214 (2d Cir. 1979) (Court restrained production of television series in which actors were to portray Oliver Hardy and Stan Laurel.).
    The right of publicity has been invoked to protect a variety of other interests as well. *See, e.g.*, Zacchini v. Scripps-Howard Broadcasting Co., 433 U.S. 562 (1977) (entire performance); Motschenbacher v. R.J. Reynolds Tobacco Co., 498 F.2d 821 (9th Cir. 1974) (materials closely related to plaintiff's personality: defendant's advertisement depicted race-car driver's likeness in a recognizable manner due to distinctive car decorations); Lahr v. Adell Chem. Co., 300 F.2d 256 (2d Cir. 1962) (imitation of actor's voice in advertisements); Haelan Laboratories v. Topps Chewing Gum, 202 F.2d 866 (2d Cir.), *cert. denied*, 346 U.S. 816 (1953) (name); Uhlaender v. Henricksen, 316 F. Supp. 1277 (D. Minn. 1970)

VALERIE B. DONOVAN

The right of publicity has been defined as a person's right to the pecuniary value of his/her name, likeness, activities, or personal characteristics.[25] This right to enjoin others from using an individual's persona can be both licensed and assigned during the life of a celebrity.[26] In this way, a celebrity is allowed full commercial exploitation of his/her persona. The assignable and transferable nature of the right of publicity has prompted commentators and courts to question whether the right constitutes a descendible property right.[27] Celebrity status represents the culmination of expenditures of money, time, and effort by the celebrity to create a "property" that has widespread public recognition. Although intangible, this property merits protection against misappropriation and should pass to heirs, beneficiaries, and assignees due to its proprietary nature.[28] Other types of property rights survive through trade-

---

(name); Wyatt Earp Enterprises, Inc. v. Sackman, Inc., 157 F. Supp. 621 (S.D.N.Y. 1958) (name); Hirsch v. S.C. Johnson & Son, Inc., 90 Wis. 2d 129 (1979) (nickname — "Crazy legs").

25. See Felcher and Rubin, *Privacy, Publicity and the Portrayal of Real People by the Media*, 88 YALE L. J. 1577, 1589 (1979).

26. Unlike a trademark license, the use of a celebrity's likeness or name need not be limited to a specific product but may be "in gross," that is, without an accompanying transfer of a business, and may be limited in duration. Haelan Laboratories v. Topps Chewing Gum, 202 F.2d 866, 867–68 (2d Cir.), *cert. denied*, 346 U.S. 816 (1953) (Permission was granted to use a baseball player's photograph to promote the sale of a product.). See Ropski, *The Right of Publicity — The Trend Toward Protecting a Celebrity's Celebrity*, 72 TRADEMARK REP. 251, 267 (1982) (The use of a name or likeness may be further limited by the type of product, or particular media.). Assignments of the right of publicity are rarely implied. Ettore v. Philco Television Broadcasting Corp., 229 F.2d 481, *cert. denied*, 351 U.S. 926 (1956). Express, written assignments will transfer the right of publicity. Estate of Presley v. Russen, 513 F. Supp. 1339, 1354–55 (D.N.J. 1981).

27. See Comment, *An Assessment of the Commercial Exploitation Requirement as a Limit on the Right of Publicity*, 96 HARV. L. REV., 1703, 1706 (1983). It is possible during life to assign one's right to the publicity value of one's name. Once a celebrity has worked hard to develop a recognizable image, the celebrity is entitled to any monetary rewards that can be reaped from that image. The property-like interest in the image allows a celebrity to prevent others from using his/her image without permission. Unauthorized use of the image would lead to unjust enrichment of the infringer. See also Zacchini v. Scripps-Howard Broadcasting Co., 433 U.S. 562, 573–77 (1977); Cepeda v. Swift & Co., 415 F.2d 1205, 1206 (8th Cir. 1969) (One has property rights in his/her name and image and may sell these rights.); Nimmer, *The Right of Publicity*, 19 LAW & CONTEMP. PROBS. 203, 216 (1954).

28. The duration of the right of publicity varies widely among states. Some courts have held that the right terminates on the death of the celebrity. Lugosi v. Universal Pictures, 25 Cal. 3d 813, 824, 603 P.2d 425, 431, 160 Cal. Rptr. 323, 329 (1979); Memphis Dev. Found. v. Factors Etc., Inc., 616 F.2d 956, 958–60 (6th Cir.) (construing Tenn. law), *cert. denied*, 449 U.S. 953 (1980). Some cases find that the right of publicity is inheritable if the celebrity exercised the right during his/her lifetime. See, e.g., Martin Luther King Jr., Center for Social Change v. American Heritage Prods., 694 F.2d 674, 682–83 (11th Cir. 1983). Others

mark and copyright protection, both of which focus on the right of the individual to reap the rewards of his/her endeavors.[29]

Some courts, however, impose limitations on the right of publicity and reject its descendibility, conceptualizing the right as an extension of the right of privacy. They also view descendibility as interfering with the protected first amendment interest in the uninhibited expression of ideas.[30] Whether the right of publicity will descend may be determined by choice-of-law decisions. A court's determination that the right is a property or a tort right will mandate which state's substantive law must be applied.[31] Consequently, the application of California law rather than New York law can dramatically affect the outcome of a case.[32]

State legislation on the right of publicity is sparse and lacks uniformity. Florida, Oklahoma, Utah, and Virginia have enacted statutes that provide a cause of action to the assignees or surviving relatives of the deceased for commercial misappropriation of the name or image of the deceased.[33] All

conclude that the right is descendible even if not exercised during the life of the individual depicted. *See, e.g.*, Hicks v. Casablanca Records, 464 F. Supp. 426, 429 (S.D.N.Y. 1978).

29. *See* Zacchini v. Scripps-Howard Broadcasting Co., 433 U.S. 562, 573 (1977) (The goals of copyright law and the right of publicity are analogous in that they both serve to encourage creative enterprise.). Name and likeness are not copyrightable, although artistic or photographic depictions of the celebrity may be copyrighted. *See infra* notes 61–82 and accompanying text (discussing copyright law).

The conceptualization of the right of publicity as a property right fails to cover some unauthorized publicity appropriations, such as emotional harm to the celebrity due to distasteful associations. The right of publicity protects against pecuniary loss, not emotional abuse. A cause of action for defamation is more appropriate in the latter case. *See infra* note 46 (discussing defamation law). *See* Memphis Dev. Found. v. Factors Etc., 616 F.2d 956, 958 (6th Cir. 1980); Lugosi v. Universal Pictures, 25 Cal. 3d 813, 818–24, 603 P.2d 425, 428–31, 160 Cal. Rptr. 323, 326–29 (1979); Note, *Publicity as an Aspect of Privacy and Personal Autonomy*, 55 S. CAL. L. REV. 727, 746–47 (1982).

30. *See* Cher v. Forum Int'l., 213 U.S.P.Q. 96 (C.D. Cal.), *rev'd in part*, 692 F.2d 634 (9th Cir. 1982) (rejecting plaintiff's right of publicity claim against a newspaper that used her name and likeness to advertise nonexistent interview, on grounds that first amendment protected newspaper's use of her identity); Paulsen v. Personality Posters, Inc., 59 Misc. 2d 444, 299 N.Y.S.2d 501 (Sup. Ct. 1968) (First amendment argument defeated suit regarding sale of "Pat Paulsen for President" posters.). *See also infra* notes 119–31 and accompanying text (discussing first amendment issues arising in right of publicity actions).

31. *See infra* note 99 and accompanying text (Multistate invasions of privacy are deemed to occur in state of plaintiff's domicile; property right choice-of-law rules are more flexible.).

32. *See infra* notes 84–89 and accompanying text (choice-of-law discussion indicating how important this distinction can be).

33. FLA. STAT. ANN., *supra* note 11; OKLA. STAT. ANN. tit. 21, § 839 (West Supp. 1980); UTAH CODE ANN. § 76-9-405 (1978); VA. CODE § 8.01-40 (1977). The Oklahoma and Utah statutes make the misappropriation a misdemeanor. It is of interest to note that California and New York, the two states most involved

four statutes adopt the view that publicity rights need not be exercised during the life of the individual in order for the right to descend.[34]

The state statutes extend the right of privacy statutes by incorporating a survivability component;[35] these are not entitled right of publicity statutes and do not refer specifically to a right of publicity.[36] Courts construe the statutes as narrowly as they see fit, thereby limiting the scope of protection.[37]

B. Other Potential Remedies

1. *Right of Privacy*

The common law right of privacy has been defined as the right to be

---

in right of publicity suits, have no statutory provisions dealing with the right.
34. See, e.g, FLA. STAT. ANN., *supra* note 11, at (1) (c). This statute provides:

> If such person is deceased, [then consent for the public use of the deceased's persona may be given by] any person, firm, or corporation authorized in writing to license the commercial use of his name or likeness, or if no person . . . is so authorized, then by any one from among a class composed of his surviving spouse and surviving children.

> *Id.*

35. *Id.* at (4) (Cause of action for unauthorized publication of name or likeness may be brought up to forty years after the death of the individual.); OKLA. STAT. ANN., *supra* note 33 (Cause of action for unauthorized publication of name or likeness may be brought up to fifty years after the death of the individual.); UTAH CODE ANN., *supra* note 33 (No limitation on survivability of the cause of action is indicated.); VA. CODE, *supra* note 33, at (B) (Cause of action for unauthorized publication of name or likeness may be brought up to twenty years after the death of the individual.).

36. For example, the Virginia statute is entitled, "Unauthorized use of name or picture of any person . . ." and reads in part:

> A. Any person whose name, portrait, or picture is used without having first obtained the written consent of such person, or if dead, of the surviving consort . . ., for advertising purposes . . . may maintain a suit in equity against the person . . . to prevent and restrain the use thereof; and may also sue and recover damages for any injuries. . . . And if the defendant shall have knowingly used such person's name . . . in such a manner as is forbidden . . . the jury . . . may award exemplary damages.
> B. No action shall be commenced under this section more than twenty years after the death of such person.

> VA. CODE, *supra* note 33.

37. *Compare* Falwell v. Penthouse Intern., Ltd., 521 F. Supp. 1204 (W.D. Va. 1981) *and* Evans v. Sturgill, 430 F. Supp. 1209 (W.D. Va. 1977) (Virginia does not recognize a common law right of privacy. Because the statute is in derogation of the common law, it must be strictly construed.) *with* Donohue v. Warner Bros. Pictures, Inc., 194 F.2d 6, 11 (10th Cir. 1952) (The court gave the statute a liberal

left alone, to have one's feelings undisturbed, and to be free from emotional upset.[38] Dean Prosser has defined the right of privacy as being comprised of four distinct torts: intrusion upon physical solitude, public disclosure of private facts, publicly placing a party in a false light, and misappropriation of one's name or likeness for another's benefit.[39] Courts have expanded on the tort of misappropriation to provide a remedy for the unauthorized use of an individual's persona. The privacy tort, however, serves the needs of the ordinary citizen whose likeness or name is misappropriated. It does not logically protect public personalities, those individuals who do not normally seek privacy.

Courts have recognized the right of privacy in most jurisdictions,[40] and have classified the right of privacy torts as personal,[41] non-assignable and

rather than narrow construction and recognized the right of publicity in Utah.).
38. See Memphis Dev. Found. v. Factors Etc., Inc., 616 F.2d 956, 957–58 (6th Cir. 1980), cert. denied, 449 U.S. 953 (1980); Carson v. Here's Johnny Portable Toilets, Inc., 498 F. Supp. 71, 78 (E.D. Mich. 1980); Uhlaender v. Henricksen, 316 F. Supp. 1277, 1282 (D. Minn. 1970); Cepeda v. Swift & Co., 291 F. Supp. 242, 245 (E.D. Mo. 1968), aff'd, 415 F.2d 1205 (8th Cir. 1969); Olan Mills v. Dodd, 234 Ark. 495, 496, 353 S.W.2d 22, 23–24 (1962). See also W. PROSSER, LAW OF TORTS § 117 (4th ed. 1971); Brandeis and Warren, The Right to Privacy, 4 HARV. L. REV. 193 (1890) (The right to be "let alone" and the concept of right to privacy was proposed and developed in this article.).
39. See W. PROSSER, supra note 38, § 117, at 804–14; accord RESTATEMENT (SECOND) OF TORTS § 652 (1977).
40. See, e.g., Memphis Dev. Found. v. Factors Etc., Inc., 616 F.2d 956, 957–78 (6th Cir. 1980) (applying Tennessee law), cert. denied, 449 U.S. 953 (1980); Gilham v. Burlington Northern, 514 F.2d 660, 662–63 (9th Cir. 1975) (per curiam) (applying Montana law); Carson v. Here's Johnny Portable Toilets, Inc., 498 F. Supp. 71, 78 (E.D. Mich. 1980); Neff v. Time, Inc., 406 F. Supp. 858, 861 (W.D. Pa. 1976); Uhlaender v. Henricksen, 316 F. Supp. 1277, 1282 (D. Minn. 1970); Cepeda v. Swift & Co., 291 F. Supp. 242, 245 (E.D. Mo. 1968), aff'd, 415 F.2d 1205 (8th Cir. 1969); Birmingham Broadcasting Co. v. Bell, 259 Ala. 656, 68 So. 2d 314, 319 (1953); Olan Mills v. Dodd, 234 Ark. 495, 496, 353 S.W.2d 22, 23–24 (1962); Korn v. Rennison, 21 Conn. Supp. 400, 401, 156 A.2d 476, 478 (Super. Ct. 1959); Barbieri v. News-Journal Co., 56 Del. 67, 68–69, 189 A.2d 773, 774 (1963); Fergerstrom v. Hawaiian Ocean View Estates, 50 Hawaii 374, 377, 441 P.2d 141, 144 (1968); Kelly v. Franco, 72 Ill. App. 3d 642, 646, 391 N.E.2d 54, 57–78 (1979); Continental Optical Co. v. Reed, 119 Ind. 643, 648, 86 N.E.2d 306, 308–09 (1949); Johnson v. Boeing Airplane Co., 175 Kan. 275, 278, 262 P.2d 808, 812–13 (1953); Jaubert v. Crowley Post-Signal, Inc., 375 So.2d 1386, 1388 (La. 1979); Nelson v. Maine Times, 373 A.2d 1221, 1223–24 (Me. 1977); Beane v. McMullen, 265 Md. 585, 590, 291 A.2d 37, 45 (1972); Palmer v. Schonhorn Enterprises, 96 N.J. Super. 72, 77–79, 232 A.2d 458, 461–62 (Super. Ct. Ch. Div. 1967); Onassis v. Christian Dior—New York, Inc., 122 Misc.2d 603, 472 N.Y.S. 2d 254 (1984); Montgomery-Ward v. Shope, 286 N.W.2d 806, 808 (S.D. 1979); Kimbrough v. Coca-Cola/U.S.A., 521 S.W.2d 719, 722 (Tex. 1975).
41. See Lugosi v. Universal Pictures, 25 Cal. 3d 813, 822, 603 P.2d 425, 430, 160 Cal. Rptr. 323, 328 (1979) (The right of publicity cannot be asserted by anyone other than the person whose privacy has been invaded.); Coverstone v. Davies, 38 Cal. 2d 315, 322–24, 239 P.2d 876 (1952) (Plaintiff must plead that his/her privacy has been infringed.). See also RESTATEMENT (SECOND) OF TORTS § 652 A, 652(c) (1977); W. PROSSER, supra note 38, § 117, at 814.

non-survivable.[42] Many states have enacted statutes creating a cause of action for invasion of privacy[43] which focus on the unauthorized appropriation of a person's name or likeness for trade or advertising purposes.[44] This statutory right does not survive or descend. In most states, a broader common law tort of privacy complements this statutory right.[45]

42. *See, e.g.*, Hanna Mfg. Co. v. Hillerich & Bradsby Co., 78 F.2d 763, 766 (5th Cir.), *cert. denied*, 296 U.S. 645 (1935) (Baseball players do not have property right to their names—fame cannot be sold.); Lugosi v. Universal Pictures, 25 Cal. 3d 813, 833 n.8, 603 P.2d 425, 437 n.8, 160 Cal. Rptr. 323, 335 n.8 (1979) (Right of privacy is personal and non-assignable.); Rosemont Enters. v. Random House, 58 Misc. 2d 1, 6, 294 N.Y.S.2d 122, 129 (Sup. Ct. 1968), *aff'd*, 32 A.D.2d 892, 301 N.Y.S.2d 948 (1969) (Privacy is purely personal and may be enforced only by the party himself.).
The term "survivable" refers to the enforceability of rights after death of the person in whom the rights were initially vested. *See* Sims, *supra* note 12, at 454. It is important to distinguish between rights that survive the right holder's death that can be asserted by executors against infringers, and the issue of whether a claim initiated during a person's life will lapse if he dies prior to completion of the legal proceedings. This article focuses on the survival of the right, not on the survival of the cause of action.

43. *See, e.g.,* CAL. CIVIL CODE § 3344 (West Supp. 1983) (prohibiting use of another's name, photograph, or likeness for advertising purposes); FLA. STAT. ANN., *supra* note 11 (prohibiting unauthorized publication of name or likeness); MASS. ANN. LAWS ch. 214, § 3A (1974) (prohibiting offenses against privacy); N.Y. CIV. RIGHTS LAW § 51 (McKinney 1976 and Supp. 1980) (prohibiting use of name, portrait, or picture of any living person for advertising purposes without obtaining written consent); OKLA. STAT. ANN. tit. 21, § 839.2 (West Supp. 1980) (prohibiting use of name, portrait, or picture for advertising without consent); R.I. GEN. LAWS § 9-1-28 (Supp. 1980) (prohibiting unauthorized use of name or picture); UTAH CODE ANN. § 76-9-406 (1978) (prohibiting offenses against privacy, abuse of personal identity); VA. CODE, *supra* note 33 (prohibiting unauthorized use of name or picture); WIS. STAT. ANN. § 895.50 (West Supp. 1980).

44. The privacy statutes grew out of Dean Prosser's privacy tort, "appropriation for the defendant's advantage of the plaintiff's name or likeness." Prosser, *Privacy*, 48 CALIF. L. REV. 383, 389 (1960).
The California privacy statute reads, in pertinent part:

> Any person who knowingly uses another's name, photograph, or likeness, in any manner, for purposes of advertising products, merchandise, goods or services, without such person's prior consent...shall be liable for any damages sustained by the person...injured as a result thereof.

CA. CIVIL CODE, *supra* note 43.
See Grant v. Esquire, Inc., 367 F. Supp. 876, 880 (S.D.N.Y. 1973). Cary Grant sued for unauthorized use of his likeness in an article on clothing styles. The court held that he had a cause of action under the New York privacy statute, and could recover damages for the monetary value of the exploitation.

45. *See* W. PROSSER, *supra* note 38, at § 117. Because New York does not have a common law tort right of privacy, a privacy claim must be presented in statutory terms. As a result, some courts have denied claims in New York that would have been actionable in other states. *See* Greenawalt, *New York's Right of Privacy— The Need for Change*, 42 BROOKLYN L. REV. 159, 160–62 (1975).

The historical protection of name and likeness under the right of privacy has confused judicial responses to the issue of a celebrity's control over the use of his/her persona. The major distinction is that a celebrity generally seeks protection for the pecuniary value of his name or likeness, rather than freedom from injured feelings.[46]

46. Another cause of action for injury to reputation and emotions is defamation. The tort of defamation consists of false and defamatory statements, either oral or written, concerning another. See L. ELDREDGE, THE LAW OF DEFAMATION 6, 14 (1978). To bring a defamation action, the plaintiff must establish pecuniary damage resulting from the defamatory statements; emotional injury may then be tacked on to the action. See generally W. PROSSER, supra note 38 § 111, at 737–44, 761; RESTATEMENT (SECOND) OF TORTS §§ 558, 575 (1977).

    The common law cause of action for defamation does not permit post-mortem vindication of non-transferable commercial interests in reputation. See, e.g., Insull v. New York World-Telegram Corp., 172 F. Supp. 615, 636 (N.D. Ill.), aff'd, 273 F.2d 166 (7th Cir. 1959), cert. denied, 362 U.S. 942 (1960) (Plaintiff could not bring a cause of action for damage to his father's reputation; action accrues only to the person against whom slander was directed.); Lee v. Weston, 402 N.E.2d 23, 26–30 (Ind. Ct. App. 1980) (Plaintiffs were not defamed by coroner's implication that their son's death was caused by drug overdose.). See also RESTATEMENT (SECOND) OF TORTS § 560, Comment a (1977); accord W. PROSSER, supra note 38 § 111, at 745. This limit on survivability of the defamation action rests on first amendment objections to obstructing newsworthy reports. See Felcher and Rubin, supra note 25, at 1596–97. Cf. MacDonald v. Time Inc., 554 F. Supp. 1053, 1054 (D.N.J. 1983). The court in MacDonald noted a trend away from non-survivability of the tort of defamation. The court stated that the mental anguish claimed in a libel action transferred to a plaintiff's family on his death. Id. at 1057. The court did not accept the common law rule that a person's reputation dies with him. "Why should a claim for a damaged leg survive one's death, where a claim for a damaged name does not. After death the leg cannot be healed, but the reputation can." Id. at 1054.

    Most states have a statutory prohibition against defamation. Statutory defamation complements common law defamation; in most states statutory protection against defamation does not survive the death of the individual. Some statutes have been expanded to protect against defamation of the dead. See, e.g., GA. CODE ANN. § 16–11–40 (a) (1982), which reads in pertinent part: "A person commits the offense of criminal defamation when, without a privilege to do so and with intent to defame another, living or dead, he communicates false matter which tends to blacken the memory of one who is dead. . . ."

    The law of defamation is premised on the notion that one's reputation is important to that individual, and society permits that person to vindicate his good name, receive compensation for harm, and deter future defamatory acts. See Note, Defamation in Fiction: With Malice Toward None and Punitive Damages for All, 16 LOY. L.A.L. REV. 99, 100 (1983). Because it protects reputation, defamation closely resembles the privacy action of public disclosure of embarrassing private facts. See supra note 39 and accompanying text (discussing the elements of the tort of right of privacy).

    In contrast, the right of publicity deals with misappropriation and the pecuniary interests of the individual. See Note, The Descendibility of the Right of Publicity: Memphis Development Foundation v. Factors Etc., Inc., 14 GA. L. REV. 831, 840 (1980). Scholars have suggested that the law of privacy may "be capable of swallowing up and engulfing the whole law of public defamation." Prosser, supra note 44 at 389. See also Wade, Defamation and the Right of

2. *Trademark Violation*

A trademark is any name, word, or symbol used by a manufacturer to identify and distinguish his goods from those of others.[47] A service mark is a mark used to identify and distinguish the services, rather than a tangible product, of one particular person.[48] The Lanham Trademark Act of 1946 codifies federal trademark law,[49] a subset of the larger doctrine of unfair competition, which prohibits fraudulently or deceptively representing the source of goods and services.[50] Unfair competition involves any violation of the total physical image created by the product and its name.[51]

A trademark provides an exclusive right in the owner to use the symbol in distinguishing his/her product. Exclusive right trademarks represent a form of property, an "intellectual bundle of rights," that are valid as long as they

---

Privacy, 15 VAND. L. REV. 1093 (1962) (concluding that majority of defamation actions can be brought for invasion of right of privacy, and thereby avoid restrictions inherent in libel and slander).

Some courts have granted relief for unauthorized publicity when the plaintiff proved defamation. *See* Ali v. Playgirl, Inc., 447 F. Supp. 723, 726–28 (S.D.N.Y. 1978); Kerby v. Hal Roach Studios, 53 Cal. App. 2d 207, 209–12, 127 P.2d 577, 579–81 (1942) (An advertising campaign using a person's name was actionable due to harm to the person's reputation.). This method of dealing with unauthorized publicity requires reputational harm and an objectively measurable offense. Courts hesitate to provide a remedy when celebrities complain of unauthorized, but inoffensive publicity. *See* Cepeda v. Swift & Co., 415 F.2d 1205, 1208 (8th Cir. 1969); O'Brien v. Pabst Sales Co., 124 F.2d 167, 170 (5th Cir. 1942); Booth v. Colgate-Palmolive Co., 124 F. Supp. 343, 349 (S.D.N.Y. 1973); Note, *Publicity as an Aspect of Privacy and Personal Autonomy*, *supra* note 29, at 749; Brandeis and Warren, *supra* note 38, at 197–98.

47. *See* 15 U.S.C. § 1127 (1982); Beech-Nut Packing Co. v. P. Lorillard Co., 273 U.S. 629 (1927).
48. 15 U.S.C. § 1127 (1982)
49. *Id.* at §§ 1051–1127 (1982). Trademark protection exists at the state and federal level. Federal and state laws generally overlap, and federal law does not preempt state law unless there is a conflict between the two. *See* 1 J. GILSON, TRADEMARK PROTECTION AND PRACTICE § 1.04, at 1–38.3 (1984); Red Devil Tools v. Tip Top Brush Co., 50 N.J. 563, 236 A.2d 861 (1967).
50. *See* Simensky, *The Law of Unfair Competition: An Alternative When the Right of Publicity is Rejected*, N.Y.L.J., September 9, 1983, at 5, col. 2.
51. *See* 1 J. MCCARTHY, TRADEMARK AND UNFAIR COMPETITION § 2:2, at 44–45 (1973). Trademark law focuses on whether a symbol functions to identify one's services and whether the use of a similar mark by another causes the public to be confused as to source or sponsorship. Unfair competition focuses on the consumer's confusion between two services based on an examination of everything that could have an impact on the purchaser. The unfair competition doctrine was designed to protect the consumer from fraud and deception. *See* Estate of Presley v. Russen, 513 F. Supp. 1339, 1372–75 (D.N.J. 1981). Unfair competition is a flexible and broad legal tool that protects against "that which a court of equity would consider unfair." Charcoal Steak House v. Staley, 263 N.C. 199, 204, 139 S.E.2d 185, 189 (1964).

are used to identify unique services.[52] The owner of a trademark has exclusive use of it or may license its use to others. He can also enjoin others from using the mark upon showing that this other use leads the public into believing that the trademark owner endorses the infringer's goods.[53]

Section 43(a) of the Lanham Act protects not only trademark interests but also interests that approximate trademarks—such as entertainers' likenesses—when used to identify the source of goods and services.[54] Section 43(a) does not require a trademark holder to own a federal trademark registration in order to sue an infringer;[55] rather it protects the right of the consumer to be told the truth.[56]

52. *See* J. MCCARTHY, *supra* note 51, § 2:6, at 54–55. Property rights have little existence independent of the service itself. After a mark owner dies, his/her service mark and trademark pass on to his/her legal representative as part of the assets of the estate. As long as the marks continue to be used actively to identify these unique services, the marks will continue to exist and not be considered abandoned. *See* Estate of Presley v. Russen, 513 F. Supp. 1339, 1365 (D.N.J. 1981).
53. *See* Simensky, *supra* note 50, at 5, col. 3.
54. *Id.* at 5, col. 2. In a claim of unfair competition under section 43(a), courts consider the total physical image created by both the products or services and their names. *Id.*, September 16, 1983, at 5, col. 1.
55. *See* J. MCCARTHY, *supra* note 51, § 27:6 at 253.
56. Section 43(a) of the Lanham Act Provides:

> Any person who shall affix,...or use in connection with any goods or services,...a false designation of origin, or any false description or representation, including words or other symbols tending falsely to describe or represent the same, and shall cause such goods or services to enter into commerce, and any person who shall with knowledge of the falsity of such designation of origin or description or representation cause or procure the same to be transported or used in commerce... shall be liable to a civil action by any person doing business in the locality falsely indicated as that of origin...or by any person who believes that he is or is likely to be damaged by the use of any such false description or representation.

15 U.S.C. § 1125(a) (1982).
See Time Mechanisms, Inc. v. Qonaar Corp., 422 F. Supp. 905, 911 (D.N.J. 1976) (Trademark rights arise from use and not registration.); N.S. Myer, Inc. v. Ira Green Inc., 326 F. Supp. 338 (S.D.N.Y. 1971); Iding v. Anaston, 266 F. Supp. 1015 (N.D. Ill. 1967); Mortellito v. Nina of California, 173 U.S.P.Q. 346 (D.C.N.Y. 1972); Germain, *Unfair Trade Practices Under Section 43(a) of the Lanham Act*, 49 IND. L.J. 84 (1973); Note, *The Present Scope of Recovery for Unfair Competition Violations Under Section 43(a) of the Lanham Act*, 53 NEB. L. REV. 159 (1978).
See also Estate of Presley v. Russen, 513 F. Supp. 1339, 1373 (D.N.J. 1981) (Elvis Presley had never used particular likenesses as service marks to advertise his entertainment services; however, the court held that the defendant's use of Presley's likeness in his product advertising violated section 43(a) despite the absence of registered trademark infringement. The likeness was used in a manner likely to cause confusion as to the origin or sponsorship of the service.).

Trademark law and section 43(a) of the Lanham Act have occasionally supplemented right of publicity claims.[57] Courts often interpret trademark law as being broader than the right of publicity. While a celebrity must often use his identity in connection with merchandising a product before the right of publicity may descend,[58] the mere false or misleading use of a performer's name or likeness may violate section 43(a).[59] The requirement that a plaintiff prove the likelihood of confusion over the source of the product or service with which the mark is used limits the use of section 43(a). Moreover, trademark law further requires the plaintiff to prove priority of use in connection with particular services.[60]

57. *See, e.g.,* Winterland Concessions Co. v. Sileo, 528 F. Supp. 1201, 1213–14 (N.D. Ill. 1981); Estate of Presley v. Russen, 513 F. Supp. 1339 (D.N.J. 1981); Hicks v. Casablanca Records, 464 F. Supp. 426 (S.D.N.Y. 1978). Entertainment groups and individual performers have used trademark law to protect their names. *See* Five Platters, Inc. v. Purdie, 419 F. Supp. 372 (D.Md. 1972); *in re* Carson, 197 U.S.P.Q. 554 (T.T.A.B. 1977) (Mere use of name to advertise his services grants valid trademark rights.). The Court of Appeals for the Second Circuit reduced right of publicity claims to trademark claims. Groucho Marx Prods. v. Day & Night Co., 523 F. Supp. 485 (S.D.N.Y. 1981), *rev'd on other grounds,* 689 F.2d 317, 322–23 (2d Cir. 1982) (Heirs must rely on trademark law to protect the goodwill that the celebrity created during his/her lifetime. A trademark owner can prevent others from using a confusingly similar trademark as long as the owner continues to use the mark commercially. The trademark can be used for an indefinite period.).

58. *See* Note, *An Assessment of the Commercial Exploitation Requirement as a Limit on the Right of Publicity, supra* note 27.

59. *See* MCCARTHY, *supra* note 51 § 10:21 C at 311. *Compare* Carson v. Here's Johnny Portable Toilets, Inc., 498 F. Supp. 71 (E.D. Mich. 1980), *aff'd in part,* 9 Media L. Rep. (BNA) 1153 (6th Cir. 1983) (reversing denial of right of publicity claim, and affirming rejection of the section 43(a) claim on the ground that consumers would not be likely to believe Carson was endorsing defendant's product) *with* Dallas Cowboys Cheerleaders, Inc. v. Pussycat Cinema Ltd., 467 F. Supp. 366 (S.D.N.Y.), *aff'd,* 604 F.2d 200 (2d Cir. 1979) (Defendant's use of plaintiff's uniform in a pornographic film would confuse the public into believing plaintiff had approved of the movie.).
    One commenter has noted that cases lost under the right of publicity might have been won under section 43(a) of the Lanham Act, because the right to the use of trademarks is descendible. *See* Simensky, *supra* note 50, September 23, 1983, at 5, col. 3. *See, e.g.,* Memphis Dev. Found. v. Factors Etc., Inc., 616 F.2d 956 (6th Cir.), *cert. denied,* 449 U.S. 953 (1980) (The ownership by Elvis Presley's estate of trademarks, after being licensed to Factors, would have given standing to Factors under section 43(a). Also, the defendant's use of Presley's likeness might have been in violation of section 43(a), if plaintiff could have shown that such use was likely to confuse consumers into thinking that Presley had approved of the replicas.). *See also* Ropski, *supra* note 26 (Right of publicity could eventually be incorporated in section 43(a).). *But cf.* Winner, *Right of Identity: Right of Publicity and Protection for a Trademark's "Persona",* 71 TRADEMARK REP. 193, 211 (1981) (advocating use of publicity right law to broaden the reach of trademark law).

60. *See* Ropski, *supra* note 26, at 273.

3. *Copyright Infringement*

Title 17 of the United States Code codifies copyright law.[61] The United States Constitution provides the basis for copyright law, granting Congress the power to "promote the Progress of . . . useful Arts."[62] Copyright laws protect the writings[63] of authors[64] fixed in a tangible medium of expression[65] against unauthorized reproduction. Copyright laws protect only the expression of a work of authorship, not the idea of the work,[66] meaning an author can copyright a book that describes an idea, but he does not have a monopoly in the use of the idea.[67] Copyrights serve the public policy of fostering intellectual creativity by protecting the value of a person's effort, time, and skill in creating an intellectual or artistic work.[68] They also provide the author with exclusive rights to reproduce the work, prepare derivative works, sell copies, and display or perform the work publicly.[69] This limited copyright

61. 17 U.S.C. §§ 101–810 (1982). Copyrights have been a recognized property interest since the Statute of Anne, 1710, 8 Anne, c. 19. *See* Cohen, *Duration*, 24 U.C.L.A. L. REV. 1180, 1192–97 (1977).
62. The U.S. Constitution in relevant part, states that: "Congress shall have power To promote the Progress of Science and useful Arts, by securing for limited Times to Authors and Inventors the exclusive Right to their respective Writings and Discoveries." U.S. CONST. art. I, § 8, cl. 8.
63. "Writings" have been defined as "any physical rendering of the fruits of creative intellectual or aesthetic labor," and are not limited to written or printed material. Goldstein v. California, 412 U.S. 546, 651, *reh. denied*, 414 U.S. 883 (1973). Writing connotes some fixation in a tangible medium of expression. 17 U.S.C. § 102 (1982). This tangible medium allows the expression to be perceived and reproduced.
64. "Author" has been held to indicate the originator of the expression. Burrows-Giles Lithographic Co. v. Sarony, 111 U.S. 53, 58 (1884) (providing definition of author in its constitutional sense—as the originator). *See also* Goldstein v. California, 412 U.S. 546 (1973) (holding that the term "author" should not be construed literally as one who writes, but rather as one who originates something).
65. Works fixed within a tangible means of expression include literary works, musical works, dramatic works, pantomimes, pictoral, graphic and sculptural works, motion pictures, recordings, and compilations and derivative works. 17 U.S.C. §§ 102(a), 103(a) (1982).
66. *See id* at 102(b). *See also* H. HENN, COPYRIGHT PRIMER 1 (1979) (Copyright protects expression as distinguished from idea.); Jacobson, *Fair Use: Considerations in Written Works*, 2 COMM. AND THE LAW 17, 20 (1980) (The taking of an idea is not a copyright infringement.). *See, e.g.*, Hoeling v. Universal City Studios, Inc., 618 F.2d 972, 975–80 (2d Cir.), *cert. denied*, 449 U.S. 841 (1980) (An author can copyright an historical account, but he does not have a monopoly over facts contained therein.).
67. *See* Note, *Copyright and the Right of Publicity: One Pea in Two Pods?* 71 GEO. L. J. 1567, 1569 (1983) (The enrichment of society is maximized by protecting only expression and not ideas.).
68. *See* Sims, *supra* note 12, at 460; Byers, *Copyright to Life: Toward Copyright Protection for Name and Likeness*, 56 CAL. ST. B.J. 52, 53 (1981). *See generally* Gordon, *Copyright Protection for the Collection and Representation of Facts*, 76 HARV. L. REV. 1569 (1963).
69. 17 U.S.C. § 106 (1982).

monopoly assures that only the artistic creator will benefit financially from the fruits of his/her labor.[70]

Copyright protection extends from the creation of the work through the life of the author plus fifty years;[71] it assumes that the death of the author does not reduce the commercial value of his/her work.[72]

Federal copyright law is uniform and preempts conflicting state statutes.[73] The judicially-created equitable defense of fair use limits the protection that copyright law potentially offers. Fair use permits others to use the copyrighted material in a reasonable manner without consent, notwithstanding the monopoly granted to the copyright owner.[74] The defense of fair use allows unauthorized use of a copyrighted work on public policy grounds for such purposes as criticism, comment, news reporting, teaching, and research.[75]

Potential conflict with the rights granted in the first amendment also limits the scope of copyright protection. Scholars are concerned that freedom of expression may be abridged by punishing speech that consists of the unauthorized use of copyrighted material.[76] The fact that copyright protects expressions of ideas rather than the ideas themselves can help limit this concern.[77] The technique of definitional balancing between speech and nonspeech

70. See Twentieth Century Music Corp. v. Aiken, 422 U.S. 151, 156 (1975) (The effect of copyright law is to assure a fair return for an author's creative effort.).
71. 17 U.S.C. § 302(a) (1982). This durational limit sets a balance between encouraging authors to produce creative works, and allowing the public dissemination that ultimately will benefit society. Twentieth Century Music Corp. v. Aiken, 422 U.S. 151, 156 (1975).
72. See Sims, *supra* note 12, at 474.
73. 17 U.S.C. § 301 (1982) (replaces the pre-1976 dual system of copyright protection: state protection for unpublished works, and federal copyright protection for published works). See N. BOORSTYN, COPYRIGHT LAW § 1:7, at 10 (1981).
74. See H. BALL, THE LAW OF COPYRIGHT AND LITERARY PROPERTY § 125 (1944); Rosenfeld, *The Constitutional Dimension of "Fair Use" in Copyright Law*, 50 NOTRE DAME LAW. 790, 807 (1975). See *infra* notes 132–40 and accompanying text (discussing defense of fair use).
75. See Leavens, *In Defense of Unauthorized Use: Recent Developments in Defending Copyright Infringement*, 44 LAW & CONTEMP. PROBS. 3, 6 (1981); 17 U.S.C. § 107 (1982). Four factors are set forth in case law to determine whether a use is fair: (1) the purpose and character of the use, including whether commercial or educational; (2) the nature of the copyrighted work; (3) the amount of the portion used compared to the copyrighted work as a whole; and (4) the economic impact on the copyright owner. See Mathews Conveyor Co. v. Palmer-Bee Co., 135 F.2d 73, 84–85 (6th Cir. 1943); M. Whitmark & Sons v. Pastime Amusement Co., 298 F. 470, 476 (E.D.S.C. 1924). See generally Jacobson, *supra* note 66, at 21–30 (discussing judicial application of fair use criteria).
76. Copyright extends only to an author's individual expression. Copyright will not protect material previously in the public domain, which has been incorporated in a copyrighted work, or mere ideas. In addition, there are notice requirements incorporated into the statute that limit copyright's scope of protection. See Felcher and Rubin, *supra* note 12, at 1130.
77. See *supra* notes 66–67 and accompanying text (discussing the idea/expression dichotomy).

interests, established by the United States Supreme Court, can provide necessary standards.[78]

Name and likeness may not receive copyrights unless they appear in the form of artistic or photographic representations.[79] Both copyright and the right of publicity arguably-serve the public policy of fostering creativity by providing increased career incentive.[80] Some courts have analogized to copyright law by requiring some tangible exercise of the celebrity's right of publicity during his/her lifetime before permitting survivability.[81] This analogy seems faulty, since copyright does not apply to intangible rights.[82] This "physicalization" of the right of publicity is not applicable when the concept of property is broadened to include protection of the legal relations among persons, as well as the protection of things.[83]

II. PROBLEMS WITH THE RIGHT OF PUBLICITY REMEDY

A. Conflict of Laws

The protection given to a person's name, likeness, and image varies

78. *See* 1 M. NIMMER, *Nimmer on Copyright* §§ 1.10(A)–(B) (1983).
79. Sims, *supra* note 12, at 460.
80. *See* Zacchini v. Scripps-Howard Broadcasting Co., 433 U.S. 562, 576–77 (1977); Goldstein v. California, 412 U.S. 546, 555 (1973); Lugosi v. Universal Pictures, 25 Cal. 3d 813, 839–41, 603 P.2d 425, 441–42 (1979); NIMMER, *supra* note 78, at § 1:03(A).
81. *See* ACME Circus Operating Co. v. Kuperstock, 711 F.2d 1538, 1544 (11th Cir. 1983); Groucho Marx Prods. v. Day & Night Co., 523 F. Supp. 485, 490 (S.D.N.Y. 1981), *rev'd on other grounds*, 689 F.2d 317 (2d Cir. 1982); Factors Etc., Inc. v. Pro Arts Inc., 579 F.2d 215, 221 (2d Cir. 1978), *cert. denied*, 440 U.S. 908 (1979), *rev'd on other grounds*, 652 F.2d 278 (2d Cir. 1981); Hicks v. Casablanca Records, 464 F. Supp. 426, 429 (S.D.N.Y. 1978); Lugosi v. Universal Pictures, 25 Cal. 3d 813, 603 P.2d 425, 160 Cal. Rptr. 323 (1979); Felcher and Rubin, *supra* note 25, at 1618–19; Sims, *supra* note 12, at 472. *See generally* Comment, *An Assessment of the Commercial Exploitation Requirement as a Limit on the Right of Publicity*, *supra* note 27 (Evidence of exploitation would be endorsement of products and intervivos assignment of right of publicity.).
82. The Act provides, in relevant part:

> (a) Copyright protection subsists, in accordance with this title, in original works of authorship fixed in any tangible medium of expression. . . .
> (b) In no case does copyright protection for an original work of authorship extend to any idea, procedure, process, system, method of operation, concept, principle, or discovery, regardless of the form in which it is described. . . .

17 U.S.C. § 102 (1982).
83. *See* Comment, *An Assessment of the Commercial Exploitation Requirement as a Limit on the Right of Publicity*, *supra* note 27, at 1713 (Right of publicity need not be exploited during a celebrity's lifetime in order to descend.).

widely from state to state, greatly diminishing the right of publicity as a remedy to unauthorized use of a deceased celebrity's persona. The lack of uniformity becomes relevant when misappropriation occurs in many states simultaneously, or when the celebrity has been domiciled in one state at the time of death, but the tortious infringement occurs in another state.[84] These situations raise difficult choice-of-law questions that the courts have not sufficiently addressed.

A court's determination of which state law to apply to a right of publicity case is critical. The doctrine of the descendibility of publicity rights is inapplicable in some states, thereby denying recovery to the injured person.[85] Other states, either by common law or statute, allow the publicity claim to pass to the injured party's heirs.[86] Without a federal statute that preempts state law regarding the right of publicity, courts will have to continue to grapple with the vagaries of the complex and evolving choice-of-law rules.[87]

Choice-of-law analysis requires a court to ascertain the nature of the

84. See supra notes 7–12 and accompanying text (providing examples of the impact of choice-of-law decisions).
85. See, e.g, Lugosi v. Universal Pictures, 25 Cal. 3d. 813, 603 P.2d 425, 160 Cal. Rptr. 323 (1979).
86. See supra notes 18– 37 and accompanying text (discussing common law and statutory right of publicity). Under New York common law, the right of publicity survives death, and assignability of the right does not require that the claimant exploit his/her right of publicity during his/her lifetime. See Groucho Marx Prods. v. Day & Night Co., 523 F. Supp. 485 (S.D.N.Y. 1980), rev'd on other grounds, 689 F.2d 317 (2d Cir. 1982); Southeast Bank, N.A. v. Lawrence, 104 A.D.2d 213, 483 N.Y.S.2d 218 (N.Y. App. Div., First Dept. 1984). New York does not recognize a statutory right of publicity, only a non-descendible right of privacy. See N.Y. CIV. RIGHTS LAW §§ 50–51 (McKinney, 1948). New York has no common law right of privacy. See Greenawalt, supra note 45, at 162. California does not recognize a descendible right of publicity available to the heirs of a person who did not exploit the right during his/her lifetime. See Lugosi, v. Universal Pictures, 25 Cal. 3d 813, 603 P.2d 425, 160 Cal. Rptr. 323 (1979); Guiglielmi v. Spelling-Goldberg Prods., 25 Cal. 3d 860, 603 P.2d 454, 160 Cal. Rptr. 352 (1979). Georgia's common law right of publicity survives the death of its owner, and the right need not have been commercially exploited to assure survival. See Martin Luther King, Jr., Center for Social Change, Inc. v. American Heritage Prods., Inc., 694 F.2d 674 (11th Cir. 1983). Compare Memphis Dev. Found. v. Factors Etc., Inc., 441 F. Supp. 1323 (W.D. Tenn. 1977), rev'd, 616 F.2d 956 (6th Cir.) (The court rejected descendibility of right of publicity.), cert. denied, 449 U.S. 953 (1980) with Commerce Union Bank v. Coors, 7 Media L. Rep. (BNA) 2204 (Tenn. Ch. Ct. 1981) (The 6th Circuit decision was held in error, and the court determined that right of publicity was descendible.) and Lancaster v. Factors, Etc., Inc., 9 Media L. Rep. (BNA) 1109(Tenn. Ch. Ct. 1982) (right of publicity terminates on death of claimant). Nebraska has no right of privacy or publicity. See Brunson v. Ranks Army Store, 161 Neb. 519, 73 N.W.2d 803 (1955) (court does not recognize an action for invasion of privacy).
87. Choice-of-law for tortious actions was traditionally the law of the state where the tort occurred. The modern trend has been to determine the applicable law by analyzing objective factors through the governmental interest approach. In this approach, the court examines the policy underlying the law of the states

problem involved, to determine the choice-of-law rule that the state would apply to the particular legal issue, and to apply the proper choice-of-law rule to the facts and determine which state's substantive law applies.[88] This process, however, leaves much room for judicial disagreement.[89]

B. Case Examples of How Choice-of-Law Decisions Limit the Descendibility of the Right of Publicity

1. *Imitation of the Marx Brothers in a Musical Production*

In *Groucho Marx Productions, Inc. v. Day & Night Co.*,[90] the estates of the Marx brothers charged that the defendants misappropriated their rights of publicity in the names and likenesses of the Marx brothers characters.[91] This alleged misappropriation took place during a musical play entitled, *A Day in Hollywood/A Night in the Ukraine*.[92] The second half of the play consisted of a depiction of how the Marx brothers would have dramatized Chekov's *The Bear*.[93] In the initial action, the district court of New York held that New York law recognized a descendible and assignable right of publicity.[94] Furthermore, the Marx brothers had adequately exploited their rights of publicity during their lifetimes for the rights to descend.[95] Finally, the court found that the musical production infringed on the Marx brothers' characters.[96]

The district court used a tort-based choice-of-law rule, holding that the law of the place of the wrong, as well as the place with the most significant contacts, controlled.[97] In making its choice-of-law decision, the court relied

involved to determine which state has a stronger interest in having its law applied. *See* Fleury v. Harper & Row, Pubs., 698 F.2d 1022 (9th Cir. 1983); Reich v. Purcell, 67 Cal. 2d 551, 432 P.2d 727, 63 Cal. Rptr. 31 (1967) (The law of the place of the wrong need not always be applied. All foreign and domestic interests must be considered to determine the applicable rule.).

88. ACME Circus Operating Co. v. Kuperstock, 711 F.2d 1538, 1540 (11th Cir. 1983).
89. It is not within the scope of this article to analyze the status of choice-of-law rules in detail. Two current cases, however, will be reviewed to provide examples of the impact of choice-of-law reasoning. *See infra* notes 90–113 and accompanying text (discussing examples of typical choice-of-law reasoning).
90. Groucho Marx Prods. v. Day & Night Co., 523 F. Supp. 485 (S.D.N.Y. 1981), *rev'd on other grounds*, 689 F.2d 317 (2d Cir. 1982).
91. *Id.* at 486.
92. *Id.*
93. Groucho Marx Prods. v. Day & Night Co., 523 F. Supp. 485 (S.D.N.Y. 1981), *rev'd on other grounds*, 689 F.2d 317, 319 (2d Cir. 1982).
94. Groucho Marx Prods. v. Day & Night Co., 523 F. Supp. 485, 489–91 (S.D.N.Y. 1981), *rev'd on other grounds*, 689 F.2d 317 (2d Cir. 1982).
95. *Id.* at 492.
96. *Id.* at 487–92.
97. *Id.* at 487 n. 1, (citing Cousins v. Instrument Flyers, Inc., 44 N.Y.2d 698, 405 N.Y.S.2d 441, 376 N.E.2d 914 (1978)) (applying law of the place of the wrong)

on the facts that all the defendants were New York residents, the play was running in New York City, and the Marx brothers' characters were originally developed in New York.[98]

On appeal, the Second Circuit reasoned that property choice-of-law rules dictated the applicable state law.[99] The court analyzed the contacts of the parties involved, and found that the California contacts were more substantial than the New York contacts.[100] The court noted that the Marx brothers were California residents when they died, and Groucho Marx had executed a contract in California to assign his right of publicity to a California corporation.[101] In light of these facts, the court held that the extent of the Marx brothers' rights must be determined under California law,[102] under which a person's right of publicity is not descendible.[103] The Marx brothers' estates, therefore, could not recover or enjoin the production.[104]

2. *Use of the Name, "Clyde Beatty Circus"*

This right of publicity action concerned the survivability of the use of the name, "Clyde Beatty" and the title, "Clyde Beatty Circus."[105] The action originated in California but was transferred to Florida, a more convenient forum.[106] The Court of Appeals for the Eleventh Circuit held that California choice-of-law governed this action because Clyde Beatty resided in California at the time of his death. Under California law, the right of publicity descends only to the extent that the right had been assigned or exploited during a person's lifetime.[107]

The court ruled that, although California choice-of-law principles applied,

---

and Babcock v. Jackson, 12 N.Y.2d 473, 240 N.Y.S.2d 743, 191 N.E.2d 279 (Ct. App. 1963) (applying law of place with most significant contacts).

98.   *Id.*
99.   *Id.* at 319. Property choice-of-law rules indicate that the law of the state where the property is situated controls. The interests of the parties in a thing are determined by the law of the state that has the most significant relationship to the thing. *See* 16 AM. JUR. 2D § 24 (1979).
100. Groucho Marx Prods. v. Day & Night Co., 523 F. Supp. 485 (S.D.N.Y. 1981), *rev'd on other grounds*, 689 F.2d 317, 320 (2d Cir. 1982).
101. *Id.*
102. *Id.* at 320–21.
103. *Id.* (citing Guiglielmi v. Spelling-Goldberg Prods., 25 Cal. 3d 860, 603 P.2d 454, 160 Cal. Rptr. 352 (1979) (Right of publicity expires on the death of the person so protected.) *and* Lugosi v. Universal Pictures, 25 Cal. 3d 813, 603 P.2d 425, 160 Cal. Rptr. 323 (1979) (California law does not recognize a descendible right of publicity unless the celebrity exploited the right during his/her lifetime.)).
104. *Id.* at 323.
105. ACME Circus Operating Co. v. Kuperstock, 711 F.2d 1538 (11th Cir. 1983).
106. *Id.* at 1538.
107. *Id.* at 1540–45.

the substantive law of California did not.[108] California applies the law of the domicile in its choice-of-law decisions in property cases.[109] The court, however, concluded that tort-based choice-of-law rules should be applied to determine whether the surviving right of publicity is infringed. California determines choice-of-law questions in tort cases under the governmental interest approach.[110] California courts examine the underlying laws of the states involved to determine which state has the greater interest in having its laws applied to the issue.[111]

Using this governmental interest analysis, the court concluded that, because California has a limited descendible right of publicity, it must be protecting a domiciliary in order to support a claim of governmental interest. The court found Florida's interests paramount; only Beatty's estate was a California domiciliary. The defendant was a resident of Florida, the circus operated out of Florida, and the unauthorized use of the name of Clyde Beatty had occurred in Florida.[112] As a result, the court applied Florida substantive law to determine whether infringement of Beatty's right of publicity had occurred.[113]

3. *Analysis*

The determination of choice-of-law, under the governmental interest approach, opens these cases to discretionary decisions by courts. The court manipulated choice-of-law in the *ACME Circus Operating Co. v.*

---

108. *Id*. at 1540. This conflict of laws theory is called the doctrine of renvoir. Under this doctrine, the court of the forum must take into account not only the local law of the other jurisdiction, but also that jurisdiction's rules as to conflict of laws. The court must then apply the law that the rules of the other jurisdiction prescribe, which may be the law of the forum. Folk v. York-Shipley, Inc., 239 A.2d 236, 239 (Del. 1968) (doctrine of renvoir not followed in torts). *See* Breslin v. Liberty Mutual Ins. Co., 134 N.J. Super. 357, 341 A.2d 342, *aff'd*, 69 N.J. 435, 354 A.2d 635 (1976) (rejecting renvoir doctrine as too confusing and circular).
109. The California Code states that, "[i]f there is no law to the contrary, in the place where personal property is situated, it is deemed to follow the person of its owner, and is governed by the law of the domicile." *See* CAL. CIVIL CODE § 946 (West 1982).
110. ACME Circus Operating Co. v. Kuperstock, 711 F.2d 1538, 1545 (11th Cir. 1983).
111. *See* Fleury V. Harper & Row Pubs., 698 F.2d 1022, 1025 (9th Cir. 1983) (California applied governmental interest rather than traditional dogma in tort cases.); Reich v. Purcell, 67 Cal. 2d 551, 553, 432 P.2d 727, 729, 63 Cal. Rptr. 31, 33 (1967) ("The forum must search to find the proper law to apply based upon the interests of the litigants and the involved states.").
112. ACME Circus Operating Co. v. Kuperstock, 711 F.2d 1539, 1546 (11th Cir. 1983).
113. *Id*.
    Florida statute § 540.08 provides for recovery of damages for infringement of a descendible right of publicity. *See supra* notes 33–37 and accompanying text (discussing right of publicity legislation).

Kuperstock[114] case so that, by any analysis, Clyde Beatty retained publicity rights to his name.

In the *Groucho Marx*[115] case, had the estate structured its suit around the tortious infringement and New York's significant interest, it is possible that the outcome would have been quite different through the application of New York law. In addition, if New York had an operable right of publicity statute, the argument for application of New York law might have been stronger.[116]

C. Affirmative Defenses to a Descendible Right of Publicity Claim: First Amendment Protection, Fair Use, and Public Domain

Legal analysts have devoted much thought to the viability of defenses to claims of descendibility of the right of publicity.[117] The potential conflict with first amendment rights presents the greatest obstacle to descendible publicity rights.[118] This article will briefly summarize the major elements of the

114. ACME Circus Operating Co. v. Kuperstock, 711 F.2d 1538 (11th Cir. 1983).
115. Groucho Marx Prods. v. Day & Night Co., 523 F. Supp. 485 (S.D.N.Y. 1981), *rev'd on other grounds*, 689 F.2d 317 (2d Cir. 1982).
116. In deciding a "governmental interest" conflict-of-law question, a California court reasoned that Oregon had exhibited the greater interest through the existence of its statutes and case law, which were directed specifically to the issue at bar. The court stated that "[t]he application of California law to the present case would substantially impair the efficacy of Oregon's law and the enforcement of its policy." Gallagher v. Koppers Co., 191 Cal. Rptr. 241, 244 (1983).

In an 11th Circuit right of publicity case, the court held that the existence of a Utah statute, granting protection for a descendible right of publicity, provided ample justification for not applying California law, which afforded no remedy to the complainant. The appellants resided in California and the exploitation occurred in California. The court stated that Utah's right of publicity statute shows no legislative intent to exclude from its reach "instances of exploitation in which the seal of privacy had already been broken in another state where no relief could be had under domestic law." Donahue v. Warner Bros. Pictures, 194 F.2d 6, 14 (10th Cir. 1952).
117. These defenses include consent (celebrity agreed to use of his/her persona), fair use, statute of limitations, public domain, and first amendment conflicts.
118. The following materials offer discussion of the first amendment affirmative defense to a descendible right of publicity. *See* Byers, *supra* note 68; Felcher and Rubin, *supra* note 12; Felcher and Rubin, *supra* note 25; Goldstein, *Copyright and the First Amendment*, 70 COL. L. REV. 1101 (1970); Jacobson, *supra* note 66; Kwall, *Is Independence Day Dawning for the Right of Publicity?* 17 U.C.D. L. REV. 191 (1983); Leavens, *supra* note 73; Saret and Stern, *Publicity and Privacy — Distinct Interests on the Misappropriation Continuum*, 12 LOY. U. CHI. L.J. 675 (1981); Shapiro, *Toward A Constitutional Theory of Expression: The Copyright Clause, the First Amendment, and the Protection of Individual Creativity*, 34 U. MIAMI L. REV. 1043 (1980); Simenski, *supra* note 50; Sims, *supra* note 12; Sobel, *Copyright and the First Amendment: A Gathering Storm?* 19 COPYRIGHT L. SYMP. 43 (1971); Treece, *Commercial Exploitation of Names, Likenesses and Personal Histories*, 51 TEX L. REV. 637 (1973); Wilson, *The Law of Libel and the Art of Fiction*, 44

defense of first amendment protection, as well as the conceptually related defenses of fair use and public domain, in order to show how protection of the public policies that they represent may be incorporated into the development of right of publicity federal legislation.

1. *First Amendment*

It is possible that the first amendment protection of free speech and press could directly conflict with a celebrity's right of publicity. Therefore, the right of publicity must be cautiously and narrowly interpreted to avoid such conflict. First amendment concerns come to the fore when courts determine that the right of publicity can survive the death of the celebrity.[119]

The Supreme Court has established a balancing test to measure the competing interests of free speech and the celebrity's commercial interest in his/her persona.[120] In *Zacchini v. Scripps-Howard Broadcasting Co.*,[121] the plaintiff sought payment for a television news broadcast of his human cannonball act, as opposed to trying to enjoin the broadcast.[122] The Court held that the first amendment privilege does not permit news media to televise a performer's entire act without his/her approval.[123] The Court also determined that the state has an interest in safeguarding a performer's proprietary and economic interest in his/her act, encouraging continuation of such performances for the public benefit and keeping the public entertained and culturally stimulated.[124] The Supreme Court seemed to suggest in *Zacchini* that property rights

LAW & CONTEMP. PROBS. 27 (1981); Note, *First Amendment Theory Applied to the Right of Publicity*, 19 B.C.L. REV. 277 (1975); Note, *Right of Publicity—Protection for Public Figures and Celebrities*, 42 BROOKLYN L. REV. 527 (1976); Note, *Descendibility of the Right of Publicity*: Memphis Foundation v. Factors Etc., Inc., 14 GA. L. REV. 831 (1980); Note, *Derivative Works and the Protection of Ideas*, 14 GA. L. REV. 794 (1980); Note, *An Assessment of the Commercial Exploitation Requirement as a Limit on the Right of Publicity*, supra note 27; Note, *Human Cannonballs and the First Amendment*: Zacchini v. Scripps-Howard Broadcasting Co., 30 STAN. L. REV. 1185 (1978); Note, *Inheritability of the Right of Publicity Upon the Death of the Famous*, 33 VAND. L. REV. 1251 (1980).

119. The affirmative defense of first amendment to the right of publicity has been considered by the U.S. Supreme Court, lower courts, and, in detail, by commentators. It is not within the scope of this article to reiterate all concerns. Major issues and their impact on model legislation composition will be considered.
120. *See* Elrod v. Burns, 427 U.S. 347, 360 (1976) (First amendment protections may be restrained for appropriate reasons.).
121. 433 U.S. 562 (1977).
122. *Id.* at 573–74.
123. *Id.* at 574–77.
124. *Id.* at 577–78. The Supreme Court has distinguished the right of publicity from the right of privacy by holding that there is a first amendment privilege in the area of false light privacy. *See* Time, Inc. v. Hill, 385 U.S. 374 (1967). The difference is in the degree of information dissemination to the public. In the right of privacy area, the individual can only be protected by stopping the spread of

are more important than reputational rights.[125]

The degree of conflict with first amendment protections greatly depends on the purpose for using the celebrity's persona. If the use informs the public, then it receives full first amendment protection.[126] If the use entertains, then the public's interest in being culturally stimulated requires first amendment protection.[127] If the use has a commercial or advertising purpose, it is not devoid of first amendment protection, but it gains more protection if it has an informative value.[128] However, in the case of unauthorized use of a celebrity's likeness to promote sales—a true commercial misappropriation— first amendment protection does not apply, and the right of publicity may be successfully asserted.[129]

Publicity cases have been successful when the unauthorized commercial use of an entertainer's persona causes identifiable harm. An advertisement that gives the false impression of a business relationship between the advertiser and the celebrity, thereby depriving the celebrity of an advertiser's usual endorsement fee, would not receive first amendment protection.[130]

The first amendment defense is particularly strong when the right of publicity is considered to be descendible. In any balancing test, the rights

---

the false information. In the right of publicity area, dissemination of information is not necessarily stopped, but rather, the parties that may do the dissemination are limited so that the celebrity can receive the commercial benefit. If in *Zacchini*, the defendant had limited his report to newsworthy detail, rather than reproducing the entire act, the first amendment privilege would have applied. *See* Note, *First Amendment Theory Applied to the Right of Publicity, supra* note 117, at 282–83.

125. *See, e.g.*, Paul v. Davis, 424 U.S. 693, 711–12 (1976) (Injury to reputational interest does not deprive an individual of liberty or property.).
126. *See* Zacchini v. Scripps-Howard Broadcasting Co., 433 U.S. 562, 578 (1977) (News enjoys first amendment protection.).
127. *See id.* at 578 (Entertainment enjoys first amendment protection.); Joseph Burstyn, Inc. v. Wilson, 343 U.S. 495, 501 (1952) (Motion pictures, sold for profit, inform as well as entertain and enjoy first amendment protection.); Whiters v. New York, 333 U.S. 507, 510 (1948) (Magazines containing violent stories are entitled to first amendment protection.).
    See Felcher and Rubin, *supra* note 25, at 1604–05 (The unauthorized biography, which is not necessarily factual or truly creative, may fall outside first amendment protection and be subject to right of publicity claims.).
128. *See* Bigelow v. Virginia, 421 U.S. 809, 818–25 (1975) (The state cannot forbid advertisement of referral service for abortions.).
129. *Compare* Factors Etc., Inc. v. Pro Arts, Inc., 579 F.2d 215, 219–22 (2d Cir. 1978) (Commercial "memorial" poster was not newsworthy or considered to be a protected mode of expression.), *cert. denied*, 440 U.S. 908 (1979) *with* Paulsen v. Personality Posters, Inc., 59 Misc. 2d 444, 449–50, 299 N.Y.S.2d 501, 507–08 (Sup. Ct. 1968) (Paulsen's poster was accorded first amendment protection because it was considered political commentary.).
130. *See e.g.*, Grant v. Esquire, 367 F. Supp. 876, 881–84 (S.D.N.Y. 1973) (rejecting a first amendment defense to a right of publicity action). *See also* Felcher and Rubin, *supra* note 25, at 1608–19 (discussion of the parameters of identifiable harm).

of society to have access to speech regarding a deceased celebrity weigh heavily against the interests of the heirs to protect a mere pecuniary interest. It is difficult to predict how a court will decide a particular case; however, an heir would be most successful if the use was purely exploitive and not informative or cultural.[131]

2. Fair Use

In copyright[132] or trademark law,[133] the defense of fair use to an infringement claim supports the public policy of protecting the free flow and use of ideas in education and cultural endeavors.[134] Courts use the equitable defense of fair use to balance the monopoly of the copyright holder with the public's access to works of universal concern.[135] This defense allows those

131. *See* International News Serv. v. Associated Press, 248 U.S. 215, 250 (1918) (Brandeis, J. dissenting) ("[K]nowledge, truths ascertained, conceptions, and ideas become, after voluntary communication to others, free as the air to common use."); Schumann v. Loew's, Inc., 135 N.Y.S.2d 361, 369 (Sup. Ct. 1954) (Court dismissed attempt by composer's heirs to enjoin production of a movie based on his life.); Felcher and Rubin, *supra* note 25, at 1596–1607 (analyzing effects of different factors on balancing test); Note, *An Assessment of the Commercial Exploitation Requirement as a Limit on the Right of Publicity, supra* note 27, at 1720–21 (As time passes, public figures may come to represent ideas that society needs for its development.).

132. The federal copyright statute codifies the doctrine of fair use as follows:

> In determining whether the use made of a work in any particular case is a fair use the factors to be considered shall include —
> (1) the purpose and character of the use, including whether such use is of a commercial nature or is for nonprofit educational purposes;
> (2) the nature of the copyrighted work;
> (3) the amount and substantiality of the portion used in relation to the copyrighted work as a whole; and
> (4) the effect of the use upon the potential market for or value of the copyrighted work.

> 17 U.S.C. § 107 (1982)

133. The fair use doctrine in trademark law is less well defined than in copyright, but operates as a defense to the contestability of a registered mark. *See* 15 U.S.C. § 115(b)(4) (1982). *Compare* Soweco Inc. v. Shell Oil Co., 617 F.2d 1178, 1185 (5th Cir. 1980) ("[T]he fair use doctrine, in essence, forbids a trademark registrant to appropriate a descriptive term for his exclusive use and so prevent others from accurately describing a characteristic of their goods.") *with* Dallas Cowboys Cheerleaders, Inc. v. Pussycat Cinema Ltd., 467 F. Supp. 366, 375 (S.D.N.Y. 1979) (In trademark there is no well-defined doctrine of fair use.).

134. *See* Rosenfeld, *supra* note 74, at 907 (Fair use effectuates constitutional protection of public access to a work.).

135. *See* Dallas Cowboys Cheerleaders, Inc. v. Pussycat Cinema, Ltd., 604 F.2d 200, 205–06 (2d Cir. 1979) (fair use considered a balancing mechanism); Meeropol v. Nizer, 560 F.2d 106, 108–09 (Areas of universal concern include art, science, history, or industry.), *cert. denied*, 434 U.S. 1013 (2d Cir. 1977).

other than the owner of a copyright to use the material in a reasonable manner without the copyright holder's consent.[136] Without the availability of a fair use doctrine,[137] a copyright holder's monopoly might hinder public access to information.[138] When the private interests of the copyright holder conflict with the constitutionally supported public right of access to a work, courts subordinate the copyright owner's exclusive use rights.[139]

Courts use the four factors set out in the 1976 Copyright Act to analyze alleged infringement.[140] The defense of fair use could be applied to limit the descendibility of the right to control the use of a celebrity's name, image, or likeness. Courts could use the four factors constituting the doctrine of fair use as a balancing test to help identify and minimize areas of conflict between the descendible right of publicity and first amendment rights.[141]

3. *Public Domain*

The claim that a name, likeness, or image is in the public domain has surfaced as a response to the current trend of courts allowing for descendibility

---

136. Rubin v. Boston Magazine Co., 645 F.2d 80, 83–84 (1st Cir. 1981).
137. *See supra* text accompanying note 74 (definition of fair use).
138. *See* Rosenfeld, *supra* note 74.
139. *See* Key Maps, Inc. v. Pruitt, 470 F. Supp. 33, 37 (D.C. Tex. 1978) (Congressional intent is to limit the excessive use of copyright through fair use.).
140. *See* MCA, Inc. v. Wilson, 677 F.2d 180, 182 (2d Cir. 1981) (Courts consider whether work was imaginative and whether it took considerable time and labor to create.); Encyclopedia Britanica Educational Corp. v. Crooks, 558 F. Supp. 1247, 1250 (W.D.N.Y. 1983) (Courts consider purpose and character of use.); Dow Jones & Co. v. Board of Trade of the City of Chicago, 546 F. Supp. 113, 119–20 (S.D.N.Y. 1982) (Court considers all four factors in determining whether use is fair); *see supra* note 132 (listing the four factors constituting fair use).
141. Courts could use the four-pronged fair use balancing test in right of publicity cases by considering the purpose and character of the use. Courts would need to consider whether the medium is an advertisement or a fictional work; fair use would be much stronger in a movie or book than in a commercial vehicle. Consideration would have to be given to the nature of the protected subject matter. If a person had created his/her own persona, rather than portraying an existing character, appropriation of the persona by another would be more fair in the latter case. If a person were also a political figure, use of his/her identity would be more fair than if the person were an author, actor, or other creative person. One court has stated that a person who has achieved fame through antisocial, criminal conduct would have no right of publicity against an author of a fictionalized account of the crime. Leopold v. Levin, 45 Ill. 434, 259 N.E.2d 250 (1970).
     Courts would also have to consider the amount and substantiality of the use. The court would need to examine whether a celebrity's entire act was being usurped, or whether only mannerisms were being appropriated. Finally, courts would have to take into account the effect of the appropriation on the person's potential market. This factor incorporates the issue of identifiable harm. Actual economic harm must be demonstrated by the celebrity before he/she can recover relief from the effects of the appropriation. It is in the analysis of this factor that the requirement of active commercial exploitation in the marketplace by the

in right of publicity cases.[142] This recent judicial protection of intellectual property (an intangible form of property) beyond the life of a celebrity may interfere with public access to the property.[143] Prior to recent developments in the right of publicity, intellectual works would fall into the public domain either through abandonment, expiration of copyright, or lack of copyright.[144] Any party could then freely use or sell the intellectual product.[145]

Public domain represents the antitheses of copyright protection in the fields of literature and the arts, because material in the public domain lacks the private property status that provides a legal right to exclude others from using a work.[146]

Without a limit on the number of years that the right of publicity can descend, intellectual property may never get into the public domain.[147] For example, in the *Lugosi*[148] and *Groucho Marx*[149] cases, there was a trend toward the protection of characters created by celebrities. If Groucho Marx, for example, had adequately exploited particular characterizations during his lifetime under California law,[150] or had these cases been decided under New York common law,[151] the property rights to the commercial use of the characterizations could have conceivably descended forever.

When dealing with celebrity-created characters, the issue becomes how much of the character the celebrity actually created, and how much existed prior to the portrayal at issue. The Dracula character, portrayed by Bela Lugosi, was well known from the original Bram Stoker novel[152] and many

celebrity of his/her persona comes into play. *See* Hoffman, *Limitations on the Right of Publicity*, 28 BULL. COPYRIGHT SOC'Y OF THE U.S.A. 111, 139–44 (1980) (suggesting application of fair use doctrine to right of publicity cases). *See infra* notes 119–130 and accompanying text (discussing parameters of the conflict between right of publicity and first amendment protections).

142. *See supra* notes 27–32 and accompanying text (discussing survivability of the right of publicity).
143. *See* Lange, *Recognizing the Public Domain*, 44 LAW & CONTEMP. PROBS. 147 (1981).
144. *See* Nathan, *Unfair Competition in Intellectual Products in the Public Domain*, 18 CLEVE. MAR. L. REV. 92, 93 (1969).
145. *See* Sears, Roebuck & Co. v. Stiffel Co., 376 U.S. 225 (1964) (An article without copyright or trademark protection is in the public domain and may be freely copied.)
146. *See* Kasililowsky, *Observations on Public Domain*, 14 BULL. COPYRIGHT SOC'Y 205 (1967).
147. *See* Lange, *supra* note 143, at 175 (Author suggests that courts should entertain a presumption against new claims within the area of descendible right of publicity.).
148. 25 Cal. 3d. 813, 603 P.2d 425, 160 Cal. Rptr. 323 (1979).
149. Groucho Marx Prods. v. Day & Night Co., 523 F. Supp. 485 (S.D.N.Y. 1981), *rev'd on other grounds*, 689 F.2d 317 (2d Cir. 1982).
150. *See supra* note 8 and accompanying text.
151. *See supra* note 9 and accompanying text.
152. B. STOKER, DRACULA (1897).

of the Marx brothers' techniques originated with other vaudeville actors.[153] Model statutory language limiting the number of years the right of publicity could descend, assuring eventual entry into the public domain, would eliminate this concern.

III. PROPOSAL: FEDERAL RIGHT OF PUBLICITY LEGISLATION

A. Suggested Language to be Considered in Drafting a Federal Right of Publicity Act

At present there is a paucity of state legislation dealing specifically with the right of publicity,[154] and the few statutes that do exist are divergent in terms of duration and scope of protection.[155] In light of the increasing number of right of publicity suits, it is an appropriate time for Congress to consider drafting a Federal Right of Publicity Act that would codify and provide a uniform duration for the right of publicity. The following language is suggested as a starting point in developing such legislation.

Section 1. Title: The Act shall be known and may be cited as the "Right of Publicity Act of 19____."

Section 2. Application: The protection of the right of publicity applies to the publishing, printing, manufacturing, performing, display or otherwise public use for purposes of trade, advertising or any commercial purpose of the name, image, likeness, or unique identifying characteristic of any natural person without the express written or oral consent to such use given by:

    a) Such person; or

    b) Any other person, firm or corporation authorized in writing by such person to license the commercial use of his/her name, image, or likeness; or

    c) If such person is deceased, any person, firm, or corporation authorized in writing to license the commercial use of his/her name, likeness, or image; or

    d) Anyone from among a class composed of his/her heirs, whoever they may be, either as designated in his/her will, or as determined by the statutory or common law rights of descent and distribution.

---

153. One commentator suggests that the celebrity's estate should prepare proof along the lines of an environmental impact statement, stating that their rights of publicity would not affect the interest of generations to come. Lange, *supra* note 143, at 176. Courts should require these assurances before permitting the "appropriation of the territory of the creative subconscious." *Id.*
154. *See supra* notes 18–34 and accompanying text (discussing status of right of publicity legislation).
155. *Id.*

Section 3. Subject matter of the right of publicity: The right of publicity protects the unauthorized use of a person's name, likeness, or image in any medium now known or later developed from which the unique, identifying characteristics of the person can be perceived. Such media include, but are not limited to:
   a)   periodical literature;
   b)   unauthorized biographies;
   c)   billboards, posters, and other advertisements;
   d)   manufactured products for public consumption;
   e)   dramatic works;
   f)   musical entertainment;
   g)   pictorial works;
   h)   motion pictures and other audiovisual works;
   i)   sound recordings; and
   j)   photographs.

Section 4. Ownership of the right of publicity:
   a)   The right of publicity vests originally in the natural person whose name, likeness, or image is being used for commercial purposes.
   b)   The right of publicity may be transferred or assigned in whole or in part by any means of conveyance or by operation of law, and may be bequeathed by will or pass as personal property by the applicable laws of intestate succession, subject to the durational limits as specified in this act.

Section 5. Limitations on the right of publicity:
The right of publicity shall not apply to:
   a)   The publication, printing, display or use of the name, likeness or image of any person in any newspaper, magazine, book, news broadcast or telecast, or other news medium as part of any bona fide news report or presentation having a current and legitimate public interest, and where such name, likeness or image is not used for advertising purposes;
   b)   The use of such name, portrait, photograph or other likeness in connection with the resale or other distribution of literary, musical or artistic productions or other articles of merchandise or property where such person had consented to the use of his/her name, portrait, photograph or likeness on or in connection with the initial sale or distribution thereof; or
   c)   Any photograph of a person solely as a member of the public and where such person is not named or otherwise identified in or in connection with the use of such photograph.

Section 6. Fair Use: The fair use of a person's name, likeness, or image for purposes such as criticism, comment, teaching, scholarship or research is permitted. In determining whether the use made of a work in a particular case is a fair use, the factors to be considered shall include:

a) the purpose and character of the use;
b) the nature of the use;
c) the amount and substantiality of the taking and;
d) the economic effect of the use.

Section 7. Duration: The right of publicity endures for a term consisting of the life of such natural person and thirty years after such person's death.

Section 8. Remedies:

a) *Injunctions:* any court having jurisdiction of a civil action arising under this Act may grant temporary and final injunctions on such terms as it may deem reasonable to restrain infringement of the right of publicity. Any such injunction may be served anywhere in the United States on the person enjoined; it shall be operative throughout the United States and shall be enforceable, by proceedings in contempt or otherwise, by any United States court having jurisdiction of that person.

b) *Impounding:* While an action under this Act is pending, the court may order the impounding of materials claimed to have been produced in violation of the right of publicity owner's rights.

c) *Damages:* The right of publicity holder is entitled to recover the actual damages suffered as a result of the unauthorized use of name, likeness, or image, including an amount which would have been a reasonable royalty, and punitive damages.

d) *Costs and Attorney's Fees:* The court in its discretion may allow the recovery of full costs by or against any party. The court may also award a reasonable attorney's fee to the prevailing party as part of the costs.

Section 9. Preemption: Nothing in this Act annuls or limits any rights or remedies under any other federal statute.

Section 10. Severability: If any section of this Act shall be declared invalid or unconstitutional, such declaration shall not effect the validity or constitutionality of the remaining portions hereof.

B. Analysis of the Proposed Federal Statute

1. *Constitutionality*

The constitutional basis for a federal right of publicity act can be found in three sections of the U.S. Constitution: the copyright and patent clause,[156]

---

156.   U.S. CONST. art. I, § 8, cl. 8.

the commerce clause,[157] and the first amendment.[158]

The language in the Constitution that enabled Congress to pass copyright laws[159] also supports legislation protecting the right of publicity. A descendible right of publicity promotes science and the useful arts by providing an incentive for entertainers to promote, develop, and refine their arts. Knowing that the fame they have gained through years of effort can pass on to their estates may act as a career incentive.

The durational limit established in a federal right of publicity act would be supported by the federal interest in free trade and commerce. In addition, the previously mentioned lack of uniformity among states' common and statutory laws would be eliminated. The federal right of publicity act would assure protection of freedom of speech and press by providing an explicit durational limit for the survivability of the right of publicity.[160] A federal statute could eliminate the possibility of overly broad state statutes, reduce the opportunity for judicial obscurity and arbitrary provisions, and assure prompt and effective relief against the infringer.

2. *Subject Matter*

Section three of the statute is intended to provide assistance to courts in determining whether the right of publicity applies to the medium in which the misappropriation occurred. It is not an exhaustive list. It emphasizes, however, that not only purely commercial media are involved.

3. *Limitations on the Right of Publicity*

First amendment protections of speech and press will not be abridged by this statute, as indicated in section five. In addition, the consideration of fair use has been incorporated into this model right of publicity act in section six.[161] This provision offers guidelines to assure fair use in education and comment. Fair use analysis enables the legal system to dismiss many suits.[162]

Section seven proposes a limited survivability for the right of publicity; this limit is less than the fifty-year duration of copyright protection after death.[163] The rationale for this reduced duration is that fame is more transitory

---

157. U.S. CONST. art. I, § 8, cl. 3.
158. U.S. CONST. amend. I.
159. *See supra* note 62 and accompanying text (discussing enabling language for copyright).
160. *See, e.g.*, UTAH CODE ANN, *supra* note 33.
161. These four factors are essentially the same as those iterated in the federal Copyright Act. *See* 17 U.S.C. § 107 (1982).
162. Under the fair use analysis, suits could be dismissed if plaintiff could not prove some identifiable harm. Relief should not be granted if burden of proof is not met.
163. *See supra* notes 71–72 and accompanying text. The right of publicity should

and ephemeral than writing or other tangible expressions of creativity. In most cases, the commercial value of publicity rights declines rapidly after the celebrity's death.[164] A fifty-year-long survivability of the right would impose too greatly on public access.[165] Survivability does not remove the celebrity-related products from the market; rather it allows for a cause of action to determine which party should be compensated for making the name, likeness, or image available.

4. *Preemption*

This model right of publicity act does not conflict with the federal Copyright Act; the congressional enactment of the copyright law was not intended to limit any of the rights or remedies under state statutes that differ in kind from copyright infringement.[166] In addition, the general issue of unfair trade practices is not a copyright concern.

IV. CONCLUSION

The celebrity's (or his/her estate's) right to control name, likeness or image has become a pervasive legal issue. The right of publicity warrants congressional consideration to determine whether a federal statute is needed to address and resolve the inconsistencies and confusion surfacing in courts across the nation. If the current, variable state common law approaches are allowed to continue evolving, they may substantially infringe upon first amendment, copyright or trademark interests. Presently, application of the law in this area remains subject to the discretion of state courts, and due to the variety of approaches to the issue, the law can be arbitrarily manipulated through choice-of-law doctrine. As a result, the rights of individuals are not being consistently protected.

---

survive the death of the person because of its proprietary nature, comparable to that of copyright. Survivability also ensures prevention of unjust enrichment.

164. See Sims, *supra* note 12, at 498; Factors Etc., Inc. v. Creative Card Co., 444 F. Supp. 279, 285 (S.D.N.Y. 1977) (The value of celebrity memorabilia is evanescent.), *aff'd sub nom*, Factors Etc., Inc. v. Pro Arts, Inc., 579 F.2d 215 (2d Cir. 1978), *cert denied*, 440 U.S. 908 (1979).

165. Survivability of the right of publicity for more than fifty years after death would interfere with the duration of copyright protection. *Cf.*, Cifelli & McMurray, *The Right of Publicity—A Trademark Model for Its Temporal Scope*, 57 CONN. B.J. 373, 386–89 (1983) (Right of publicity should exist for as long as it is distinctive and not abandoned.).

166. 17 U.S.C. § 301(b)(3) (1982). *See also* H.R. REP. No. 1476, 94th Cong., 2d Sess. 1, 132, *reprinted in*, 1976 U.S. CODE CONG. & AD. NEWS 5659, 5748 (The laws of privacy, publicity, defamation, and fraud are unaffected by copyright law as long as they contain elements that are different in kind from copyright infringement. "Misappropriation" is not synonymous with copyright infringement.).

Federal legislation would relieve the courts of constant re-analysis of the law to determine what kind of right, if any, is involved. It could also relieve the administrative burden caused by application of improper law, which necessitates re-hearings. Most importantly, the setting of a standard durational limit by the legislature for the right of publicity will eliminate the proliferation of concern about first amendment infringement and intrusion into the public domain.

ADDENDUM

New York State Privacy/Publicity Cases

Christie Brinkley v. Casablancas, 80 A.D.2d 428, 438 N.Y.S.2d 1004 (1981).

Goelet v. Confidential, Inc., 5 A.D.2d 266, 171 N.Y.S.2d 431 (1958).

Frosch v. Grosset & Dunlap, Inc., 75 A.D.2d 768, 427 N.Y.S. 828 (1980).

Wojtowicz v. Delacorte Press, 43 N.Y.2d 858, 43 N.Y.S.2d 218, 374 N.E.2d 129 (1978).

Stephano v. News Group Publications, Inc., 98 A.D.2d 287, 470 N.Y.S.2d 377 (1984).

Onassis v. Christian Dior-New York, Inc., 122 Misc.2d 603, 472, N.Y.S.2d 254 (1984).

Mario Andretti v. Rolex Watch U.S.A., Inc., 56 N.Y.2d 284, 452 N.Y.2d 5, 437 N.E.2d 264 (1982).

Hill v. Hayes, 27 Misc.2d 863, 207 N.Y.S.2d 901 (1960)

Hemingway v. Random House, Inc., 23 N.Y.2d 341, 296 N.Y.S.2d 771, 244 N.E.2d 250 (1968).

Davis v. High Society Magazine, Inc., 90 A.D.2d 374, 427 N.Y.S.2d 308, *dismissed*, 58 N.Y.2d 1115 (1982).

Lombardo v. Doyle, Dane & Beinbach, 58 A.D.2d 620, 396 N.Y.S.2d 32, 396 N.Y.S. 661 (1977).

Joe Namath v. Sports Illustrated, A Division of Time, Inc., 48 A.D.2d 487, 371 N.Y.S.2d 10, *aff'd*, 39 N.Y.2d 897 (1975).

Delan v. CBS, Inc., 111 Misc.2d 928, 445 N.Y.S.2d 898 (1981).

Spahn v. Julian Messner, Inc., 43 Misc.2d 219, 250 N.Y.S.2d 529 (1964).

Schneiderman v. New York Post Corp., 31 Misc.2d 697, 220 N.Y.S.2d 1008 (1961).

DECKLE MCLEAN

Press and Privacy Rights Could Be Compatible

Deckle McLean is a member of the journalism faculty at Western Illinois University. He has also been a writer for the *Providence Journal-Bulletin* and the *Boston Globe.*

Courts and the mass media might be more eager to protect privacies from invasion if the United States Supreme Court had interpreted press freedom during this century along lines suggested by Alexander Meiklejohn.

Meiklejohn was a political scientist and academic administrator who died in 1964 after a half-century of public disputation, first with Oliver Wendell Holmes and Louis D. Brandeis, then with the Fred M. Vinson Supreme Court of the early fifties. Meiklejohn insisted there are two kinds of freedom of speech. One kind, he said, pertains to issues with which voters must wrestle in order to govern themselves. This kind, he said, is absolute and protected by the first amendment. The other kind, pertaining to other forms of speech, is not absolute and is protected by the fifth amendment, he said.[1]

Meiklejohn's theory, although once well known, has received little public discussion in recent decades, and there is no incentive to invoking it now as a viable legal option. Too much water has passed over the dam. But a reexamination of his theory—and its rejection by leading jurists — gives a useful perspective on our current view of the first amendment. It also gives helpful background on the intensifying criticisms

---

1.   MEIKLEJOHN, ALEXANDER, POLITICAL FREEDOM (1960).

and self-criticisms of the mass media for invading privacies, because if Meiklejohn's theory had become legal policy, we would not be in our present pickle of having to defend the media's right to invade privacies as part and parcel of our defense of the first amendment.

Meiklejohn insisted that his approach made the first amendment more vital by giving speech total protection — making it as completely free as the words of a senator on the floor of the U.S. Senate — with regard to all politically significant expression.

The Meiklejohn spirit was caught by the U.S. Supreme Court in its opinion in *Cohen v. California* in 1971: "The constitutional right of free expression is designed and intended to remove government restraints from the arena of public discussion. . . ."[2]

But the first amendment has been interpreted, contrary to Meiklejohn's hopes, also to protect speech that is not public discussion. Editors and judges therefore fear that any curbs on nonpublic discussion will increase the likelihood of curbs on public discussion—and they are right. In striving to secure maximum protection for essential public discussion, they must endorse greater protection for nonpublic discussion than the latter deserves. Meanwhile, the need to curb some nonpublic speech, for example, privacy invasions, threatens the freedom of public discussion.

This impasse could be broken by making a distinction between public and nonpublic discussion and by applying different standards to each. This is what Meiklejohn advocated. The first amendment, he said, was meant to absolutely protect public discussion necessary for self-government and has nothing to say about nonpublic speech. The fifth amendment, he said, was meant to give nonpublic speech a qualified protection by insuring that it won't be curbed without due process of law.

These distinctions, he said, could have been carried into fourteenth amendment protections against state action if the fourteenth amendment had been interpreted to embody the first amendment in its "privileges and immunities" clause and the fifth amendment in its "due process" clause.[3] The first section of the fourteenth amendment includes the words: "No State shall make or enforce any law which shall abridge the privileges or immunities of citizens of the United States; nor shall any State deprive any person of life, liberty, or property, without due process of law. . . ." But the Supreme Court has interpreted the fourteenth amendment to embody both the first and fifth amendments in its "due process" clause.

2. Cohen v. California, 403 U.S. 14, 24 (1971).
3. MEIKLEJOHN, *supra* note 1, at 53.

The result, according to Meiklejohn, was that the first amendment lost its absoluteness in protecting public discussion, and, in effect, was swallowed by the fifth amendment's qualified standard.[4]

Another result was that some nonpublic discussion, like privacy invasion, was able to hitchhike to constitutional legitimacy on the back of the kind of public discussion the first amendment was meant to protect.

The impasse in protecting privacy from mass media invasion stems in part from the fact that after 1965, the right to privacy developed as a constitutional right itself, also interpreted to be embodied in the fourteenth amendment's due process clause, and as a widely recognized common law tort right.[5] But court interpretation of the first amendment has fixed matters so that privacy can be defended only at the risk of threatening the media's freedom to report on public discussion.

Meiklejohn's theories have the virtue of reminding first amendment partisans that the defense of privacy is compatible with the defense of first amendment press freedom, and that under the proper framework, the two go together comfortably. But raising Meiklejohn also suggests that the great first amendment developments of the twentieth century were wrong to a degree: wrong in pitting the essential values of privacy and press freedom against one another; and strategically wrong in inadvertently encouraging Americans to strike out against the first amendment due to a viscerally felt need to be respected in their privacies.

Recent privacy invasion cases do appear to be manageable under Meiklejohn's interpretations of the first and fifth amendments. Some seem to fall into the category of affecting "self-government" and might be appropriate for the absolute first amendment privilege. Some of the others clearly do not touch matters essential for self-government, and would be decided under a qualified fifth amendment privilege. In the fact situations which fall under Meiklejohn's fifth amendment, a privilege to invade privacies might or might not be recognized; but in this class of cases, a judge would be free to deny the privilege without fear that his or her doing so would weaken the first amendment privilege.[6]

4. *Id.* at 54.
5. The U.S. Supreme Court first recognized a constitutional privacy right in *Griswold v. Connecticut* (381 U.S. 479 (1965)), striking down a state anti-birth control law as invading the privacies of married couples.
6. In *McCormack v. Oklahoma Publishing Company,* (613 P. 2d 737) (1980)), the Oklahoma Supreme Court affirmed the dismissal of a suit by a rehabilitated man whose career as a criminal twenty years earlier was disclosed in a magazine article. For Meiklejohn, this would probably have been a fifth amendment case, and the dismissal of the suit might not have appeared so imperative.

The handling of some privacy invasion cases as fifth amendment rather than first amendment cases does not mean the mass media defendants would lose all of them. It does mean, however, that courts would be freer to rule against the mass media defendants if policy considerations dictated such a result. Such policy considerations might be: a public interest in encouraging rehabilitation of criminals; or a privacy value in allowing householders to keep unwanted intruders off their premises. The handling of some privacy cases as first amendment cases, in Meiklejohn's terms, would insure that no privacy invasion lawsuit could succeed under those circumstances.

The most crucial decision under Meiklejohn's terminology would be whether a fact situation fell under the first amendment. This decision

---

In *Gilbert v. Medical Economics* (665 F. 2d 305 (1981)), a federal circuit judge in Colorado ruled against a suit by a doctor described in an article as incompetent for psychiatric reasons. In *Lerman v. Chuckleberry* (521 F. Supp. 228 (1981)), a federal district judge in New York found that publication of an actor's portrait on a picture of a nude woman invaded the actor's privacy. Both of these were probably fifth amendment cases, in Meiklejohn's terms.

In *Dresbach v. Doubleday* (518 F. Supp. 1285 (1981)), a man sued after being described in a book as an accomplice when his brother murdered their parents many years before. A federal judge in Washington, D.C. ruled the plaintiff could win privacy invasion damages if he could prove the publisher was negligent in falsely describing him as an accomplice. This would have been a fifth amendment case.

In *McCall v. Courier-Journal* (623 S.W.2d 882 (1981)), the Kentucky Supreme Court ruled it found possible proof of actual malice, in effect giving a chance to win privacy invasion damages to a lawyer described in a newspaper article as planning to fix a case by bribing a judge. This appears to be more of a gray area case. Because it almost involves the conduct of a public officer, a judge, maybe it is a first amendment case, according to Meiklejohn's interpretation.

Herrel v. Twin Coast, (7 MEDIA L. REP. 1216 (1981)), a California case, even more directly involved conduct of public officials. Policemen sued for privacy invasion after a newspaper reported they had been suspended for allegedly sexually attacking a woman in a police van. They had been absolved of wrongdoing. This was possibly a straight-away first amendment case, in Meiklejohn's terms. A California appeals court must have been thinking along the same line because it upheld the dismissal of the lawsuits on grounds that public interest in policemen's qualifications made the publications newsworthy and therefore privileged.

In *Fitzgerald v. Penthouse* (639 F. 2d 1076 (1981), a Maryland federal district judge ruled against a privacy suit by a scientist who was discussed in a magazine article on the Pentagon's military use of dolphins. Later, a federal circuit court ruled a genuine dispute existed as to whether the magazine had recklessly disregarded the truth. The involvement of the Pentagon in the story might have put the case under Meiklejohn's first amendment.

would be made by testing whether a case involved information essential for self-government. Some people might argue that in the era of the global village's seamless web, all information bears upon self-government. Others would limit the concept to political information touching political officials or public forums.

Meiklejohn suggested that because self-government is intellectually demanding, it won't work without the right intellectual starting points. Other forms of government, being stupid, don't make such demands, he indicated. They are easy to understand. The rulers simply compel the ruled.[7] Self-government is more complicated, he said, because people must agree to exercise some absolute freedoms in order to govern themselves, and then, as governors, may give themselves some qualified "liberties" or "privileges" which they would like to have. The same people give and receive the qualified liberties, and employ the absolute freedoms in deciding what to give and what ought to be received. This is the subtle balancing act that makes self-government possible, said Meiklejohn. If the absolute freedoms are reduced, people don't have the wherewithal to govern and must be governed by someone else—a ruling elite. If qualified liberties are mistaken to be absolute freedoms, anarchy results. Self-governent is not anarchy, a "dialectical free-for-all" or a "Hyde Park," he said.[8]

Meiklejohn went back to Plato for his own starting point. Socrates, judged guilty, asserted his independence in thought and speech, and was therefore given the hemlock; but he wouldn't dispute the state's right to put him to death. Self-governing people arrive at decisions through free

---

In *Rafferty v. Hartford Courant* (416 A. 2d. 1215 (1980)), a Connecticut court faced a suit by a man whose private party had been crashed by a reporter without invitation. The reporter had then written and published an article about the party. The appeals courts asked for a determination as to whether the reporter could be considered to have been invited. In *Boyd v. Thompson Newspapers* (6 MEDIA L. REP. 1020 (1980)), a federal district judge in Arkansas ruled against a public disclosure lawsuit. The suit stemmed from a newspaper's publishing of the name of a child who died while a malpractice suit defendant was giving anesthesia. In *Cape Publications v. Bridges* (423 So. 2d 426 (1982)), a Florida court ruled against a woman photographed undressed after having been held hostage by her former husband. The woman's privacy suit had met with some success in a lower court. The photo had been published and had won prizes. These three cases would have been fifth amendment cases, in Meiklejohn's understanding.

7. MEIKLEJOHN, *supra* note 1, at 11.
8. *Id.* at 25.

thought and free speech, but if you belong to the polity, you must go along with the decisions.[9]

Meiklejohn argued that one proof, or model, of first amendment absoluteness is in article I, section 6, of the Constitution. This provision gives representatives in the House and Senate an absolute speech right. The language here, Meiklejohn said, is similar to that of the first amendment in being blunt and unqualified.[10] Article I, section 6, says: "(F) or any speech or debate in either House, they (senators or representatives) shall not be questioned in any other place." The first amendment says: "Congress shall make no law. . .abridging the freeom of speech, or of the press. . . ."

Further proof that the first amendment was meant to be absolute, Meiklejohn argued, was that the fifth amendment did grant a qualified speech right. The fifth amendment reads: "No person. . .shall. . .be deprived of life, liberty, or property without due process of law. . . ." Part of this liberty was freedom of speech; therefore, said Meiklejohn, two kinds of speech were recognized in the Bill of Rights. This led him to conclude, "The constitutional status of a merchant advertising his wares, of a paid lobbyist fighting for the advantage of his client, is utterly different from that of a citizen who is planning for the general welfare."[11]

Elsewhere Meiklejohn defined the two kinds of speech as: (1) an individual interest in expressing opinions—protected by the fifth amendment; and (2) a social interest in attaining truth so the country can follow the wisest course — protected by the first amendment.[12]

Meiklejohn's underlying point was that the purpose, the challenge, and the bracing emotional thrust of the first amendment had been lost in twentieth century court interpretations of the amendment. The Supreme Court, he said, had failed in its responsibility to educate Americans about the meaning of the amendment. The essence of the amendment was lost, he argued, when leading jurists elevated the interest in national self-preservation to the status of a competing force to be balanced against the "search for truth." The Constitution requires, Meiklejohn argued, that the interest in public safety or the inherent power of the government or nation to protect itself never be used to justify curbing the search for truth. Balancing one against the other, he said, is short-sighted.[13]

---

9. *Id.* at 23.
10. *Id.* at 35.
11. *Id.* at 37.
12. *Id.* at 54.
13. *Id.* at 56.

Furthermore, he argued, the first amendment in its present form means we've agreed to risk permitting speech to be free even where the ideas expressed seem to threaten our self-preservation. The only way to repudiate this agreement is with a formal alteration of the amendment.

The meaning of the first amendment has been lost, said Meiklejohn, because it has been interpreted with too much reference to self-interested individualism. The twentieth century view has been, he said, that we all have a right to assert our self-interest and that, in line with this, the powerful have a right to suppress anything that jeopardizes their power. In enlightened self-interest, we know that in the long run our self-interest will be better served if we forego suppressions in the short run. This attitude, Meiklejohn argued, makes it impossible to understand the first amendment. The amendment, he argued, represents an agreement to see dignity in others, seek the truth, and govern ourselves. This, he indicated, is a deal made for cooperation. It doesn't excuse people from searching for the truth. It doesn't let people relinquish the search for truth to the marketplace of ideas on the assumption that they needn't make any effort themselves because the marketplace will take care of it.[14] The deal, he said, can be understood only by those who serve the common welfare, not by those who seek personal advantage.[15]

The history of the first amendment in the twentieth century has been an effort by judges to covertly keep the amendment alive while political pressures threatened to kill it. The interpretation of the amendment has been a snatching of victory from the jaws of defeat, but perhaps only a partial victory. The pressures have mainly come from the fear of communism, in the name of which Americans have been willing to sacrifice the freedom to engage in public discussion of matters important to self-government. It was the fear and the struggle against communism in the teens, twenties, thirties, fourties, and fifties that threw the first amendment out of joint. The amendment's interpretation has been such that now we can't say "no" to privacy invasions without seeming to threaten the whole amendment. But it is not demands for privacy protection that have weakened the first amendment: it is compromises of the amendment made for the purpose of silencing public debate on scary political issues. We're paying a price now in the privacy protection field for judicial timidity in the past. But on reflection, it may appear that the judges had no choice, and that the form of their timidity was brilliant, strategic, and inspired.

14. *Id.* at 73, 74.
15. *Id.* at 66.

During World War One and around the time of the Russian Revolution, Congress passed an espionage act.[16] Under this act, several thousand Americans were severely punished for criticizing government actions regarding the Great War in Europe and the Revolution in Russia. The most famous court cases under the act were *Schenck v. U.S.*[17] and *Abrams v. U.S.*,[18] decided by the U.S. Supreme Court in 1919. The Supreme Court allowed both men to be away on long prison terms. Schenck's offense was publishing and distributing anti-draft leaflets after the U.S. had entered World War One. Abrams' offense was publishing and distributing leaflets criticizing the government for sending U.S. troops to Russia to oppose the Bolsheviks. The cases are famous because in them, Justice Oliver Wendell Holmes described and first used his "clear and present danger" test. After more than sixty years, this test is still generally regarded as a device for bolstering first amendment rights, even though technically it was a justification for curbing those rights.

To Meiklejohn, Holmes led the country astray in first amendment interpretation by admitting that the amendment's speech and press rights were qualified, not absolute.[19] According to Meiklejohn, the rights to air issues that affect self-government might still be absolute if Holmes had not compromised by saying the rights could be curbed when words used create a clear and present danger of bringing about some evil that government can legitimately suppress.

In the *Schenck* case, Holmes argued that first amendment speech protection obviously was qualified because a person would not be allowed to falsely shout "fire" in a crowded theatre. Meiklejohn's response was that falsely shouting "fire" in a crowded theatre is not the kind of speech essential to self-government; is not related to the first amendment; is covered by the fifth amendment's due process clause; and definitely is not absolute. But speech affecting political decisions, according to Meiklejohn, is protected by the first amendment and is absolutely free.[20]

In retrospect, Meiklejohn's analysis is persuasive. But let's consider the political reality in which Holmes worked. Congress, the American public generally, and the Supreme Court were ready to curb any speech that criticized government during a period of national patriotic fervor.

16. Espionage Act of June 15, 1917, 40 STAT. at L. 217.
17. Schenck v. U.S., 249 U.S. 47 (1919).
18. Abrams v. U.S., 250 U.S. 616 (1919).
19. "The philosophizing of Mr. Holmes has, I think, led us astray... it has in effect led to the annulment of the First Amendment rather than to its interpretation." MEIKLEJOHN, *supra* note 1, at 33.
20. *Id.* at 39.

Holmes wrote the Supreme Court's majority opinion in *Schenck,* but later court decisions indicate the other justices didn't vote with him because they believed in his clear and present danger test. Instead, they believed speech and press rights were not absolute, and they were ready to curb them when they reasonably conflicted with governmental policies.

In the *Schenck* case, Holmes said interfering with the military draft through leafletting during a declared war was a real danger, a clear and present danger. But in the *Abrams* case, Holmes was opposed to the conviction, and had to write a dissenting opinion saying that criticism of troop movements when there was no declared war created no clear and present danger. The Court majority upheld Abrams's conviction on grounds that it was a reasonable exercise of government power.

Six years later, the Supreme Court majority said the same thing in upholding a conviction under a state sedition and espionage act. The decision, *Gitlow v. New York,*[21] was an important step in the development of the first amendment because in it, the Court said the fourteenth amendment's due process clause protects persons against state infringement of their first amendment rights. But the Court majority said the socialist "manifesto" published and distributed by Gitlow could reasonably be considered an interference with state policy in keeping the peace. They upheld Gitlow's conviction without using the clear and present danger test. Holmes wrote a dissenting opinion, arguing that in prosecutions under such statutes, judges must always decide for themselves whether a clear and present danger has been presented.

Holmes's reality in 1919 and 1925 was that the first amendment was being curbed for the purpose of suppressing public discussion of socialism, communism, and violent anti-government rhetoric. If he had tried then to endorse a Meiklejohn-like view of first amendment absolutism, he might have gotten nowhere. In *Whitney v. California* in 1927,[22] Justice Louis Brandeis,[23] who had become Holmes's colleague on behalf of the clear and present danger test, concurred in upholding a state conviction of a socialist who had spoken in favor of terrorism. By interpreting the clear and present danger test to support this conviction, Brandeis secured the test a place in American constitutional law.

According to Meiklejohn, Holmes's dissenting opinions in *Abrams* and *Gitlow,* and Brandeis's concurring opinion in *Whitney* reflected the

21. Gitlow v. New York, 268 U.S. 652 (1925).
22. Whitney v. California, 274 U.S. 357 (1927).
23. American privacy law began in 1890 with an article, *The Right to Privacy,* in 4 Harv. L. Rev. 193, by Brandeis and a colleague, Samuel D. Warren.

alarm of these two Supreme Court justices upon finding that their clear and present danger test had backfired. According to Meiklejohn, they discovered that their colleagues were more than willing to use the test backwards by agreeing that whenever an utterance creates a clear and present danger to public safety, it may be forbidden and punished.

Brandeis's opinion in *Whitney,* Meiklejohn argued, went so far in counteracting the interpretation other judges were giving the test that it actually departed from the clear and present danger test offered by Holmes in *Schenck.*[24] This was a good development, said Meiklejohn. Brandeis's test has been called an "emergency test." Brandeis defined a clear and present danger as an emergency, and argued that only in an emergency could speech rights be curtailed. Brandeis then defined an emergency as a situation in which there is no opportunity for full discussion. It was this definition of "emergency," Meiklejohn said, that made Brandeis's test an improvement over Holmes's. Under Brandeis's emergency test, Meiklejohn argued, speech freedom could be reduced only when there was no time to discuss ideas. But under Holmes's clear and present danger test, said Meiklejohn, a dangerous idea could be suppressed at the same time a safe idea was being discussed. The emergency test, Meiklejohn said, was really a new test, much closer to first amendment absoluteness.

In addition, Meiklejohn challenged the clear and present danger test as unworkable. In testimony to a Senate subcommittee in 1955, he read from Judge Learned Hand's federal district court opinion in the *U.S. v. Dennis* case of 1950.[25]

> The phrase "clear and present danger". . .is a way to describe a penumbra of occasions, even the outskirts of which are undefinable, but within which, as is so often the case, the courts must find their way as they can. In each case, they must ask whether the gravity of the evil, discounted by its improbability, justifies such an invasion of free speech as is necessary to avoid the danger.[26]

To this, Meiklejohn commented:

> These words, coming from the penetrating and powerful mind of Learned Hand, show how intolerable it is that the

24. MEIKLEJOHN, *supra* note 1, at 48–9.
25. U.S. v. Dennis, 183 F. 2d 201 (1950).
26. *Id.* at 212.

most precious, most fundamental, value in the American plan of government should depend, for its defense, upon a phrase which not only has no warrant in the Constitution but has no dependable meaning, either for a man accused of crime or for the attorneys who prosecute or defend him or for the courts which judge him. That phrase does not do its work.[27]

Meiklejohn's view might be right in the abstract, but under the political heat of the moment, Holmes and then Brandeis may have been doing all they possibly could. Meiklejohn, after all, was a college professor — he wasn't on the judicial hotseat.

The first amendment took its most severe beating during the 1950s, again in the name of the struggle against communism. The chief case of the era was *Dennis v. U.S.* in 1951,[28] in which the U.S. Supreme Court upheld the convictions of some American communist party members under the Smith Act,[29] a federal sedition and conspiracy statute originally passed in 1940. In its *Dennis* opinion, the Supreme Court removed the braking effect of the clear and present danger test, by holding that application of the test had to be reasonable, and that it wasn't reasonable to ask the government to forbear until a radical coup was underway or to take into consideration the potential success of any possible overthrow attempt. Holmes had drafted the clear and present danger test to replace the use of reasonableness tests in first amendment cases.

Meiklejohn disputed with the *Dennis* majority opinion on grounds that the Supreme Court was wrong in giving the governmental duty of self-preservation equal status with the first amendment political freedoms. The constitutional imbalance in favor of political freedoms, he said, can be changed by action of the people (presumably through constitutional amendment), but cannot be changed by action of the legislature (through laws like the Smith Act) or of the judiciary (through interpretation of the Smith Act in the *Dennis* opinion).[30]

The Dennis case opinion made possible a series of convictions of communist-connected persons. In 1957, the Supreme Court bailed out of the pattern it had struck in 1951 by ruling in *Yates v. U.S.*[31] that the advocacy of abstract doctrine, as opposed to violent action, was not the

---

27. MEIKLEJOHN, *supra* note 1, at 121.
28. Dennis v. U.S., 341 U.S. 494 (1951).
29. 54 STAT. 671 (1940), 18 U.S.C.A. (1951).
30. *What Does the First Amendment Mean?* 20 U. CHI. L. REV. 461, 479 (1952).
31. Yates v. U.S., 354 U.S. 298 (1957).

kind of speech meant to be suppressed.

The suppression of communism by curbing speech freedoms has not been an admirable chapter in the American story. Commentators on the United States Constitution have stressed that the document was made for the intrepid. But with respect to communism, Americans' nerve failed.

The price of suppressing communists has been to weaken the first amendment so that privacy interests can't be protected for fear the already weakened amendment would suffer too much.

But, in Meiklejohn's terminology, privacy invasions by media don't have anything to do with the first amendment. They get qualified constitutional protection under the fifth amendment and can be curbed. When, on the other hand, private matters touch issues that must be publicly aired for effective self-government, discussions of them are absolutely privileged by the first amendment.

If Meiklejohn's theory had been adopted by judges, much of what is now called first amendment press law would be found under the fifth amendment — much of libel law, privacy invasion law, free press/fair trial law, law justifying broadcast regulation, and obscenity law, to name a few areas. Much of the law would be devoted to sorting fifth amendment speech from first amendment speech. But some of what Meiklejohn sought to achieve might be accomplished without dividing speech and press law between two amendments, but instead by working his distinctions into interpretations of the first amendment.

For example, the actual malice test,[32] so important in libel and "false light" privacy invasion cases, might be reserved for fact patterns in which the information published or broadcast does not touch a matter essential to self-government. Where information concerns a matter essential for self-government, it might be considered absolutely privileged without regard to the actual malice test, or to the fault test used in libel cases where the plaintiff is a "private person."[33] The unconscionability test in

32. The test, first stated in *New York Times v. Sullivan* (376 U.S. 254 (1954)), excuses the mass media for libels of public figures, or "false light" inaccurate depictions of newsworthy persons, except where the media has lied knowingly or recklessly disregarded the truth.
33. Under the rules stated in *Gertz v. Welch* (418 U.S. 323 (1974)), a private person libel plaintiff may win damages if (s)he can show that the mass media defendant was faulty — usually defined as negligent — and that the plaintiff was injured.

public disclosure privacy invasion cases might be handled the same way.[34]

Difficulties might arise in describing just what it is that makes a matter essential for self-government. However, the definition, to be faithful to Meiklejohn, might be along the lines of anything pertaining to: politics; political ideologies or platforms; political parties; the actions of legislatures, executives, or courts; the political actions or statements of public officeholders or candidates for elective or appointive public office; public expenditures; or governmental involvement with the economy.

In such an environment of absolute privilege, discussion and mass media commentary on political matters might get wild, reckless, and frightening. But at least we would know we had freedom of speech and press. We would not find it so urgently important to give ourselves the impression of having this freedom by defending publication of nude photos of a woman who does not choose to be naked in public, or excusing throes-of-grief interviews in the mass media with the relatives and close friends of war dead.

Meiklejohn's ideas are important because we still need to make a workable distinction between the kind of speech that is absolutely free and the kind that is qualifiedly free. Lumping the two together weakens the first amendment by eliminating the chance to call any kind of speech absolutely free; and it cheapens the first amendment by making it a slick battle cry for those whose statements, publications, and broadcasts are obviously without redeeming social or political value.

There is an emotional component in Meiklejohn. He remained true to the basic spirit of the first amendment, even if his doubling of the speech rights seems tortured. He told us that any two-bit country can put its self-preservation above free speech, and that in the twentieth century, the U.S. broke down and became just such a two-bit country by denying the belief that people can govern themselves through free public discussion. This is a troubling message, but it explains backhand why we now make such a show of protecting offensive and personally damaging speech which doesn't bear on government. It is because we refused for decades to let political debate play itself out according to the constitutional plan.

---

34. The unconscionability test blocks victory to a plaintiff suing due to public disclosure of true but embarrassing private facts, unless the plaintiff can show that the mass media defendant's disclosure shocked the community's sense of decency.

MICHAEL D. SHERER

Photojournalism and the Infliction of Emotional Distress

Michael D. Sherer is an assistant
professor of journalism in the Department
of Communication, University of Nebraska
at Omaha. He received his Ph.D. in
journalism from Southern Illinois
University-Carbondale in August 1982.
He is also Chairman of the Freedom
of Information Committee for the
National Press Photographers Association.

There is little doubt; photojournalism is a powerful medium. News photograph lets the viewer "share in a vicarious but vivid sense the excitement, the tragedy, or the exultation being experienced by the person caught up in the news."[1] In this sharing process, emotions play a critical role. The ability to arouse a viewer's emotions, often cited as one of photojournalism's greatest strengths,[2] is a concept that has been demonstrated by recent research.[3]

1. J. HULTENG, THE MESSENGER'S MOTIVES: ETHICAL PROBLEMS OF THE NEWS MEDIA 59 (1976). For additional comments on the power of pictures, see also, H. EVANS, PICTURES ON A PAGE 5 (1978); W. LIPPMANN, PUBLIC OPINION 92 (1922); S. SONTAG, ON PHOTOGRAPHY 5–6 (1978).
2. EVANS, supra note 1, at 5; HULTENG, supra note 1, at 59.
3. Thompson, Clarke & Dinitz, Reactions to My-Lai: a Visual-Verbal Comparison, 58 SOC. & SOC. RESEARCH 122, 125 (1974). Additional research, although not directly concerned with the emotional element of photography, has investigated viewers reactions to and/or interpretations of photography. See cf., ADAMS, COPELAND, AND FISH & HUGHES, The Effect of Framing on Selection of Photographs of Men and Women, 57 JOURNALISM Q. 463 (1980); FEDLER, COUNTS & HIGHTOWER, Changes in Wording of Cutlines Fail to Reduce Photographs' Offensiveness, 59 JOURNALISM Q. 633 (1982); Hazard, Responses to News Pic-

The emotional impact of news photography may act as a double-edged sword. Viewers may be moved by images that cut to the soul with emotionally gripping messages. Those captured in these images, however, may experience emotional distress by being photographed and displayed before the public in a manner they find objectionable. Persons seeking redress for damages done to their emotional well-being often turn to the courts, thus setting up a classic confrontation: the right of an individual to be free from emotional distress versus the photojournalist's right to communicate newsworthy information. This article is an examination of reported state and federal court decisions which have involved photojournalism and the question of infliction of emotional distress.[4]

I. THE NATURE OF THE TORT

The idea that an individual may seek legal redress for the infliction of emotional distress is not new. In 1875, the Wisconsin Supreme Court affirmed a lower court judgment awarding a school teacher $1,000 as compensation for her mental suffering caused by an over amorous railroad conductor.[5] Over a half-century later, William Prosser noted that the "courts have created a new tort. . . .It is something very like assault. It consists of the intentional, outrageous infliction of mental suffering in an extreme form."[6]

---

tures: A Study in Perceptual Unity, 37 JOURNALISM Q. 515 (1960); Hightower, *A Study of the Messages in Depression-Era Photos,* 57 JOURNALISM Q. 495 (1980); Hightower, *The Influence of Training On Taking and Judging Photos,* 61 JOURNALISM Q. 682 (1984); Kerrick, *The Influence of Captions On Picture Interpretation,* 32 JOURNALISM Q. 177 (1955); Kerrick, *News Pictures, Captions and the Point of Resolution,* 36 JOURNALISM Q. 183 (1959); MacLean & Hazard, *Women's Interest in Pictures: the Badger Village Study,* 30 JOURNALISM Q. 139 (1953); Nesterenko & Smith, *Contemporary Interpretations of Robert Frank's "The Americans,"* 61 JOURNALISM Q. 567 (1984); Shoemaker & Fosdick, *How Varying Reproduction Methods Affects Response to Photographs,* 59 JOURNALISM Q. 13 (1982); Van Tubergen & Mahsman, *Unflattering Photos: How People Respond,* 51 JOURNALISM Q. 317 (1974); Woodburn, *Reader Interest in Newspaper Pictures,* 24 JOURNALISM Q. 197 (1947).

4. Although the primary focus of this article is on cases involving photojournalists working for both print and broadcast media, additional cases involving written communication and the question of infliction of emotional distress will also be included.

5. Craker v. The Chicago & N.W. Railway Co., 36 Wisc. 657 (Wisc. 1875).

6. Prosser, *Intentional Infliction of Mental Suffering: A New Tort,* 37 MICH. L. REV. 874 (1939). For an updated account of how the infliction of emotional distress

Photojournalism and the Infliction of Emotional Distress

The use of this tort in suits against the news media, however, has only recently emerged in the courts and attracted the attention of media scholars.[7] With the recent publicity surrounding the Reverend Jerry Falwell's suit against *Hustler* magazine publisher Larry Flynt, and a jury's award of $200,000 in damages to Falwell for emotional distress caused by an ad parody in *Hustler,* it is likely that others may seek similar awards for the infliction of emotional distress.[8]

The problem with the Falwell verdict, media attorney Floyd Abrams noted, was that the verdict could lead "to an end run around constitutional protections for people who want to bring libel suits but know they can't win."[9] In making this "end run" around libel litigation, the focus of damage done centers upon the emotional well-being of an individual as compared to a person's reputation, which is the focus of libel litigation.[10]

Under the general concept of infliction of emotional distress, photojournalists may find themselves confronted with suits alleging intentional and/or negligent infliction of emotional distress. Nearly all of the reported cases to date have centered on the question of intentional infliction of emotional distress, a tort that involves four elements: (1) the conduct complained of must be extreme and outrageous; (2) the conduct must be intentional or reckless; (3) the conduct must cause emotional distress;

---

tort has been applied to several areas of the law, *see, e.g.,* Bell, *The Bell Tolls: Toward Full Tort Recovery for Psychic Injury,* 36 U. Fla. L. Rev. 333 (1984); Note, *Negligent Infliction of Emotional Distress: Developments in the Law,* 14 U. Balt. L. Rev. 135 (1984); Note, *Negligent Infliction of Emotional Distress: Formulating the Psycho-legal Inquiry,* 18 Suffolk U. L. Rev. 401 (1984).

7. Among the few articles concerned with the general question of emotional distress and the news media are: Drechsel, *Mass Media Liability for Intentionally Inflicted Emotional Distress,* 62 Journalism Q. 95 (1985); Mead, *Suing Media for Emotional Distress: A Multi-Method Analysis of Tort Law Evolution,* 23 Washburn L. J. 24 (1983); Stevens, *The "Tort of Outrage": A New Legal Problem for the Press,* 5 Newspaper Research J. 27 (1984); Stevens, *Media Tort Liability for Emotional Distress,* 54 Journalism Q. 157 (1977).

8. For a brief discussion of and reaction to the Falwell/Flynt lawsuit, *see Rev. Falwell Loses Libel Verdict, but Wins Damages,* Editor & Publisher, Dec. 15, 1984, at 34. *See also* Omaha World-Herald, Feb. 5, 1985, at 33, col. 5 for an account of a farmer filing a four million dollar law suit against two newspapers and three television stations, claiming that he suffered severe distress, embarrassment, humiliation, public scorn, loss of income, loss of sleep, etc., when photographers and reporters entered his land "without consent" and photographed dead animals.

9. *Rev. Falwell Loses Libel Verdict, supra* note 8, at 34.

10. Mead, *supra* note 7, at 27.

and (4) the distress must be severe.[11]

The element of extreme and outrageous conduct is not critical in a negligent infliction of emotional distress action.[12] This allows a finding that the conduct complained of, which may have amounted to something less than extreme outrage, may still cause emotional distress.[13] However, to support a claim of negligent infliction of emotional distress, there must also be an element of bodily harm that resulted from the negligent infliction of emotional distress.[14]

II. A QUESTION OF CONDUCT

The critical consideration in intentional infliction of emotional distress suits filed against photojournalists focuses on a question of conduct, *i.e.,* conduct which is so extreme, so "beyond all possible bounds of decency. . . .and utterly intolerable in a civilized community."[15]

A. Communication as Conduct

The most common complaint in intentional infliction of emotional distress suits filed against photojournalists is the act of communication. Many reported decisions have turned on the question of whether the publication of a photograph or the broadcast of a film or video tape constituted an act of outrageous conduct. The Federal Court of Appeals, Sixth Circuit, for example, said that photographing an undercover police officer and publishing the picture, along with his identity, was not extreme and outrageous conduct that would constitute an intentional infliction of emotional distress.[16] The publication of a photograph of a woman being rescued from a hostage situation while clutching a dish towel to her body in order to conceal her nudity also "did not meet the test of outrageousness."[17] The court added that the photograph "revealed little more than could be seen had appellee been wearing a bikini and somewhat less than some bathing suits seen on the beaches. . . .The published photograph is more a depiction of grief, fright, emotional tension and

11. RESTATEMENT (SECOND) OF TORTS § 46 (1965).
12. RESTATEMENT (SECOND) OF TORTS § 312 (1965).
13. *Id.* at comment b.
14. *Id.* at comment a.
15. RESTATEMENT (SECOND) OF TORTS § 46 comment d (1965).
16. Ross v. Burns, 612 F.2d 271, 274 (6th Cir. 1980).
17. Cape Publications v. Bridges, 8 MEDIA L. REP. 2535, 2536 (Fla. Dist. Ct. App. 1982).

flight than it is an appeal to other sensual appetites."[18]

Several other courts have offered similar rulings. The reaction of a woman upon seeing a published photograph of herself when she was "stoutish," for example, also was not an intentional infliction of emotional distress because there was no showing of extremely outrageous conduct.[19] "There is no occasion," the court noted, "for law to intervene in every case where someone's feelings are hurt."[20] A photographer's effort to sell pictures of two children who had suffocated in a refrigerator did not constitute an intentional infliction of emotional distress for the parents because "the constitutionally protected right to publish articles on subjects within the area of public concern affords a clear legal justification" for the photographer's acts.[21] The broadcast of a five-second film clip of a man and his female co-worker holding hands on a public street also was not an intentional infliction of emotional distress in that it could not "be said to be unusual conduct transcending the norms tolerated by a decent society."[22] The republication of a crab fisherman's photograph used with an article discussing organized crime in wholesale fish markets was also not considered to be an act of extremely outrageous conduct.[23] Several courts have issued similar rulings in intentional infliction of emotional distress suits filed against print journalists.[24]

---

18. *Id.* at 2535.
19. McManamon v. Daily Freeman, 6 Media L. Rep. 2245, 2248 (N.Y. Sup. Ct. 1980).
20. *Id.*
21. Costlow v. Cusimano, 311 N.Y.S. 2d 92, 95–96 (N.Y. App. Div. 1970).
22. De Gregorio v. CBS, Inc., 473 N.Y.S. 2d 922, 925–26 (N.Y. Sup. Ct. 1984). One can perhaps better understand De Gregorio's sense of emotional distress by considering that he was married to another woman, his co-worker was engaged to another man, and that he had told the camera crew that it would not "look good" to have the film shown on television. *Id.* at 923.
23. Morrell v. Forbes, 11 Media L. Rep. 1869, 1871 (D. Mass 1985).
24. Andren v. Knight-Ridder Newspapers, 10 Media L. Rep. 2109, 2112 (D. Mich. 1984) (stating that a newspaper's use of direct quotes from a murder victim's diaries did not constitute an act of extremely outrageous conduct); Galvin v. Gallagher, 401 N.E. 2d 1243, 1246 (Ill. App. Ct. 1980) (stating that an article on drug abuse, although it contained the writer's opinions, was not an act of extremely outrageous conduct); Beresky v. Teschner, 381 N.E. 2d 979, 983 (Ill. App. Ct. 1978) (stating that the publication of a two-month series of stories on drug abuse and the death of a youth was not an act of extremely outrageous conduct); Fry v. Ionia Sentinel-Standard, 300 N.W. 2d 687, 691 (Mich. Ct. App. 1980) (stating that publishing the names of a man and woman who perished in a fire was not an act of extremely outrageous conduct, even though the man was married to another woman); Watkins v. Campbell, 8 Media L. Rep. 1039, 1040 (Mich. Cir. Ct. 1982) (stating that the publication of an advertisement seeking information about an individual was not an act of outrageous conduct); Eaton v. Beach, 11 Media L. Rep. 1229, 1231 (N.Y. Sup. Ct. 1984) (stating that the broadcasting of newsworthy information was not an act of

The concept of publishing privileged information has also been cited as justification for defeating an intentional infliction of emotional distress suit filed against a television station. A woman whose testimony during a rape trial was broadcast on an evening news report found her suit for intentional infliction of emotional distress dismissed. The court noted that her testimony was offered in open court in which no attempt was made by the state to protect or prohibit her testimony from being taped.[25] Similar rulings have also been issued by courts when print reporters have based their stories on official public records.[26]

B. Mistakes Made as Outrageous Conduct

In the process of pursuing and publishing newsworthy information, photojournalists have occasionally made mistakes which have later played a key role in a court's decision. The mislabeling of a photograph that accompanied a story on crimes committed by a former mayor was not considered to be an act of extremely outrageous conduct.[27] A plaintiff's mistaken claim that a televised report was an act of intentional infliction of emotional distress, rather than an act of libel, led to the dismissal of a suit filed against a television and its reporter.[28] Mistakes

---

extremely outrageous conduct, even though the information was based upon a sealed grand jury report); Reichenbach v. Call-Chronicle, 9 MEDIA L. REP. 1438, 1440 (Pa. Ct. Common Pleas 1982) (stating that a newspaper's graphic description of a hospital emergency room procedure was not an act of extremely outrageous conduct).

25. Doe v. Sarasota-Bradenton Florida Television Co., Inc., 436 So. 2d 328, 329–30 (Fla. Dist. Ct. App. 1983). *Cf.* S. Barber, *The Big Dan's Rape Trial* 7, No. 2 COMM. AND THE LAW 3 (1985).
26. Kilgore v. Younger, 640 P. 2d 793, 797 (Cal. 1982) (stating that the publication of an individual's name and picture in connection with a newspaper article on organized crime was not an intentional infliction of emotional distress); Williams v. New York Times, 10 MEDIA L. REP. 1494, 1497 (Fla. Cir. Ct. 1984) (stating that the publication of a sexual assault victim's name was not an intentional or negligent infliction of emotional distress); Brennan v. Globe Newspaper Co., 9 MEDIA L. REP. 1147, 1149 (Mass. Sup. Ct. 1982) (stating that the publication of an individual's name in connection with an article on tax delinquency was not an intentional infliction of emotional distress).
27. Brennan v. Globe Newspaper Co., 9 MEDIA L. REP. 1147, 1149 (Mass. Sup. Ct. 1982).
28. Boyles v. Mid-Florida Television Corp., 431 So. 2d 627, 636 (Fla. Dist. Ct. App. 1983) (stating that the act complained of described the tort of libel and did not set forth an independent tort of infliction of emotional distress). *See also,* Kaplan v. Newsweek, 10 MEDIA L. REP. 2142, 2143 (D. Cal. 1984) (stating that only one action for libel and not an additional action for intentional infliction

made by print journalists during the reporting process have also not been considered to be acts of extremely outrageous conduct.[29]

Not all mistakes made in the reporting process, however, have resulted in "not guilty" verdicts for photojournalists. A free-lance journalist, for example, recovered damages for intentional infliction of emotional distress when the publisher of *Cinema-X* magazine used the journalist's name as identification for a photograph of a nude woman in a section featuring "aspiring erotic actors and actresses."[30] In this case, the court noted that the misidentification of the photograph "was published with his [the publisher's] knowledge and approval."[31]

The fundamental mistake of using obnoxious behavior while pursuing a subject was cited by a federal district court as an act of intentional infliction of emotional distress.[32] Some of the photographer's obnoxious activities included photographing his subject, Jackie Onassis, while remaining hidden behind a coat rack in a restaurant, jumping out from behind bushes into the path of the subject's children, flicking a camera strap at his subject while grunting "Glad to see me back, aren't you Jackie?" and paying a man to dress in a Santa Claus suit and attempt to embrace the subject while the photographer said, ". . .come on, Jackie, be nice to Santa, won't you? Come on, Jackie, snuggle up to Santa."[33]

C. Coping with Conflicting Testimony

When confronted with conflicting testimony regarding the photo-

---

of emotional distress may be based upon any single publication). *But cf.,* MacDonald v. Time, 7 Media L. Rep. 1981, 1983-84 (D.N.J. 1981) (stating that there may be some overlapping of libel and emotional distress torts, especially when they flow from the same act). *See also,* MacDonald v. Time, Inc., 554 F. Supp. 1053, 1054-55 (D.N.J. 1983) (stating that although the individual who originally filed suit in the case just cited had died, his relatives could continue the suit on his behalf).

29. Tumminello v. Bergen Evening Record, Inc., 454 F. Supp. 1156, 1158 (D.N.J. 1978) (stating that a mistake that could have been detected by confirming the story with another source was not an act of extremely outrageous conduct); Rubinstein v. New York Post, 11 Media L. Rep. 1329, 1331 (N.Y. Sup. Ct. 1985) (stating that the mistaken publication of an individual's obituary did not constitute an act of negligent infliction of emotional distress). *See also,* Wolford v. Herald-Mail, 11 Media L. Rep. 1426, 1427 (Md. Cir. Ct. 1984) (stating that the mistaken publication of an obituary was not a negligent infliction of emotional distress because the state had not recognized the tort).
30. Clifford v. Hollander, 6 Media L. Rep. 2201, 2202 (N.Y. Civ. Ct. 1980).
31. *Id.*
32. Galella v. Onassis, 353 F. Supp. 196, 231 (D.N.Y. 1972), *modified,* 487 F.2d 986 (2d Cir. 1973), *enforced,* 533 F. Supp. 1076 (D.N.Y. 1982).
33. *Id.* at 353 F. Supp. 207-8.

MICHAEL D. SHERER

journalists's conduct, the courts have ruled that the issue of infliction of emotional distress should be decided by a jury. A federal district court, for example, said that a dispute concerning a photograph used with a story on prostitution made the granting of summary judgment for the newspaper inappropriate.[34] The story involved in this case was also the subject of an infliction of emotional distress suit. Here, too, the federal district court noted that the dispute concerning the conduct of the reporter toward his subject did not make the matter appropriate for summary judgment in favor of the newspaper.[35] The manner in which a photographer depicted a soldier undergoing prisoner of war training also led to a dispute and the denial of summary judgment for a newspaper faced with an intentional infliction of emotional distress suit.[36] A magazine's request for summary judgment was denied by a federal district court because the judge felt that the caption used with the photograph may be found by a jury to be extremely outrageous conduct.[37]

D. An Absence of Outrageous Conduct

Although most of the infliction of emotional distress suits filed against photojournalists have been based upon a question of outrageous conduct, an additional problem is raised with the negligent infliction of emotional distress tort. Unlike the tort of intentional infliction of emotional distress, the negligent infliction of emotional distress tort does not

---

34. Parnell v. Booth Newspapers, Inc., 572 F. Supp. 909, 920 (D. Mich. 1983). The newspaper and the photojournalist argued that the woman in the picture could not be identified because the picture had been retouched. The woman in the photograph, however, told the court that her mother and friends were able to identify her in the picture and thus connected her to the subject of prostitution discussed in the story. *Id.* at 913. A second point of conflict centered around the decision to photograph the woman in question. The newspaper and photojournalist argued that they had no idea of who the woman was, nor was there any information which indicated that the woman was not a prostitute. The woman countered with the argument that she had legitimate reasons for being in the area and was not a prostitute. Given this, the court stated that the matter was not appropriate for summary judgment. *Id.* at 915–16.
35. Apostle v. Booth Newspapers, Inc., 572 F. Supp. 897, 908 (D. Mich. 1983).
36. Pierson v. News Group Publications, Inc., 549 F. Supp. 635, 643 (D. Ga. 1982). The soldier claimed that the photographs which depicted him clad only in underwear, "strung up between two trees, handcuffed to another tree, being hosed down and being carried to an ambulance" caused him to suffer humiliation, embarrassment, and mental distress. *Id.* at 638, 643.
37. Martin v. Municipal Publications, 510 F. Supp. 255, 260 (D. Pa. 1981). The

involve the question of outrageous conduct. The key consideration here is that the conduct, although not of an outrageous nature, does result in illness or other bodily harm. [38]

Although not an often raised issue, there are a few instances in which suits have been filed against photojournalists and other reporters for negligent infliction of emotional distress. The publication of a photograph concerning prostitution, for example, allegedly caused a woman in the photograph to suffer such things as loss of appetite, nausea, tremor, and shakes, all of which the court said constituted "a definite and objective physical injury." Because of this, the court said that a jury should decide if the photojournalist was guilty of negligent infliction of emotional distress. [39] Similar complaints of bodily harm such as high blood pressure, chest pains, slight heart fibrillation, and involuntary gritting of teeth have also been blamed upon the publication of news stories. [40] Beyond these few instances, however, the use of negligent infliction of emotional distress suits against the media has been rare.

III. SUMMARY AND CONCLUSIONS

The harm suffered, whether it is mental and/or physical, has formed the basis of several infliction of emotional distress suits filed against photojournalists and other reporters. This relatively recent trend may be in response to the perceived power of photojournalism in particular and the news media in general. "To live in this day and age of advanced communication," a federal district court judge noted, "is to recognize the awesome power of the press. It can destroy a person with a banner headline or a thirty-second moment on television." [41]

In nearly all of the emotional distress suits filed against photojournalists and other reporters, the courts have carefully scrutinized the

---

photograph was of a man wearing a "Mummers" costume. The caption read, "Dead animal of the month: A New Year's tribute here to all ostriches who gave their tails to make the world free for closet transvestites from South Philly to get themselves stinking drunk." *Id.* at 260.

38. RESTATEMENT (SECOND) OF TORTS § 312 (1965).
39. Parnell v. Booth Newspapers, Inc., 572 F. Supp. 909, 917–18 (D. Mich. 1983).
40. Apostle v. Booth Newspapers, Inc., 572 F. Supp. 897, 901 (D. Mich. 1983). *See also* Rubinstein v. New York Post, 11 MEDIA L. REP. 1329 (N.Y. Sup. Ct. 1985) (where the plaintiff claimed that the mistaken publication of an obituary caused him "severe and painful injuries, both internal and external").
41. MacDonald v. Time, Inc., 554 F. Supp. 1053, 1054 (D.N.J. 1983).

conduct of those gathering and disseminating newsworthy information. When there has been clear evidence of extremely outrageous conduct, the decision has often gone against the media.[42] In situations where there is a dispute regarding the photojournalist's conduct, the courts have been reluctant to dismiss the suits, turning instead to a full trial in an attempt to reconcile the conflict.[43] When the photojournalist's conduct has not been considered by the courts to be of an extremely outrageous nature, intentional infliction of emotional distress suits have failed.[44] Clearly, the critical factor in intentional infliction of emotional distress suits has been the photojournalist's conduct used in the pursuit and publication of newsworthy information. The use of an extremely outrageous conduct test provides the photojournalist with adequate protection in intentional infliction of emotional distress suits.

A note of caution, however, must be offered in the area of negligent infliction of emotional distress suits. Although only a few cases have been based upon this tort to date, the application of this tort to suits against photojournalists and other reporters can become troublesome. By allowing plaintiffs to allege bodily harm caused by the publication of newsworthy information, the courts can lower the standard of fault from one of outrageous conduct to that of negligent behavior, *i.e.*, to a standard in which the photojournalist should have realized that the gathering and publication of images would result in bodily injury.[45]

To allow negligent infliction of emotional distress suits against photojournalists to proceed to full trials may well dampen the entire news communication process. The courts should recognize that the public's need to be informed on issues and events may be greater than the need to protect individuals from conduct by the press which is less than extremely outrageous. The comments of William Prosser offered over forty years ago on the issue of infliction of emotional distress are as valid today. "The rough edges of our society," Prosser wrote, "are in need of a great deal of filing down, and the plaintiff in the meantime must necessarily be expected and required to be hardened to a certain amount of rough language, and to occasional acts that are definitely inconsiderate and unkind."[46] To do less would certainly undermine one of photo-

42. *See supra* text accompanying notes 30–33.
43. *See supra* text accompanying notes 34–37.
44. *See supra* text accompanying notes 16–29.
45. *See supra* text accompanying notes 38–40.
46. Prosser, *supra* note 6, at 887.

journalism's greatests strengths: the ability to communicate the news via a truly powerful medium.

DECKLE MCLEAN

Recognizing the Reporter's Right to Trespass

Deckle McLean is a member of the journalism faculty at Western Illinois University. He has also been a writer for the
Providence Journal-Bulletin and the
Boston Globe.

Courts may eventually have to recognize a first amendment right to gather news that includes not only the right of access to criminal trials endorsed by the U.S. Supreme Court in 1980,[1] but also a right to follow protest demonstrations onto public or quasi-public property without fear of trespass suits or prosecutions.

Traditional rulings refusing to extend the first amendment's protections to newsgathering have created a mechanism with which public and quasi-public officials can control the flow of information on public issues, at least where protest demonstrations or other organized or unorganized crowd actions develop. As a result, what began as a construction of the first amendment to hold journalists accountable for their torts and crimes has become in some circumstances an affirmative instrument of information control.

One cure for this problem would be to make a right to follow demonstrations onto public and quasi-public property a second exception to the rule denying first amendment protection to newsgathering, the first exception being the already recognized right to attend criminal trials.

Scenarios here include crowd actions on installations run by the government or on behalf of it: at nuclear power plants, military bases, arsenals, parks, dams, and government buildings, to name a few. Those who operate these installations are now in a position, when offended by reporting or commentary about them on issues raised by protesting groups, to either bar reporters from the grounds during protest actions or to assign reporters to unreasonably

---

1. Richmond Newspapers v. Virginia, 448 U.S. 555 (1980).

distant observer stations, and then to prosecute or sue the press for trespass or privacy invasion if the reporters leave the assigned areas.

Such protest actions often result in trespasses; yet if reporters follow the trespassing protesters to cover the developing events, they may be rounded up with protesters and subjected to civil or criminal process. While such protest actions do not occur every day, they are a recurrent feature of the political scene. Although they do not receive as much media attention now as they did twenty years ago, they happen often and involve a wide variety of issues. Such events can be called journalistically routine, in that no reporter can be surprised when he or she is asked to cover one. Yet, if those who operate an installation do not like the media coverage they are getting, they can discourage coverage of a protest event by invoking the threat of court action against reporters.

Just such a situation occurred in Oklahoma in 1979 and led to an Oklahoma Criminal Appeals Court ruling in 1983.[2] Reporters entered onto a nuclear power plant site while covering an antinuclear demonstration. The plant contained a public viewing area inside the fence, but reporters did not stay within it. They were convicted of criminal trespass and fined $25 apiece. The appeals court ruled that their convictions did not violate the first amendment. The court said the first amendment does not reach newsgathering but only publication and distribution. It cited for this proposition a list of cases frequently cited in support of this idea.[3]

In this Oklahoma case, *Stahl v. Oklahoma*, a dissenting judge noted that the trial court specifically found that the power company's reason for limiting press coverage was to control the kind of news story the press would distribute to the public.[4] The judge argued that the trial court should have given greater weight to this finding because, the judge said, this was a quasi-governmental body prohibiting communication merely because they disapproved of the speaker's views.[5] The dissenting judge also said the power plant protest was newsworthy and coverage of it was at the core of first amendment protection; the authorized press access was not reasonable; and the information the press sought was the type people have a right to know.[6]

---

2. Stahl v. Oklahoma, 665 P.2d 839, MEDIA. L. REP. 1945 (Okla. Crim., 1983).
3. *Id.* at 841–842. The cases listed are Galella v. Onassis, 353 F. Supp. 196 (S.D.N.Y. 1972); Dietemann v. Time, 449 F.2d 245 (1971); Anderson v. WROC-TV, 441 N.Y.S.2d 220, 7 MEDIA L. REP. 1987 (1981); Prahl v. Brosamle, 295 N.W. 2d 768 (Wis. 1980); Le Mistral v. CBS, 420 N.Y.S.2d 815, 3 MEDIA L. REP. 1913 (N.Y. 1978); Branzburg v. Hayes, 408 U.S. 665 (1972); Houchins v. KQED, 438 U.S. 1 (1978); Pell v. Procunier, 417 U.S. 817 (1974).
4. 665 P.2d at 848.
5. *Id.* at 848–849.
6. *Id.* at 847.

Wrote Judge Tom Brett:

> On the press's [*sic*] side of the scale is the media's newsgathering right to reasonable access to newsworthy events. This right is constitutionally protected. It is premised on the significance of a free press for the maintenance of our political system. See *Richmond, Gannett, Saxbe, Branzburg,* and *Houchins,....* It is an uncontroverted fact that the news media is an integral part of our national communications system by which the public obtains information to form their judgments about national politics. The press has a constitutionally recognized role to inform and educate, offer criticism and provide a forum for public discussion and debate.[7]

Brett's discussion has a familiar ring. It is a version of the argument often identified with former U.S. Supreme Court Justice Potter Stewart, who set it out famously in his dissent in the *Branzburg* case[8] and again in a speech at Yale Law School.[9] It is the argument that the first amendment does more than create a speech right for the press; in addition, it establishes the press

---

7. *Id.* at 846–847.
8. Branzburg v. Hayes, 408 U.S. 665, 725 (1972).
9. At the Yale Law School Sesquicentennial Convocation in 1974, Justice Stewart said:

> It seems to me that the Court's approach to all these cases has uniformly reflected its understanding that the free press guarantee is, in essence, a structural provision of the Constitution. Most of the other provisions in the Bill of Rights protect specific liberties or special rights of individuals: freedom of speech, freedom of worship, the right to the counsel, the privilege against compulsory self-incrimination, to name a few. In contrast, the free press clause extends protection to an institution. The publishing business is, in short, the only organized private business that is given explicit constitutional protection.
>
> This basic understanding is essential, I think, to avoid an elementary error of constitutional law. It is tempting to suggest that freedom of the press means only that newspaper publishers are guranted freedom of expression.
>
> They are guaranteed that freedom, to be sure, but so are we all, because of the free speech clause. If the free press guarantee meant no more than freedom of expression, it would be a constitutional redundancy. Between 1776 and the drafting of our Constitution, many of the state constitutions contained clauses protecting freedom of the press while at the same time recognizing no general freedom of speech. By including both guarantees in the First Amendment, the Founders quite clearly recognized the distinction between the two....The primary purpose of the constitutional guarantee of a free press was...to create a fourth institution outside the government as an additional check on the three official branches.

Twentieth Century Fund Task Force on Justice, Publicity, and the First Amendment, background paper by Alan Barth, in RIGHTS IN CONFLICT 104 (1976).

in the structure of the American governmental system to assure that the system works properly.

In *Allen v. Combined Communications* in 1981,[10] a Colorado judge used a similar approach in dismissing a trespass suit against T.V. reporters. The reporters had gone onto the property of a "livery stable." The judge ruled that a balancing test must be used in such trespass cases, a first amendment balancing test: "(T)he importance of the activity and degree and type of restraint against the governmental interest which tends to infringe upon First Amendment rights."[11]

The judge said that common law strict liability damages media interests in these cases, and recommended that a test similar to the one used for libel plaintiffs under *Gertz v. Welch*[12] be used in trespass suits against the press: there should be no liability without convincingly clear proof that the reporter knew he or she was trespassing or recklessly disregarded the fact. In addition, there should be no liability without proof of damage to the plaintiff.[13]

The distinction between news gathering and publication is not so valid anymore, said the judge.

> The work of the modern reporter is most realistically viewed as a continuum, consisting of components (i.e. finding the story, researching the story, composing it for delivery to the public and publication of broadcast) which may or may not occur simultaneously depending upon the nature of the story, the nature of the medium and the choice of the reporter and his/her editors. In this context a chilling effect on speech could occur whenever there is a substantial risk of liability for activities necessary to acquisition of the story.[14]

I. THE TRADITIONAL VIEW

The traditional view of newsgathering has been to distinguish it from publishing and distribution and to limit full first amendment protection to the latter two. This has meant giving little or no protection to newsgathering.

Frequently cited to support this view has been *Zemel v. Rusk*,[15] a 1965 travel freedom case. A journalist sought a passport to Cuba, even though the State Department at the time had banned travel by Americans to the island. The journalist claimed the first amendment gave him a right to travel to Cuba

---

10. 7 MEDIA L. REP. 2417 (Colo. Dist. Ct. 1981).
11. *Id.* at 2420.
12. 418 U.S. 323 (1974).
13. 7 MEDIA L. REP. at 2419–2420.
14. *Id.* at 2420.
15. 381 U.S. 1 (1965).

because he would collect material there for articles and books. The U.S. Supreme Court upheldthe state department's denial to him of a passport. It said, "The right to speak and publish does not carry with it the unrestrained right to gather information."[16]

This theme was reiterated in a series of cases in which journalists sought to interview prison inmates and to select the inmates they would interview. In *Pell v. Procunier* in 1974,[17] the U.S. Supreme Court upheld a California law denying such opportunities in that state's prisons.

"Newsmen have no constitutional right of access to prisons or their inmates beyond that afforded the general public," wrote the Court.[18]

Also in 1974, the Court decided *Saxbe v. Washington Post,*[19] in which the newspaper challenged the constitutionality of a Federal Bureau of Prisons regulation barring interviews between newspeople and inmates designated by them. Lower federal courts had ruled against the regulations. The Court ruled for the regulations. It said the case was controlled by *Pell.*[20]

In 1978, the Court upheld a sheriff's exclusion of the press from a county jail in California. In *Houchins v. KQED,*[21] the Court cited *Zemel, Pell,* and *Saxbe* and said, "The issue is a claim of special privilege of access which the Court rejected in *Pell* and *Saxbe,* a right which is not essential to guarantee the freedom to communicate or publish."[22]

A few years earlier, the Court in *Branzburg v. Hayes,*[23] a landmark 1972 source protection case, rejected a reporter's argument that the first amendment protected his promises of confidentiality to news sources. The Court took the view that promises to news sources were newsgathering events and that the first amendment did not reach far enough to provide the protection the reporter demanded.

The traditional view also determined the outcome of *Dietemann v. Time,*[24] a 1971 trespass privacy invasion case. *Life* magazine reporters had entered a nature healer's office in disguise carrying a concealed camera and a hidden microphone. After *Life* published an article, the doctor sued the company and won. Time argued in its defense that first amendment protections developed in libel cases and in privacy invasion cases in which the grievances arose from publication applied to trespass cases in which the grievance arose from newsgathering. The Ninth Circuit Court of Appeals rejected this argument,

---

16. *Id.* at 17.
17. 417 U.S. 817 (1974).
18. *Id.* at 834.
19. 417 U.S. 843 (1974).
20. *Id.* at 850.
21. 438 U.S. 1 (1978).
22. *Id.* at 12.
23. 408 U.S. 665 (1972).
24. 449 F.2d 245 (9th Cir. 1971).

reiterating that constitutional defenses developed for publishing cases did not extend to newsgathering cases.[25]

The *Dietemann* rationale served as the basis for an even better known physical privacy invasion case a year later, *Gallela v. Onassis*.[26] Constitutional defenses were unavailable to Galella in his unsuccessful attempt to defend himself against an injunction request. This was to stop him from trespassing in his efforts to photograph Jacqueline Onassis and her children.

The most visible break in this tradition came in 1980 when the U.S. Supreme Court, in deciding *Richmond Newspapers v. Virginia*,[27] ruled the press had a right of access under the first amendment to attend criminal trials. The ruling was interpreted as being potentially groundmoving in impact[28] because in it, the Court clearly indicated that at least one form of newsgathering, that in crimial trials, would receive abundant first amendment protection.

II. SKIRTING THE FIRST AMENDMENT QUESTION

Courts have tried to avoid stretching the first amendment to cover trespass privacy invasions by handling these cases in terms of other theories. These efforts to skirt the first amendment question have not worked.

One of the best known of these efforts, in *Florida Publishing Company v. Fletcher*,[29] promised that the press would do well under alternative approaches. But courts turned against the implied consent theory as it was used in *Florida Publishing. Florida Publishing* has been known as the "Silhouette of Death" case. A Florida woman vacationing in New York saw a news photo, cutlined "Silhouette of Death," showing the outline left on a charred floor by the body of a person who had died in a housefire. The person killed was the woman's daughter; the house was the woman's own. She sued the newspaper company for which the photographer worked, claiming he had invaded her privacy by trespassing on her property to take the picture.

The Florida Supreme Court ruled there was no privacy invasion because the photographer had gone onto the disaster site at the invitation of public officials and according to customary practice. The court said there was no trespass because consent had been implied by custom and usage.[30]

25. *Id.* at 249–250.
26. 353 F. Supp. 196 (S.D.N.Y. 1972).
27. 448 U.S. 555 (1980). In endorsing the right of newspeople to attend criminal trials, the U.S. Supreme Court laid heavy stress on an American historical pattern of openness in trials and of press reporting from them. A similar argument might be made that a historical pattern supports mass media reporting of crowd actions.
28. *Id.* at 582. Stevens wrote: "This is a watershed case. Until today the Court has accorded virtually absolute protection to the dissemination of information or ideas, but never before has it squarely held that the aquisition of newsworthy matter is entitled to any constitutional protection whatsoever."
29. 340 So. 2d 914 (Fla. 1976).
30. *Id.* at 918–919.

Other courts promptly rejected the implied-consent-by-custom rationale. In *Prahl v. Brosamle* in 1980,[31] a Wisconsin appellate court wrote: "We will not imply a consent as a matter of law. It is of course well known that news representatives want to enter a private building after or even during a newsworthy event within the building. That knowledge is no basis for an implied consent by the possessor of the building to entry."[32]

A broadcast reporter had followed a SWAT team to the site of a shooting. He filmed the police as they approached the building. Then he went inside to film the confiscation of guns. He had been told by police that he could come forward when the situation was under control. The Wisconsin court discussed *Florida Publishing Company*. It said that in the case before it, no evidence of custom comparable to that presented in *Florida Publishing Company* had been offered.[33]

The Wisconsin court added:

> Because of reasonable expectations, landowners commonly post their lands against trespassers. Businesses, professionals and homeowners are known to post their buildings against anticipated solicitations. Few private persons anticipate, however, that an unplanned newsworthy event will occur on their property. An advance objection to entry under remotely possible circumstances need not be made, and it is unreasonable to require an objection after entry under distracting circumstances, especially when the identity of the intruder is unknown.[34]

After disposing of the implied consent argument, the Wisconsin court also rejected an argument that newspeople should get a privilege to trespass under the first amendment.

The Wisconsin court cited *Le Mistral v. CBS*,[35] a 1978 New York case which had not been fought over the implied consent issue. In *Le Mistral*, CBS had claimed a first amendment right to trespass while gathering news. A New York appellate court rejected this assertion. A CBS news team had entered a restaurant cited for health code violation with camera rolling and lights on. The trial court had set aside damages but upheld a jury's finding that this was a trespass. The appeals court reinstated compensatory damages and remanded the case for a trial on punitive damages.

The Wisconsin appeals court in *Prahl* seemed to be using *Le Mistral* to make the point that the implied consent issue was not the central one, the

31. 295 N.W.2d 768 (Wis. 1980).
32. *Id.* at 780.
33. *Id.* at 780.
34. *Id.* at 780.
35. 3 MEDIA L. REP. 1913, 402 N.Y.S.2d 815 (N.Y. 1978).

first amendment issue was central, and that on the first amendment issue the media defendant could not have victory.

Also in 1978, the implied consent rationale suffered a backhanded loss in another New York court. *People v. Berlinger*[36] was a criminal trespass prosecution against reporters and photographers who had entered the "Son of Sam" apartment.[37] The reporters went to the apartment without encountering police restraint. The door was posted, "Do not enter, crime scene." They went in anyway. Police arrived and arrested them, and then claimed a trespass had been committed against them. The city court in Yonkers dismissed the charges. It said police in an apartment on a search warrant did not have a possessory interest strong enough to support a trespass charge.[38] The media won the case, but the implication was that police also do not have enough possessory interest under such circumstances to grant permission to the press to enter.

The strongest repudiation of *Florida Publishing Company* came in *Anderson v. WROC-TV* in 1981.[39] This New York case developed after T.V. reporters and camera people went into a Rochester animal owner's house with humane society workers. The workers had obtained a search warrant and had invited the news crew to join them. A news story was later broadcast. The householder sued the T.V. station for trespass. The plaintiff, seeking summary judgment, asked that the defendants' defenses be dismissed. The Monroe County Supreme Court here granted the plaintiff's motion.

The court discussed and rejected *Florida Publishing Company*. "The gathering of news and the means by which it is obtained does not authorize, whether under the First Amendment or otherwise, the right to enter into a private home by an implied invitation arising out of a self-created custom and practice."[40] The court also noted that here affidavits comparable to those offered in *Florida Publishing* were not provided to support the claim of a customary implication of consent.[41]

Also in the *Anderson* opinion, the court said of first amendment elements in the case: "What must be remembered is that news people do not stand in any favored position with respect to newsgathering activity."[42] It wrote, "Assessing the degree of the intrusion against the newsworthiness of the story is a test that is too vague and subjective to counter-balance the predominant interest served in protecting the rights of individuals in a free society against invasion of their privacy or their home."[43]

---

36. 3 MEDIA L. REP. 1942 (Yonkers City Court 1978).
37. "Son of Sam" and "44 Caliber Killer" were aliases of David Berkowitz, who confessed in 1977 to a series of lovers' lane murders.
38. 3 MEDIA L. REP. at 1943–1944.
39. 441 N.Y.S.2d 220, 7 MEDIA L. REP. 1987 (Sup. Ct. 1981).
40. *Id.* at 223.
41. *Id.* at 227.
42. *Id.* at 223.
43. *Id.* at 224.

III. NEWSGATHERING AND THE FIRST AMENDMENT

The implied consent theory and the theory that the first amendment protects newsgathering both took beatings in the *Prahl, Le Mistral, Berliner,* and *Anderson* cases. Of the two theories, the latter, as measured by *Richmond Newspapers* and a second review of pertinent U.S. Supreme Court opinions, still has vitality in it. Implied consent appears to have little future in media trespass cases except in fact patterns identical to that in *Florida Publishing*— that is, where proof of a customary practice is available and is offered. Even when offered, however, such proof may not be sufficient. In terms of the *Anderson* opinion, there can be no implied consent if the custom is "self-created" by the press. In terms of the *Allen* opinion, however, the media is better off without the implied consent theory. The *Florida Publishing* ruling skirted the central issue by relying on the implied consent theory, the Colorado lower court said in *Allen*.[44]

These cases bring a clash of fundamental constitutional rights—to free speech and press, on the one hand, to privacy, on the other. The clash is not new; it is a characteristic of this era. Court decisions indicate that both rights must be viewed as essential to free institutions and democratic government. These are rights which sometimes must go head-to-head. But in the situation of the trespasses during newsgathering, a resolution of the conflict may be available. It lies in making the same kind of public-private distinction familiar in defamation cases. The strength of privacy interests might be considered diminished where public or quasi-public property is involved. The first amendment protections extended to the press might be correspondingly greater under these circumstances.

If the first amendment protection of newsgathering were regarded as substantial in cases of trespasses on public or quasi-public property, then the central policy problem raised by this kind of case—information control through the threat of trespass suits or prosecutions—would be reduced in severity.

Support for extending protection to newsgathering can be found in the same opinions typically cited for the nearly opposite purpose of limiting the first amendment protection of newsgathering.

"The right to speak and publish does not carry with it the unrestrained right to gather information," said the U.S. Supreme Court in *Zemel*,[45] but this implies that the right to publish does carry a restrained right to gather. Similarly, other major opinions imply a constitutional right to gather news.

"We do not question the significance of free speech, press or assembly to the country's welfare. Nor is it suggested that news gathering does not qualify

44. 7 MEDIA L. REP. 2417 at 2419.
45. 381 U.S. 1 at 17.

for First Amendment protection; without some protection for seeking out the news, freedom of the press could be eviscerated," wrote the Court majority in *Branzburg*.[46] In his dissent in *Branzburg*, Justice Stewart noted, "News must not be unnecessarily cut off at its source, for without freedom to acquire information the right to publish would be impermissibly compromised. Accordingly, a right to gather news, of some dimensions, must exist."[47]

In *Houchins*, the Court majority said: "There is an undoubted right to gather news 'from any sources by means within the law,'…but that affords no basis for the claim that the First Amendment compels others—private persons or governments—to supply information."[48] In his dissent in *Houchins*, Justice Stevens commented:

> It is not sufficient…that the channels of communication be free of governmental restraints. Without some protection for the acquisition of information about the operation of public institutions such as prisons by the public at large, the process of self-governance contemplated by the Framers would be stripped of its substance.
>
> For that reason information gathering is entitled to some measure of constitutional protection.[49]

In addition, the *Pell* opinion,[50] on which *Houchins* was based, was written by Justice Stewart, who consistently advocated first amendment protection for newsgathering. As a result, *Pell* cannot be understood to be a blanket rejection of constitutional protection for newsgathering, but instead as a ruling, roughly limited to the facts of the case, that states authorities don't have to grant reporters special access to prison inmates.

The Ninth Circuit Court's language in the *Dietemann* case is discouraging to press interests in physical privacy invasion cases: "The First Amendment has never been construed to accord newsmen immunity from torts or crimes committed during the course of newsgathering. The First Amendment is not a license to trespass. …"[51] But the impact of *Dietemann* is counterbalanced by the U.S. Supreme Court's ruling in *Richmond Newspapers*, recognizing that newsgathering gets first amendment protection in a class of cases, and that the press right involved can be defeated only by a showing of "overriding interest."[52]

46. 408 U.S. 665 at 681.
47. *Id.* at 728.
48. 438 U.S. 1 at 11.
49. *Id.* at 32.
50. 417 U.S. 817 (1974), discussed in text at notes 17 and 18.
51. 449 F.2d 245 at 249.
52. 448 U.S. 555 at 581.

IV. A BALANCING TEST

The test advocated in the *Allen* opinion was a first amendment balancing test. The *Allen* court said, "The balancing test has two parts: First, whether the state is acting pursuant to a compelling interest; second, whether the state's activity bears a substantial relationship to that interest."

The broad pattern created by first amendment decisions in the twentieth century indicates that the balancing test provides only moderate protection to those claiming press or free speech rights. The protection it provides is not as complete as that provided by the clear and present danger or actual malice tests. The balancing test is a conservative test in terms of media interests.[53]

Courts might employ a balancing test for all trespass privacy invasion claims, recognizing that where the claimed trespass was to public or quasi-public property, privacy interests would not weigh heavily in the balance. Courts might as an alternative restrict the balancing test to cases where public or quasi-public property was involved, handling private property cases by a more rigid standard such as the traditional rule denying first amendment protection to newsgathering.

Use of a balancing test would provide outcomes like that in *New Jersey v. Lashinsky* in 1979,[54] a case the press did not win but about which it should not complain. Decisions such as the one in *Lashinsky* are the best the media can ask for in this area. They would go a long way toward protecting reporters, such as those caught in the *Stahl* case, who face efforts by public and near-public officials to use trespass and privacy invasion law to control news coverage of protests and demonstrations about crucial public issues. In *Lashinsky*, a news photographer would not leave the scene of a fatal car accident. A policeman, organizing the accident scene by backing up an unruly crowd, asked the photographer to back up with the crowd. When the photographer refused, he was arrested and charged with disorderly conduct. He claimed in his defense that his press status protected him.

The New Jersey Supreme Court ruled that the press does get constitutional protection to gather news, but that under appropriate circumstances these constitutional protections must yield to other legitimate governmental interests. The court identified reasonable time, place, and manner regulation

---

53. The clear and present danger test prohibits the reduction of a person's speech rights without proof of a government emergency. *See* Schenck v. U.S., 249 U.S. 47 (1918), *and* Whitney v. California, 274 U.S. 357 (1927). The actual malice test protects mass media libel defendants from liability unless there is proof of an extreme degree of culpability, namely knowing falsehood or reckless disregard for the truth. By comparison, the balancing test is mild and flexible.
54. 404 A.2d. 1121, 5 MEDIA L. REP. 1418 (N.J. 1979).

as an interest that might outweigh press rights in these cases. It ruled that the balance of interests was against the press in the case at hand.[55]

Used in cases in which reporters cross public or quasi-public property lines to cover protest demonstrations, the *Lashinsky* test would provide a needed exception to the theory that newsgathering is outside constitutional free speech protection.

---

55. *Id.* at 1127–1129.

ROY L. MOORE

The 1978 Right to Financial Privacy Act and U.S. Banking Law

Roy L. Moore is an associate professor in the School of Journalism at the University of Kentucky.

Although the U.S. Supreme Court ruled in a decision 100 years ago that the fourth and fifth amendment afford protection against government invasions of the "sanctity of a man's home and the privacies of life,"[1] the Court did not recognize a broad constitutional right to privacy until 1965. In *Griswold v. Connecticut,* a majority of the justices contended that this right was one of the "penumbras, formed by emanations" from the guarantees in the Bill of Rights.[2]

As a dissenting opinion noted,[3] the majority opinion made specific reference to six amendments within the Bill of Rights without pointing to any one of them as having been infringed upon by the state law in question. In spite of the obliqueness and vagueness of the majority opinion, this decision clearly established a constitutional right to privacy.[4]

The U.S. Supreme Court is not alone in its concern over privacy rights. Public interest in this issue has apparently increased dramatically in the last decade, as witnessed by a 1979 Lou Harris Opinion Poll, which found that more than three-fourths of Americans feel that the right of privacy should be included as a fundamental right alongside the rights of life, liberty, and

1. Boyd v. U.S., 116 U.S. 630 (1886).
2. Griswold v. Connecticut, 381 U.S. 479 (1965). In this decision, the Supreme Court overturned the convictions of the executive director and other officials of the state Planned Parenthood League for disseminating birth control information to married individuals in violation of the state law prohibiting the use of "any drug, medicinal article or instrument for the the the purpose of preventing conception" and restricting any person from promoting contraception.
3. J. Stewart, joined by J. Black.
4. See W. E. FRANCOIS, MASS MEDIA LAW AND REGULATION 206 (4th ed. 1986).

the pursuit of happiness.[5] Eighty-one percent believed that law enforcement authorities should not be permitted to peruse the bank records of members of a group never convicted of a crime,[6] and 91 percent agreed that it was "very important" for financial institutions and organizations, such as insurance companies and credit card issuers, to secure a consumer's consent prior to providing information from his/her file to other organizations.[7]

A spate of litigation and legislation has spewed forth since privacy became a major public concern in the 1960s, thanks to the so-called "information explosion" and the unparalleled government intrusions, illegal and otherwise, into the private affairs of individuals, which culminated in the Watergate investigations and prosecutions.[8]

Watergate aside, "public concern today about privacy ultimately derives from the impact of modern technology on the collection, storage, and retrieval of information. Modern business transactions require an increasing amount of individual financial data to be collected and maintained."[9] Another factor in this information explosion is the economic efficiency with which "the amount of personal data...can be...maintained and retrieved, and the speed with which information can be transmitted over great distances."[10] In essence, the collection and use of personal information can often reap dividends for financial institutions and government agencies.

As Fischer notes:

> Over the last two decades rapid advances in the technology of information storage, indexing, and retrieval have permitted both government and business to maintain records on individual citizens that are vastly more accurate, complete, and accessible than ever before. Both government and business have adopted new means for storage and interchange of data. At the same time the complexity and interdependence of both governmental and private institutions have grown enormously. Governmental and private institutions now maintain a tremendous volume of records on the financial and other private affairs

5. Louis Harris & Assocs. & A. Westin, The Dimensions of Privacy, A National Opinion Research Survey of Attitudes Toward Privacy 15 (1979).
6. *Id.* at 69.
7. *Id.* at 90.
8. An incredible array of convictions resulted from the Watergate investigation, including seven men for conspiracy, burglary and unlawful attempt to intercept wire communications in connection with the break in of the Democratic National Committee's offices in the Watergate building. Three White House officials, including Attorney General John Mitchell and White House aides H.R. Haldeman and John Ehrlichman, were also convicted of various charges.
9. L. R. Fischer, The Law of Financial Privacy: A Compliance Guide 6-1 (1983).
10. *Id.*

of individuals, which may reveal intimate details of each individual's life.[11]

Public concern over compilation and use of financial records was not aroused until 1970 when Congress passed the Bank Secrecy Act,[12] which ironically was designed not to maintain secrecy but to avoid secrecy by requiring financial institutions, such as banks, to retain detailed records of customers' transactions and to report certain kinds of such transactions to the Secretary of the Treasury.[13] Before this egregious Act saw the light of day, banks and other financial institutions had routinely kept records of customers' accounts, including photocopies of checks, deposit slips, and other documents, on a voluntary basis but for confidential, internal use only.[14]

While the Act was an attempt to assist law enforcement agencies in their tax, criminal, and regulatory investigations,[15] the requirement that microfilmed copies be made of all transactions of $100 or more and be retained for at least five years forced most banks to make copies of all transactions, including those under $100.[16] In other words, the expense of sorting checks of $100 or more from smaller checks was greater than the cost of microfilming all records.[17] The result was the accumulation of an unprecedented amount of financial and personal information about customers and their activities, much of which was now available to the government.[18]

Thanks to increasing public concern with privacy, the fallout from the Watergate investigations, and pressure from financial institutions, civil libertarians, and consumer groups, Congress passed several privacy bills. These included the Privacy Act of 1974,[19] which heavily regulated information systems

11. *Id.* at 2–4 (footnote omitted).
12. Bank Secrecy Act, Pub. L. No. 91–508, 84 Stat. 1114 (1970) [codified at 12 U.S.C. §§ 1730d. 1829b, 1951–1959, 31 U.S.C. § 1051–1062, 1081–1083, 1101–1105, 1121, 1122 (1976 and Supp. 1982)].
13. *See* FISCHER, *supra* note 9, at 4-2 and 8 K.M. LAPINE & B. A. BASH, BANKING LAW 162-5 (1986).
14. L. K. Davitt, *The Right to Financial Privacy Act: New Protection for Financial Records*, 8 FORDHAM URB. L.J. 597 (1980).
15. 12 U.S.C. § 1819 (b) (a) (1976).
16. Davitt, *supra* note 14, at 598.
17. *Id.*
18. The Bank Secrecy Act was enacted over the vigorous opposition of bankers who objected to being placed in the no-win situation of being forced to disclose records that customers expected to be confidential. Before the Act was passed, governmental officials had become concerned that financial institutions had stopped making copies of checks and other documents due to increased expenses. As noted in LAPINE & BASH, *supra* note 13, at 162-5 (1986), "These records were a useful and irresistible source of information to governmenral [sic] agencies in the investigation and prosecution of violations or evasions of criminal, tax, and other regulatory laws. Governmental authorities could walk into a bank, flash their badges, and expect bank officers to divulge customer account records."
19. Privacy Act of 1974, Pub. L. No. 93-579, 88 Stat. 1897 (1974), as amended by Pub. L. No. 95-38, 91 Stat. 179 (1977) (codified at 5 U.S.C. § 552a).

operated or controlled by the U.S. government and which created a seven-member Privacy Protection Study Commission to evaluate the effectiveness of the Act and to consider whether similar legislation was warranted to control state and local government agencies and private business.

Before the Privacy Protection Study Commission had a chance to issue a report (which came in 1977), the U.S. Supreme Court struck a blow in 1976 to the idea that the U.S. Constitution, specifically the fourth amendment, offers protection against government intrusion into the financial records of individuals maintained by private institutions. Two years earlier, the Court had upheld the constitutionality of the Bank Secrecy Act of 1970 in *California Bankers Association v. Schultz.*[20] But in *United States v. Miller,*[21] the U.S. Supreme Court went further, holding in a seven-to-two decision that customers have no legitimate "expectation of privacy" in the contents of their records held by financial institutions.[22]

The defendant, Mitchell Miller, had been indicted by a federal grand jury for conspiracy to defraud the U.S. government of tax revenues in the production and possession of distilled spirits.[23] Before Miller's indictment, federal authorities had subpoenas served on the defendent's bank to produce records of his financial transactions, and the bank complied without notifying Miller. The records were used at trial to convict Miller, who claimed the government's actions had violated his fourth amendment right "against unreasonable searches and seizures." Miller also argued that the subpoenas used by the government to obtain the bank records were defective.[24] The Fifth Circuit U.S. Court of Appeals held that while the petitioner's challenge to the constitutionality of the Bank Secrecy Act had been precluded by the U.S Supreme Court's decision in *California Bankers Association*, the officials had used a faulty subpoena *duces tecum,* which thereby constituted an unwarranted invasion of Miller's privacy.[25] (The appeals court also cited other grounds for the suppression of the records as evidence and granted the appellant a new trial.)

Upon appeal, the U.S. Supreme Court reversed the U.S. Court of Appeals by holding that Miller had no legitimate expectation of privacy in the bank records, since the checks involved were negotiable instruments, conveyed voluntarily as part of a commercial transaction, rather than as confidential communication.[26] The Court reasoned that a customer assumes the risk that such information will be transmitted to the government. Citing an earlier

---

20. California Bankers Assoc. v. Schultz, 416 U.S. 31 (1974).
21. United States v. Miller, 425 U.S. 435 (1976).
22. *Id.* at 442.
23. United States v. Miller, 500 F.2d 751 (5th Cir. 1974), *rev'd*, 425 U.S. 435 (1976).
24. *Id.*
25. *Id.*
26. *Id.* at 442.

decision, the Court said the documents were business records and since they were knowingly exposed to the public by Miller, they did not have fourth amendment protection.[27] "The effect of the *Miller* decision was to grant the government unrestricted access to a customer-depositor's financial records through administrative subpoenas."[28]

I. THE IMPETUS FOR THE RFPA

A. *United States v. Miller*

The reaction by Congress, state legislatures, consumer groups, and even financial institutions to *Miller* was swift and furious. Several states passed statutes granting consumers the right to notice of requests by the government for financial records and the right to contest such subpoenas.[29] Unfortunately, these laws could affect only "non-federal requests made on state-chartered institutions."[30] Even before the long-awaited report of the Privacy Protection Study Commission (hereinafter "Privacy Report")[31] could be issued, many privacy bills were introduced in Congress. In fact, more than 100 privacy bills were introduced during the 95th Session (1977–78).[32]

B. Report of the Privacy Protection Study Commission

On June 30, 1977, a dozen congressmen introduced legislation that ultimately became, in modified form, the Right to Financial Privacy Act (RFPA) of 1978.[33] Twelve days later, the Privacy Protection Study Commission (hereinafter "The Privacy Commission") issued its report. The Privacy Commission, with a budget of $1,750,000,[34] had spent two years conducting its study, including two months of hearings and testimony from more than 300 individuals.[35] In its 654-page final report, the Privacy Commission concluded the government continued to pose the most serious threat to individual privacy and thus a major revision of federal privacy laws was warranted. According to Lapine and Bash:

---

27. United States v. Katz, 389 U.S. 347 (1967).
28. Davitt, *supra* note 14, at 607.
29. LAPINE & BASH, *supra* note 13, at 162-10.
30. *Id.*
31. PRIVACY PROTECTION STUDY COMMISSION, PERSONAL PRIVACY IN AN INFORMATION SOCIETY (1977).
32. LAPINE & BASH, *supra* note 13, at 162-12.
33. Right to Financial Privacy Act, Pub. L. No. 95-630, Tit. XI, 92 Stat. 3697 (1978) [codified at 12 U.S.C. §§ 3401-3422].
34. FRANCOIS, *supra* note 4, at 261.
35. LAPINE & BASH, *supra* note 13, at 162-14.

The report identified a number of problems and made specific recommendations. Three basic objectives for privacy legislation were set forth. These were
  (1) minimizing intrusiveness;
  (2) maximizing fairness; and
  (3) creating legitimate and enforceable expectations of confidentiality.
To implement these objectives, the Privacy Commission recommended that
  (1) individuals be informed of the needs for and methods of collecting information in advance;
  (2) certain information not be collected (i.e., arrest records for use in hiring and promotions);
  (3) false interviews by private sector information-collecting organizations be made a criminal offense;
  (4) individuals be given access to their records for purposes of review, copying, correcting, or amending to provide some control over collections and disclosure;
  (5) organizations be responsible for notifying individuals that records have been or will be created about them; and
  (6) reasonable procedures be adopted for assuring accuracy, timeliness, completeness, and relevancy of records maintained.[36]

While "there was broad bipartisan support for the essential principles" of the RFPA,[37] Congress attempted to balance the need of individuals for confidentiality of financial records with the need of government agencies to have access to such records in conducting investigations of possible illegal activities. Four groups particularly vied with one another, according to Lapine and Bash: federal bank supervisory agencies, which generally supported the legislation so long as it "did not interfere with their supervisory and regulatory functions;" civil libertarians, who were concerned with *Miller*'s erosion of first, fourth and fifth amendment protection; bankers, who wanted to resolve the bind of answering government requests for information while preserving customer's privacy; and state and federal law enforcement officials,[38] who provided the only real opposition to the bill because they were concerned

36. *Id.* at 162-11-62-12.
37. FISCHER, *supra* note 9, at 2-7.
38. LAPINE & BASH, *supra* note 13, at 162-14.

that it would interfere with their investigations, especially white-collar and organized crime.[39]

The result was a compromise bill that "generally prohibits disclosure by a financial institution of information in customer records to federal government authorities"[40] while including several exceptions, as discussed previously. The Act directly implements several of the Privacy Commission's recommendations, such as the right of the consumer to challenge a summons or subpoena, while modifying some of the Commission's recommendations, such as that the government be limited to access to customer information only by legal process or customer consent.[41]

II. APPLICABILITY OF THE RFPA

A. Overview

Even though *Miller* provided the impetus for Congress to express concern about governmental intrusion into financial records, the RFPA "does little to hinder such intrusions. The act does not repeal ... *Miller*."[42] The major impact of the Act is to restrict (but not prohibit) government access to financial records of individuals held by all financial institutions—banks, savings and loan associations, credit card issuers, credit unions, consumer finance firms, and trust companies. A federal agency (the Act does not apply to state and local agencies) may gain access to customer records only for legitimate purposes (specified in the Act) and only through the use of specific procedures. The consumer may challenge the government request and if the information is improperly obtained or disclosed, he or she may seek civil liability. Government access can be obtained only by consumer authorization,[43] administrative subpoena or summons,[44] search warrant,[45] judicial subpoena,[46] or by formal written request under specified conditions.[47]

B. Types of Records

For purposes of the RFPA, financial record is defined as "an original of, a copy of, or information known to have been derived from, any record

39. FISCHER, *supra* note 9, at 2-7.
40. *Id.* at 2-9, citing Right to Financial Privacy Act (hereinafter "RFPA"), §3402, 3403 (a).
41. *See* A.E. BRILL, THE RIGHT TO FINANCIAL PRIVACY ACT: A COMPLIANCE GUIDE FOR FINANCIAL INSTITUTIONS 2 (1979).
42. J.C. CONBOY JR., LAW AND BANKING 347 (1982).
43. RFPA § 3402 (1).
44. *Id.* § 3402 (2).
45. *Id.* § 3402 (3).
46. *Id.* § 3402 (4).
47. *Id.* § 3402 (5).

held by a financial institution pertaining to a customer's relationship with the financial institution."[48] The act applies only to records of individuals or of partnerships of five or fewer persons[49] and only to those records held by a "financial institution," which is defined as "any office of a bank, savings bank, [credit] card issuer ..., industrial loan company, trust company, savings and loan, building and loan, or homestead association (including cooperative banks), credit union, or consumer finance institutions."[50] Thus, the Act is very broad in its coverage of types of records and types of institutions and is equally broad in its covered locations, which include "any State or territory of the United States, the District of Columbia, Puerto Rico, Guam, American Samoa, or the Virgin Islands."[51]

C. Specific Government Agencies

Although Congress encouraged states to enact their own right-to-financial-privacy statutes,[52] it chose not make the RFPA itself applicable to state and local governments. While several states have followed the advice and passed such legislation,[53] only requests from federal government authorities ("any agency or department of the United States, or any officer, employee, or agent thereof")[54] are affected. The Act clearly does not apply to agents or officials of state or local governments nor to requests for records by private businesses. In effect, "[r]egardless of the person's title, be it 'agent,' 'officer,' 'special agent,' 'deputy secretary,' or anything else, if they work for the United States Government, they must comply with the provisions of the Act."[55]

One of the exceptions under the Act includes "any supervisory agency [examining or disclosing] ... financial records or information in the exercise of its supervisory, regulatory, or monetary functions with respect to a financial institution."[56] Supervisory agency is defined in the Act as "any of the following which has statutory authority to examine the financial condition of the business operation of the institution—

(A) the Federal Deposit Insurance Corporation;
(B) the Federal Savings and Loan Insurance Corporation;
(C) the Federal Home Loan Bank Board;

48. *Id.* § 3401 (2).
49. *Id.* § 3401 (4).
50. *Id.* § 3401 (1).
51. *Id.*
52. *See* U.S. CODE CONG. & AD. NEWS 9376.
53. According to Davitt, *supra* note 14, at 617, these states include California ("the most comprehensive state legislation enacted this far"), Illinois, and Maryland.
54. RFPA §3401 (3).
55. BRILL, *supra* note 41, at 7.
56. RFPA § 3413 (b).

(D) the National Credit Union Administration;

(E) the Board of Governors of the Federal Reserve System;

(F) the Comptroller of the Currency;

(G) the Security and Exchange Commission;

(H) the Secretary of the Treasury, with respect to the Bank Secrecy Act and the Currency and Foreign Transactions Reporting Act ...; or

(I) any State banking or securities department or agency."[57]

According to the legislative history of the RFPA, Congress intended to exclude credit reporting agencies, since their records were already regulated by the Fair Credit Reporting Act,[58] but state-chartered financial institutions are included even though "there is no specific language in the statute to that effect."[59] Application of the provisions of the Act would, however, be limited by the Commerce Clause of the U.S. Constitution.[60]

Although corporations, trusts, estates, unions, clubs, partnerships, and other entities with more than five persons are not covered by the RFPA, most of these groups, especially larger corporations and partnerships, "are usually provided with notice of government requests for their records by their financial institution and are usually well aware of any legal proceedings concerning them."[61] Thus, this exemption is probably not a serious problem for such entities.[62]

D. Exceptions

1. *Financial Records Not Identified with a Particular Customer*

The RFPA specifically mentions ten "exceptions," although other exceptions are implied or created within various provisions of the statute. The first major exception is "the disclosure of any financial records or information which is not identified with or identifiable as being derived from the financial records of a particular customer."[63] The reasoning of Congress in including this exception is that the major purpose of the Act is to protect the financial privacy of individual customers, whose privacy would not be invaded by disclosures that do not specifically identify them.[64] This exception would

---

57. *Id.* § 3401 (6).
58. H.R. Rep. No. 1383, 95th Cong., 2d Sess. 49 (1978) (cited in FISCHER, *supra* note 9, at 2-14).
59. FISCHER, *supra* note 9, at 2-14.
60. U.S. Const. art. 1 § 8. As noted in *id.* at 2-15, "Challenges to the commerce power have become virtually extinct."
61. Davitt, *supra* note 14, at 623.
62. See *id.* at 623–624 for a discussion of this issue, including the potential expense for the financial institution.
63. RFPA § 3413 (a).
64. See FISCHER, *supra* note 9, at 2-54.

presumably include "statistical summaries, graphs, charts, and other aggregate data" as well as the disclosure of "summary information in connection with a legislative or administrative investigation of proposed laws favorable to that institution."[65]

For example, the U.S. Court of Appeals ruled in *Donovan v. National Bank of Alaska*[66] that compliance by a bank with a subpoena by the U.S. Department of Labor requesting general information about employee benefit plans was not a violation of the RFPA.[67] The court reasoned that the plans were not "customers" under the Act, but that the Act would apply to a disclosure of the records of individual bank customers subscribing to the plans.[68]

2. Financial Information Necessary to Bank Regulatory Authorities

The second major exemption, as discussed previously, allows "any supervisory agency" to gain access to financial records and information so long as such access is in the exercise of their "supervisory, regulatory, or monetary functions with respect to a financial institution."[69]

3. Financial Information under the Internal Revenue Code

Under the third exception ("disclosure of financial records in accordance with procedures authorized by the Internal Revenue Code"),[70] the Internal Revenue Service is excluded from the provisions of the RFPA. The legislative history of the Act indicates that Congress felt that the Tax Reform Act of 1976 already made IRS access and disclosures "subject to privacy safeguards."[71] Section 7609 of the Internal Revenue Code, for example, requires the IRS to notify the taxpayer within three days of a third-party summons, with the notice including a copy of the summons and directions for staying compliance.[72] As Fischer notes, "Thus, the procedures and restrictions of the tax privacy provisions are mutually exclusive, and only the latter govern IRS summonses."[73]

Section 7609 of the Internal Revenue Code grants the IRS the authority is to issue summonses to anyone or any organizations, including financial

---

65. *Id.* at 2-55.
66. Donovan v. National Bank of Alaska, 696 F.2d 678 (9th Cir. 1983).
67. *Id.* at 683.
68. *Id.* at 683-84. Ironically, as FISCHER, *supra* note 9, 1985 Supp. at S2-16 points out, "[T]he court did not discuss the fact that the Department of Labor's subpoena requested information regarding the name and address of each plan sponsor."
69. RFPA § 3413 (b).
70. *Id.* § 3413 (c).
71. *See* 124 Cong. Rec. H11734 (daily ed. Oct. 5, 1978) (remarks of Mr. LaFalce) (cited in FISCHER, *supra* note 9, at 2-60).
72. I.R.C. § 7609 (9) (1). *See* discussion in Davitt, *supra* note 14, at 619.
73. FISCHER. *supra* note 9, at 2-60.

institutions, to compel the production of records.[74] Once the summons is served on both possessor of the records and on the affected taxpayer, the IRS must wait fourteen days before actually demanding the records. If the taxpayer does not raise objections within the fourteen-day period, the financial institution or other holder can then provide the IRS with the information.[75] On the other hand, if the taxpayer objects, he or she must notify the institution or other holder, and the record holder cannot release the information unless ordered to do so by a court or unless the taxpayer gives written consent.[76]

The Tax Reform Act of 1976 also controls use of "John Doe" summonses (requesting information about the tax affairs of unidentified persons) by requiring the IRS to obtain court approval of such summonses before service.[77]

At least one writer has questioned whether Congressional reliance on the provisions of the Tax Reform Act of 1976 as an excuse for exempting IRS from the RFPA is justified.[78]

4. *Financial Information Required to be Reported under Federal Statute or Regulations*

Another exception under the RFPA is the disclosure of information "required to be reported in accordance with any federal statute or Rule."[79] The purpose of this exception is to permit the disclosure of records and reports required by acts such as the Internal Revenue Code, the Bank Secrecy Act, the Federal Deposit Insurance Act, the National Housing Act, and the Currency and Foreign Transactions Reporting Act.[80]

5. *Information Sought through Judicial Discovery Procedures*

Information "sought by a Government authority under the Federal Rules of Civil or Criminal Procedure or comparable rules of other courts in connection with litigation to which the Government authority and the customer are parties"[81] is also exempt under the RFPA. This exemption of records sought through judicial discovery procedures was included by Congress since "[u]nder

---

74. I.R.C. § 7609 (d) (1).
75. *Id.*
76. *Id.* § 7609 (d) (2).
77. *Id.* § 7609 (f).
78. Davitt, *supra* note 14, at 618. *See* this student comment at 618-621 for a more detailed discussion of the RFPA and the IRS.
79. RFPA § 3413 (d).
80. *See* H.R. No. 95-138, 95th Cong., 2d Sess. (1978) (cited in LAPINE & BASH, *supra* note 13, at 162-35.
81. RFPA § 3413 (e).

these circumstances, the process of disclosure is already under direct judicial supervision."[82]

6. *Administrative Proceedings Against a Customer*

Similar reasoning would seem to apply to the sixth exception (administrative proceedings against a customer),[83] since any administrative subpoena would have to be issued by an administrative law judge and would be controlled by the provisions of the Administrative Procedures Act.[84] Such a proceeding must be "an adjudicatory proceeding subject to section 554 of title 5, United States Code, and to which the Government authority and the customer are parties."[85] The legislative history of the Act indicates that Congress felt that, as in civil and criminal litigation, "the customer's privacy rights would be protected by the administrative law judge's supervision of discovery proceedings."[86]

7. *Name, Address, Account Number and Type of Account of a Customer Associated with a Financial Transaction with a Foreign Country*

Provision [g] under Section 3413[87] of the RFPA provides that the notice requirements of the Act, the customer challenge provisions,[88] and the use of information provisions[89] "shall not apply when a Government authority by a means described in section [3402] and for a legitimate law enforcement inquiry is seeking only the name, address, account number, and type of account of any customer" associated with a financial transaction with a foreign country when a federal agency has authority over foreign accounts in the United States.[90] The legislative history of the Act reveals that this exception primarily covers disclosure of the limited type of information contained on the signature card.[91]

---

82. LAPINE & BASH, *supra* note 13, at 162-36.
83. RFPA § 3413 (f).
84. *See* 5 U.S.C. § 554.
85. RFPA § 3413 (f).
86. H. R. Rep. No. 1383, 95th Cong. 2d Sess. (1978) (cited in FISCHER, *supra* note 9, at 2-61).
87. RFPA § 3413 (g).
88. *Id.* § 3410.
89. *Id.* § 3412.
90. *Id.* § 3413 (g) (1)–(2)
91. H.R. Rep. No. 95-138, 95th Cong., 2d Sess. (1978) (cited in LAPINE & BASH, *supra* note 13, at 162-36.)

8. Financial Records Sought in Connection with an Investigation of the Financial Institution Itself

The eighth exception focuses on (1) financial records sought by a federal agency "in connection with a lawful proceeding, investigation, examination, or inspection directed at the financial institution" in possession of such records or at a legal entity which is not a customer[92] and (2) in connection with the "authority's consideration or administration of assistance to a customer in the form of a government loan, loan guaranty, or loan insurance program."[93]

In both instances, the records may be disclosed, so long as two safeguards against abuse are met. First, the government agency must provide the financial institution with a certificate of compliance, as required under Section 3403 (b) of the Act.[94] Second, "[f]inancial records pursuant to this subsection may be used only for the purpose for which they were originally obtained, and may be transformed to another agency or department only when the transfer is to facilitate a lawful proceeding, investigation, examination, or inspection directed at the financial institution in possession of such records, or at a legal entity which is not a customer."[95] The exception is when those records are "needed by counsel representing a Government authority in a civil action arising from a Government loan, loan guaranty, or loan insurance agreement,"[96] or for a "Government authority providing assistance to a customer in the form of a loan, loan guaranty, or loan insurance agreement," when use or transfer is "necessary to process, service or foreclose a loan, or to collect" on a debt to the government resulting from the customer's default.[97]

9. Federal Grand Jury Proceedings

The penultimate exception is for "any subpoena or court order issued in connection with proceedings before a grand jury."[98] Although this exception applies to the procedural requirements of the Act, it does not apply to the section that allows for cost reimbursement to financial institutions,[99] as discussed previously, nor to the section that imposes special procedures for compliance with grand jury subpoenas.[100] Thus, the RFPA's ordinary notice, waiting period, and challenge procedures do not apply to customer financial records sought by federal grand juries, the government is not required to

92. RFPA § 3413 (h) (1) (A).
93. *Id.* § 3413 (h) (1) (B).
94. *Id.* § 3413 (h) (2).
95. *Id.* § 3413 (h) (4).
96. *Id.* § 3413 (h) (4) (A).
97. *Id.* § 3413 (h) (4) (B).
98. *Id.* § 3413 (i).
99. *Id.* § 3415.
100. *Id.* § 3420.

provide a certificate of compliance with the Act, and the civil liability provisions do not apply to disclosure by financial institutions in response to federal grand juries.[101]

The reasoning of Congress in providing this exception was that "judicial scrutiny inherent in grand jury proceedings, coupled with the secrecy rules governing these proceedings, would adequately protect the privacy interests of customers" and that "the consititutional status of grand juries and the need to protect grand jury secrecy militate[d] against permitting the delay and confusion involved in notice and challenge procedures."[102] As the legislative history of the Act notes, the grand jury is the " 'single most effective tool of criminal law enforcement,' " and "its procedures are already subject to judicial scrunity."[103]

The Act does require that "[f]inancial records about a customer obtained from a financial institution pursuant to a subpoena issued under the authority of a Federal grand jury"[104] must "be returned and actually presented to the grand jury"[105] and may "be used only for the purpose of considering whether to issue an indictment or presentment" or for "prosecuting a crime for which that indictment or presentment is issued, or for a purpose authorized by rule 6(e) of the Federal Rules of Criminal Procedure."[106] The Act requires that the records "be destroyed or returned to the financial insititution if not used for one of the purposes specified."[107] It also specifies that if the records or content descriptions are maintained by any government authority, they must be placed "in the sealed records of the grand jury, unless...used in the prosecution of a crime for which the grand jury issued an indictment or presentment or for a purpose authorized by rule 6 (e) of the Federal Rules of Criminal Procedure."[108]

10. *Financial Records from the General Accounting Office*

Finally, the RFPA exempts "financial records...sought by the General Accounting Office pursuant to an authorized proceeding, investigation, examination or audit directed at a government authority."[109]

---

101. FISCHER, *supra* note 9, at 2-71.
102. *Id.* at 2-71 to 2-72, citing H.R. Rep. No. 1383, 95th Cong., 2d Sess. 228 (1978) (views of Mr. LaFalce).
103. LAPINE & BASH, *supra* note 13, at 162-39 [citing H.R. Rep. No. 95-138, 95th Cong., 2d Sess. (1978) at 9358].
104. RFPA § 3420.
105. *Id.* § 3420 (1).
106. *Id.* § 3420 (2).
107. *Id.* § 3420 (3).
108. *Id.* § 3420 (4).
109. *Id.* § 3413 (j).

III. MEANS OF ACCESS

The RFPA provides five basic procedures by which the government may obtain access to financial records: customer authorization,[110] administrative subpoena and summons,[111] search warrants,[112] judicial subpoena,[113] and formal, written request.[114] The requirements vary somewhat with each method, but all of the five require that the government order or request reasonably describe the information sought, and except for customer authorization or search warrants, the customer must be notified in advance, and he or she has the right to protest the disclosure unless one of the exceptions applies. The government does have the opportunity to secure an *ex parte* order to delay notice to the customer for a specified time if it can demonstrate exigent circumstances.[115] Once the order has been granted, neither the financial institution nor the government agency can notify the customer until the restrictive order has ended. In most cases, the government has to provide the financial institution with a certificate of compliance with the Act before the institution provides the records,[117] and the financial institution incurs no liability if it can prove that it relied in good faith on the certificate.[118]

A. Customer Authorization

A customer may authorize disclosure to the government of his or her financial records, but such authorization:

- must be signed and dated[119]
- cannot permit disclosure for a period of more than three months[120]
- must state that the customer may revoke such authorization at any time before the financial records are disclosed[121]
- must identify the specific records involved[122]

110. *Id.* § 3404.
111. *Id.* § 3405.
112. *Id.* § 3406.
113. *Id.* § 3407.
114. *Id.* § 3408.
115. *Id.* § 3409.
116. *Id.* § 3409 (b) (1).
117. *Id.* § 3403 (b).
118. *Id.* § 3417 (c).
119. *Id.* § 3404 (a).
120. *Id.* § 3404 (a) (1).
121. *Id.* § 3404 (a) (2).
122. *Id.* § 3404 (a) (3).

- must indicate the specific purposes for which the records are sought and the specific government authority to which the records are to be disclosed[123] and
- must state the customer's rights under the RFPA.[124]

The gist of this section of the Act is to allow a customer to voluntarily work with a government agency investigating his or her affairs.[125] This section prohibits a financial institution from requiring this type of customer authorization "as a condition of doing business."[126]

The customer does have the right—unless the government agency obtains a delayed notice[127]—to obtain a copy of the record that must be kept by the financial institution anytime it discloses information to a government agency pursuant to a customer authorization.[128] This record must identify the specific agency to which the information was disclosed.[129]

B. Administrative Subpoena and Summons

Before a government agency can obtain records through an administrative subpoena or summons, three conditions must be met. First, the authority must have "reason to believe that the records sought are relevant to a legitimate law enforcement inquiry."[130] Second, the customer must have been served or mailed a copy of the subpoena or summons on or before the date on which the document was served on the financial institution, along with a specific notice (the wording of which is contained in the statute) that indicates the nature of the law enforcement inquiry.[131] Finally, the agency must wait at least ten days from the serving of the notice or fourteen days if the notice is mailed.[132] During this period, the customer has the right to file a sworn statement and motion to quash in court or to challenge the request or order under the "Customer Challenge Provisions" of the Act.[133] If the customer does not exercise these rights during this period and the first two requirements have been fulfilled, the government agency can obtain the records sought.

As Lapine and Bash point out, the "reasonable belief" standard is "considerably less than, and conceptually different from, the standard of probable

---

123. *Id.* § 3404 (a) (4).
124. *Id.* § 3404 (a) (5).
125. LAPINE & BASH, *supra* note 13, at 162-18.
126. RFPA § 3404 (b).
127. *Id.* § 3409.
128. *Id.* § 3404 (c).
129. *Id.*
130. *Id.* § 3405 (1).
131. *Id.* § 3405 (2).
132. *Id.* § 3405 (3).
133. *Id.* § 3410.

cause," but the "legitimate purpose" requirement is "an important safeguard that is intended to prevent an agency from acting outside the scope of its statutory authority...as well as from pursuing an investigation in bad faith to harass or intimidate its subject."[134]

Such summonses by the Internal Revenue Service are exempt from this provision, since the RFPA does not apply to the disclosure of financial records in accordance with procedures authorized by the Internal Revenue Code.[135]

C. Search Warrants

The standard by which the government may justify gaining access to financial records through the third method, a search warrant, is probable cause as required under the fourth amendment. Such a warrant may be obtained only in accordance with the Federal Rules of Criminal Procedure.[136] Under this provision, the government agency must mail a copy of the search warrant to the customer no later than ninety days after the warrant is served on the financial institution.[137] The copy must include a notice (the wording of which is specified in the Act) indicating that the information has been obtained and that the customer may have rights under the RFPA.[138]

Under Rule 41 of the Federal Rules of Criminal Procedure, the search warrant may be issued only under the supervision of a federal magistrate or state judge in the district in which the records are located, usually after an *ex parte* hearing. The search must be conducted within the time specified in the warrant but no longer than ten days. There are also certain procedures that apply to the service and execution of the warrant.[139]

This provision of the Act does permit the court to grant, upon government request, a delay in the mailing of the notice beyond the normal ninety days, but the delay cannot be for more than 180 days after service of the warrant[140] and the court must find that:

> (1) the investigation being conducted is within the lawful jurisdiction of the Government authority seeking the financial records;
> (2) there is reason to believe that the records being sought are relevant to a legitimate law enforcement inquiry; and
> (3) there is reason to believe that such notice will result in...endangering life or physical safety of any person; flight from

---

134. LAPINE & BASH, *supra* note 13, at 162-18.
135. RFPA § 3413 (c).
136. *Id.* § 3406 (a).
137. *Id.* § 3406 (b).
138. *Id.*
139. *See* FISCHER, *supra* note 9, at 2-30, for a general discussion of this issue.
140. RFPA § 3406 (c).

prosecution; destruction of or tampering with evidence; intimidation of potential witnesses; or otherwise seriously jeopardizing an investigation or official proceeding to the same extent as [above].[141]

The above provisions are in the section entitled "Delayed Notice—Preservation of Records" and apply in several circumstances, as specified in the Act.

D. Judicial Subpoena

Under the RFPA, the government may obtain financial records in response to a judicial subpoena only if the "subpoena is authorized by law and there is reason to believe that the records sought are legitimate law enforcement inquiry"[142] and a copy of the subpoena has been served on the customer or mailed to him or her by the time the subpoena is served on the financial institution.[143] The copy of the subpoena must bear a notice informing the customer of his or her rights under the RFPA, with the exact wording provided in the Act. The customer then has ten days from service or fourteen days from mailing of the notice to file a sworn statement and motion to quash in the appropriate court or contest the subpoena under the challenge provisions of the Act.[144]

Once this period has expired and the consumer has not exercised his or her rights, the government agency may obtain the records. As Fischer notes, however, the financial institution should receive a certificate of compliance from the agency *before* complying with the subpoena since, as with administrative subpoenas and summonses, the institution incurs no liability for disclosure if it relied in good faith on the certificate.[145]

E. Formal Written Request

The final procedure by which the government may obtain access to financial records is through a formal, written request. This method requires procedures that are very similar to those for the other methods, but its enforceability and legal effect are "strikingly different."[146] Such a request is considered a "new, non-coercive procedure"[147] to be used only if "no administrative summons or subpoena authority reasonably appears to be available

---

141. *Id.* § 3409 (a) (1)–(3) (A)–(E).
142. *Id.* § 3407 (1).
143. *Id.* § 3407 (2).
144. *Id.* § 3407 (3).
145. FISCHER, *supra* note 9, at 2-34.
146. *Id.* at 2-37.
147. LAPINE & BASH, *supra* note 13, at 162-19.

to that Government authority to obtain financial records for the purpose for which such records are sought."[148] Thus, this procedure is not

> a general grant of authority to all government agencies that have the authority to investigate violations of law but lack the power to issue administrative summons or subpoenas with a means of gaining access to financial records required to fulfill their responsibilities.[149]

The request must be "authorized by regulations promulgated by the head of the agency or department," [150] there must be "reason to believe the records sought are relevant to a legitimate law enforcement inquiry,"[151] and a copy of the request must be served on or mailed to the customer by the date on which the request is made to the financial institution.[152] The copy must also include a notice that states "with reasonable specificity the nature of the law enforcement inquiry" and notifies the customer of his or her rights under the RFPA (the exact wording is specified in the section).[153]

As with the other methods, this procedure requires a waiting period of ten days from service or fourteen days from date of mailing of the copy of the request to the customer, during which time he or she can file "a sworn statement and an application to enjoin the Government authority in an appropriate court" or contest the request under the challenge provisions of the Act.[154]

The major difference between this method and the other procedures lies in its legal effect. Compliance by the financial institution is discretionary—it is *not* required to meet the formal, written request. This provision clearly states that "the records may be made available" or "may be transferred to other Government authorities,"[155] while the "Administrative Subpoena and Summons" section and "Judicial Subpoena" section provide that the requested information "will be made available."[156]

IV. REQUIREMENTS FOR COMPLIANCE

The primary responsibility of financial institutions under the RFPA is to keep detailed records, including dates on which records were disclosed

---

148. RFPA § 3408 (1).
149. LAPINE & BASH, *supra* note 13, at 162-19 (citing RFPA § 3408 (1) and H.R. Rep. No. 95-1383 at 9324 and 9351.)
150. RFPA § 3408 (2).
151. *Id.* § 3408 (3).
152. *Id.* § 3408 (4).
153. *Id.* § 3408 (4) (A).
154. *Id.* § 3408 (4) (B).
155. *Id.* § 3408 (4) (A).
156. *Id.* § 3405 (2) and § 3407 (2).

and the government agencies involved.[157] There are very few limitations placed on those institutions that want to notify their customers of government requests for their financial records. If a court order is granted to the agency to prevent customer notice or if the agency is exercising financial controls over foreign accounts in this country under the Trading with the Enemy Act, the International Emergency Economic Powers Act, or section 5 of the United Nations Participation Act,[158] delayed notice can be granted. Such a delay is also permitted when the agency is conducting "foreign counter- or foreign positive-intelligence activities"[159] when the Secret Service is involved.[160]

Financial institutions are required, of course, to keep financial records of customers confidential except in accordance with the Act.[161] The institution must not release the records "until the Government authority...certifies in writing...that it has complied with the applicable provisions" of the Act.[162]

V. CUSTOMER CHALLENGES

The RFPA provides detailed procedures by which a consumer can judicially challenge a government agency's request for access to his or her financial records.[163] This right and the procedures involved must be given in writing with the notice that the agency must provide to the customer. Once the notice is received, the customer has the right to file a motion in federal district court with an affidavit indicating why he or she believes the records requested are not relevant to a legitimate law enforcement inquiry or that "there has not been substantial compliance" with the RFPA.[164]

Once the motion to quash or application to enjoin has been filed, the court will "order the Government authority to file a sworn response."[165] The court can then decide the issue or order further proceedings to be completed within seven days of the filing of the government response.[166] If the court finds "there is a demonstrable reason to believe that the law enforcement inquiry is legitimate," there is "a reasonable belief that the records sought are relevant to that inquiry" and there has been substantial compliance with the Act, it shall deny the motion and thus permit access to the records.[167] There is also an appeals procedure provided within the Act.[168]

---

157. *Id.* § 3413 (h) (6).
158. *Id.* § 3409 (b) (1).
159. *Id.* § 3414 (a) (1) (A).
160. *Id.* § 3414 (a) (1) (B).
161. *Id.* § 3403 (a).
162. *Id.* § 3403 (b).
163. *Id.* § 3410.
164. *Id.* § 3410 (a) (1)–(2).
165. *Id.* § 3410 (b).
166. *Id.*
167. *Id.* § 3410 (c).
168. *Id.* § 3410 (d) and (e).

VI. REIMBURSEMENT OF COSTS

Except for certain types of records, including those under the "exceptions" section[169] and those involving the perfection of a security interest, bankruptcy, government loans, etc.,[170] the government agency must reimburse the financial institution for "such costs as are reasonably necessary and which have been directly incurred in searching for, reproducing, or transporting books, papers, records, or other data required or requested to be produced."[171]

The Federal Reserve System's Board of Governors is granted the authority to set the rates and conditions for reimbursement.[172]

VII. ENFORCEMENT

Both financial institutions and government agencies can be held liable for violation of the provisions of the RFPA. There are no criminal penalties, but both civil penalties and equitable relief are available. The civil penalties include:

(1) $100 without regard to the volume of records involved;
(2) any actual damages sustained by the customer as a result of the disclosure;
(3) such punitive damages as the court may allow, where the violation is found to have been willful or intentional; and
(4) in the case of any successful action to enforce liability under this section, the costs of the action together with reasonable attorney's fees as determined by the court.[173]

The Civil Service Commission is granted the authority to recommend the appropriate disciplinary action when an officer or employee of a government agency has willfully or intentionally violated the Act.[174]

In addition to damage, injunctive relief is also avaialbe to ensure compliance with the act, along with reasonable attorney's fees.[175]

VIII. CONCLUSIONS

Although at least one law review comment has concluded that "[i]t is apparent that the [R]FPA has reversed the holding of *Miller*," the same

169. *Id.* § 3413.
170. *Id.* § 3403 (d).
171. *Id.* § 3415 (a).
172. *Id.*
173. *Id.* § 3417 (a).
174. *Id.* § 3417 (b).
175. *Id.* § 3418.

comment also concludes that "there has been virtually no immediate change in banking procedures as a result of the [R]FPA" and that "[t]hus far the [R]FPA does not seem to have hindered law enforcement activities."[176] In all honesty, the statute does not really reverse *Miller* but rather limits the effects of that decision. Consumers now have a legitimate expectation of privacy in their records held by financial institutions, but this right is very limited, thanks to the many exceptions under the Act.

Very few states have chosen to enact their versions of the RFPA, and only federal government agencies, not private businesses (other than financial institutions which receive government requests), are bound by the Act.

The various civil penalties and the injunctive relief provided do give the statute some "bite," especially since individual government employees can be disciplined for willful or intentional violations.

The Right to Financial Privacy Act is clearly a major step toward providing a clearly needed right of customers to protect their records from unwarranted government intrusion, but it represents only one step down a road that will probably prove to be circuitous and long.

---

176. Davitt, *supra* note 14, at 626.

DECKLE MCLEAN

Unconscionability in Public Disclosure Privacy Cases

Deckle McLean is a member of the journalism faculty at Western Illinois University. He has written for the *Providence
Journal-Bulletin* and the *Boston Globe.*

Unconscionability is the key to understanding and redressing privacy invasions by public disclosure of true but embarrassing private facts. Where there
is no unconscionability, there is no invasion. Courts have recognized that con-
scionability is the basis of the grievance—though few have explicitly used the
word "unconscionability"—since at least 1931.[1] The authoritative *Restatement
of Torts* also employs the concept, not explicitly, in its section on privacy
invasions by public disclosure. This section reads: "One who gives publicity
to a matter concerning the private life of another is subject to liability to the
other for invasion of his privacy, if the matter publicized is of a kind that
(a) would be highly offensive to a reasonable person and (b) is not of legitimate
concern to the public."[2]

Nevertheless, the utility of the unconscionability concept is lost when
lawyers and judges attempt to import the actual-malice test—or an actual-
malice "variant"—into public disclosure cases; procedurally separate the components of the unconscionability test, making one a matter of law and another
a matter of fact; or resist placing the label "public disclosure" on that type
of privacy invasion suit that turns on unconscionability, for fear that doing
so will stifle the creative growth of privacy invasion law generally.

The result is murkiness and the absence of a conceptual handle in a corner
of law which can be, and needs to be, clear.

Here are some basics about the public disclosure form of privacy invasion:

1. *See* Melvin v. Reid, 297 P. 91 (Cal. App. 1931).
2. Restatement (Second) of Torts, § 652D (1977).

- Even those who reject William Prosser's widely accepted dissection of the privacy invasion lawsuit into the four "separate torts" of misappropriation, physical intrusion, false light, and public disclosure[3] must acknowledge that some privacy invasions are caused by the distribution of facts that are true.

- Fault in privacy invasions by true statements cannot be assessed by means of the actual-malice test created in *New York Times v. Sullivan*[4] because the *Sullivan* actual-malice test was designed to measure the fault behind false statements. This test defines actual-malice as publication of knowing falsity or reckless disregard for the truth.

- The use of the words "reckless disregard" in a test formulation does not convert the test into a version of the actual-malice test unless the words "reckless disregard" refer to behavior with respect to truth. As a result, formulations such as "reckless disregard for privacy interests" or "reckless disregard for the community's standards of decency" are not versions of the *Sullivan* actual-malice test, although, like the *Sullivan* test, they include the words "reckless disregard."

- The only standard from the *Sullivan* defamation opinion that is clearly at work in public disclosure privacy invasion cases is the interpretation that the first amendment prohibits "chilling" impacts on the press.[5] A parallel concern for press freedom has been part of privacy invasion common law for most of its history, and accounts for the almost—but not quite—impossible odds plaintiffs face in public disclosure cases.

- The unconscionability concept reasonably can be understood to contain elements of newsworthiness, community mores,[6] logical nexus,[7] and legitimacy of public interest.

- Unconscionability, when used as a test, probably should be used in one place, a judge deciding the whole as a matter of law or passing the whole on to a jury as a matter of fact; rather than in two pieces, the judge, for example, reserving logical nexus questions while passing to a jury newsworthiness questions.

- Malice by common-law definition of animosity or ill-will remains available as a traditional grounds for awarding punitive damages in privacy invasion lawsuits. As a result, some sorting out is needed to distinguish common-law malice from the kind of fault implied by unconscionability. Clarification is needed of whether a finding of unconscionability, by whatever

---

3. William Prosser first offered his four "separate torts" of privacy invasion in Prosser, *Privacy* 48 CAL. L. REV 383 (1960).
4. 376 U.S. 254 (1964).
5. *Id.* at 277–279.
6. *See* Virgil v. Time, 527 F.2d 1122 (9th Cir. 1975).
7. *See* Campbell v. Seabury Press, 614 F.2d 395, 5 MEDIA L. REP. 2612 (5th Cir. 1980); and Dresbach v. Doubleday, 518 F. Supp. 1285, 7 MEDIA L. REP. 2105 (D.C.D.C. 1981).

terminology, justifies an award of punitive damages, or whether in addition common law malice must be shown.

I. PROSSER'S CRITICS

An example of resistance to the Prosser and *Restatement* classifications of privacy torts can be found in *The Law of Torts* (2nd edition 1986) by Fowler v. Harper, Fleming James, Jr., and Oscar S. Gray. After recognizing the *Restatement*'s wide popularity in privacy invasion tort law, the authors note:

> [The Restatement formulation's] principal drawback is that, as usually presented, it overparticularizes common law developments, reducing them, undesireably in our view, to a misleading semblance of statutory precision. This threatens to stultify common law growth. The potential for further generalization from basic principles may be limited by excessive deference to the specific terms of the Restatement provisions.... The formulation tends to obscure the existence of an underlying privacy concept.... The recognition of such a general principle...has been diluted by the notion that the decisions reflect "not one tort, but a complex of four."[8]

Harper, James, and Gray advocate a different four-way classification: interests in (a) seclusion, (b) personal dignity and self-respect, (c) privacy of name, likeness, and life history, and (d) sentimental associations.[9] The *Restatement* categories cross-cut these four, public disclosure cases potentially touching all four.

Harper, James, and Gray do, however, indirectly acknowledge a class of true-fact privacy invasion cases. They do so in a discussion of *Sidis v. F-R Publishing*[10] and newsworthiness. All of the cases mentioned in this passage are true-facts cases. The authors conclude, "[Stale news interests] rank low on any scale of civilized values, it is submitted, in comparison with the private individual's dignitary interest in avoiding unwanted publicity."[11] With a little adjustment to protect fresh news interests, this would amount to an unconscionability test.

---

8. 2 HARPER, JAMES & GRAY, THE LAW OF TORTS sec. 9.6, n. 3, pp. 633–634 (2d ed. 1986).
9. *Id.* at 635–641.
10. 113 F. 2d 806, 1 MEDIA L. REP. 1775 (1940).
11. *Supra* note 8, at 652.

II. NO FALSITY, NO ACTUAL MALICE

The actual-malice test was developed in defamation law, a field in which truth is a defense. Although the test is usually traced only to the U.S Supreme Court's *Sullivan* decision, it has roots in earlier libel cases. The Supreme Court itself cited *Coleman v. MacLennan*, a 1908 Kansas decision,[12] in its *Sullivan* majority opinion.

The Supreme Court explained in *Sullivan* why it was adding the actual-malice test to libel law. To prevent a chilling effect on journalists, contrary to first amendment intent, it said,[13] it was creating a class of cases in which journalists could publish defamatory falsities and yet not be subject to libel damages. Previously, journalists, like others, were liable for all defamatory falsities. But, with the change made in *Sullivan,* they would not be liable for publications about public officials, except in a narrow class of cases. The actual-malice test, then, singles out a particular type of falsity from others a journalist can get away with; and for this particular type of falsity, it imposes liability. The test, in short, defines an unacceptable falsity.

In the area of public disclosure privacy invasions, by contrast, the central challenge is to define an unacceptable truth. As a result, the actual-malice test is the wrong tool.

Logic, then, dictates that the actual-malice test cannot be introduced into public disclosure cases. But logic has not carried the day. Even in *Modern Tort Law* by James A. Dooley, there appears a comment that the actual-malice concept has been used in public disclosure privacy.[14] For this proposition, *Cox v. Cohn* is cited—but this reader cannot find the support in *Cox*.[15]

Why then has the actual-malice test been brought into the public disclosure area?

One reason is that some persons have regarded the "reckless disregard" language of the test to be its essence. Such persons would regard any test that contains the concept "reckless disregard" to be an actual-malice test, even when the test is not geared to reckless disregard for the truth. The essence of the *Sullivan* actual-malice test, however, as indicated above in terms of its evolution in defamation law, is not reckless disregard, which is a timeless legal concept often captured in the words "gross negligence" and applied to a variety of extreme departures from prudent, thoughtful, or sensitive practices. Instead, the essence of the actual-malice test is one particular kind of

---

12. 78 Kan. 711, 98 P. 281 (1908).
13. 376 U.S. 254 at 277–279.
14. J. DOOLEY, MODERN TORT LAW sec. 35.09, pp. 14–15 (1984 revision of vol. 3 by Barry A. Lindahl).
15. Cox v. Cohn, 420 U.S. 469, 43 L.Ed2d 328 (1975). The Court in *Cox* refers to the actual-malice test in acknowledging that the test applies when a plaintiff claims privacy invasion due to publication of false and misleading information about one's affairs. 43 L.Ed2d at 346.

reckless disregard, namely reckless disregard for the truth. This focus on falsity removes it from the broad category of timeless concepts. It makes it special to defamation law, in which never before had a rule allowed a party to defame another with a falsity and get away with it.

Another reason why actual malice has been brought into public disclosure law is a failure to distinguish clearly between false light privacy invasion and public disclosure privacy invasion. False light invasions caused by publication of falsities turn on the same question as defamation: what is an unacceptable falsity in a statement otherwise protected by free press rights?[16] The actual-malice test is therefore appropriate to these cases. Difficulty in distinguishing these cases from public disclosure cases may stem from recognition, intuitive as well as explicit, that the real but unstated grievance in false light cases is sometimes not the falsity but instead the disclosure. In the famous *Time v. Hill case*,[17] for example, the plaintiffs sued on the basis of fictionalizations in their public portrayal, but it seems likely that they were at least equally upset by the disclosure of the unfictionalized elements in their portrayal. Because dual false light and public disclosure motives can be assumed in plaintiffs no matter what legal theories they actually base their claims on, judges and others may be reluctant to distinguish sharply between the lawsuits. Yet the public disclosure lawsuit has no identity unless the distinction is made.

Another reason for the introduction of actual malice into public disclosure may be that when perfunctorily applied in public disclosure cases, the actual-malice test does not disturb the outcomes even as it muddies the theoretical waters. According to the actual-malice test, no plaintiff can recover damages in a protected area—defined in current libel law as any matter touching the plaintiff if he or she is a public figure, and in current false light privacy invasion law as any matter touching a public issue—unless the defendent lied knowingly or recklessly disregarded the truth. Applied to a public disclosure case, the test means there can be no recovery, period, in a protected area because the offending statement is true and therefore not a lie or the result of reckless disregard for truth.

As a result, the actual-malice test when applied in a public disclosure case simply says that the plaintiff can't win damages when the offending statement is on a legitimate public issue—when false light is the model—or at least when the plaintiff is a public figure —when defamation is the model.

---

16. In a strictly logical taxonomy, false light privacy invasion is an umbrella concept that includes defamation. Such an invasion can be defined as depriving a person of control over his or her public image by means of a falsehood. Defamation is a deprivation of control over a single element of public image, namely reputation, as a result of a falsity. All other deprivations of control due to falsity are false light privacy invasions. Technically, a false positive statement might be such an invasion.
17. 385 U.S. 374 (1967).

This effect neither adds to nor detracts from the public disclosure lawsuit in its *Restatement* form. According to the *Restatement,* a public disclosure is not actionable if it is about a legitimate public issue.[18] In fact, the *Restatement* position on public disclosure privacy invasions can be very simply stated: There can be no recovery for a true statement about a matter of legitimate public interest. When there is no public interest, the *Restatement* calls for consideration of unconscionability.[19]

The importation of actual malice into public disclosure is easy because it is inexpensive—it does not cause much ostensible trouble. But it does cause trouble on a higher level, where it disrupts conceptual clarity, shifting the focus away from unconscionability onto what in these cases is an irrelevancy, damaging the uniqueness of the public disclosure lawsuit, which works best when understood as a special cause of action for a special problem.

In public disclosure cases we are a long way from the land of lying, intentional or accidental. We are in the land of truth, struggling to discern what kind of fault would actually bring liability upon a speaker of truth. It must be a terrible fault. Rules designed to assess falsification must be considered foreign to such a rarified zone. Something different is needed. "Revelations may be so intimate and so unwarranted in view of the victim's position in society as to outrage the community's notions of decency," according to the *Sidis* opinion.[20] "The use of appellant's true name in connection with the incidents of her former life...was unnecessary and indelicate, and a willful and wanton disregard of that charity which should activate us in our social intercourse, and which should keep us from unnecessarily holding another up to the scorn and contempt of upright members of society," wrote the judge in *Melvin v. Reid*.[21]

Actual malice has nothing to do with this problem.

In *Deaton v. Delta Democrat* in 1976, the Mississippi Supreme Court ruled that the U.S. Supreme Court had never said any kind of malice, including knowledge of falsity or reckless disregard of the truth, was an essential element in these cases.[22]

III. RECKLESS DISREGARD

The term "reckless disregard" and its equivalents are regularly used without reference to truth in public disclosure cases and usually need not be read as intended to connect these cases to *Sullivan* actual malice.

---

18. *Supra* note 2.
19. *Id.* The *Restatement* phraseology is "highly offensive to a reasonable person."
20. 113 F.2d 806 at 809, 1 MEDIA L. REP. 1775 at 1777.
21. 297 P. 91 at 93.
22. 326 So.2d 471 (Miss. 1976).

For example, in *Myers v. U.S. Camera,* a New York court said it was grossly negligent and reckless to publish a full body photo of a nude woman revealing her identity without her written consent.[23] In *Briscoe v. Readers Digest,* a California court wrote, "[W]e find it reasonable to require a plaintiff to prove, in each case, that the publisher invaded his privacy with reckless disregard for the fact that reasonable men would find the invasion highly offensive."[24] And in *Melvin,* the phraseology was "...willful and wanton disregard of that charity...."[25] However, a federal court in a later ruling in *Briscoe* wrote, "One may not recover for invasion of privacy if the publication was published in a non-malicious, nonreckless manner,"[26] and cited *Sullivan.*

These references to recklessness not geared to truth are not the actual-malice test. If the phraseology was chosen to be resonant of *Sullivan*—as the explicit citation of *Sullivan* indicates was the intent of the federal court in *Briscoe*—the intent was probably to incorporate, or at least remind of, an element in *Sullivan* deeper than the actual-malice test, namely that the first amendment prohibits chilling impacts on the press. *Melvin,* of course, was decided long before *Sullivan,* but was within the common-law tradition of taking press freedom seriously.[27]

IV. THE SPIRIT OF *SULLIVAN*

While the actual malice test itself does not belong in the public disclosure area, the spirit of the *Sullivan* case does. As a result, citations of *Sullivan* in public disclosure cases are not symbolic citations of the actual-malice test. *Sullivan* belongs in public disclosure cases as a reminder that press freedom has a strong constitutional basis.

In his exhaustive 1976 law review article "Defamation and Privacy Under the First Amendment," Alfred Hill[28] wrote:

> But that aspect of fault known as scienter, which has been the Court's virtually exclusive preoccupation in the defamation cases, and which served as a convenient basis for the decision in *Time v. Hill,* is normally not in issue in privacy cases (apart from the false light category). Typically, the defendant is acting

---

23. 167 N.Y.S.2d 771, 774 (N.Y.C. 1957).
24. 483 P.2d 34, 43–44 (Cal. 1971); 1 Media L. Rep. 1845, 1851–1852.
25. 297 P. 91 at 93.
26. 1 Media L. Rep. 1853, 1854 (C.D. Cal. 1972).
27. Hill, *Defamation and Privacy Under the First Amendment,* 76 Col. L. Rev. 1205 (1976). Hill argued that first amendment concerns have been concerns of the common law all along and that the common law can be relied upon to protect freedom of expression in libel and privacy cases.
28. *Id.*

willfully in the sense that it knows exactly what it is doing in terms of invasion of privacy. The search here is for the kinds of fault that may constitutionally warrant liability in this area.[29]

Later in the article, Hill wrote:

First Amendment issues are very prominent in the privacy area. The fault requirement is basic here, as in defamation, but the Supreme Court's decisions on fault are unhelpful in those common situations in which the defendant knows exactly what it is doing in terms of invasion of privacy. The distinctive types of communicative behavior that may lead to invasion of privacy call for distinctive approaches for resolution of the omnipresent issues of freedom of expression.[30]

Sullivan has a place within Hill's framework to emphasize the prominence of first amendment issues, but not with regard to the scienter with which the Court has been preoccupied in defamation cases.

The Ninth Circuit Court of Appeals conveyed a similar message in the public disclosure case *Virgil v. Time.*[31] The court referred to *Sullivan* in its opinion, saying evidence in the *Virgil* case "must be measured against the standard of *New York Times v. Sullivan.*" The *Virgil* court could not have been referring to the actual-malice test. Its opinion followed closely the Restatement formulation on public disclosure, and focused hard on whether the disclosures pertained to a legitimate public interest, deciding to pass the legitimacy question on to a jury for a finding based on community mores.[32] The opinion did not discuss actual malice, and contained language indicating that to this court, the Sullivan standard meant simply balancing first amendment press rights against the rights claimed by the plaintiff.[33]

V. COMPONENTS OF UNCONSCIONABILITY

Unconscionability, a term rarely used in the cases, embraces terms that regularly do appear in the cases: newsworthiness, community mores, logical nexus, legitimate public interest. It is unfortunate that the word "unconscionability" is not used more often in the cases; it more closely captures the essence of the public disclosure suit than the cooler terms often used.

29. *Id.* at 1255.
30. *Id.* at 1312.
31. 527 F.2d 1122, 1 MEDIA L. REP. 1835.
32. *Id.* at 1128–1130.
33. *Id.* at 1130–1131.

A precise and forceful synopsis of this lawsuit would be: public disclosure of a truth is actionable when it is unconscionable, and unconscionable means unrestrained by conscience, unscrupulous, beyond prudence or reason, excessive, contrary of what one's conscience feels is right, outrageous.[34] Nevertheless, the Restatement's formulation—stating that public disclosure of the truth is actionable when the matter publicized is not of legitimate concern to the public and would be highly offensive to a reasonable person—is equivalent.

The legitimacy of public interest has been a pivot in court discussions of public disclosure. Newsworthiness has often been considered only a component of legitimate public interest,[35] the remainder being made up of first amendment policy considerations and local standards regarding how much exposure a member of society should be required to put up with. Community mores in the colloquial sense are logically part of the legitimacy question. But the term "community mores" has not often been used in the cases, presumably because it has become a term of art referring to the community mores test under which determinations of community standards have been sent to juries in obscenity cases.[36] In public disclosure cases judges have generally preferred to decide the legitimacy question themselves as a matter of law and have avoided "community mores" language. However, the court in *Virgil,* willing to pass the problem along to a jury, used the term community mores.

The logical nexus concept is also tied to legitimacy of public interest. If there is a logical nexus connecting the life of a private person to a proper public issue, then this person must put up with exposure even if he or she has not been directly or intentionally involved in the issue. The logical nexus rule was outlined in 1980 when the Fifth Circuit Court of Appeals said the sister-in-law of a civil rights leader was a legitimate part of a public discussion of the leader. The woman's relationship with the leader's brother affected the relationship of the brothers which affected the leader's public performance, the court said.[37]

The other half of unconscionability by the *Restatement* definition, great offensiveness to a reasonable person, has received less attention in recent cases. In fact, one is tempted to conclude that in the thinking of some judges the two components of the Restatement formulation on public disclosure are really only one, that a finding that public interest was legitimate means there was

34. These definitions are drawn from *American Heritage Dictionary* (2d College Edition 1985), and *Oxford American Dictionary* (1980).
35. The South Carolina Supreme Court said in Hawkins v. Multimedia, 344 S.E.2d 145, *cert. den.* 107 S.Ct. 685 (1986), that public or general interest does not mean mere curiosity, and newsworthiness is not necessarily the test. 344 S.E.2d at 146.
36. Hamling v. U.S., 418 U.S. 87 (1974).
37. 614 F.2d 395.

no offensiveness, and that a finding of no legitimate public interest means a reasonable person would be offended by the disclosure. Only a few examples of offensiveness have appeared in the case literature. The leading ones are in *Melvin v. Reid*,[38] *Barber v. Time*,[39] and *Briscoe v. Readers Digest*.[40]

In *Melvin*, the court ruled that identification of a woman by name in a movie based on her earlier career as a prostitute was, in effect, unconscionable, since six years before the film's release the woman had rehabilitated herself, married, and entered into a circle of acquaintances who knew nothing of her past.

In *Barber*, a court ruled in effect unconscionable a published description, with photograph, of a hospitalized woman with a glandular problem as a starving glutton who ate for ten.

In *Briscoe*, a state court ruled in effect unconscionable a published disclosure of a man's conviction years earlier for truck hijacking, a conviction not known to his children or friends.

A recent example came in the 1986 South Carolina case, *Hawkins v. Multimedia*.[41] In *Hawkins*, a boy indentified in a newspaper article as an unwed, teenaged father won $1,500 in actual damages and $25,000 in punitive damages. The boy's name had been given to the reporter by an unwed, teenaged mother. The reporter did not ask permission to identify the boy as the father or to quote him, but she did talk with him. The state supreme court upheld the verdict. The U.S. Supreme Court denied *certiorari*.

VI. UNIFIED UNCONSCIONABILITY TEST

When used as a test, unconscionability probably should not be split into components, some to be handled as questions of law, others as questions of fact. The most obvious reason for keeping the test unified procedurally is tidiness.

Tradition dictates that unconscionability be handled as a question of law for judges. Newsworthiness, when raised as a defense in privacy invasion lawsuits, has been decided by judges themselves. Similarly, where logical nexus has been recognized as an issue, judges have decided it as a question of law. The breaks in this tradition have been decisions (of which *Virgil v. Time*[42] is the best known) in which courts have given the newsworthiness question to juries. In *Hawkins*,[43] legitimacy of public interest was submitted to the jury

38. 297 P. 91.
39. 159. S.W. 2d 291 (Mo. 1942).
40. 483 P.2d 34.
41. 344 S.E.2d 145, *cert. den.* 107 S.Ct. 658 (S.C. 1986).
42. 527 F.2d 1122.
43. 344. S.E.2d 145.

as a fact question. The state supreme court in *Hawkins* said this was not error;[44] and, as happened after a similar ruling in *Virgil,* the U.S. Supreme Court declined to review the case.[45] The passing on of this question to juries represents an importation into public disclosure cases of a practice developed in obscenity cases; since the early 1970s, determinations of what a reasonable person would regard as prurient have been made by juries applying community mores.[46]

A contrary theme, however, also runs in the U.S. Supreme Court's obscenity cases and was stated in Justice William Brennan's authoritative dissent in *Paris Theatre v. Slaton.*[47] The decision on what is obscene cannot be left to jurors, Brennan said, because jurors, in their zeal, would impose penalties for speech properly protected under the first amendment.[48] A similar theme has been dominant policy in public disclosure cases. Courts have apparently believed that if juries decided newsworthiness, they would in effect be deciding whether a privacy invasion had occurred, and that they would frequently penalize speech that deserved protection. Clearly, an element of condescension infects this reasoning. It is based on the assumption that ordinary people, the kind that make up juries, do not know what is good for them, are apt to destroy their own speech and press freedoms in the emotional heat of a provocative fact situation, and as a result should not be given central questions . However, the assumption has been solidly established in public disclosure cases.

Hill argues in his law review article on privacy and defamation that unconscionability should be handled as question of law.[49] For support, he cites *Monitor Patriot v. Roy,* a 1971 U.S. Supreme Court defamation decision.[50] In the *Monitor* case, a candidate for the U.S. Senate who had been called a "former small-time bootlegger" by a New Hampshire newspaper, sued the newspaper for libel and won $20,000 in the trial court. However, the jury had been allowed to decide whether *New York Times v. Sullivan* principles applied to the case and whether the report on the earlier criminal charge of bootlegging against the candidate was relevant to the campaign coverage. Because of these jury instructions, the Supreme Court reversed the judgment.

The trial judge in *Monitor* instructed the jury that if the publication was in the "private sector," one possible defense for the newspaper would be "justification," which, the judge instructed, would prevail if the jury found

---

44. *Id.* at 146.
45. 527 F.2d 1122, *cert. den.*
46. *See* Miller v. California, 413 U.S. 15 (1973).
47. 413 U.S. 49 (1973).
48. *Id.* at 101–102.
49. *Supra* note 27, at 1205, 1269.
50. 401 U.S. 265 (1971).

that the article was both true and published on a "lawful occasion."[51] The jury was given latitude to base its verdict on "justification" or its absence if it chose, without indicating in the verdict whether this or some alternate basis had been used.

The instruction, then, even though this was a defamation case, allowed the jury to find the defendent liable even if the published fact was true, provided it was not also proper for publication. As a result, the trial judge created for the jury a situation almost identical to those in public disclosure privacy invasion suits.

The Supreme Court's response was:

> A standard of "relevance"..., especially such a standard applied by a jury under the preponderance-of-the-evidence test, is unlikely to be neutral with respect to the content of speech and holds a real danger of becoming an instrument for the suppression of those "vehement, caustic, and sometimes unpleasantly sharp attacks"...which must be protected if the guarantees of the First and Fourteenth Amendments are to prevail.[52]

Hill noted, *"Monitor Patriot v. Roy* strongly suggests that application of the 'unconscionability' standard should be by the court rather than the jury." He also noted this result would be consistent with *Barber,* in which the court ruled that newsworthiness was to be decided as a question of law.[53]

VII. PUNITIVE DAMAGES?

Unconscionability may provide a test that is both workable as a measure of culpability and conceptually compatible with the gravamen of the public disclosure complaint, but it does not solve the problem of when to award punitive damages. In the *Barber v. Time* ruling, so important here because it offers one of the clearest examples of an unconscionable publication, the plaintiff was directed to remit punitive damages awarded by the lower court.[54] The appeals court in *Barber* characterized the publication as a "serious, unreasonable, unwarranted and offensive interference,"[55] but said it nevertheless fell short of being "express malice."[56] The court said: "Certainly the acts of the reporters shown in this case would be sufficient to prove express

---

51. *Id.* at 269 and 269 n.2.
52. *Id.* at 276–277.
53. *Supra* note 27, at 1205, 1269.
54. 159 S.W.2d 291, 296.
55. *Id.* at 295.
56. *Id.* at 296.

malice.... However, it was not shown that these persons had any connection with the defendant or that defendant knew what they had done and no such contention is even made."[57] The material used in the offending *Time* article was from the *New York Daily News* and United Press.

The message of *Barber,* then, is that unconscionability is the proper fault standard for determining compensatory or actual damages, but that punitive damages will be available only upon proof of common law malice, namely animosity, ill-will, wantonness, or intent to victimize.[58] In *Hawkins,* punitive damages were awarded on a finding of common-law malice.[59]

If this structure derived from *Barber* were applied regularly in public disclosure cases, the line-up of fault requirements in the various privacy invasion and defamation lawsuits would be as follows:

- In libel suits by private-person plaintiffs, simple negligence would be required in most jurisdictions for actual and compensatory damages, actual malice for punitive damages.[60]
- In libel suits by public-figure plaintiffs, actual malice would be required for actual and compensatory damages, and also for punitive damages if these were allowed.[61]
- In false light privacy invasion suits decided under the rule currently endorsed by the U.S. Supreme Court, actual malice would be required for any damages if the matter involved were a public issue.[62]
- In false light privacy invasion suits decided under a growing rule as yet not endorsed by the U.S Supreme Court, false light damages would be handled under a persons test just as libel damages are now handled.[63]
- In public disclosure privacy invasion cases, unconscionability would be required for actual and compensatory damages, common-law malice for punitive damages.
- In physical intrusion privacy invasion suits and also in misappropriation suits, no fault showing would be required for actual or compensatory damages; common-law malice would be required for punitive damages.[64]

These fault standards may not make a neat package of the personality-

---

57. *Id.* at 296.
58. *See also* Doe v. Roe, 400 N.Y.S. 2d 668, 679 (Sup. Ct. N.Y.C 1977).
59. 344 S.E.2d 145.
60. Gertz v. Welch, 418 U.S. 323 (1974).
61. *Id.*
62. Time v. Welch, 385 U.S. 374 (1967); *cf.* Arrington v. New York Times, 55 N.Y.2d 433, *cert. denied,* 459 U.S. 1146.
63. Rinsley v. Brandt, 446 F. Supp 850 (D.C. Kan. 1977); Dresbach v. Doubleday, 518 F. Supp. 1285 (D.C.D.C. 1981).
64. Dietemann v. Time, 449 F.2d 245 (9th Cir. 1971); Summit Loans v. Pecola, 288 A.2d 114 (Ct. App. Md. 1972); Zacchini v. Scripps-Howard, 433 U.S. 562 (1977).

damage torts, but at least for most of them—and for the public disclosure tort in particular—they make sense in terms of the specific grievances involved.

Clarification of privacy invasion suits for publication of true facts requires that such suits be regarded as unique, as Prosser suggested. Thinking appropriate to false light privacy suits or defamation suits does not belong in true-facts cases. Unconscionability must be the guiding concept here. It must have a luminescence here comparable to that of *Sullivan* actual malice in false-facts cases, but it cannot be confused with *Sullivan* malice because a true-fact grievance is fundamentally different from a false-facts grievance.

TIM A. PILGRIM

Docudramas and False-Light Invasion of Privacy

Tim A. Pilgrim is a doctoral candidate at the School of Communications of the University of Washington. He is also on leave as the director of the journalism program at North Idaho College.

In 1960, William Prosser noted in his seminal article in the *California Law Review*[1] that privacy as a legal concept in the United States had already evolved into four distinct subcategories—divisions which he incorporated in 1964 into the *Handbook of the Law of Torts*. Those subcategories— privacy appropriation, intrusion, public disclosure of private facts, and non-defamatory falsehood (commonly called false-light invasion of privacy)— have subsequently become accepted legal categories of privacy.[2]

At present, *Restatement (Second) of Torts* indicates that false-light invasion of privacy occurs when the publication or broadcast of some matter concerning a person places the individual before the public in such a way that it meets two criteria: (1) the portrayal is highly offensive to a reasonable person, and (2) the material was published or broadcast with knowledge of its falsity or with reckless disregard as to its falsity.[3]

U.S. Supreme Court recognition of the false-light area came in 1967 when the *Time, Inc. v. Hill*[4] decision provided one of the two basic criteria for false light as it is presently listed in *Restatement*. The court ruled in *Time, Inc.* that the plaintiff in such actions must prove that the portrayal in question demonstrates knowledge of falsity or shows reckless disregard as to the truth.[5]

In American broadcasting, historical roots of a genre of programming known as the docudrama can be traced to early newsreels being produced around the turn of the century, as well as early motion pictures that are based on real people and actual events. Modern examples of the docudrama

1. Prosser, "Privacy," 48 CALIF. L. REV. 383, 383–423 (1960).
2. *Id.*
3. RESTATEMENT (SECOND) OF TORTS 652E (1977) (hereinafter cited as RESTATEMENT).
4. 385 U.S. 374 (1967).
5. *Id.*

range from attempts to dramatize recent events, such as the Atlanta child murders, to efforts to bring historical figures such as Christopher Columbus to life on television, the so-called "bio-vid." The genre involves a merging of "documentary," an objective, factual interpretation of real persons or events, and "drama," which can be defined as a "creative, subjective interpretation of a human situation."[6]

Docudramas can be said to include at least three different program formats: (1) a format that is predominantly fictional (NBC's *Holocaust* and ABC's *The Trial of Lee Harvey Oswald*); (2) a format that is predominantly factual (NBC's *King*, a program about Dr. Martin Luther King, Jr.); and (3) a format that uses fiction to fill large or small gaps left empty by the absence of historical documentation (ABC's *Roots*).[7]

As such formats indicate, the essence of the docudrama is fictionalization of factual material, and when a docudrama is broadcast, it immediately fulfills the second criteria for a successful false-light invasion of privacy suit. The material is presented with the knowledge of its falsity. Indeed, it is the falsity of the program, the adding of fictional elements to the otherwise true story, which makes the docudrama attractive to television producers and audiences. Program-makers can paper over the dull parts of the story with spiced-up dialogue or intriguing relationships.

False-light legal action involving what can be seen loosely as docudramas has been a part of the American legal system since the *Binns v. Vitagraph*[8] decision in 1913. Moreover, beginning as early as the 1906 *Riddle v. MacFadden*[9] case, U.S. legal decisions have been made that have contained in general the qualities of false-light invasion of privacy.

On the surface, it would appear that docudramas would be particularly susceptible to false-light privacy litigation. An individual who believes events in his or her life have been fictionalized or falsified would seemingly seek recovery for invasion of his or her privacy. In addition, the process of intentionally falsifying factual material by fictionally portraying real persons and events would seem to lend itself to the conclusion that the docudrama producer had the requisite "knowledge of falsity" called for by *Restatement*.[10]

However, in the years since the enunciation of the false-light privacy category by Prosser, false-light litigation involving docudramas have been based on defamation, as well as on other privacy claims (i.e., the publication of private facts).[11] Such a discrepancy is unusual, and the lack of clarity concerning the relationship between docudramas and false-light invasion of

---

6. McKerns. "Television Docudramas: The Image as History," 7 Journalism History 24 (1980).
7. *Id.* at 3.
8. 103 N.E. 1108 (N.Y. Ct. App. 1913).
9. 101 N.Y.S. 606 (Sup. Ct. 1906).
10. Restatement, *supra* note 3.
11. *Id.*

privacy is puzzling, because docudramas are increasingly becoming a staple of network television programming.

In exploring this disparity, it is desirable to examine briefly the history of false-light invasion of privacy, the history of docudrama, and the various underpinnings and intersections. By including a tangential examination of current television network policies concerning the production of docudramas, additional knowledge will allow determination as to whether network policies are so comprehensive that they adequately protect the networks from false-light privacy suits.

Evaluation of such research allows the formation of some preliminary conclusions about the relationship between false light and docudramas, as well as about why defamation is often the action of choice when docudramas are involved.

I. EVOLUTION OF FALSE LIGHT

The legal origin of the false-light tort can be traced to 1816 in England when Lord Byron succeeded in enjoining the circulation of a poem being attributed to him that was considered to be degrading and inferior.[12] In the United States, false light can be traced to court actions just after the turn of the century.

In 1906, the New York Supreme Court Appellate Division ruled in *Riddle* that Felicite Riddle had a cause of action under the New York Civil Rights Law of 1903. Ms. Riddle had hired a photographer to take her picture, a photo which was supposed to be limited to her personal use. However, the defendants used the photo to advertise a book, *New Hair Culture*, and Riddle sued, claiming that her picture had been used without consent for trade purposes. She successfully claimed that the photograph was used to mislead the public into believing that the defendants had treated her hair in the manner cited in the book.[13]

Another early action with false-light qualities can be seen in *Binns*. In 1909, two steamships, Republic and Florida, collided at sea. The Republic was equipped with an early version of wireless telegraphy equipment, and John Binns, who was the telegrapher, communicated with the steamship Baltic and with a telegrapher on Nantucket Island.[14]

Because of the messages sent by Binns, the Baltic was able to rescue hundreds of passengers and crew and transport them safely to New York. It was the first such rescue made possible by use of the wireless. Soon after, Vitagraph Company of America produced a series of photographs that depicted the incident. In the photos, Vitagraph used settings and actors to

12. Lord Byron v. Johnston, 2 Mer. 29, 35 Eng. Rep. 851 (1816).
13. 101 N.Y.S. 606.
14. 103 N.E. 1108 at 1109.

recreate the rescue, and one of the actors portrayed Binns, whose name was used without his consent. Moving pictures with subtitles were prepared from the pictorial series and were exhibited throughout New York, which prompted Binns to seek an injunction and ask for damages.[15]

The Court of Appeals of New York noted that the news value of the pictures of Binns had passed. Further, the decision said the pictures involved a false portrayal of Binns and were used by the defendant for profit, contrary to the prohibition of the New York 1903 privacy statute.[16] That New York law deals mainly with appropriation and permits recovery by a plaintiff if his or her name, portrait, or picture is used for advertising or trade purposes without prior written consent.[17] In ruling the portrayal of Binns to be "a product of the imagination," the courts said the plaintiff was not merely the victim of appropriation, but, in effect, had been cast in a false light—one of the first rulings dealing with false light through fictionalization.[18]

In both cases, although the incidents are dissimilar, the plaintiffs are portrayed in a manner that is not accurate—that is, in a manner which paints a false picture of the plaintiff's life or habits. In *Riddle*, Ms. Riddle had been portrayed as one who had her hair treated by the product her picture seems to advertise. In *Binns*, the plaintiff's name and role as ship telegrapher had been taken over by an actor in the fictional recreation of the dramatic sea rescue. Neither portrayal was accurate.

In addition, these two cases share an intent to fictionalize—or what can be seen as a conscious decision on the part of the defendant to represent the plaintiff in a fictitious manner. In *Riddle*, the defendants consciously decided to appropriate the Riddle picture and to portray her in a manner that suggested she treated her hair in a way that she in fact did not.[19] In *Binns*, the fictionalization is even more obvious, because the defendants intentionally used the plaintiff's name and part in the sea rescue to create their own fictional version of the event.[20]

A. The Middle Years

False-light qualities can be seen in a number of cases in the years between the *Binns* case and the tort's first inclusion of false light as a branch of privacy. The 1931 *Melvin v. Reid*[21] resulted from a false portrayal of the plaintiff, a woman who in her youth had been a prostitute and who was tried in a sensational murder trial and then acquitted. As a happily married

---

15. Binns v. Vitagraph Co. of America, 124 N.Y.S. 515 (Sup. Ct. 1910).
16. 103 N.E. 1108 at 1110.
17. N.Y. Civil Rights Law, art. 5, § 50, 51 (McKinney, 1976).
18. 103 N.E. 1108 at 1110.
19. 101 N.Y.S. 606.
20. 103 N.E. 1108.
21. 297 P. 91 (Cal. Dist. Ct. App. 1931).

woman, she sued the defendant after the defendant produced and exhibited *The Red Kimono*, a motion picture about her earlier life.[22] Although the court based its decision on Melvin's constitutional right to pursue and obtain happiness, not on invasion of privacy, it also ruled that in the context of her new and respectable life as a married woman, the movie served to cast Melvin in a false light.[23]

Subsequent court actions that are based on false portrayals include the 1939 *Mau v. Rio Grande Oil, Inc.*[24] decision (story of man shot and wounded during hold-up recreated including use of name without consent on radio program, *Calling All Cars*);[25] the 1941 *Hinish v. Meier & Frank Co.*[26] case (state employee's name used without his permission for political endorsement);[27] the 1942 *Kerby v. Hal Roach Studios*[28] decision (former actress/singer name used without permission as signature to 1,000 seductive letters mailed to men as part of movie promotion);[29] and the 1944 *Cason v. Baskin*[30] decision (woman portrayed favorably for most part in a novel but not identified by name).[31]

A slightly different version of false light resulted in the 1948 *Peay v. Curtis Pub. Co.*[32] decision, a ruling stemming from an instance in which an unrelated photograph of a cab driver was used to illustrate an article in *Saturday Evening Post* about taxi drivers and their tendencies to cheat patrons. In ruling on the action for libel and slander, as well as false-light privacy, the court did not focus directly on the false portrayal of Muriel M. Peay but instead based the refusal to grant summary judgment for the magazine on a right of privacy enjoyed by private persons.[33]

Three years later, the third U.S. Circuit Court ruled in *Leverton v. Curtis Publishing Co.*[34] that Eleanor Leverton's privacy had been invaded a decade after she had been in the news as a 10-year-old accident victim. An old photo of Leverton, who had nearly been killed in the accident caused by a careless driver, was used to illustrate an article on the dangers posed by careless pedestrians.[35] The ruling noted that the use of the picture had

22. *Id.*
23. *Id.*
24. 28 F. Supp. 845 (N.D. Cal. 1939).
25. *Id.* at 846.
26. 113 P.2d 438 (Or. Sup. Ct. 1941).
27. *Id.*
28. 127 P.2d 577 (Cal. Dist. Ct. App. 1942).
29. *Id.*
30. 20 So.2d 243 (Fla. Sup. Ct. 1944).
31. *Id.*
32. 78 F. Supp. 305 (D.D.C. 1948).
33. *Id.*
34. 192 F.2d 974 (3d Cir. 1951).
35. *Id.*

nothing to do with Leverton's accident, that it misrepresented the facts, and that it was an example of "garnishment and embellishment."[36]

Other early 1950s decisions with false-light qualities include *Garner v. Triangle Publications, Inc.*[37] (detective magazine article about husband and wife whose murder conviction was later reversed);[38] *Gill v. Curtis Pub. Co.*[39] (use of photo, caption, and story of husband and wife implying they were married because of sexual attraction);[40] and *Metzger v. Dell Publishing Co., Inc.*[41] (unrelated photograph used to illustrate magazine article on the conditions which created gang activity in Brooklyn).[42]

In 1958, a California U.S. District Court ruled in *Strickler v. NBC*[43] that NBC's inaccurate and dramatized portrayal of Kenneth Strickler during a plane crash and subsequent rescue, gave him a cause of action. Strickler, a Navy commander, had been a passenger on a commercial airliner that developed engine trouble and had to make an emergency landing at sea. He claimed that the telecast portrayed him in a false light when it repeatedly showed him smoking a pipe and cigarettes and wearing a Hawaiian shirt instead of his Navy uniform. Strickler also objected to NBC's failure to depict his part in helping to evacuate those aboard the airliner.[44]

About a year before Prosser's article outlining the four categories of privacy, the Pennsylvania Supreme Court ruled in *Aquino v. Bulletin*[45] that falsehoods destroyed newsworthiness in an action resulting from an article about a young girl's marriage and annulment. The girl's parents successfully claimed that exaggerations in the article were "embellished and fictionized."[46]

B. The Prosser Connection

In examining the evolution of false-light invasion of privacy, it is also important to note that William Prosser, who was dean of the law school at the University of California, did not suddenly concoct false-light invasion of privacy in 1960 when he published "Privacy."[47] Undoubtedly, however, his role of reporting on privacy influenced the development of the tort. Both the 1941 and 1955 editions of Prosser's *Handbook of the Law of Torts*, which were quite widely used by attorneys and judges, discussed—in terms akin to false light—privacy cases which would be among those on which

36. *Id.* at 978.
37. 97 F. Supp. 546 (S.D.N.Y. 1951).
38. *Id.*
39. 239 P.2d 630, 632 (Cal. Sup. Ct. 1952).
40. *Id.*
41. 136 N.Y.S.2d 888 (Sup. Ct. 1955).
42. *Id.*
43. 167 F. Supp. 68 (S.D. Cal. 1958).
44. *Id.*
45. 154 A.2d 422, 427 (Pa. Super. Ct. 1959).
46. *Id.*
47. Prosser, *supra* note 1.

the category was based in "Privacy" and in the 1964 edition of *The Handbook of the Law of Torts*.

In the 1941 edition, Prosser asserted the existence of a cause of action in publicity which violates ordinary decencies. This assertion, although it embodies the first hints of the false-light subcategory, tended to be largely based on litigation that involves unreasonable publicity given to a person's private life, another accepted subcategory of privacy.[48] Prosser cited both *Melvin*[49] and *Mau*[50] as support of this category, but he also cited cases that have little to do with false light. These cases include one involving publication of a photo of a plaintiff's deformed child,[51] one involving a stolen picture of plaintiff in connection with a report of an attempted double suicide,[52] and one involving a plaintiff's picture that had been included in a rogue's gallery before he had been convicted.[53]

However, in the 1955 edition of the *Handbook of the Law of Torts*, Prosser gave the false-light division a boost toward its formal establishment. Calling it a form that had made a "rather amorphous appearance in several cases," Prosser dealt with false light separately from publication of private facts.[54] He said the division "apparently consists of putting the plaintiff in a false but not necessarily defamatory position in the public eye. . . ."[55] In writing of intrusion, publication of private facts, and false light together, Prosser observed:

> It is obvious that all three of these torts are primarily concerned with the protection of a mental interest, and that they are only a phase of the larger problem of the protection of peace of mind against unreasonable disturbance. . . . As in other cases of mental disturbance, the tendency is still to find some other basis of liability, such as defamation, a breach of an express or an implied contract, or the invasion of some property right, upon which to base the action. There remains, however, a large and growing field in which privacy becomes important because no other remedy is available.[56]

48. W. PROSSER, HANDBOOK OF THE LAW OF TORTS 1055–56 (1941).
49. 297 P. 91.
50. 28 F. Supp. 845.
51. Douglas v. Stokes, 149 S.W. 489 (Ky. Ct. App. 1912). *See also* Bazemore v. Savannah Hospital, 155 S.E. 194 (Ga. Sup. Ct. 1930) as a case where photos were obtained in breach of confidence.
52. Peed v. Washington Times, 55 WASH L. REP. 182 (D.C. Sup. Ct. 1927).
53. Itzkovitch v. Whitaker, 39 So. 499 (La. Sup. Ct. 1905).
54. W. PROSSER, HANDBOOK OF THE LAW OF TORTS 638 (2d. ed. 1955).
55. *Id.* at 638.
56. *Id.* at 639 (notes omitted).

To support the 1955 edition, Prosser listed *Hinish* (signing plaintiff's name to a public telegram),[57] *Kerby* (signing plaintiff's name to letter),[58] *Leverton* (attributing to plaintiff views he/she does not hold),[59] and *Itzkovitch* (including plaintiff's picture in a rogue's gallery after his/her acquittal),[60] while also citing *Marks v. Jaffa*,[61] an 1893 case in which the plaintiff was entered unknowingly in an embarrassing popularity contest.[62]

By 1960 Prosser had refined his classification of the four subcategories of privacy. He asserted in "Privacy" that false-light cases differ from those of disclosure of private facts or intrusion.[63] He noted that only recently had it begun to receive independent recognition.[64] Prosser wrote:

> The principle frequently, over a good many years, has made a rather nebulous appearance in a line of decisions in which falsity or fiction has been held to defeat the privilege of reporting news and other matters of public interest, or of giving further publicity to already public figures.[65]

Both the element of false portrayal and that of intent to fictionalize—elements seen in the early cases of *Riddle* and *Binns*—are referred to in the phrase "falsity or fiction." However, by using "or," Prosser noted that the two elements may not have equal weight in false-light cases. One or the other may dominate and thus expand the boundary for the types of cases ultimately considered to be false-light actions. This inequality is a factor in the evolution of the tort and contributes to its schizoid nature.

In the 1964 *Handbook of the Law of Torts*, Prosser transferred most of the false light in the public eye category from his 1960 article with very few alterations. In *Torts*, as he had in "Privacy," Prosser said that false-light action generally takes three forms:

1. publicly attributing opinion or utterance to the plaintiff
2. using the plaintiff's picture to illustrate an article or book with which the plaintiff had no reasonable connection (with the implication that such a connection exists)

57. 113 P.2d 438.
58. 127 P.2d 577.
59. 192 F.2d 974.
60. 39 So. 499.
61. 26 N.Y.S. 908 (Super Ct. 1893).
62. *Id.*
63. Prosser, *supra* note 1, at 400.
64. *Id.* at 398.
65. *Id.* at 398 (notes omitted).

3. including the plaintiff's photo, name, or fingerprints in a public "rogue's gallery" of convicted criminals when there has not been a conviction.[66]

In addition, Prosser reiterated that the false light need not be defamatory, although it very often is. Among other cases, he cited *Bennett v. Norban*,[67] a 1959 action in which the plaintiff suffered public accusation of theft,[68] and *Martin v. Johnson Publishing Co.*,[69] a 1956 action in which a New York justice found that the use of the plaintiff's photo with a lurid story entitled "Man Hungry" libeled her and invaded her privacy.[70]

Carlisle v. Fawcett Publications, Inc.[71] is one of the first actions to refer to false-light invasion of privacy as proposed by Prosser. The ruling denied a libel and privacy action based on the division as outlined by Prosser.[72] However, since acceptance of the four subcategories of privacy, the number of false-light actions has increased rapidly, with forty-eight cases occurring between 1964 and 1974.[73] An additional ninety-four have been recorded by various appeals court case reporters between 1974 and 1988.[74]

C. Time for *Time Inc.*

Such mushrooming of the tort is due partially to the *Time, Inc.* decision, which brought the U.S. Supreme Court into the false-light arena. The decision stemmed from an incident in 1952 when James Hill and his family were held hostage for nineteen hours by three escaped convicts, who released the family unharmed. The convicts were later cornered, and two of them died in a gun battle with law enforcement officials.[75] The incident received wide media coverage, and a year later, Random House published a novel (later made into a play and a motion picture) by Joseph Hayes.[76]

When the play was being produced in Philadelphia, *Life* magazine sent the cast to the former Hill home for a photo session and in 1955 published "True Crime Inspires Tense Play," which prompted Hill to sue for invasion

---

66. W. PROSSER, HANDBOOK OF THE LAW OF TORTS 837–38 (3d. ed. 1964).
67. 151 A.2d 476 (Pa. Sup. Ct. 1959).
68. *Id.*
69. 157 N.Y.S.2d 409 (Sup. Ct. 1956).
70. *Id.*
71. 20 Cal. Rptr. 405 (D. Ct. Ap. 1962).
72. *Id.*
73. Susan Elizabeth Nessler, False Light Privacy and the Press: An Analysis of Selected Cases, 1960–1974 (1976) (unpublished thesis available from Indiana University).
74. Tim Alfred Pilgrim, Docudramas and False Light Invasion of Privacy: An Inquiry into the Scarcity of Legal Intersections (1987) (unpublished thesis available from the University of Washington). The number of false-light actions cited has been updated to include those reported through mid-January, 1988.
75. 385 U.S. 374 at 374.
76. *Id.*

of privacy on the argument that inaccuracies in the article amounted to fictionalization.[77] After eleven years of litigation, the U.S. Supreme Court ruled that the Hills were public figures and had to prove that the editors of *Life* had knowledge of falsity or had acted in reckless disregard as to the falsity when the photo-story was published.[78]

In a second false-light decision, the U.S. Supreme Court ruled in *Cantrell v. Forest City Publishing Co.*[79] in 1974 that Margaret Cantrell could recover damages after the defendant's newspaper published knowing or reckless falsehoods about the Cantrell family in an article about the impact upon the family of the death of the father in a bridge collapse. Besides containing several inaccuracies and false statements, the story gave the false impression that the reporter had interviewed the mother for the story, when, in fact, he had not.[80]

In recent years, cases that have been decided in the false-light area follow the refinements offered by the American Law Institute under 652E, "Publicity Placing Person in False Light" in *Restatement*.[81] Widely used by attorneys and judges, *Restatement* presents the general common law, including law developed by judicial decision, as well as that evolving from application of statutes by the courts. It is here in a section prepared by Prosser that the current understanding of false light is summarized:

> One who gives publicity to a matter concerning another that places the other before the public in a false light is subject to liability to the other for invasion of his privacy, if
> (a) the false light in which the other was placed would be highly offensive to a reasonable person, and
> (b) the actor had knowledge of or acted in reckless disregard as to the falsity of the publicized matter and the false light in which the other would be placed.[82]

Restatement indicates that false light is contingent on the published material being false—a requirement quite similar to the element of false portrayal noted above. In terms of its relation to defamation, false light protects the interest of the individual in not being cast publicly in an objectionable false light or false position. Many times publicity is defamatory, so plaintiffs can proceed upon either false light or defamation, or both, but can have only one recovery for a single instance of publicity. Damage to reputation—or defamation—is not necessary. It is sufficient that plaintiffs

77. *Id.*
78. *Id.* at 374.
79. 95 S. Ct. 465 (1974).
80. *Id.*
81. RESTATEMENT, *supra* note 3.
82. *Id.*

are given "unreasonable and highly objectionable publicity" that attributes to them conduct, characteristics, or beliefs that are false.[83]

Restatement notes that publicity given the plaintiff must be of a highly offensive nature if he or she is to be cast in a false light.[84] Privacy is not invaded, the institute maintains, when unimportant false statements are made, even if they are made deliberately; instead, major misrepresentation of character, history, activities, or beliefs—misrepresentations that result in plaintiffs as reasonable people being seriously offended—bring about a cause of action.[85]

D. A Division for False Light

Actions concerning false light have, thus, been present since the early part of the century and are now an accepted subcategory of the privacy tort. However, the subcategory of false light lends itself more readily to two further subdivisions: 1) those that deal with some newsworthy event or issue in which a person is inadvertently cast in a false light, and 2) those that deal with some event or issue in which fictionalization is involved.

Examples of inadvertent false-light litigation include the use of a photo of an innocent person to illustrate a story on an unrelated subject (i.e., using a photo of any cab driver as artwork in an article on cab driver corruption—*Peay*),[86] or it can involve a situation in which an auto-pedestrian accident victim is portrayed as having caused the accident when, in reality, the auto that struck her had run a red light (*Leverton*).[87]

Such inadvertent false-light actions closely mirror defamation actions. In fact, such false-light actions often appear to have more in common with defamation than with privacy, especially when compared to the other three privacy subcategories—instrusion, appropriation, and public disclosure of private facts. Discussion of the similarities in *Restatement* attempts to address this overlap. This kind of false-light action, it seems, would be better categorized as libel because it usually deals more with publicity—placing people in the public view but in a false manner. However, inadvertent false-light actions are largely unrelated to docudramas.

---

83. *Id.*
84. *Id.*
85. *Id.*
86. 78 F. Supp. 305. *But see* Arrington v. New York Times, 433 N.Y.S.2d 164 (Sup. Ct. 1980); *aff'd, modified*, 449 N.Y.S.2d 941 (Ct. App. 1982), in which a newspaper's unauthorized publication on the cover of a plaintiff's photograph to illustrate an article on upward mobility by the black middle class was ruled not to be so highly offensive as to give rise to a cause of action for false-light invasion of privacy. However, in a dissenting opinion, Judge J. P. Kupferman argued that the plaintiff should be able to plead such a cause of action.
87. 192 F.2d 974.

The second type of false-light action does have relevance for docudramas. These center around incidents that embody both false portrayal and a much more vigorous intent to fictionalize. This type of action can be a feature story embellished with fictional dialogue (*Aquino*),[88] although it does not always result in a successful litigation, or it can be a situation in which a real person is the basis for a person in a work of fiction (*Strickler*).[89] In addition, it can involve a dramatic recreation of an incident similar to the one cited in *Binns* or *Time, Inc.*, in which the real person being portrayed is placed in fictitious situations or given false actions or dialogue.[90]

It is in this second type of false light action—the type that has not only the element of false portrayal but also a clear-cut intent to fictionalize—that litigation concerning docudramas would seem to fit most easily. Indeed, some court actions based on the privacy tort have, over the years, involved fictionalization in film and television. In such actions, the results have been mixed.

In 1935, a New York Supreme Court, Appellate Division, affirmed the findings but reduced the damages of a lower court, which awarded damages to Sidney Franklin, an American bullfighter about whom newsreel shots had been included without his permission in a Columbia Pictures short subject movie called *Throwing the Bull*. Justice Glennon wrote in *Franklin v. Columbia Pictures Corporation*[91] that the lower court's decision allowing Franklin to recover for three actions—privacy, libel, and slander—was a technicality that ought not to be altered.[92] The decision noted: "It is undoubtedly true that respondent could have obtained all the damages he suffered in a cause of action based solely upon a violation of his civil rights [privacy]."[93]

In 1944, *Levey v. Warner Bros. Pictures, Inc.*[94] involved a complaint by Ethel Levey that *Yankee Doodle Dandy*, a fictional biographic presentation of her one-time husband, George M. Cohan, invaded her privacy. Although the suit is largely one involving appropriation, it has false-light qualities in that the ruling asserts that Levey was not identified by name or sufficiently in any other way to have suffered invasion of privacy.[95]

In a 1952 action, a California District Court of Appeals affirmed a lower court ruling in *Stryker v. Republic Pictures Corporation*,[96] which denied a privacy claim by a former U.S. Marine. In the case, Louis Stryker,

---

88. 154 A.2d 422.
89. 167 F. Supp. 68.
90. *See, e.g., Binns*, 103 N.E. 1108, and *Time, Inc.*, 385 U.S. 374.
91. 284 N.Y.S. 96 (Sup. Ct. 1935). *See also* Nizer, "The Right of Privacy: A Half Century's Developments," 39 MICH. L. REV. 526, 546 n.63 (1941).
92. *Id.*
93. 284 N.Y.S. 96, at 97.
94. 57 F. Supp. 40.
95. *Id.*
96. Stryker v. Republic Pictures Corporation, 238 P.2d 670 (Cal. Dist. Ct. App. 1952).

who had been portrayed fictionally in a positive way as war hero in *Sands of Iwo Jima*, failed to state adequately a cause of action.[97]

E. Enter Television

In 1955, NBC was granted a summary judgment in *Bernstein v. NBC*[98] from a claim of invasion of privacy by a man who had been convicted of first-degree murder, sentenced to death, but pardoned several years before NBC produced a *Big Story* television episode fictionalizing his ordeal but not using his name.[99]

Another case resulting from a *Big Story* episode that was a dramatic re-enactment of a bank robbery committed by William Miller also was dismissed by a U.S. District Court judge in *Miller v. NBC*[100] in 1957. As in the Bernstein dramatization, NBC fictionalized an incident that had been widely publicized but that did not use the plaintiff's name in the dramatization.[101]

In *Youssoupoff v. Columbia Broadcasting System Inc.*,[102] stemming from the 1963 CBS television motion picture, *If I Should Die*, the court ruled that sufficient evidence existed to submit the case to a jury to determine the issues of fact. Prince Felix Youssoupoff, a man who as a member of the former Russian royal family had murdered the monk Rasputin, successfully claimed in the case that the motion picture about the event did not accurately depict his motivation in the murder, his relationship with the Princess Irina, or dialog at the time of the assassination.[103]

In a 1969 privacy and defamation action, *DeSalvo v. Twentieth Century-Fox Film Corporation*,[104] a U.S. District Court judge ruled in Massachusetts that a film about Albert DeSalvo, known as the Boston Strangler, could not be restricted from release.[105] DeSalvo had earlier signed an agreement allowing the release of his story, but changed his mind and tried to prevent the release. The court ruled that because of the extreme amount of publicity in the case, DeSalvo's attorneys needed to show that the strangler's portrayal was "knowingly false or falsely made with reckless disregard for the truth."[106]

A case decided by the Supreme Court of Illinois in 1970 upheld a lower court ruling which said that a book and motion picture were reasonably

97. *Id.*
98. 29 F. Supp. 817 (D.D.C. 1955).
99. *Id.*
100. 157 F. Supp. 240 (D. Del. 1957).
101. *Id.*
102. 244 N.Y.S.2d 1 (Sup. Ct. 1963); *aff'd*, 244 N.Y.S.2d 701 (Sup. Ct. 1963); 265 N.Y.S.2d 754 (Sup. Ct. 1965).
103. *Id.*
104. 300 F. Supp. 742 (D. Mass. 1969).
105. *Id.*
106. *Id.* at 742.

comparable to the facts of public record surrounding the infamous murder and kidnapping of a 14-year-old boy by Richard Loeb and Nathan Leopold, who were attempting to commit the perfect crime. In *Leopold v. Levin*,[107] the court openly recognized that the novel and movie titled *Compulsion* were based on the notorious crime by Leopold and Loeb, although their names were not used in the works but were used in related advertising. Justice Ward maintained that the two works sufficiently fictionalized Leopold's portrayal so that it would not outrage a community's sense of decency.[108]

II. EVOLUTION OF THE AMERICAN DOCUDRAMA

The term, "docudrama," summons to mind a broadcast genre associated largely with television. Programs such as *King* (Martin Luther King, Jr.), *Young Joe: The Forgotten Kennedy*, and *The Atlanta Child Murders* seem to fit the format. Moreover, the docudrama genre appears, on the surface, to be a relatively recent development, perhaps taking shape only two decades ago. However, additional research suggests that the genre has historical roots—roots which run much deeper.

If studied in a broad context, the earliest beginnings of docudrama could probably be traced in literature to Shakespeare and many of his historically based plays, such as *Henry IV* and *Richard II*. Perhaps, as some scholars suggest, the history goes back further to the story of the Trojan War as related in *Trojan Women* by Euripides.[109] Even Homer's *Iliad* might be interpreted as a fictionalized account of the Trojan War, and perhaps the Old English retelling of the heroic slaying of Grendel in *Beowulf* could also be seen as an early influence on the docudrama. However, it is sufficient here to acknowledge that much fiction has been based on real events and on the people involved in those events. Such a practice has been a long-standing part of oral and print literary traditions.

A solid definition of docudrama is somewhat elusive. Some scholars suggest that it is a format which "openly mixes" fact and fiction.[110] Others say it is drama based on real people and actual events.[111] Some say it is a format that uses real people (rulers, presidents, celebrities, etc.) as central characters to enhance and lend credibility to fictionalized events.[112] Still others maintain it is a genre attempting to educate viewers in the facts and

---

107. 259 N.E.2d 250 (Ill. Sup. Ct. 1970).
108. *Id.*
109. Salerno, "Politics, the Media and the Drama," 1 J. AM. CULTURE 189, 189 (1978).
110. B. CARTER, M. FRANKLIN, & J. WRIGHT, THE FIRST AMENDMENT AND THE FIFTH ESTATE: REGULATION OF ELECTRONIC MASS MEDIA 515 (1986).
111. Rintels, "In Defense of the Television 'Docu-Drama,'" N.Y. Times, April 22, 1979, at § 2, 1, col. 6.
112. Kovner, "The Great Docudrama Controversy—Elizabeth Taylor and ABC," 1 COM. LAWYER 1, 1 (1983).

events of history.[113] And, more skeptical observers see it as "slickly confected hybrids of fact and fancy."[114]

It is at least safe to say, however, that docudramas are presented to audiences under a guise of being historical offerings. Docudramas blend fiction and fact in an entertaining, dramatic format. At its foundation, the genre merges the terms "documentary" and "drama." "Documentary" can be called an objective, factual interpretation of real persons or events presented through broadcast media, and "drama" can be termed a subjective, creative interpretation of a human situation.[115]

However, the merging of these two terms into one has not resulted in only one, easily identifiable format. Instead, as the genre has evolved, major characteristics of each of the root terms have surfaced in a variety of forms that vary in the amount of fictionalization involved. Thus, docudrama has become a term describing at least three different program formats.[116]

The first is a presentation that is predominantly fictional, although it uses a well-known event or person as a springboard to create interest. One example of this is NBC's 1978 miniseries, *Holocaust*, a program about two fictional families, one German and one Jewish, set in the context of the Nazi attempt to exterminate the Jews.[117]

Another example is the NBC production of *The Court-martial of George Armstrong Custer*, a program dealing with what might have happened if Custer, a flamboyant Army general killed by the Sioux, had survived the Battle of the Little Bighorn in 1876. The only indication viewers were given that the program was not historical was a message flashed briefly on the screen at the conclusion of the film stating that the program was a work of fiction.[118]

A second format is that which uses much fiction—although less than the category above—to fill gaps left empty by the absence of historical documentation. ABC's *Roots*, which was broadcast by ABC in January 1977, is an example of such a format. Even Alex Haley, whose family beginnings *Roots* purported to trace, described the program as "faction," a term combining "fact" and "fiction."[119] Another example, ABC's *Young Joe: The Forgotten Kennedy*, is based quite loosely on Hank Searls's book, *The Lost Prince*, a work about John F. Kennedy's brother, Joseph Jr., who was

---

113. Harris, "Docudramas Unmasked," TV GUIDE, March 4, 1978, at 6.
114. Waters, "Recipe for Paranoia," NEWSWEEK, Oct. 3, 1977, at 64.
115. McKerns, *supra* note 6, at 24. For discussions of docudrama in relation to the right of publicity—not false light—*see* Manson, *The Television Docudrama and the Right of Publicity*, 7 COM. & THE LAW 41 (Feb. 1985) and Lawrence, *Television and the Right of Publicity: Too Bad Liz, That's Show Biz*, 8 COM./ENT L.J. 257 (Winter 1986).
116. *Id.* at 24–25, 40.
117. Waters, "'Holocaust' Fallout," NEWSWEEK, May 1, 1978, at 72.
118. Harris, *supra* note 113, at 9.
119. McKerns, *supra* note 6, at 24. *See* Kaplan, "Roots Under Attack," 1 COM. & LAW (Spring 1979).

killed in World War II. The fiction incorporated in the docudrama falsely depicted Joe Kennedy as a fun-lover who played tricks on John Kennedy, stole his girlfriend, and volunteered for dangerous missions in a semisuicidal effort to become a hero.[120]

A third type of docudrama is even less a work of fiction and relies more heavily on factual information. In such a docudrama, fictionalization is present, but its quantity and use vary from production to production. Such productions attempt to re-enact actual events and fill in with fictional material as needed. The difference between this type of docudrama and the "faction" of the second type centers on the more strict adherence to factual re-enactment in this third category. NBC's *King*, a 1978 program about Dr. Martin Luther King, Jr. that even included some actual news film footage, is one example.[121] CBS's *The Defection of Simas Kudirka*, a depiction of a Lithuanian seaman's attempt to defect to a Coast Guard ship from a Soviet trawler, is another.[122] ABC's *Friendly Fire*, a program based on C.D.B. Bryan's investigation of the accidental death in Vietnam of an American soldier, also qualifies for this category.[123]

A. The Docudrama-Newsreel Connection

Beginnings of docudrama in American broadcast media can be traced to the years just prior to the turn of the century. Early newsreel films first appearing in the 1890s provide the early fact/fiction connection, for they often re-enacted news events or faked them in some way. During the 1894 to 1900 period, nearly every major film producer faked some news film as a matter of common practice. The first fake film was the newsreel of the 1894 Corbett-Courtney fight, which was arranged specifically for the news-film camera. The fight is said to have included prearranged incidents in each round, as well as a preordained denouement.[124]

Among other faked events in the pre-1900 period were the sinking of the Maine in 1898 and the Jeffries-Sharkey, Corbett-Jeffries, Fitzsimmons-Jeffries, Jeffries-Ruhlin, Kid McCoy-Maher, and Palmer-McGovern prize fights of 1899.[125] One particularly ambitious faked film was one of the Battle of Santiago Bay in 1898, which was recreated by both Vitagraph and by Edwin H. Amet. Amet's project made the Vitagraph production look amateurish, for Amet recreated Santiago Bay in a tub and used highly detailed model ships, as well as electrically controlled devices to create waves and

120. Harris, *supra* note 113, at 8.
121. McKerns, *supra* note 6, at 24.
122. *Id.* at 25.
123. A. McNeil, Total Television: A Comprehensive Guide to Programming from 1948 to the Present 770 (2d. ed. 1984).
124. R. Fielding, The American Newsreel 1911–67 at 38 (1972).
125. *Id.* at 38–40.

move the ships and guns. Some motion picture histories apparently tell of the Spanish government in Madrid purchasing a print of Amet's film because it believed the newsreel to be authentic.[126]

Newsreel fakery was not only widespread, but it also was widely erratic in its application—variation that creates a four-category spectrum of faked news films. Embodying similarities to the divisions of the docudrama, turn-of-the-century newsreels included:

1. Theatrically staged re-creations of famous events, based roughly upon the original but not intended or likely to fool audiences.
2. Realistically staged re-creations of famous events, based upon reliable information and duplicating insofar as possible the location, participants, and circumstances of the original. These films were generally made to deceive audiences.
3. Rough re-creations of famous events, made without attempting to duplicate known particulars of the events. These films were also generally designed to deceive audiences.
4. Outright manufacture of unverifiable activities alleged to have been associated with famous events—always intended to deceive audiences.[127]

The newsreel telling of the sinking of the Maine was not intended to deceive and is representative of the first category. However, the newsreel of the Jeffries-Sharkey fight embodies the qualities of the second category, while the Battle of Santiago Bay is an example of the third category. Because it was staged for the news film camera, the Corbett-Courtney fight fits easily into the fourth category.

As such categories indicate almost without exception, faked productions involved an intent to deceive audiences, as well as an element of fictionalization. If events were not staged with actors and actresses or re-enacted with the real participants, then, much like docudramas, entirely fictionalized events roughly associated with a famous event were created.

The 1908 Selig Polyscope production of *Hunting Big Game in Africa* was such an outright fictional production attempting to capitalize on President Theodore Roosevelt's 1908 expedition to that continent. Produced in Chicago, the film featured a toothy impersonator of Roosevelt, as well as a scene of the shooting of an old lion that had actually gotten out of hand on the set. The film was released when Roosevelt's real expedition began to

126. *Id.* at 40.
127. *Id.* at 37.

make headlines. Selig did not mention Roosevelt in the picture title or publicity, but the film enjoyed considerable success. Roosevelt was reportedly less than pleased.[128]

Among other reconstructions after 1900 which illustrate the continuation of such fakery were the assassination of President McKinley in 1901, the coronation of Edward VII in 1901, and the San Francisco earthquake and fire of 1906.[129]

An early newsreel production also resulted in the first privacy ruling, the *Binns* decision. In testimony, an officer of the Vitagraph Company stated that the company's method of producing such pictures was to gather all the data possible from every reliable source and to "weave" it into a "scenario" for a picture story by using imagination "just as a playwright writes a play or an author writes a story."[130]

Other docudrama-newsreel connections can be seen in the 1930s with productions that used actors and actresses to recreate news events. Created by the Time, Inc. organization, the motion picture newsreel series, *The March of Time*, patterned after the radio versions by the same name, was launched in 1935 and is normally considered in studies of the documentary genre. However, its format of combining actual sequences of news events with dramatizations, including re-enactments complete with dialogue by professional actors, makes it distinctly different from documentaries and also links it firmly to the docudrama as defined above.[131] Henry Luce, head of Time, Inc., said the style of *The March of Time* was "fakery in allegiance to the truth,"[132] a characterization that in itself might be asserted as having suitable qualities for a definition of the docudrama.

B. Docudramas and Television

In television, the first productions embodying the docudrama format can be seen in some programming in the late 1930s and in the early and mid-1940s. For example, NBC presented fifteen historical dramas in a series called *The Chronicles of America*, which featured programs on Columbus, Daniel Boone, Abraham Lincoln, and Alexander Hamilton among others.[133]

---

128. *Id*. at 51.
129. *Id*. at 37–42.
130. 103 N.E. 1108, 1110.
131. E. BARNOUW, DOCUMENTARY: A HISTORY OF THE NON-FICTION FILM 121 (1974). The radio version of *The March of Time* ran from 1931 to 1945 and was known for the impersonation of well-known personalities. *See* Lichty & Bohn, "Radio's March of Time: Dramatized News," 51 J. Q. 458 (1974). See also *Mau*, 28 F. Supp. 845 for information based on another docudrama-like presentation on radio titled *Calling All Cars*.
132. BARNOUW, *supra* note 131, at 121–22.
133. W. HAWES, AMERICAN TELEVISION DRAMA: THE EXPERIMENTAL YEARS 106–07, 172–238 (1986).

Later, the 1950s saw productions of docudrama-like series such as *The Big Story*, which dramatized actual stories.[134]

In 1957, NBC dramatized the emergency landing and subsequent Coast Guard rescue of passengers on a commercial aircraft flying from Honolulu to San Francisco—an early docudrama which resulted in the *Strickler* decision[135] and which fits the third category of docudrama defined above.

Of course, several motion pictures over the years have focused on subject matter that dovetails nicely into the various docudrama divisions.[136] Consequently, as the genre gained popularity, films based on fact (i.e., *Compulsion* and *The Boston Strangler*) were produced more and more frequently. As with other later productions that fit the docudrama definition,[137] these films embody the qualities of a docudrama subcategory, as they are dramatized yet fictionalized versions of well-known events.

After its sporadic beginning, the docudrama genre, espcially in television, became a staple of programming. Although the 1960s offered only a very few television docudramas such as *The Sacco-Vanzetti Story* (NBC) in 1960 and *This is Sholom Aleichem* (NBC) in 1969,[138] the genre saw its real blossoming beginning in 1971 with the production of *Brian's Song*, an ABC movie about Chicago Bears halfback and cancer victim, Brian Piccolo.[139]

Just a few months after *Brian's Song, The Crucifixion of Jesus*, a CBS production, was presented.[140] Subsequently, the genre caught fire. *Portrait: The Woman I Love*, a biographical drama about Edward VIII and Wallis Warfield, was shown by NBC in December 1972. *The Last King of America*, a CBS drama with King George III interviewed by Eric Sevareid, followed in February 1973. That year also saw *Pueblo*, an ABC docudrama about the capture of an American Navy vessel by North Korea, and *Portrait: A Man Whose Name Was John*, an ABC production about Pope John XXIII, among others.[141]

The 1970s generated an array of docudramas that could be placed in all the subcategories of the genre. The decade saw not only *Kill Me If You Can* (a production about condemned California sex criminal Caryl Chess-

---

134. E. BARNOUW, THE IMAGE EMPIRE: A HISTORY OF BROADCASTING IN THE UNITED STATES, Vol. III—from 1953, at 22 (1970). *See also Bernstein*, 129 F. Supp. 817.
135. 167 F. Supp. 68.
136. *See generally The Red Kimono, Yankee Doodle Dandy*, and *Look for the Silver Lining*. Descriptions can be seen in *Melvin*, 297 P. 91, *Levey*, 57 F. Supp. 40, and Donahue v. Warner Bros. Pictures, 194 F.2d 6 (10th Cir. 1952).
137. See generally television network motion pictures and other motion picture docudramas of the last eighteen years, including *The Boston Strangler, Judge Horton and the Scottsboro Boys*, and *Missing*. Actions resulting from them include *DeSalvo*, 300 F. Supp. 742, Street v. NBC, 7 MEDIA L. REP. 1001 (6th Cir. 1981), Davis v. Costa-Gavras, 10 MEDIA L. REP. 1257 (S.D.N.Y. 1984).
138. McNEIL, *supra* note 123, at 748–59.
139. *Id.* at 762.
140. *Id.* at 763.
141. *Id.* at 763–65.

man), *The Trial of Lee Harvey Oswald, Young Joe: The Forgotten Kennedy, Friendly Fire, Roots, King,* and *Holocaust,* but also, *The Lindbergh Kidnapping Case, Eleanor and Franklin,* and *Judgment: The Court-Martial of Lieutenant William Calley* among others. In fact, at least thirty-five ABC, NBC, or CBS 1970s programs qualify as docudramas.[142] Conversely, the 1940s, 1950s, and 1960s saw fewer than ten docudrama-like productions by the major networks.[143]

Not surprisingly, docudramas continue to enjoy success in the 1980s. At least twenty-five programs qualify as docudramas between 1980 and 1984,[144] and the years since have seen continued popularity. Nearly each week, one network or another offers a production fitting the docudrama genre. Along with motion pictures fitting the format (such as *Missing*),[145] *The Deliberate Stranger*, NBC's 1986 two-part docudrama about murderer Ted Bundy,[146] and *At Mother's Request*, a 1987 docudrama by CBS about a woman who convinces her son to kill her own father, are just two recent productions.[147]

III. INTERSECTIONS OF FALSE LIGHT AND DOCUDRAMA

The call for a legal protection of privacy is generally credited to Samuel D. Warren and Louis D. Brandeis and their December 1890 *Harvard Law Review* article, "The Right to Privacy."[148] That article, which refers to the threat of "instantaneous photographs" and "numerous mechanical devices," as well as newspaper enterprise, said the press was overstepping the obvious bounds of propriety and decency.[149] The privacy issue gained momentum after the Warren and Brandeis proposal and boiled over after a June 1902 New York Court of Appeals decision. In *Roberson v. Rochester Folding Box Company*,[150] the court said it could not award damages to Abigail Roberson, whose portrait had been published without permission on posters advertising flour.[151]

142. *Id.* at 760–71.
143. *Id.* at 741–60.
144. *Id.* at 772–78.
145. *Missing* is the motion picture that prompted the defamation action, *Davis*, 10 MEDIA L. REP. 1257, 13 MEDIA L. REP. 876 (S.D.N.Y. 1986), 13 MEDIA L. REP. 2112 (S.D.N.Y. 1987). *See supra* note 137.
146. Larsen, "Bundy: Reel and Reality," Seattle Times, May 4, 1986, at § K, 1, cols. 1–5.
147. Voorhees, "'At Mother's Request': Don't Waste Your Time on It," Seattle Times, Jan. 4, 1987, at TV Times §, 2, cols. 1–5.
148. Warren & Brandeis, "The Right to Privacy," 4 HARV. L. REV. 193 (1890).
149. *Id.* at 195–96.
150. 64 N.E. 442 (N.Y. Ct. App. 1902).
151. *Id.*

Subsequently, in November 1902, Denis O'Brien criticized the *Roberson* decision in a *Columbia Law Review* article and helped to bring about the nation's first privacy statute in New York in 1903.[152] O'Brien wrote:

> He cannot, if he would, escape the camera or the kodak. If concealment were possible it would, instead of adding anything to his happiness, aggravate his misery. . . . The artist who by the use of modern appliances is enabled in a moment of time to secure a likeness of a man or woman for some purpose of his own may be impertinent, but it is not so certain that it would be wise to enact a penal statute to punish him for such an act or to empower the courts to grant an injunction to prevent it.[153]

Indictments based on taste were evidently leveled at early newsreels as well, probably because of their insensitive content. One fake newsreel produced by Vitagraph in 1911 showed alleged atrocities committed by the Italians against the Turks. It received so much criticism that Vitagraph was forced to recall the film and apologize to the Italian consul.[154]

The practice of photographing newsworthy people and events also received criticism in a 1905 *American Law Review* article by Elbridge L. Adams, who used wording similar to Warren and Brandeis in listing taking and vending of instantaneous photographs, among other press practices, as being quite annoying to sensitive people and deserving of calls for censure.[155]

Binns privacy decision can definitely be seen as a privacy complaint over portrayal in what can be called a docudrama format. In a court action which began in 1909, Binns sued for both libel and invasion of privacy. The appellate division of the New York Supreme Court ruled in favor of Binns's libel action, but denied recovery in the privacy action. The lower court said that it could not allow a double recovery on the basis of a single act.[156] The New York Court of Appeals ruled that Vitagraph had used Binns's name and picture, thus violating the New York privacy statute. An important part of the ruling asserted that a picture need not be a photograph of a living person, but could be any representation.[157] Thus, the use by Vitagraph of an actor portraying Binns in the pictorial series constituted identification.

Binns provided an early precedent for cases in which a person's name and likeness are used without his or her permission in a fictional production.

---

152. D. PEMBER, PRIVACY AND THE PRESS: THE LAW, THE MASS MEDIA, AND THE FIRST AMENDMENT 66–67 (1972).
153. *Id.* at 446.
154. FIELDING, *supra* note 124, at 39.
155. Adams, "The Right of Privacy, and Its Relation to the Law of of Libel," 39 AM. L. REV. 37, 38–39 (1905).
156. 132 N.Y.S. 237, 240 (Sup. Ct. 1911).
157. 103 N.E. 1108 at 1110.

Moreover, the judgment that a picture is not necessarily a photograph but can be any fictional representation of a person influences the very essence of the docudrama genre—the element of fictional portrayal. If fictional identification had been ruled to be unacceptable, it is likely that false-light action involving docudramas or other types of fictionalization would not have developed as they did, for fictionalized newsreels would have been exempt from privacy action by plaintiffs who had been portrayed in these docudramas.

A. Wigmore's False Attribution

Three years later, John H. Wigmore examined what he called the right against false attribution of belief or utterance. Wigmore grouped cases in which defendants falsely attributed some utterances to plaintiffs, and he listed five categories as being special and as not fitting the normal under-standing of defamation.[158] While four of them have little to do with docu-dramas and false-light invasion of privacy, one addresses the concept of fictionalization:

> Finally there is the common situation (but not yet, apparently, represented by any decisions) in which the defendant falsely attributes to the plaintiffs the possession of some opinion. This is unlike the third class, in that it does not attribute any statement or utterance of the opinion. And it is unlike the fourth class, in that it does not attribute any act of invention or authorship. But it is a not uncommon form of injury in current journalistic practice. The irresponsible vendors of sen-sations, moved by the meanest motives of mankind, will recklessly attribute to this or that personage some view on current affairs which is alien to his actual thoughts and is calculated to make hard feelings that never can be assuaged by protestation.[159]

Wigmore's "meanest motives" wording is somewhat predictive of the *Re-statement* phrase, "reckless disregard as to the falsity of the published material."[160]

Moreover, Wigmore also included in this category basic tenets that call for relief from being cast in a fictional manner:

---

158. Wigmore, "The Right Against False Attribution or Belief or Utterance," 4 KENTUCKY L.J. 3, 4 (1916).
159. *Id.* at 7.
160. RESTATEMENT, *supra* note 2.

> The essential thing is that I do not entertain the convictions
> falsely ascribed me . . . and that I am entitled to be protected
> against such an unauthorized misrepresentation of my
> personality.[161]

Two other early privacy court actions involve motion picture productions having tangential docudrama characteristics. One of those, *Kunz v. Allen*[162] in 1918, deals with a portrayal that is accidental. The court ruled that a newsreel on weight reduction did not ridicule a group of fat women who were exercising.[163] In the other action, *Humiston v. Universal Film Mfg. Co.*[164] in 1919, a privacy claim involving a motion picture with docudrama characteristics was denied when the court ruled that the dramatization of a New York woman attorney who had helped solve a murder was legitimate news.[165]

The 1931 *Melvin* action is the first intersection after *Binns* in which the plaintiff recovered from being portrayed falsely in a docudrama production. As had been the case in *Binns*, Melvin was identified by her married name in promotional material for the motion picture, although her maiden name was used in the film.[166] Also, as it had been in *Binns*, the issue revolved around the propriety of spreading facts—in a fictional way—of the plaintiff's past. In *Binns*, those facts could have been ruled to be newsworthy, but the narrowness of the New York privacy statute provided for Binns' recovery largely because Vitagraph appropriated his name, likeness, and actions for commercial gain.[167] In *Melvin*, the material could have been ruled to have been privileged since they were largely from court documents, but the court ruled in Melvin's favor and noted that she had a right guaranteed by the California Constitution to pursue and obtain happiness.[168]

Two decades later, one of the earliest television false-light intersections resulted in *Bernstein*.[169] NBC's production of the episode and its publicity about the production did not use his name in the production. Nonetheless, Bernstein claimed that the actor portraying him was similar in looks and in speech. The court ruled, however, that Bernstein was not identified, and furthermore, the decision asserted that if the telecast were more fiction than

161. Wigmore, *supra* note 158, at 8.
162. 172 P. 532 (Kan. Sup. Ct. 1918). But in another decision just after *Melvin*, 297 P. 91, Blumenthal v. Picture Classics, Inc., 257 N.Y.S. 800 (Sup. Ct. 1932), found that a short movie, *City Life,* made a street vender it accidentally included in the film look foolish and undignified.
163. 172 P. 532.
164. 178 N.Y.S. 752 (Sup. Ct. 1919).
165. *Id.*
166. 297 P. 91 at 91–93.
167. 103 N.E. 1108.
168. 297 P. 91 at 93–94.
169. 129 F. Supp. 817.

fact, Bernstein had no grounds for recovery, since the production still did not identify or defame him.[170]

Strickler represents the earliest victory for a plaintiff in a television docudrama–false-light court action.[171] Unlike *Bernstein*, the false portrayal at issue stemmed from NBC's use of Strickler's real name and identity in the dramatized version of the aircraft crash and rescue of its passengers; in addition, the production in general portrayed Strickler in a positive manner, but he successfully pleaded that the portrayal was incomplete and offensive.[172]

Moreover, the wording of Strickler's claim in the decision is akin to a false-light description although false light was not classified as a tort until six years later; District Judge Westover wrote: "Plaintiff claims he was placed in a false position by the telecasts and has experienced humiliation, embarrassment and great mental pain and suffering."[173]

B. A Widening of Attention

Although the inclusion of false light as a subcategory of privacy in the 1964 *Handbook of Torts* did not immediately increase docudrama-related litigation using such a claim, the 1967 *Time, Inc.* decision brought national attention to privacy because it was the first U.S. Supreme Court decision involving privacy.[174]

Fictionalization was an integral part of the decision in that it involved an instance much like the *Strickler* situation in that the Hill family had been portrayed fictionally, but in a largely positive manner. In ruling that Hill needed to prove that errors were published with careless disregard for the truth, the court in essence extended the protection given defamatory falsehoods in 1964 to nondefamatory falsehoods.[175]

In the decision, Justice Brennan noted the difficulty of categorizing fiction and refused to allow the case to be based solely on whether the play depicting the Hill family crisis was fictional or not. Brennan also pointed out that the trial judge in the case had apparently wrongly construed fictionalization to be synonymous with falsity and did not consider the knowledge element of falsity or the concept of negligence.[176] The court's stance on the element of fictionalization seems to say clearly that first amendment considerations outweigh any individual rights of privacy when a person is falsely depicted. In short, the production in question must have very little informative potential for society before the courts will grant privacy relief.

---

170. 129 F. Supp. at 817, 817–37.
171. 167 F. Supp. 68.
172. *Id.*
173. *Id.* at 69.
174. 385 U.S. 374.
175. *Id. See also* New York Times v. Sullivan, 376 U.S. 254 (1964).
176. 385 U.S. 374, 391–96.

In spite of the increase in docudrama production beginning in the 1970s, false-light invasion of privacy cases involving such productions have not expanded as rapidly. In the years immediately following the *Time, Inc.* decision, only *DeSalvo* and *Leopold* were false-light decisions involving docudramas.[177] Moreover, neither of these was concerned purely with a question of false light. In *Leopold*, the ruling said that the portrayal was not highly offensive to a reasonable person.[178] Both the *DeSalvo* and *Leopold* decisions indicate that the public's right to be informed outweighs the individual's privacy right, especially if the fictional portrayal is not highly offensive.

A 1972 study by Don R. Pember, *Privacy and the Press*, suggested precautions that could prevent lawsuits in the area of false light and fictionalization: If an individual's life is going to be the basis for a drama, use of the real name should be avoided; if the person is named, the portrayal should be factual.[179] Pember also noted that to that point, many courts had found it difficult to accept the concept of nondefamatory falsehood and had often rejected such suits as being foreign to traditional Anglo-American legal principles.[180] However, this trend is changing.

Of course, *Restatement* itself represents a major intersection in that its guidelines lay out clearly the two criteria for false light: 1) false light must be highly offensive to a reasonable person, and 2) there is reckless disregard as to the falsity of the publicized matter.[181]

Restatement notes that the second criterion applies only when publicity casts plaintiffs in a false light that is highly offensive in nature. Privacy is not invaded if the false statements are unimportant, even if they are made deliberately. Major misrepresentations of character, history, activities, or beliefs that result in plaintiffs being seriously offended bring about a cause of action.[182]

More recently, the false light/docudrama connection has been discussed by Victor A. Kovner in *Communications Lawyer*. Kovner asserted that docudramas try to give the illusion that they are more historical than they really are. These productions differ from fiction or allegories, Kovner argued,

---

177. *See, e.g., DeSalvo,* 300 F. Supp. 742, and *Leopold,* 259 N.E.2d 250. *But see Davis,* 10 Media L. Rep. 1257, 13 Media L. Rep. 876, 13 Media L. Rep. 2112; Aquilar v. Universal City Studios, 12 Media L. Rep. 1485 (Cal. Ct. App. 1985); *Street,* 7 Media L. Rep. 1001; American Broadcasting-Paramount Theatres, Inc. v. E. L. Simpson, 126 S.E.2d 873 (Ga. Ct. App. 1962) and Kelly v. Loew's Inc., 76 F. Supp. 473 (D. Mass. 1948) are some cases involving docudramas and based totally or partially on defamation as a cause of action.
178. *See, e.g., Leopold,* 259 N.E.2d 250 and Restatement, *supra* note 3.
179. Pember, *supra* note 152, at 245.
180. *Id.* at 247.
181. Restatement, *supra* note 3.
182. *Id.*

in that they often purport to give a "substantially accurate historical account" and to use names and places with a "concomitant aura of authenticity."[183]

183. Kovner, *supra* note 112, at 1. *See also* Felcher & Rubin, "Privacy, Publicity, and the Portrayal of Real People by the Media," 88 YALE L.J. 1577 (1979) *and* Zimmerman, "Real People in Fiction: Cautionary Words About Troublesome Old Torts Poured into New Jugs," 51 BROOKLYN L. REV. 355 (1985) for articles indirectly related to false light and docudrama. In a discussion of privacy, publicity, and portrayal of real people by the media, Felcher and Rubin asserted social policies (of which they list the first amendment as being the most important) influence the principles that courts use in reaching their decisions.

The primary principle is that if a portrayal serves an informative or cultural function, then it will be immune from liability. If the portrayal serves no such function but merely exploits the individual portrayed, immunity will not be granted. A second principle is based on identifiable harm. If courts see that a person is able to demonstrate some type of harm, relief will be granted. However, if there is no apparent harm, relief is denied.

In addition, Felcher and Rubin pointed out that media portrayals of real persons have three possible purposes: to inform, sell, or to entertain. Informative portrayals are often called news and involve such examples as newspaper and television reporting. Portrayals that sell are commercial in nature and sell a specific product. Entertaining portrayals are more artistic and involve fictionalized history, stage, motion picture, or television simulations of real events, as well as other purely fictionalized productions set against an historical background. This portrayal as entertainment appears to be a wholesale lumping of all the docudrama formats into a single category.

Zimmerman asserted that doubt and confusion in the laws dealing with real people and fiction exist partially because of uncertainty about the difference between fiction and falsehood. Falsehood, Zimmerman wrote, is usually presented under the guise of a literal rendering of reality, but fiction is usually not. She noted that fiction is meant to refer to works that are intended to be nonliteral. Fictionalization—imaginary dialog and scenes in works that are otherwise factual—is sometimes treated as genuine fictional work.

Zimmerman noted that in both the U.S. Supreme Court decisions related to false-light cases (*Time, Inc.* and *Cantrell*), falsehood has only been dealt with in the context of otherwise factual speech, for in both decisions the publications in question were dealing with factual reporting. In short, both *Time, Inc.* and *Cantrell* lie mainly in the area of inadvertent false-light portrayal—not directly in the area of fictionalization and, thus, docudramas.

She also asserted that the two Supreme Court decisions seem to be statements saying privacy is not as strong a social value as is reputation—which would mean defamation would be chosen as a cause of action, not privacy. To some extent, then, it is somewhat paradoxical to say that privacy can be invaded by fiction. She argued:

> If the character is involved in scenes of great intimacy or shown in a light that is believed by the model on whom it is based to be inaccurate or unfair, the author's response can be that the character was never meant to be "accurate," except in an artistic or psychological sense. Even when the parallels are strong enough that the plaintiff can readily be recognized, either by himself or herself or by others, as the source of the character, the author, by announcing that the work is fiction, is nonetheless stating that the portrait is not journalistic but is instead a product of the imagination—that is, a reworking of the raw material of reality. . . . Even in false-light actions, when the communication that causes the injury is untrue, the publication ordinarily at least

To circumvent legal problems arising from such portrayals, Kovner listed four precautions that producers of docudramas should consider in order to avoid legal problems: 1) use a clear characterization of the work as fiction, and in areas that involve facts, prepare to defend the accuracy of the material; 2) change names to disguise identity, but understand that such changes may strengthen a perception by the audience that the events portrayed should not be taken literally; 3) place disclaimers in the introductory material and make them explicit; and 4) limit the use of nonconsenting living persons to peripheral roles and make those portrayals "indisputably accurate and nondefamatory" in nature.[184]

C. The ABC Approach

Some of Pember's and Kovner's ideas can be seen in the policies of the three major television networks. However, those standards-and-practices policies of the American Broadcasting Company, the Columbia Broadcasting System, and the National Broadcasting Company, Inc. also provide a different perspective on the intersection of false light and docudrama.

ABC's Department of Broadcast Standards and Practices uses an eighteen-page guidebook to monitor productions falling within the framework of docudramas. The guidelines say docudramas, "sometimes also called 'dramatization based on fact,' 'theatre-in-fact,' or 'historical recreation,' " must adhere to the rules if the overall presentation imparts authenticity.[185] It makes no difference if dramatic license has been used in character portrayal or if composites of people or events have been used to meet time limitations.[186]

For ABC, docudramas fall into five different categories: legendary characters; interpretations of historical figures or events; memoirs/stories of private individuals; personal stories about public individuals; and factual backdrops. In discussing these categories, the guidelines stress that ABC's general docudrama rules apply to all fact-based programming.[187]

---

purports to convey truth about the real world. Fiction fits uneasily into this construct because it raises questions about how reasonable it is for the plaintiff or anyone else to treat the publication as though it were, in any sense, "about" a real person. If the work is not treated as informational, then, arguably, the claim that it invades privacy is specious.

Id. at 370.
According to Zimmerman, false-light and other nondefamation torts are less likely to be successful for plaintiffs than is defamation with its hundred years of common-law baggage and its twenty years of Constitutional refining.
184. Kovner, *supra* note 112, at 9.
185. American Broadcasting Company, Department of Broadcasting Standards and Practices, Docudrama Programming Guidelines, 1, 1 (rev. ed. 1985).
186. *Id.*
187. *Id.* at 12–15.

ABC places the burden upon the producer to demonstrate that facts and events are portrayed fairly. Projects involving significant historical events require more detailed substantiation. In addition, projects which originate from items outside of current interest or which only loosely reflect current events must be classified as fiction. Programs with a fictitious story line against a historical backdrop can be treated as fiction also, but the producer must provide documentation that the backdrop is accurately portrayed.[188]

The guidelines state:

> The objective of the guidelines is to enable such dramatization to be presented within the bounds of authenticity, as a fair interpretation of the facts, within the time limits of the dramatic form, and in such a manner as not to mislead, deceive or be untruthful to the facts or events as presented to the viewer.[189]

Among examples listed by ABC as programs that meet this objective are *Eleanor and Franklin, Young Joe: the Forgotten Kennedy*, and *Friendly Fire*.[190]

In addition, factual backdrops cannot be misrepresented or distorted in such a way as to confuse or misinform the viewer about actual events. Fictitious characters in programs defined as fiction cannot change, affect, or distort the course of history.[191]

The ABC guidelines place importance on the "reasonable basis"— adequate substantiation to justify attitudes and/or actions.[192] ABC specifies:

> For example, a scene between individuals for which there is no verifiable proof may be found to have a "reasonable basis" if it is in keeping with the individual's known attitudes and behavior patterns and if it does not contradict known facts. Similarly, if sound circumstantial evidence places an individual in a given situation, but there is no conclusive "proof" he was there, "reasonable basis" may nevertheless make it acceptable for that individual to be depicted as present. If an event is of key historical significance, more information/sources will be necessary to allow for a "reasonable basis" than if a scene depicts the interfamilial actions of non-public individuals.[193]

188. *Id.* at 2.
189. *Id.* at 3.
190. *Id.* at 3.
191. *Id.* at 14.
192. *Id.* at 6.
193. *Id.* at 6–7.

By specifically requiring adherence to accuracy in fictionalized scenes and disallowing inaccuracies that are offensive to reasonable people, ABC appears to be monitoring productions so that it does not fall prey to the false-light area or other tort areas, such as defamation.

Disclaimers are listed as being of key importance in docudrama production because they disclose the basis of the dramatization and establish the type and degree of substantiation and documentation that was used. ABC requires that docudramas provide disclaimers at the beginning of the first act. These notices must be both audio and video, but other disclaimers during the course of the program may be voice-overs. In all, eleven types of disclaimers dealing with variations on the five types of docudramas are listed in the guidelines.[194]

Of course, the ABC guidelines provide supplementary rules that also are aimed at ensuring the denial of any recovery in a false light action:

1. Sensitive subjects—sexual, religious, political, or controversial in nature—are required to have multiple sources of verification.

2. Representative events must be attributable to specific, participating persons and must have enough substantiation to permit accurate representation.

3. Actual names should be used in docudramas unless legal considerations dictate a name change in the program.

4. Names of composite characters must be changed to avoid using the dual names of any individuals in the composite.

5. If an individual demands a name change before he/she will consent to a release, the broadcast standards office must be notified.

6. Releases must be obtained from individuals depicted in a significant fashion.

7. Fictional dialogue that has a circumstantial basis requires reasonable substantiation to establish that it represents the attitudes and beliefs of the people portrayed.

8. Any court documents used in docudrama must be cleared by Standards and Practices personnel. Although court documents are a primary research source, court transcripts of testimony may need additional substantiation.[195]

D. CBS and NBC Rules

The CBS guidelines are found on two pages of the CBS Program Practices manual, *CBS Program Standards*. CBS also asserts that its docudrama productions should represent clearly to viewers the genre and frame

194. *Id.* at 15–18.
195. *Id.* at 3–5.

of reference.[196] Noting that docudramas are particularly challenging, the guidelines state:

> Its material factual components should be accurate and cannot be changed merely to enhance dramatic value. Fictionalized elements consistent with the events being presented may amplify or enhance the story, so long as they do not materially alter or distort history.[197]

CBS provides five specific guidelines to ensure the integrity of its docudrama form:

1. The only unsubstantiated elements that may be used are those that do not distort the factual elements of the historical record.

2. It is not acceptable to omit historical information which materially distorts the perception of an historical event.

3. Editing or condensation in a portrayal should maintain the accuracy or value of the events. Distortions of time, changes in sequence of events, and composite events which materially alter the historical record must be avoided.

4. Production techniques should not be used that will alter or distort the historical record.

5. Characters, including composite characters, must accurately reflect the real persons and their actual roles and behavior. Furthermore, composite or fictional characters must be monitored so that they do not undermine the overall accuracy of the historical events portrayed.[198]

Found in *NBC Broadcast Standards for Television*, NBC's guidelines dealing directly with docudramas are by far the most brief. These guidelines forbid dramatizations that give the false impression that the material constitutes an actual event occurring at the time of presentation.[199] The only other reference that could be linked to docudrama states simply: "Dramatized or reenacted events must be clearly disclosed as such and may be utilized only when based on an actual occurrence."[200]

These guidelines provide no definition of docudrama, nor do they deal with specific placement of disclaimers, methods of fictionalization, treatment of the historical record, or necessity of obtaining releases.

Taken together, however, the three network policies governing the production of docudramas constitute an adequate beginning for dealing with

196. CBS Television Network, CBS Program Standards, 7 (n.d.).
197. *Id.* at 7.
198. *Id.* at 8.
199. National Broadcasting Company, NBC Broadcast Standards for Television, 4 (1986).
200. *Id.* at 15.

legal issues as outlined in *Restatement* and for staving off any bevy of successful lawsuits. Although lacking definition, as well as substantive and current legal documentation, the policies of both ABC and CBS cover the basics and emphasize accuracy in portrayal of historical events and wariness in dealing with fictional or composite characters. If such extensive codification is desirable, NBC's policy, however, appears to be too abbreviated and general to provide adequate guidance for those producing docudramas.

IV. CONCLUSIONS

Such an examination of false-light invasion of privacy and docudramas ultimately gives rise to a central question: Why is it that plaintiffs do not choose to use false light as a cause of action? The reasons appear to be fivefold.

First, it is often difficult to prove the offensive nature of the portrayal. Law books such as *Restatement* tend to consider false-light privacy actions commonly,[201] but as noted earlier, false-light falls into two distinct categories. A legal action may result when someone is inadvertently portrayed in a false light by the mass media. Most frequently, such suits stem from news coverage.[202] The main legal issues in such cases are generally: 1) was the plaintiff portrayed in a false light, and 2) if so, did the defendant do so with reckless disregard for the truth or falsity of the matter.

A second type of false-light suit, usually resulting from intentional false portrayal, is more commonly associated with a drama, such as a film or play, or a television docudrama.[203] Since the falsity of the portrayal is assumed in such a case—after all, the presentation is largely fiction even though based on fact—the key issue in such actions centers on whether or not the false portrayal would be highly offensive to a reasonable person.

Moreover, such an offensive portrayal need not necessarily be one that is negative or offensive only to the audience. It could be one in which the plaintiff is portrayed in too positive a manner—so positively, in fact, that the portrayal would become offensive to any reasonable person. For example, if a docudrama were produced about child-hater W.C. Fields that portrayed him as a baby-kissing adorer of small children, a reasonable person who knew of the child-hating qualities of the real Fields would be likely to view such a positive portrayal as casting Fields in a false light.

It is wariness of the element of offensiveness that seems to have influenced the development of broadcast industry standards attempting to eliminate excessively negative or positive portrayals. The guidelines of the three major television networks are aimed at reducing the chances that a person

201. RESTATEMENT, *supra* note 3.
202. *See, e.g., Peay,* 78 F. Supp. 305, and *Leverton,* 192 F.2d 974.
203. *See, e.g., Melvin,* 297 P. 91, *Time, Inc.,* 385 U.S. 374, and *Strickler,* 167 F. Supp. 68.

portrayed in a docudrama will be depicted falsely in a manner that is hightly offensive. For example, ABC requires that fictionalized scenes have a "reasonable basis," to make them acceptable,[204] and CBS requires that characters, including composite characters, accurately reflect the real persons and their actual roles and behaviors.[205]

Of course, some false-light cases won by plaintiffs were decided before offensiveness was refined. For instance, *Strickler* was based on a portrayal that was largely positive in nature.[206] However, subsequent refinement in the requirement for offensiveness suggests that if *Strickler* were decided today, the decision would probably not allow recovery because the portrayal is not highly offensive in either a positive or negative way. In fact, an illustrative case in *Restatement* is based on *Strickler,* but the example serves to point out a nebulous portrayal in which the portrayal is not a clear-cut instance of false-light invasion of privacy. *Restatement* notes that in a case such as *Strickler,* different juries would most likely decide differently as to whether the portrayal were highly objectionable or not.[207]

A. The Importance of Importance

A second factor limiting false light/docudrama legal action is based on the requirement that falsity in the portrayal in question must focus on a material matter. *Restatement* stresses that a plaintiff's privacy is not invaded when unimportant false statements are made, "even when they are made deliberately."[208] Furthermore, major misrepresentations of character, history, activities, or beliefs must be present, resulting in serious offense being taken by a reasonable person.[209]

These restrictions, reflected in current television network guidelines cited above, would probably preclude recovery in cases such as *Strickler* if such actions were to be pursued today. Strickler's portrayal as being dressed in a Hawaiian shirt and as praying and comforting other passengers while the airliner made its landing, although false, would not likely be construed to be important enough details or dialog to be highly offensive. Thus, plaintiffs are prevented from successfully using false light as a cause of

---

204. *See, e.g., ABC, supra* note 185, at 6–7.
205. *See, e.g., CBS, supra* note 196, at 8.
206. 167 F. Supp. 68.
207. *See* RESTATEMENT, *supra* note 3. But, cases such as Spahn v. Julian Messner, Inc., 221 N.E.2d 543 (N.Y. Ct. App. 1966), resulting from a larger-than-life portrayal of baseball player Warren Spahn in a fictional biography, support the concept that a highly offensive portrayal can be positive as well as negative. *See also* Molony v. Boy Comics Publishers, Inc., 98 N.Y.S.2d 119 (Sup. Ct. 1950); *Cason,* 20 So.2d 243, Sutton v. Hearst Corporation, 98 N.Y.S.2d 233 (Sup. Ct. 1950), and Zolich, "Laudatory Invasion of Privacy," 16 CLEV.-MAR. L. REV. 532 (1967).
208. RESTATEMENT, *supra* note 3.
209. *Id.*

action if the dialogue or actions objected to—whether intentional or not—are not major misrepresentations.

A third reason for the few false light/docudrama actions is that courts tend to be more lenient in cases involving matters of public interest and importance. Only in three earlier false light/docudrama cases—*Binns, Melvin,* and *Strickler*—have plaintiffs been allowed recovery.[210] It is in those cases that courts found in part that privacy considerations outweighed the public interest in the docudramas.

However, other similar actions involving docudramas have denied plaintiff claims. Newsworthiness, which relates to the public's right to know or to public interest,[211] has generally been a factor mentioned in such decisions. Those docudramas based on court records, as well as those based on events that received much publicity, tend not to have false-light actions sustained against them. For example, *Bernstein* involved a largely inoffensive fictionalized portrayal based on an incident that had been in the public domain.[212]

Furthermore, the *Binns, Melvin,* and *Strickler* recoveries all came before false light was listed as a subcategory of privacy in the 1964 *Handbook of the Law of Torts.* Perhaps more important, they were all decided before decisions such as *Time, Inc.* noted the gravity of risk to a free society if freedom of press is restricted. Justice Brennan noted:

> We hold that the constitutional protections for speech and press preclude the application of the New York statute to redress false reports of matters of public interest in the absence of proof that the defendant published the report with knowledge of its falsity or in reckless disregard for the truth.
>
> The guarantees for speech and press are not the preserve of political expression or comment upon public affairs, essential as those are to healthy government. Exposure of the self to others in varying degrees is a concomitant of life in a civilized community. The risk of this exposure is an essential incident of life in a society which places a primary value on freedom of speech and press. . . . A broadly defined freedom of the press assures the maintenance of our political system and an open society.[213]

A fourth reason why false-light action is not chosen is because the fictional portrayal in question may be so fictional that the plaintiff is not

---

210. *See, e.g., Binns,* 103 N.E. 1108, *Melvin,* 297 P. 91, and *Strickler,* 167 F. Supp. 68.
211. Pember, "Privacy and the Press: The Defense of Newsworthiness," 45 J.Q. 14 (1968).
212. 129 F. Supp. 817, 837.
213. 385 U.S. 374 at 387–89.

clearly identified. Indeed, the plaintiff may not be able to convince the court that the portrayal in question is of and concerning him or her. Over the years, those plaintiffs in false light/docudrama cases that have managed to recover have been those whose real names were used in connection with the docudrama. *Binns, Melvin,* and *Strickler* all involved the use of plaintiffs' names.[214]

In cases such as *Stryker* and *Bernstein,* the court denied recovery for plaintiffs partially because their identity in the portrayal was not quite so clearly ascertained.[215] In *Stryker,* Judge David Sachs noted that Louis B. Stryker did not prove that he was the same person as a sergeant with the same surname in a World War II film called *The Sands of Iwo Jima.*[216] In *Bernstein,* the court tied public interest to identity in denying Bernstein recovery. It ruled that if the telecast based on facts from Bernstein's life were factual, Bernstein had no cause of action because it was taken from material in the public interest. Furthermore, the court noted, if the material were adequately fictionalized, Bernstein had no cause of action because he was not identified.[217]

Because of such decisions and perhaps partially because of warnings by media law experts to change names in fictional portrayals,[218] docudrama producers began to take the simple precaution of requiring that names of characters in the productions be changed. For instance, ABC guidelines governing docudramas require that names be changed for composite characters and all other characters for which legal problems are foreseen. In addition, ABC requires releases from characters it portrays in docudramas.[219] This precautionary tendency to alter names seems to be a factor motivating plaintiffs not to pursue false light.

Finally, the long-standing preference by attorneys and judges for defamation is a reason why plaintiffs do not choose false light as a cause of action. Although its advice is not applicable in states not recognizing false light as an acceptable tort area, *Restatement* notes that the publicity given to the plaintiff in false-light actions is usually also defamatory and that the plaintiff can proceed upon either action (or both) but can have only one recovery.[220] In such instances, *Restatement* advises:

---

214. *See, e.g., Binns,* 103 N.E. 1108, *Melvin,* 297 P. 91, and *Strickler,* 167 F. Supp. 68. It is important to note in *Melvin* that only Melvin's maiden name, Gabrielle Darley, was used in the motion picture, but advertisements for the film stated that the story was based on the life of Gabrielle Darley Melvin.
215. *See, e.g., Stryker,* 238 P. 670, and *Bernstein,* 129 F. Supp. 817.
216. 238 P. 670 at 673.
217. 129 F. Supp. 817 at 837.
218. *See, e.g.,* PEMBER, *supra* note 152, at 245 and Kovner, *supra* note 112, at 9.
219. ABC, *supra* note 185, at 7–9.
220. RESTATEMENT, *supra* note 3.

> It is arguable that limitations of long standing that have been
> found desirable for the action for defamation should not be
> successfully evaded by proceeding upon a different theory of
> later origin, in the development of which the attention of the
> courts has not been directed to the limitations.[221]

Although somewhat qualified, such a comment clearly urges that plaintiffs who have a choice should not choose false light as a cause of action.

Furthermore, privacy has less than a century of legal development while defamation is a cause of action with a legal history several centuries old. The larger number of libel cases stemming from docudrama portrayals seems to suggest that attorneys and judges are more comfortable with the more elaborate, more detailed, and more familiar nature of defamation.[222] In fact, a *Yale Law Journal* article asserted that libel is a more promising cause of action because once a plaintiff proves his/her identity with a fictional character, actual falsity and the awareness thereof required will follow readily.[223]

Thus, it seems that the relationship between false light and docudrama is not one involving—or promising—frequent intersection. Largely because of these five reasons, false-light invasion of privacy is not a choice of legal action by plaintiffs who believe they have been portrayed falsely in docudramas. Furthermore, these reasons suggest that false-light invasion of privacy will not see a dramatic increase in much litigation concerning docudramas but will be largely limited to cases involving plaintiffs who have been inadvertently cast in a false light by news-oriented stories and broadcasts.

---

221. *Id. See also* PROSSER AND KEETON ON THE LAW OF TORTS 864 (5th ed. 1984), which asserts that plaintiffs have a better chance of recovery in defamation if such an action is possible.
222. Recent examples of courts focusing on defamation include *Davis,* 10 MEDIA L. REP. 1257, 13 MEDIA L. REP. 876, 13 MEDIA L. REP. 2112; *Aquilar,* 12 MEDIA L. REP. 1485; *Street,* 7 MEDIA L. REP. 1001; Geisler v. Petrocelli, 616 F.2d 636 (2nd Cir. 1980); and Cohn v. NBC, 4 MEDIA L. REP. 2533. Earlier examples include Wright v. R.K.O. Radio Pictures, 55 F. Supp. 639 (D. Mass. 1944); *Kelly,* 76 F. Supp. 473 (D. Mass. 1948); and *American Broadcasting-Paramount Theatres, Inc.,* 126 S.E.2d 873.
223. Smirlock, " 'Clear and Convincing' Libel: Fiction and the Law of Defamation," 92 YALE L.J. 520 (1983). However, at least one scholar has noted that false light may be a better cause of action because it is less difficult to prove damage to reputational interests than to prove an inaccurate and offensive portrayal. *See* Lebel, "The Infliction of Harm through the Publication of Fiction: Fashioning a Theory of Liability," 51 BROOKLYN L. REV. 293 (1985).

Readings from COMMUNICATIONS AND THE LAW, 1

The articles collected in *Defamation: Libel and Slander* were published in the following issues of COMMUNICATIONS AND THE LAW.

"Herbert v. Lando: No Cause for Alarm," by Howard E. Goldfluss, originally appeared in vol. 1, no. 3, pp. 61-68, © 1979.

"Herbert v. Lando: Threat to the Press, Or Boomerang for Public Officials?" by Andre E. Briod, originally appeared in vol. 2, no. 2, pp. 59-92, © 1980.

"Fashioning a New Libel Defense: The Advent of Neutral Reportage," by Donna Lee Dickerson, originally appeared in vol. 3, no. 3, pp. 77-86, © 1981.

"The Future of Strict Liability in Libel," by F. Dennis Hale, originally appeared in vol. 5, no 2, pp. 23-37, © 1983.

"Protecting Confidential Sources in Libel Litigation," by Anthony Green, originally appeared in vol. 6, no. 3, pp. 39-51, © 1984.

"Retraction's Role Under the Actual Malice Rule," by Donna Lee Dickerson, originally appeared in vol. 6, no. 4, pp. 39-51, © 1984.

"Libel and the Long Reach of Out-of-State Courts," by Donna Lee Dickerson, originally appeared in vol. 7, no. 4, pp. 27-43, © 1985.

"Problems in Libel Litigation," by Erik L. Collins, Jay B. Wright and Charles W. Peterson, originally appeared in vol. 7, no. 5, pp. 41-57, © 1985.

"Avoiding the Chilling Effect: News Media Tort and First Amendment Insurance," by Robert L. Spellman, originally appeared in vol. 7, no. 6, pp. 13-27, © 1985.

"'Innocent Construction' Rule Survives Challenge," by Kyu Ho Youm and Harry W. Stonecipher, originally appeared in vol. 7, no. 6, pp. 43-60, © 1985.

"'Single Instance' Rule as a Libel Defense," by Kyu Ho Youm, originally appeared in vol. 9, no. 4, pp. 49-65, © 1987.

"Libel as Communication Phenomena," by Jeremy Cohen and Albert C. Gunther, originally appeared in vol. 9, no. 5, pp. 9-30, © 1987.

"Fact or Opinion: Where to Draw the Line," by Robert L. Spellman, originally appeared in vol. 9, no. 6, pp. 45-61, © 1987.

"Constitution Provides Limited Libel Protection to Broadcast Commentators," by Don Sneed, Whitney S. Mandel, and Harry W. Stonecipher, originally appeared in vol. 10, no. 2, pp. 19-30, © 1988.

Readings from COMMUNICATIONS AND THE LAW, 2

The articles collected in *Privacy and Publicity* were published in the
following issues of COMMUNICATIONS AND THE LAW.

"The Public and the Fair Credit Reporting Act," by Blair C. Fensterstock,
     originally appeared in vol. 2, no. 1, pp. 31-43, © 1980.
"Resolving the Press-Privacy Conflict: Approaches to the
     Newsworthiness Defense," by Theodore L. Glasser, originally
     appeared in vol. 4, no. 2, pp. 23-42, © 1982.
"Motor Vehicle Records: Balancing Individual Privacy and the Public's
     Legitimate Need to Know," by Leslie G. Foschio, originally
     appeared in vol. 6, no. 1, pp. 15-20, © 1984.
"The Television Docudrama and the Right of Publicity," by Deborah
     Manson, originally appeared in vol. 7, no. 1, pp. 41-61, © 1985.
"The Big Dan's Rape Trial: An Embarrassment for First Amendment
     Advocates and the Courts," by Susanna R. Barber, originally
     appeared in vol. 7, no. 2, pp. 3-21, © 1985.
"The Freedom of Information Act Privacy Exemption: Who Does It
     Really Protect?," by Kimiera Maxwell and Roger Reinsch,
     originally appeared in vol. 7, no. 2, pp. 45-59, © 1985.
"Privacy Invasion Tort: Straddling the Fence," by Deckle McLean,
     originally appeared in vol. 7, no. 3, pp. 5-30, © 1985.
"Unauthorized Use of Deceased's Persona: Current Theories and the Need
     for Uniform Legislative Treatment," by Valerie B. Donovan,
     originally appeared in vol. 7, no. 3, pp. 31-63, © 1985.
"Press and Privacy Rights Could Be Compatible," by Deckle McLean,
     originally appeared in vol. 8, no. 2, pp. 13-25, © 1986.
"Photojournalism and the Infliction of Emotional Distress," by Michael D.
     Sherer, originally appeared in vol. 8, no. 2, pp. 27-37, © 1986.
"Recognizing the Reporter's Right to Trespass," by Deckle McLean,
     originally appeared in vol. 9, no. 5, pp. 31-42, © 1987.
"The 1978 Right to Financial Privacy Act and U.S. Banking Law," by
     Roy L. Moore, originally appeared in vol. 9, no. 6, pp. 23-44, ©
     1987.
"Unconscionability in Public Disclosure Privacy Cases," by Deckle
     McLean , originally appeared in vol. 10, no. 2, pp. 31-44, ©
     1988.
"Docudramas and False-Light Invasion of Privacy," by Tim A. Pilgrim
     originally appeared in vol. 10. no. 3, pp. 3-37, © 1988.

Readings from COMMUNICATIONS AND THE LAW, 3

The articles collected in *Censorship, Secrecy, Access, and Obscenity* were published in the following issues of COMMUNICATIONS AND THE LAW.

Readings from COMMUNICATIONS AND THE LAW, 4

The articles collected in *Advertising and Commercial Speech* were published in the following issues of COMMUNICATIONS AND THE LAW.

"The First Amendment Protection of Advertising in the Mass Media," by Bradford W. Scharlott, originally appeared in vol. 2, no. 3, pp. 43-58, © 1980.

"Comparative Advertising Law and a Recent Case Thereon," by Patricia Hatry and Jeffrey C. Katz, originally appeared in vol. 3, no. 2, pp. 35-47. © 1981.

"Implications of First Amendment Doctrine on Prohibition of Truthful Price Advertising Concerning Alcoholic Beverages," by Gary B. Wilcox, originally appeared in vol. 3, no. 2, pp. 49-66, © 1981.

"False and Comparative Advertising Under Section 43(a) of the Lanham Trademark Act," by A. Andrew Gallo, originally appeared in vol.. 8, no. 1, pp. 3-29, © 1986.

"Alcoholic Beverage Advertising and the Electronic Media," by Gary B. Wilcox, Dorothy Shea and Roxanne Hovland, originally appeared in vol. 8, no. 1, pp. 31-41, © 1986.

"The Future of Alcoholic Beverage Advertising," by Roxanne Hovland and Gary B. Wilcox, originally appeared in vol. 9, no. 2, pp. 5-14, © 1987.

"The Commercial Speech Doctrine: *Posadas* Revisionism," by Denise M. Trauth and John L. Huffman, originally appeared in vol. 10, no. 1, pp. 43-56, © 1988.

"The First Amendment Defense to Negligent Misstatement," by Robert L. Spellman, originally appeared in vol. 10, no. 3, pp. 59-72, © 1988.

"The Tobacco Advertising Debate: A First Amendment Perspective," by David D. Vestal, originally appeared in vol. 11, no. 1, pp. 53-67, © 1989.